D0553937

PRINCIPLES OF PHONOLOGY

Published under the auspices of
The Center for Research in Languages and Linguistics
University of California, Los Angeles

N. S. TRUBETZKOY

PRINCIPLES OF PHONOLOGY

Translated by Christiane A. M. Baltaxe

Berkeley and Los Angeles
University of California Press
1969

University of California Press
Berkeley and Los Angeles, California
University of California Press, Ltd.
London, England
Translated from *Grundzüge der Phonologie* (Göttingen: Vandenhoeck
& Ruprecht, 1958; third edition, 1962)
This translation by permission of the German publishers
Copyright © 1969 by The Regents of the University of California
Library of Congress Catalog Card Number: 68-16112
Designed by Claudia Canerdy
Printed in the United States of America

SBN   520-01535-5

TRANSLATOR'S FOREWORD

Trubetzkoy's *Grundzüge*, like de Saussure's *Cours* and Bloomfield's *Language*, ranks as a classic in linguistic literature. Just as the name Bloomfield in American linguistics is associated with such terms as behaviorism and mechanism, so is the name Trubetzkoy in European linguistics associated with such terms as functionalism and structuralism. It may not even be an exaggeration to say that for some linguists the words Trubetzkoy and *Grundzüge* are almost synonymous with Prague phonology.

Yet, despite his great contributions to linguistics as a compiler, systematizer, and theoretician, Trubetzkoy's works have remained relatively inaccessible to many English readers. *Grundzüge* in particular, originally published in German, is a difficult book to read. It has become somewhat more accessible through Cantineau's French translation. More recently, a Russian translation has also become available.

When I was a graduate student in linguistics at the University of California, Los Angeles, I conceived the idea of translating *Grundzüge* into English. Professor Jaan Puhvel, who was director of the Center for Research in Languages and Linguistics, lent the project his active support. I was thus able to undertake the translation soon thereafter.

Grundzüge is Trubetzkoy's major work. It represents the culmination of the author's prior work in synchronic phonology and phonological theory. The book may be regarded as more than a summation of personal accomplishments, however; it may also be considered a final synthesis of phonological ideas and linguistic trends that existed before the disruptive forces of World War II took their toll of an unfolding linguistic community.

In deciding to translate *Grundzüge*, I felt that the book held considerably more than historical interest. A shift in linguistic goals and concerns in recent years has placed many of Trubetzkoy's accomplishments directly in the present. It was he, for example, who first reduced vowel systems to a few oppositions. His oppositions were not entirely binary, however. Many of the problems studied now were first recognized and investigated by Trubetzkoy, and notions first elaborated by him now take a central place in linguistic theory. As examples we might take the concept of neutralization and the theory of markedness as it is now being expanded in generative grammar.

Closely linked with the name of Trubetzkoy is that of Roman Jakobson, his friend and collaborator. He was to become the principal exponent of Prague phonology in the United States. His theory of "distinctive features" in many ways parallels Trubetzkoy's theory of distinctive oppositions. A constant interchange of ideas existed between the two scholars. However, Jakobson had not quite convinced the author of *Grundzüge* of his theory of binarism at the time Trubetzkoy was writing his book.

Approximately twenty pages were still needed to complete *Grundzüge* when Trubetzkoy died at the age of forty-eight. It was Roman Jakobson who after the author's untimely death saw to it that *Grundzüge* was published. He made a hurried attempt at editing it. The confusion and conditions created by the outbreak of World War II and Germany's invasion of Czechoslovakia caused fear that the book might be lost or confiscated. Rather than run such a risk, Jakobson made hurried preparations for publication in the book's existing state. Thus the book was left almost completely unedited.

Several decisions basic to the task of translating *Grundzüge* had to be taken. Because of the immensity of the task, I did not feel I could edit the book, nor did I think it was my function as translator to do so, except to correct minor printing errors. The unevenness of the prose and the shifting of style are indicative of the unedited character of the original. They are, in particular, a reflection of the book as a synthesis that contains large portions of text taken almost verbatim from Trubetzkoy's earlier publications of varying attitude and style. What made the task of translation especially difficult was the apparent switching between what seemed to be impressionistic and what seemed to be scientific in observation and terminology.

In my choice of terms, I made an effort to stay within the terminology current at publication of the original, or still current with respect to the Prague School. For example, the terms *interchangeable* (vertauschbar) and *noninterchangeable* (unvertauschbar) were preferred over *commutable* and *noncommutable.* Although commutation was a basic operation in Prague phonology, the term itself was not used by members of that school and was originally associated with glossematics. Again, the terms *combinatory variant* (kombinatorische Variante) and *facultative variant* (fakultative Variante) were selected over *allophone* and *free variant* because of association of usage. The term *phonology* (Phonologie) as in the work's title was chosen over *phonemics* despite the author's own suggestion, because of the association of the former term with the Prague School.

Some of the terms used by Trubetzkoy were without an established form in English. It was therefore necessary to decide on equivalent terms. Where these terms were descriptive in nature, I chose to give a direct "descriptive" translation, which is not always elegant in English but which I hope will convey the author's intentions. For example, for the term *"Überwindungsarteigenschaften,"* a direct descriptive translation into *properties based on the manner of overcoming an obstruction* was chosen.

The terms *binary* and *distinctive feature* were purposely avoided, as it was Roman Jakobson who gave these terms their specific meaning in the United States. Where it was thought helpful, terms that seemed to need an explanation were footnoted in the translation.

Previous publications in English of the Prague School, or publications concerning the School, as well as Josef Vachek's *Dictionnaire de linguistique de l'École de Prague,* served as helpful sources for the terminology.

A comprehensive bibliography of Trubetzkoy's publications, which also comprises topics other than linguistics, is included as an appendix to the translation. I felt that inclusion of such a bibliography would give the reader a better idea of the wide range of Trubetzkoy's interests, and perhaps afford him easier access to source material.

I would like to thank Professor Roman Jakobson for his valuable aid and assistance in terminology and background information and for his help with the Russian bibliographical material. I am also indebted to Professor Josef Vachek for his kind suggestions, and to Professors Henrik Birnbaum, František Daneš, Paul Schachter, and Peter Ladefoged.

My very special thanks go to Professor Jaan Puhvel for reading a draft of the translation and for his valuable comments and support throughout.

Christiane A. M. Baltaxe

FOREWORD TO THE FIRST GERMAN EDITION

BY THE PRAGUE LINGUISTIC CIRCLE

The present book, on which N. S. Trubetzkoy worked untiringly until the
final weeks of his life, remains unfinished. According to the late author's
estimation, approximately another twenty printed pages were still to
follow. They would probably have contained a chapter on boundary
signals for sentences and a conclusion. The text of the book has
not had a final revision. In particular the author had intended to
expand the bibliographical footnotes, revise, supplement, and formulate
individual chapters with more precision, and dedicate the book to Roman
Jakobson.

In the course of·the preparation for this work Trubetzkoy studied
approximately two hundred phonological systems, and he intended to use
part of the collected data for illustrations of the theses of his principal
work in the form of a series of supplementary expositions under the
general heading *Extracts from My Phonological Dossier*. Although Trubetzkoy worked out these sketches in detail in his mind, only the beginning of
the first—on the phonological system of the Dungan language—was dictated from his deathbed and taken down for Volume VIII of the *Travaux
du Cercle linguistique de Prague*.

The author also had plans to work on a second volume of *Principles of
Phonology*, in which the major questions of historical phonology, linguistic
geography, and morphonology, as well as orthography and its relation to
the phonological structure of language, were to be discussed. Originally it

had been intended to develop a uniform system of symbols for phonological transcription and to use it in this book. This plan was not realized, however, and in most cases the phonemic symbols that were customary for the description of the various language groups were retained.

For Roman Jakobson

CONTENTS

PART I
THE THEORY OF DISTINCTIVENESS
The Distinctive or Meaning-differentiating Function of Sound

xiii

PART II
THE THEORY OF DELIMITATIVE ELEMENTS
The Delimitative Function of Sound

INTRODUCTION

1 PHONOLOGY AND PHONETICS

Each time that someone says something to someone else there exists an *act of speech*. An act of speech is always concrete and takes place in a specific locale at a specific time. Its prerequisites are a specific speaker (a "sender"), a specific addressee (a "receiver"), and a specific subject matter to which the act relates. All three of these elements—sender, receiver, and subject matter—vary from one act of speech to another. But an act of speech has still another prerequisite: so that the addressee may understand the speaker, both must speak the same language; and the existence of a language in the consciousness of the members of a speech community is the prerequisite for each and every act of speech. In contrast with the act of speech, which is always unique, language, or the *system of language*, is something general and constant. The system of language exists in the consciousness of all members of a particular speech community and forms the basis for innumerable concrete acts of speech. At the same time, the system of language has no other reason for existence than to make the acts of speech possible. It exists only insofar as the concrete acts of speech relate to it, that is, insofar as it is actualized in concrete speech events. Without concrete acts of speech, the system of language would not exist. Speech event and system of language accordingly presuppose each other. They are inseparably linked and should be considered as two interrelated aspects of the same phenomenon "language." Still, they are quite different in nature and must, therefore, be studied separately.

1

The distinction between act of speech (*parole*) and system of language (*langue*) was first recognized most clearly by the Swiss linguist Ferdinand de Saussure* (see his *Cours de linguistique générale* [Lausanne, 1916]). Among subsequent writings on the same subject, mentioned here are only Alan H. Gardiner, *Speech and Language* (Oxford, 1932), and particularly K. Bühler, "Axiomatik der Sprachwissenschaft" (*Kant-Studien*, XXXVIII) and *Sprachtheorie* (Jena, 1934), in which additional literature is listed. We will use the term *glottic* proposed by Otto Jespersen (*Linguistica* [Copenhagen, 1931]) to signify "pertaining to the system of language."

Anything that is part of language, that is, the act of speech as well as the system of language, has two aspects, according to Ferdinand de Saussure: *le signifiant* (the signifier) and *le signifié* (the signified).† Language is thus always a combination or an interrelation of the signified and the signifier. In the act of speech the signified is always a concrete communication, meaningful only as a whole, while the signified in the system of language consists of abstract syntactic, phraseological, morphological, and lexical rules. For even the meanings of words as they exist in the system of language are nothing but abstract rules or conceptual schemes to which the concrete meanings that appear in the act of speech relate. The signifier aspect of the act of speech is the concrete sound flow, a physical phenomenon that can be perceived aurally. What then is the signifier aspect of the system of language? If the signified aspect of the system of language consists of rules according to which the world of meanings is cut into pieces and the resulting pieces are ordered, the signifier aspect of the system of language can consist only of rules according to which the phonic aspect of the act of speech is ordered.

---

* *Translator's note:* The terms *Sprachgebilde* and *Sprechakt* are often rendered in English by Saussure's original terms *langue* and *parole* (cf. N. Chomsky, *Current Issues in Linguistic Theory* [The Hague, 1966], pp. 23, 26). For *langue* "system of language" and "language system" are also used (cf. J. Vachek, *The Linguistic School of Prague* [Bloomington, 1966], pp. 22–26). *Langue* is sometimes also rendered by "linguistic pattern" (cf. Paul Garvin, *A Prague Reader on Esthetics, Literary Structure and Style* [Washington, 1958], pp. vii, 52) and "linguistic system." For *parole* the terms "act of speech" (cf. Paul Garvin, *op. cit.*, p. 1), "speech act," "speech event," and "utterance" are also found. Among other terms for *langue* and *parole* used in English are "language" and "speaking" (cf. W. Baskin, trans. de Saussure, *Course in General Linguistics* [New York, 1959], pp. 17 ff.), "language" and "speech" (cf. A. H. Gardiner, *Speech and Language* [Oxford, 1932]), and "code" and "message" (cf. R. Jakobson, *Selected Writings* I, 465 [The Hague, 1962]).

† *Translator's note:* The terms *das Bezeichnete* (*le signifié*) and *das Bezeichnende* (*le signifiant*) are rendered variously in English. The translations "signified" and "signifier" used here are rather common (cf. W. Baskin, trans. de Saussure, *Course in General Linguistics*, pp. 65–70). The original *le signifié* and *le signifiant* are retained quite often as well (cf. S. Ullmann, *The Principles of Semantics*, 1959, p. 31). Also found are *significatum* and *significans* (cf. E. Palmer, trans. A. Martinet, *Elements of General Linguistics*, p. 24) and *signatum* and *signans* (cf. R. Jakobson, *Selected Writings*, I, 292 f., 295 ff).

The number of different concrete concepts and ideas which can be expressed in the various speech events is infinite. But the number of lexical meanings that exist in the system of language is limited, and "mastery of a language" consists precisely in being able to express all concrete concepts, ideas, and their combinations by an always limited number of semantic and grammatical means made available by the system of language. In contrast with the signified aspect of the act of speech, the signified aspect of the system of language thus consists of a finite (enumerable), limited number of units. But this same relationship between system of language and act of speech also obtains for the signifier aspect. The articulatory movements, and the phonations corresponding to them which occur in the different acts of speech, are infinitely varied. The phonic norms, however, which constitute the units of the signifier aspect of the system of language, are finite (enumerable) and limited in number.

Since *langue* or the system of language consists of rules or norms, it is a system, or better, several partial systems, as compared with *parole* or the act of speech. The grammatical categories form a grammatical system, the semantic categories various semantic systems. All these systems are properly balanced, so that all parts lend support to one another, complement one another, and relate to one another. It is only for this reason that it is possible to relate the infinite variety of concepts and ideas that appear in the act of speech to the components of the subsystems of the language system. This is also true for the signifier aspect. The sound flow of the concrete speech event is an uninterrupted, seemingly unordered sequence of sound movements merging into each other. The units of the signifier aspect of the language system, on the other hand, form an ordered system. And due to the fact that individual elements or moments of the sound flow realized in the speech event can be related to individual units of that system, the sound flow is ordered.

As can be seen from what has been said, the various aspects of the speech process are so disparate that their study must be divided into several subsciences. It is particularly clear that the signified and the signifier aspects of speech must be assigned to different disciplines. The "study of sound," that is, the science concerned with the elements of the signifier, has therefore always formed a special branch of linguistics, carefully differentiated from the "study of meaning." But we have seen above that the signifier of the system of language is something quite different from that of the act of speech. Accordingly it would be advisable to institute in place of a single "study of sound" two "studies of sound," one directed toward the act of speech, the other toward the language system. According to their subject matter, both studies of sound would

have to use quite different methods of investigation: the study of sound
pertaining to the act of speech, which is concerned with concrete physical
phenomena, would have to use the methods of the natural sciences, while
the study of sound pertaining to the system of language would use only
the methods of linguistics, or the humanities, or the social sciences respectively. We designate the study of sound pertaining to the act of speech
by the term *phonetics*, the study of sound pertaining to the system of
language by the term *phonology*.

Linguists arrived only gradually at the separation of phonetics and
phonology. J. Winteler, in his well-known work *Die Kerenzer Mundart des
Canton Glarus* (Leipzig, 1876),[1] seems to have been the first to recognize
correctly that there are phonic oppositions that are used to differentiate
the meaning of words, in a given language, and others that cannot be
used for this purpose. But he did not as yet conclude from this fact that
the study of sound should be divided into two separate sciences. To reach
this conclusion was even less possible for Winteler's contemporaries;
although his book attracted attention and received recognition as a first
attempt to describe a dialect with phonetic precision, his thoughts on
distinguishing two types of phonic oppositions were not taken up, and
possibly even went unnoticed. Subsequently, and it appears independently
of Winteler, the famous English phonetician Sweet expressed the same idea
on several occasions and passed it on to his students. This insight was
stressed in particular by Otto Jespersen, the most outstanding of Sweet's
students. Yet Sweet as well as his students treated all phonic oppositions
in the same manner, regardless of whether these oppositions served to
distinguish meaning or not. The method used was that of scientific observation. Ferdinand de Saussure, who recognized and clearly formulated the
importance of the difference between *langue* and *parole*, also recognized,
as he himself expressed it, the intangible nature of the signifier pertaining
to *langue*. Nevertheless, he did not expressly insist on the necessity of
distinguishing between the study of sound pertaining to the act of speech
(*parole*) and that pertaining to the system of language (*langue*). In his *Cours
de linguistique générale* this thought is merely hinted at. It seems that
the founder of the Geneva School considered the distinction between the
study of sound pertaining to *parole* and the study of sound pertaining
to *langue* as being less important than the distinction between the descriptive and the historical study of sound. (Incidentally, the distinction
between the study of sound pertaining to *parole* and the study of sound
pertaining to *langue* was subsequently stressed sufficiently clearly by some
of de Saussure's students, in particular by A. Meillet, Ch. Bally, and A.
Sechehaye.) It was only J. Baudouin de Courtenay, however, who arrived

at the idea that there should be two distinct types of descriptive sound study, depending on whether concrete sounds were to be investigated as physical phenomena or as phonic signals used by a speech community for purposes of communication. Baudouin de Courtenay's students were principally Russian, but there were also some Poles. He himself was Polish, although he spent most of his life teaching at Russian universities, first in Kazan, then in St. Petersburg. Among these students L. Ščerba and E. Polivanov especially must be credited with broadening and spreading the ideas of their teacher on the phonological aspect of languages. Outside this limited circle of disciples, however, Baudouin de Courtenay's views on general linguistics were little known and little appreciated. It thus happened that the distinction between two separate branches of sound study did not gain any followers prior to the First World War. This idea began to become popular only in the postwar period. At the First International Congress of Linguists in The Hague in 1928 three Russian scholars, none of whom happened to be from the school of J. Baudouin de Courtenay, formulated a short program in which the distinction between the study of sound pertaining to the act of speech and the study of sound pertaining to the system of language was clearly and distinctly set forth. These scholars, further, called for a holistic point of view, a study of the structural laws of the phonological systems, and an extension of these principles not only to the descriptive but also to the historical study of sound. They were R. Jakobson, S. Karcevskij, and the present writer. The program met with warm approval. Several linguists from various countries joined in it. The Prague Linguistic Circle (*Cercle linguistique de Prague—Pražský linguistický kroužek*), which had been founded in 1926 and which already prior to the congress in The Hague had some eager proponents of this new idea, was especially active in this direction.[2] In 1929 the first two volumes of the *Travaux du Cercle linguistique de Prague* appeared. They were devoted to phonology in the sense of study of sound pertaining to the system of language. A year later a phonological conference was organized in Prague, in which representatives of nine countries participated.[3] It was decided to found an international association for phonological studies. At the Second International Congress of Linguists in Geneva in 1931 a plenary session was devoted to "phonology" in the above sense, which revealed that this new science held the interest of wide circles. Today the International Association for Phonology has members in numerous countries.[4]

It would be wrong, however, to assume that the distinction between the study of sound pertaining to the act of speech and the study of sound pertaining to the system of language has at the present time become a generally accepted idea. There are many scholars who do not even recognize the difference between act of speech and system of language. For some, such nonrecognition is based on conscious conviction rooted in a particular world view (so for W. Doroszewski; see his essay "Langue et parole," in *Prace filologiczne*, XIV [1930]). For others, and probably for most, such nonrecognition is simply a consequence of inertia, mental lethargy, and stubborn rejection of any new thought. Whatever the reason, it is quite natural that scholars who reject the distinction between act of speech and system of language cannot recognize phonetics and phonology in the above sense either. But there are also linguists who may recognize the difference between act of speech and system of language, as well as the difference between distinctive and nondistinctive phonic oppositions, who nevertheless do not want to separate phonology from phonetics. One likes to refer to the classic handbooks of the British school, to Sweet and Jespersen, who treated phonology and phonetics as a whole, although they were fully aware of the fundamental difference between phonic oppositions differentiating meaning and phonic oppositions not differentiating meaning. But similar arguments could be voiced against any advance in science. The absence of a sharp division between phonology and phonetics was a methodological shortcoming of the classic handbooks on phonology, which had the consequence of slowing down the development of phonetics as well as phonology; there is no reason to repeat this shortcoming in the future.

But there have also been more serious attempts to reconcile the difference between phonology and phonetics. E. Zwirner believed that he would be able to achieve this end by replacing the two sciences by a single new one to which he gave the name "phonometry."* In his view the study of individual concrete speech events as an end in itself is pointless and unnecessary "as the science of linguistics has never considered as its task to differentiate among the very clear acoustic differences of individual speakers of the same speech community" ("Aufgaben und Methoden der Sprachvergleichung durch Mass und Zahl, Phonometrie," in *Zeitschrift für Mundartforschung*, XII, 2, 78).[5] "Not only is linguistics not interested in what a certain Mr. X spoke into a microphone or megaphone on a certain day in some laboratory . . ., but also what . . . was spoken by *any* person at *any one* time is of absolutely no scientific interest whatsoever" (*ibid.*, p. 69). Language for Zwirner is only "a system of norms, of audible signs

---

* *Translator's note:* In the preface to the second edition of *Grundfragen der Phonometrie* Zwirner denies that it has ever been his intention to replace the above two sciences by phonometry, and that this statement by Trubetzkoy is due to a misunderstanding on Trubetzkoy's part.

formed by the human organs and serving the purpose of communication . . .
These norms can fulfill their task of serving communication only if both
speaker and hearer relate to them within . . . the same speech community.
. . . They are valid for the formation as well as for the perception of those
signs; and their linguistic character is not due to their production by the
vocal organs but to their reference to those traditional norms intended in
speaking and hearing" (*ibid.*, p. 77). Thus, as is evident, Zwirner wants to
understand via language only the system of language. Only the conventional and, given a particular speech situation, fixed norms can be the
object of scientific study, not the "observable, nonrecursive (and innumerable!) realizations of these norms." But Zwirner draws an unexpected
conclusion: "Since these conventionalized norms for the production of
speech sounds cannot be realized twice in exactly the same way by the
vocal organs, a shift from the study of these norms to the study of the
speech event itself carries with it a shift from language history to a *statistical
conception of speech variation* as related to language history" (*ibid.*, p. 77).
By following a special procedure, the mean values of the individual sounds
are determined. The variations of a sound, recorded mechanically with
precision, are scattered around this mean value in accordance with the
familiar Gaussian curve. On the basis of this curve, the mean values are
closely examined, and only those mean values that have undergone such
close examination would be of linguistic value. Here Zwirner is in error.
What can be obtained by his phonometric method is by far not yet the
norm to which the speakers relate in the production or perception of a
certain sound. They are "norms," but in a quite different sense: norms of
a particular pronunciation, norms of realization, that is, in final analysis,
norms of the speech event, not of the system of language. "Norms" of
this type can, of course, only be mean values. They should, however, not be
equated with the values of the system of language. "*k*" in German is
articulated differently before consonants and before vowels, and differently
before stressed vowels and before unstressed vowels; its timbre and
articulation vary, depending on the quality of the vowel immediately
preceding or following it. For each of these variants phonometric mean
values can be computed, and the correct German pronunciation of
each of these variants "is scattered" around this mean value in accordance
with the Gaussian curve. But for "*k* in general" no such mean value can be
determined. Before stressed vowels *k* is aspirated (and the degree of aspiration varies greatly). Before unstressed vowels it is unaspirated. If all
occurrences of *k* in this text were to be studied carefully as to their degree of
aspiration, if this degree were expressed numerically in each individual
case, and the mean value of aspiration of *k* were then to be determined, the

resulting mean value would not correspond to reality: it would at most symbolize the relative frequency of occurrence of k before stressed vowels in a particular text. Unambiguous results could be obtained only if one would compute two different mean values: the one for k before stressed vowels, the other for k before unstressed vowels. But the referent norm for speakers is "k in general," and this cannot be determined by measurements and computations. To be sure, an exact determination of the average normal pronunciation of a sound in a particular environment is indeed welcome, and the application of biostatistical methods, as used by Zwirner, is certainly to be hailed as great progress. But it would be erroneous to assume that all tasks of phonology would thereby be solved. The problems of phonology remain completely untouched because the system of language is outside the scope of "measurement and number." But neither are the objectives of phonetics exhausted by phonometry. In contrast with Zwirner, we must emphasize that the phonetician must deal not only with the norms valid for a speech community but also with individual differences between speakers and with modifications in the pronunciation of individual sounds resulting from a change in the speech situation. In this area, too, one must look for regularities of a special type. Linguistics must deal not only with the system of language but also with the speech event, that is, with the entire area of the speech event. It is important, however, to keep the two objects of linguistic study, the speech event and the system of language, strictly separate.

As regards the designations given to the study of sound pertaining to the act of speech and the study of sound pertaining to the system of language, it should be noted that the terms "phonetics" and "phonology" used by us are not used with the same meaning by all linguists. Ferdinand de Saussure, who himself had first suggested such a differentiation in terms, subsequently modified them so that the term "phonology" applied to the static (synchronic) or descriptive study of sound, and the term "phonetics" to the historical (diachronic) study of sound, that is, to the history of sound changes that have taken place in a language.[6] It appears that, apart from M. Grammont, nobody followed his example. To the Swedish linguist Noreen, phonetics meant the "science of the acoustic, physiological, and anatomical prerequisites of language," while phonology meant "the science of the physical material of language, of the produced speech sounds," and this terminology was adopted by his colleagues. The English and Americans often use the term "phonology" to mean "historical study of sound" or "study of the use of sounds in a specific language"; whereas the term "phonetics" is always used to designate the study of the physical or physiological constitution of speech sounds. In recent times the British have employed the term "phonemics" in the sense in which we use the term "phonology." Since in English the term "phonology" has already received another meaning, the term "phonemics"* will be retained for English speakers. It would, perhaps, be useful to introduce this term into Swedish as well. But in other languages in which the term "phonology" does not have another meaning, it shall be used in the sense proposed by us. In any case, the term "psychophonetics" proposed by J. Baudouin de Courtenay must be rejected since phonetics (which Baudouin de Courtenay wanted to designate "physiophonetics") is much more concerned with psychic phenomena than is phonology, the latter dealing with supra-individual social values.

Not all is said by defining phonology as the study of sound pertaining to the system of language, and phonetics as the study of sound pertaining to the act of speech. The difference between the two sciences must be shown in greater detail.

Since the signifier of the act of speech is a nonrecurring natural phenomenon, that is, a flow of sounds, the science in which it is studied must use the methods of the natural sciences. Depending on whether the object of study is the constitution or the production of sounds—though actually both aspects must be studied simultaneously—either the purely physical, acoustic aspect or the physiological articulatory aspect of the sound flow can be studied.

The two branches of phonetics, that is, acoustic and articulatory phonetics, need not be strictly kept apart. In "auditory phonetics," in which sounds are studied without the use of special instruments, but solely with the aid of the human senses subjected to special training, acoustic and articulatory phonetics are not kept separate: the "auditory phonetician" evaluates the acoustic value of the sound under study by ear. At the same time he investigates the manner in which it is produced with the aid of his eyes, his sense of touch, and by kinetics. A distinction between acoustic and articulatory phonetics is found only in what is called experimental (more precisely, instrumental) phonetics, and in that field also only as regards some methods that have lately been under frequent attack. A synthesis of acoustic and articulatory phonetics is reestablished by the X-ray method. An investigation into the nature and production of speech sounds accordingly constitutes not two separate tasks of phonetics, but a single one.

---

* *Translator's note:* Despite the author's suggestion, the term "phonology" has been chosen instead of "phonemics" to render *Phonologie* in the translation, since "phonology" is established usage in English with reference to the Prague School of Linguistics.

The sole task of phonetics is to deal with the question of speech production. This question can be answered only by stating exactly how the sounds are perceived (or, translated into physical terms, into what sound fractions, sound waves, etc., a specific sound complex can be broken down), and in what manner, that is, by what movements of the vocal organs, a particular acoustic effect is achieved. Sound is a physical phenomenon perceptible by the sense of hearing; and in studying the acoustic aspect of a speech event the field of phonetics borders on the psychology of perception. The production of speech sounds is a semiautomated, but intentional, centrally controlled activity; and in investigating the articulatory aspect of the speech event phonetics borders on the psychology of automated actions. But even though the area of phonetics actually lies in the domain of psychology, the methods of phonetics are purely those of the natural sciences: this is related to the fact that the adjacent areas of experimental psychology also employ the methods of the natural sciences as they involve rudimentary, rather than higher, psychic processes. For phonetics an orientation toward the natural sciences is absolutely necessary.

Particularly characteristic of phonetics is the complete exclusion of any reference to the lexical meaning of the sound complexes under study. The special training of ear and sense of touch which a good "auditory phonetician" has to undergo consists in getting accustomed to listening to sentences and words and to probing his vocal organs during the production of sentences and words without regard to their meaning, that is, he must get accustomed to perceiving only their phonic or articulatory aspect, as a foreigner would who does not understand the particular language. Phonetics may therefore be defined as the *science concerned with the material aspect (of sounds) of human speech.*

The signifier of the system of language consists of a number of elements whose essential function it is to distinguish themselves from each other. Each word must distinguish itself by some element from all other words of the same system of language. The system of language, however, possesses only a limited number of such differential means, and since their number is smaller than the number of words, the words must consist of combinations of discriminative elements ("marks" in K. Bühler's terminology). Moreover, not all conceivable combinations of discriminative elements are permissible. Their combination is subject to specific rules, which are different for each language. It is the task of phonology to study which differences in sound are related to differences in meaning in a given language, in which way the discriminative elements (or marks) are related to each other, and the rules according to which they may be combined into words and sentences. It is clear that these objectives cannot be attained by the methods of the natural sciences. Rather, phonology must use the same methods as are used in the study of the grammatical system of languages.

The speech sounds that must be studied in phonetics possess a large number of acoustic and articulatory properties. All of these are important for the phonetician since it is possible to answer correctly the question of how a specific sound is produced only if all of these properties are taken into consideration. Yet most of these properties are quite unimportant for the phonologist. The latter needs to consider only *that aspect of sound which fulfills a specific function in the system of language.*

This orientation toward function is in stark contrast to the point of view taken in phonetics, according to which, as elaborated above, any reference to meaning of the act of speech (i.e., any reference to signifier) must be carefully eliminated. This fact also prevents phonetics and phonology from being grouped together, even though both sciences appear to deal with similar matters. To repeat a fitting comparison by R. Jakobson, phonology is to phonetics what national economy is to market research, or financing to statistics.

In addition to the definition of phonetics as the study of sound pertaining to the speech event, and phonology as the study of sound pertaining to the system of language, another definition could be given in which phonetics would be a purely phenomenalistic study of speech sounds, with phonology the study pertaining to the linguistic function of the same sounds. In a book titled *Die Phonetik und ihre Beziehungen zu den Grenzwissenschaften* (Publicationes Instituti Phonetici Universitatis Helsingforsiensis, no. 4—*Annales Academiae Scientiarum Fennicae*, XXXI, 3 [Helsinki, 1936]), which, incidentally, is highly recommendable reading, Arvo Sotavalta tried to show that the latter definition, already accepted in 1930 by the Prague Conference on Phonology and reprinted in the "Projet de terminologie phonologique standardisée" (*TCLP*, IV), is the only correct one. He concedes that phonology moves exclusively within the realm of the system of language; yet he believes that the relationship of phonetics to the act of speech is not as essential. The "starting point" for phonetics "is concrete, namely, it is human speech. . . . But this is true of any scientific study: individual animals serve as the basis for zoology, individual plants for botany, etc. In spite of this fact, it is not the knowledge and the study of these *individual* objects that is the *proper* objective of science: what is important are the general concepts that are to be reached by means of these objects." Similarly "phonetics," which has the act of speech (*parole*) as its basis, endeavors "to grasp the essence of a concept more general than that of the act of speech, namely, that of the system of language (*langue*)." Phonetics investigates "the immediate prerequisites, the production, the direct effects, and the perception of language." It attempts to "gain full knowledge of the *component parts* of the system of language (*langue*)" (p. 34). This is clearly a misconception. It appears to be a result of the fact that Arvo Sotavalta considers the natural sciences, in which there is no equivalent for the dichotomy "system of language"/"act of speech," as a parallel. The elements of the act of speech alone can be produced and perceived. The system of language is neither produced nor perceived. It must already be present and serves as a frame of reference for both speaker and hearer. Those "more general concepts" which are arrived at in phonetics by observation of actual spoken sounds and sound sequences, and which can be compared with the various species of animals in zoology or with species of plants in botany, are the different types of sound or articulation. But phonetics can never reach its linguistic function if it chooses to remain a purely phenomenalistic science. Phonetics will, therefore, always remain in the domain of the act of speech, while phonology, as conceded by Arvo Sotavalta, will always remain in the sphere of the system of language. The definitions are parallel: phonology is the study of sound pertaining to the system of language, phonetics the study of sound pertaining to the act of speech. Phonology, of necessity, is concerned with the linguistic function of the sounds of language, while phonetics deals with their phenomenalistic aspect without regard to function. The basis for this distinction is that the system of language as a social institution constitutes a world of relations, functions, and values, the act of speech, on the other hand, a world of empirical phenomena. There is no parallel for this in the natural sciences, such as botany and zoology. Therefore, these cannot be considered for comparison. But the same type of relation is found in all the social sciences insofar as they deal with the social evaluation of material things. In all such cases the social institution per se must be strictly distinguished from the concrete acts in which it finds expression, so to speak, and which would not be possible without them. The institution must be examined with regard to its relations and functions, while its referent act must be examined in its phenomenalistic aspect.

E. Otto's attempt to define phonology as the study of sound from an acoustic point of view, and phonetics as the study of sound from an articulatory point of view, must be considered completely mistaken.[7] Strange as it may seem, Otto combines this view with the quite correct insight that phonology is the study of sound pertaining to the system of language, while phonetics is the study of sound pertaining to the act of speech. But Otto assumes that for the system of language, the acoustic aspect is the more important, while it is the articulatory aspect of speech sounds which is more important for the act of speech. Here he is definitely wrong. In his above-mentioned book Arvo Sotavalta presents a very good outline of the various branches of phonetics, so that we do not have to go into detail here. In passing, it is merely noted that both the articulatory and the acoustic aspect of speech sounds are natural phenomena and can only be studied by the methods of the natural sciences. This places both in the sphere of phonetics. The data for the study of the articulatory as well as the acoustic aspect of speech sounds can only be gathered from concrete speech events. In contrast, the linguistic values of sounds to be examined by phonology are abstract in nature. They are above all *relations*, oppositions, etc., quite intangible things, which can be neither perceived nor studied with the aid of the sense of hearing or touch.

A clear distinction between phonology and phonetics is necessary in principle and feasible in practice. Such a distinction is in the interests of both sciences. This should not prevent, of course, either one from profiting from the findings of the other. But limits should be recognized. This, unfortunately, is not always the case.

The sound flow studied by the phonetician is a continuum that can be divided into an arbitrary number of segments. The endeavor of some phoneticians to isolate "speech sounds" within this continuum had its basis in the phonological projection of the written letter. Since in reality it is very difficult to isolate speech sounds, some phoneticians arrived at the concept of "nuclear sounds," and "transitional sounds" which are found between nuclear sounds. The nuclear sounds that corresponded to phonological elements were described in detail, while the transitional sounds were usually not described since they were obviously regarded as less important or even as quite unimportant. Such a segmentation of the elements of the flow of speech cannot be justified from a purely phonetic point of view. It is based on an incorrect application of phonological concepts to the field of phonetics. Some elements of the sound flow are indeed unimportant for the phonologist. But among these are not only "transitional sounds" but also individual properties and marks of "nuclear sounds." The phonetician, on the other hand, cannot take this view. Only the meaning of the act of speech is of no importance to him, while all other elements or segments of the flow of human speech are equally essential and important. The phonetician will, of course, always consider certain typical positions of the vocal organs or their respective acoustic phenomena as base elements of phonation. Consequently he will adhere to describing typical articulatory positions and sounds (*Schallgebilde*—see note, p. 36) taken from the articulatory and sound continuum. But this is only true as regards the study of the base elements of his science. Another part must follow, in which the structure of larger phonetic entities is investigated. It is quite natural that in describing the phonetic structure of a language its phonological system is taken into consideration with regard to the base phonetic elements, inasmuch as phonologically distinctive oppositions of sound are treated in more detail than the nondistinctive ones.

As regards phonology, it is clear that it must make use of certain phonetic concepts. For instance, the claim that in Russian the contrast between voiced and voiceless obstruents is used to differentiate between words, belongs to the field of phonology. The terms "voiced" and "voiceless" and "obstruents" themselves, however, are actually phonetic. In starting any phonological description the distinctive sound oppositions in the language in question have to be uncovered. The phonetic transcription of the particular language must be taken as a point of departure and serve as data, though further higher levels of the phonological description, that is, the systemic study and the study of combinations, are quite independent of phonetics.

Despite their fundamental independence, a certain amount of contact between phonology and phonetics is therefore inevitable and absolutely necessary. But only the introductory sections (i.e., the sections on the base elements) of a phonological and a phonetic description should take each other into account. Here, too, the limit of what is absolutely necessary should not be overstepped.[8]

2   PHONOLOGY AND PHONOSTYLISTICS

Since the prerequisites for human speech are always a speaker, one or several hearers, and a topic to be discussed, each linguistic utterance has three aspects: it is at once a *manifestation* (or an expression) of the speaker, *an appeal* to the hearer or hearers, and *a representation* of the topic. It is to the great merit of Karl Bühler that this apparently simple, yet so long overlooked, fact was put into its true perspective.[9]

Bühler's scheme also holds for the phonic aspect of speech. When we hear somebody speak, we perceive *who* is speaking, his *intonation* and *pitch*, and *what* he says. In reality only one single acoustic impression is given. But we divide it into its components. We always do this from the point of view of Bühler's three functions of speech: we interpret certain properties of the sound we perceive as a manifestation or characteristic of the speaker (e.g., his pitch). We consider certain other properties as means of evoking a certain response on the part of the hearer, and still others as marks by which words and their specific meanings as well as the sentences composed of these words are recognized. Likewise, we project the various properties of the speech sounds we perceive onto three different planes: the plane of expression, the plane of appeal, and the plane of representation.

Whether it is the task of phonology to study all three of these planes is problematic. It becomes immediately clear, however, that the representation plane belongs to the sphere of phonology. The content of an observed sentence can be understood only if its constituent words are related to the lexical and grammatical elements of the system of language; and the signifier aspect of these elements necessarily consists of phonological units. The relationship between the expression plane and appeal plane to phonology is less certain. At first glance these planes seem to lie exclusively in the domain of the act of speech, and therefore appear to be suited only for phonetic, not phonological, study. Yet upon closer examination this view proves mistaken. Among the acoustic impressions by which we recognize the identity of the speaker, as well as the emotional impression he intends to make upon the hearer, there are also those impressions that must be related to the norms established in the particular language in order to be interpreted correctly. These norms must be regarded as linguistic values; they are part of the system of language and must therefore be dealt with in phonology.

In the early phonological studies little attention was paid to the expression plane and the appeal plane. In general there prevailed a tendency to overestimate the role of phonetics in this area.[10] Julius v. Laziczius was apparently the first expressly to call attention to the inadequacy of this view. Since phonology, in contrast with phonetics, must deal with the functions of the phonic aspect of human speech, it cannot be limited to the representative function.* According to Laziczius, it should also investigate the expressive and the appeal function of sound. In this connection the Hungarian phonologist pointed out that the use of individual phonations with an expressive or an appeal function is just as fixed and conventionalized as their use for purposes of differentiating meaning: a means of expression or appeal that fulfills precisely such a function in a specific language cannot simply be transferred to another language.[11]

What seems to follow from this argument of Julius v. Laziczius is that now two new subdivisions of phonology are to be created, namely, a phonology of expression and a phonology of appeal. The creation of such subdivisions is certainly associated with great difficulties, especially in view

---

* *Translator's note: Darstellungsfunktion.* Other terms used in English for this function are "communicative function," "referential function," and "ideational function"; for *Appellfunktion* (appeal function) another term used is "conative function." Cf. Josef Vachek, *The Linguistic School of Prague*, p. 34.

of the lack of reliable collected data. Only in very rare cases can information on the means of expression and appeal in a particular language be found in a detailed description of the sound system of that language. Some such data could be gleaned from works on elocution. However, since such writings are generally oriented toward purely practical goals and, of course, do not differentiate between the act of speech and the system of language, they cannot be used indiscriminately. Upon closer inspection, it usually turns out that the material offered is of little value. In view of the present state of research, only little can thus be said with regard to the phonology of the expression and the appeal plane. Only a few general thoughts will be offered.

The expressive function of human speech consists in characterizing the speaker. Anything in speech that serves to characterize the speaker fulfills an expressive function. The elements performing this function can therefore be very diverse. For example, the circumstance that the speaker belongs to a particular human type, his physical and mental characteristics, etc., all these are recognizable from his voice, his diction, and from the entire style of his speech, including choice of words and sentence structure. But we are only interested in phonological *means of expression*, that is, in means of expression belonging to the phonic aspect of the formal system of signs which constitutes the system of language.

A large part of the diagnostic phonic elements of human speech must therefore be excluded at the outset from our field of investigation. We must especially exclude natural characteristics and those features that are purely psychologically conditioned. It is quite possible to recognize by the voice of the speaker not only his sex and age but at times even his state of health. Indeed, it is possible to determine whether he is fat or skinny without actually seeing him. But all this has nothing to do with phonology. For, although perceptible to the ear, these features are not part of the formal system of signs of a particular language. They retain their distinctive force in extralinguistic vocal activities as well. This is also true of many properties of human speech from which conclusions as to the speaker's character can be drawn. Only conventionally determined means pertaining to the linguistic characterization of a speaker belong to the phonology of expression. And since language is, above all, a social institution, only those phonic means that characterize speakers as belonging to particular types or groups of persons, important for the existence of the particular speech community, are specified by convention. These means may indicate, for example, membership of the speaker in a particular age group or social class. They may further be indicative of his sex, degree of education, and the region of his origin. All these properties are important for the internal grouping of the speech community and for the content and form of verbal interaction. The division of people into fat and skinny ones, into phlegmatics and sanguines, etc., is on the other hand of no significance for the life of the speech community as expressed in the different types of speech behavior. Accordingly it does not require any formal *linguistic* characterization ("glottic" in the sense of Otto Jespersen): if features of the latter type can be surmised from speech behavior, such a surmise involves an extralinguistic psychological process.

The phonology of expression may thus be compared to the study of costumes in folklore. The difference between fat and skinny or between tall and small people is very important to the tailor, whose job it is to make a particular costume. But from the point of view of folklore these differences are quite insignificant: only the conventionally specified form of the costume is important. The clothing of a sloppy person is dirty and rumpled. Absentminded persons do not always have all their buttons fastened. All these characteristics are of no significance for the study of costumes in folklore. Folklore is interested in every characteristic, however minute, by which in accordance with prevailing custom the dress of a married woman is distinguished from that of a single girl, etc. People belonging to groups customarily characterized by ethnologically relevant differences in dress are also often distinguished by linguistic ("glottic") characteristics and especially by peculiarities pertaining to the "phonology of expression." Compare, for example, sex and age groups, social classes or occupational groups, educational classes, city dwellers and peasants, and regional groups.[12]

The details naturally depend on the social structure of the particular people or speech community. In speech communities with little or no social stratification, the realization of individual speech sounds is particularly affected by differences in age and sex. In the Darchat dialect of Mongolian, the articulation of all back and central vowels is slightly fronted in female speech. *u*, *o*, and *a* of male speech correspond to female *ü*, *ó*, and *á*, and *ü*, *ò*, and *á* of male speech correspond to female *ü*, *ö*, and *ä*; further, the fricative *x* in male speech corresponds to the stop *k* in female pronunciation.[13] VI. Bogoraz reports of the Chukchi (now Luorawetlans) on Kamchatka that a certain sound in their language is realized as *č'* (palatalized *č*) by adult males but as *c* (= *ts*)[14] by women and children. According to V. Jochelson, there are some sounds in the language of the Yukaghir (now "Odules") in Northeastern Siberia which are realized as palatalized plosives *t* and *d* by adult males of hunting age, as affricates *c*, *ʒ* (*ts*, *dz*) by children and women of childbearing age, and as palatalized *č'* and *ʒ'* by old people.[15] In all these cases the people are nomads or nomadic hunting (or fishing) tribes, in which sex groups (or sex and age groups) form very sharply delimited bodies, and where these groups practically constitute the only internal structure of society. But differences of speech in accordance with sex and age groups are also found in cases where peoples have a developed social structure, though they are usually less pronounced here. For instance, there is a general tendency in Russian, in articulating accented *o*, to increase its rounding initially and to decrease it toward the end, so that the vowel *o* always sounds like a kind of diphthong with decreasing lip rounding. But while the difference between the beginning and end of the *o* sound in standard male pronunciation is only very slight, in fact hardly noticeable, it is quite great in female speech. Some women actually say *u͡o* instead of *o*. This, however, is considered somewhat vulgar. The difference between male and female speech here consists only in the degree of diphthongization. When *o* is pronounced by a man with the degree of rounding considered normal for female speech his diction immediately stands out as effeminate and affected.[16] Such subtle formal differences between male and female pronunciation can probably be discovered in almost any language when examined more closely. A detailed description of the phonological system of a language must take this circumstance into account. As regards formal differences in the pronunciation of different age groups, they too are found in most languages. Often they are expressly mentioned by observers. One must be careful, however, not to confuse formal differences with differences that are innate or developmental. In certain speech communities children substitute some sounds for others because they acquire the correct pronunciation of these sounds only gradually. However, this, as well as all cases of pathological speech defects, is not a matter to be dealt with in the phonology of expression. A phenomenon pertaining to the phonology of expression is present in those cases where a child is able to imitate the pronunciation of adults quite well, yet intentionally fails to do so, or where a young person, in order not to appear old-fashioned or ridiculous, purposely avoids the pronunciation of old people, though it would not otherwise cause him any difficulty. Sometimes this involves quite subtle nuances, such as "intonation," and so on.

In speech communities with a marked social stratification, differences in pronunciation that are due to class or professional structure, or to the cultural structure of society, are quite prominent. They exist not only in the languages of India, where they are anchored in the caste system (e.g., in Tamil the same speech sound is said to be pronounced as either *č* or *s*, depending on the caste of the speaker), but are found in other parts of the world as well. Colloquial Viennese in the mouth of a government official is quite different from that spoken by a salesman. In prerevolutionary Russia the spirantized pronunciation of g (as γ) was characteristic of members of the priesthood, although in other respects they spoke pure standard Russian. Further, there existed a special pronunciation of standard Russian as spoken by the nobility, and another as used by the merchant class. Differences in the pronunciation of city and country dwellers, or in the speech of the well educated and the uneducated, probably exist in all languages. One frequently also finds a special "stylish" pronunciation, used by dandies and fops of all kinds, which is characterized by sloppy enunciation.

Regional differences in pronunciation are likewise found in all languages. People at a country fair are sometimes able to recognize the native village of a particular speaker by these differences. As for the more cultured speaker of a normalized written language, it is probably impossible to make precise predictions as to his place of origin. But even in the case of those speakers it is possible, along general lines, to surmise what part of a language area they come from.

Conventional phonic means of expression do not always characterize what the speaker is in reality, but often only how he would like to appear at a given moment. For many people the pronunciation used in public address is highly distinct from that of normal conversation. There are special marks that are characteristic of a sweetly pious and flattering pronunciation. The affectedly naive, twittering way of speech of some ladies shows a number of formal sound marks. All phonological means of expression that, within a speech community, serve to characterize a specific group of speakers, form a system. Their sum total may be designated as the style of expression of the respective group. A speaker need not always use the same style of expression. He may sometimes use the one, sometimes the other, depending on the content of the conversation, or the nature of the hearer. In short, his usage conforms to the prevailing customs of the speech community in question.

A special type of phonological means of expression is represented by "permissible sound substitution." In addition to the normal sounds used by all "average speakers," every language has some sounds that are only used by a few speakers as substitutes for certain normal sounds for which they have a dislike. The reason for such a "dislike" is sometimes a particularly common speech defect, sometimes a kind of fad. The difference between "substitute" and "normal sound" may be big or small: sometimes, as in the case of the various r substitutions in many European languages, it can be noticed by any observer; sometimes a well-trained ear is needed. It is significant that these sound substitutions are *permitted* by the speech community, that is, that they are not pushed aside but continue to exist side by side with the normal sounds. Insofar as individual speakers adopt such substitute sounds and always, or almost always, use them, these sounds become the personal means of expression of these speakers.

Besides those means with a purely expressive function, there are also others that additionally fulfill a specific representational function. The speech of a group of speakers may frequently be distinguished from the usual speech pattern in that it neglects a distinctive phonological opposition (i.e., an opposition relevant to the representational plane) or, vice versa, in that it shows distinctiveness where this is not found in the speech of other groups of speakers. An example would be the nondistinctiveness of the opposition tenues and mediae, even for speakers of standard German, which is characteristic of some parts of the German-speaking area; further, the coalescence of š and s, and ž and z characteristic of the inhabitants of Marseille, and the distinction between unaccented o and a which characterized the pronunciation of the older generation of priests in prerevolutionary Russia. (This was, of course, especially pronounced in the regions of Central and South Great Russia where the distinction between unaccented o and a was lost for the other social strata.) From the standpoint of representational function, the cases cited involve different dialectal phonological (or phonetic) systems. From the viewpoint of the expressive function, they involve different expressive forms of the same system. Nevertheless, these cases need to be carefully distinguished from others in which specific socially or regionally distinct groups of speakers are characterized solely by a difference in the realization of the same phonemes and not by the number of differentiated phonemes.

From the phonological means of expression, it is necessary to distinguish the phonological *means of appeal* or *the conative means*. The means of appeal or conative means serve to evoke or "release" certain emotions in the hearer. Ostensibly the speaker often experiences these emotions himself. It is important, however, that the hearer be infected. Whether the speaker actually experiences these emotions or whether he only simulates them is not significant. It is not the intent of the speaker to manifest his own feelings but to provoke these or corresponding feelings on the part of the hearer.

The phonological means of appeal must therefore again be carefully distinguished from any natural expressions of emotion, even where these are only simulated. When a speaker stutters out of actual or imagined fear or excitement, or when his speech is interrupted by his sobs, this has nothing to do with phonology. These are symptoms that occur even in extralinguistic behavior. Phenomena such as the exaggerated lengthening of consonant and vowel in the German word "schschöön!" uttered in rapture, on the other hand, are obviously linguistic (glottic). First, they can be observed only in linguistic, not extralinguistic, expressions; second, they have a definite function; and third, they are conventional in nature like all other linguistic means that fulfill definite functions. They are therefore part of the phonology of appeal. (They involve the evoking of a specific emotional response on the part of the hearer.)

At the present stage of research it is difficult to say what methods should be followed in a "phonology of appeal." From a theoretical viewpoint, a complete inventory of all phonological means of appeal, in other words, of all conventionalized means serving to evoke feelings and emotions, should be set up for every language. But it is not always clear what is to be considered as a single means of appeal, and how these means of appeal are to be delimited. The problem of distinguishing between language and speech, between system of language and act of speech in this context, is particularly ticklish and difficult. We have already mentioned the exaggerated lengthening of the stressed vowel and the pretonic consonant in German. The example given was "schschöön!" as it would be pronounced in rapture. The same means may, however, also be used to evoke different emotions. Pronounced in such a way, "schschöön!" need not only signal rapture but can also signal irony; "schschaamlos!" can signal indignation, "lliieber Freund!" delight, irony, indignation, persuasion, grief, or regret, etc. In each case the intonation is different. However, the question remains as to how these different intonational nuances are to be interpreted. Are they all part of the phonology of appeal, and do they belong to the system of language at all? Or are they only part of the act of speech? And are they really conventionalized at all? Emotionally stressed intonation frequently also occurs in extralinguistic expressions, for example, in indeterminate arbitrarily articulated exclamations. The actual emotions intended to be evoked are easily recognizable. It seems that this type of extralinguistic intonation, intended as an appeal to emotion, has the same pitch and intensity structure as words of equivalent emotional signification, though this matter has never been examined closely. It can further be observed that many of these types of intonation with an appeal to emotions have the same connotation in the most distant languages of the world.[17] The exaggerated lengthening of a stressed vowel and the preceding consonant, on the other hand, presupposes the presence of vowels and consonants as well as the presence of stressed and unstressed syllables. It is therefore by nature confined exclusively to purely linguistic expressions. Further, it is only valid for specific languages.

It appears that most phonological means of appeal are constituted in this way. Actually they do not bear any direct relation to the release of any specific emotion. They merely make the release of several different emotions possible. Their choice depends on the speech situation. The arousal of emotions is brought about by an innumerable variety of diverse unconventional vocal behavior. It is not within the task of the phonology of appeal to collect, describe, and systematically classify this type of emotional vocal behavior, and to assign it to actual specific emotions. Disregarding this type of vocal behavior, the task of the phonology of appeal is only to determine those conventional phonic marks by means of which emotionally tinged speech is distinguished from emotionally neutral, tranquil speech. Thus one can say that lengthening of stressed long vowels and pretonic consonants in German, lengthening of initial consonants and utterance of final vowels in Czech, lengthening of short vowels (under retention of their specific open lax quality) in Hungarian, lengthening of the first consonant of a word (accent d'insistance) in French, etc., are signs of emotional speech. They are phonological means of appeal, for the peculiarities mentioned in these languages occur only for purposes of arousing an emotion. Their use is not permissible in ordinary emotionally neutral speech. They are quite obviously conventional as contrasted, for example, with the intonation of terror. The latter is quite universal, so to speak, though in any given language it can only be used with those words already provided with conventional means of appeal (such as lengthening of the pretonic consonant in German).[18]

It is not always easy to distinguish the means of appeal from the means of expression. Some styles of expression are characterized by the increased use of the appeal function, others by its decreased use. In cases of this kind the degree of intensity of the appeal function becomes itself a means of expression. Compare, for example, the exaggerated, emotionally charged way of speech of an affected woman with the solemn, apathetic way of speech of an important elderly dignitary. Certainly both these styles of expression do have their individual specific characteristics which are exclusively part of the phonology of expression. But to be added to these characteristics is the way the means of appeal are used. It will probably be the task of future research to separate carefully the expressive function from the conative function within the various styles of speech. As yet this is not possible. For the present, data must be collected from as diverse languages as possible with this purpose in mind.

At any rate, one cannot permit that the possibility of distinguishing the means of expression from those of appeal be bypassed, as is done by J. v. Laziczius in the article referred to. Laziczius would like to keep separate three types of elements belonging to the phonic aspect of the system of language: *the phonemes*, which have all three functions (expression, appeal, and representation), *the emphatics*, which have an expressive and a conative function, but lack the function of representation, and *the variants*, which, it is claimed, fulfill an expressive function only. Everything that we consider expressive and conative is regarded as "emphatics" by Laziczius. However grateful we may be to him for having called attention to the need for a phonological study of Bühler's three functions, we cannot agree with his conception of a distinction between phoneme "emphatic" and phoneme "variant." In the concrete speech event all three functions are interrelated and mixed. However, the hearer analyzes this complex into its components. Each of these components has only one function, and each of these functional elements relates to, and identifies with, a corresponding element of the system of language. As an example Laziczius cites the Hungarian word "ember" (human being). But let us assume that this word is pronounced by a sophisticated dandy in a "tone of reproach." In this particular case all five phonemes (ε, m, b, ε, r) are necessary for lexical distinction. None of them is substitutable without rendering the word unrecognizable or changing its meaning. The emphatic lengthening of the initial ε is a means of appeal having to do with the "tone of reproach." Its absence would change the emotional content (i.e., the content of appeal) of the utterance since the latter would then have to be made in a completely neutral tone. Finally, the characteristic nondescript degree of aperture of the vowels, the sloppy articulation of the consonants, and the uvular r, all are expressive means by which a dandy is recognized. Any utterance can be analyzed in this way. If, at times, it is easier to abstract the phonemes from the phonic properties with an expressive and a conative function than it is to separate the means of expression from the means of appeal, this should be no reason to relinquish such a separation.[19]

We therefore insist on a careful separation of the means of expression from the means of appeal. Accordingly two separate branches of phonology should be created, one dealing with the means of expression, the other with the means of appeal. To these a further and third branch should be added, constituting the part of phonology that deals with the phonological means of representation. Prior to the article by Laziczius it was this part of phonology that had been investigated almost exclusively in the studies of phonologists. However, if one compares these three branches with one another, one is struck particularly by the lack of proportion in their relationship. The "phonology of representation" would cover an enormous area, while each of the other two branches of phonology would only deal with a small amount of factual material. Further, the phonology of expression and the phonology of appeal would share certain features that would distinguish them from the phonology of representation. The problem of keeping natural and conventional features apart actually exists with respect only to the phonology of appeal and expression. It plays no role whatsoever for the phonology of representation. Only direct imitations of sound, insofar as these do not consist of conventional speech sounds, could at most be considered as nature-given phonic properties of representation. However, insofar as these are really not conventional but natural, such imitations of sound do not come within the framework of language at all. If someone narrates a hunting adventure and, in order to illustrate his story, imitates some animal cry or some other natural sound, he must *interrupt* his speech at that point: the imitated sound of nature is a foreign particle which is external to normal representational human speech.[20] The situation is quite different with respect to the plane of expression or the plane of appeal of language, where conventional and natural means are interwoven. The conventional lengthening of consonants or vowels relevant to the plane of appeal occurs only in connection with a particular natural emotional intonation; the special pronunciation of some sounds traditionally proscribed for women in some languages always occurs together with the physiologically conditioned female voice, etc. It can probably be assumed that the number of conventional means of expression and appeal is always smaller than the number of natural means of expression and appeal. Thus, while the entire area of phonic means relevant to representation is studied by the "phonology of representation," the remaining two branches of phonology deal only with a small part of the phonic means pertaining to expression and appeal. Accordingly, on the one hand, the question may be raised whether one can really consider the above three branches of phonology of equal rank and importance. On the other hand, it may be asked whether it is expedient to separate the conventional from the natural means of expression and appeal and include them in the field of phonology.

These difficulties can probably be solved most easily if one assigns the investigation of the expressive and conative phonic means to a special branch of the science, namely, that of *phonostylistics*. This branch could then be subdivided into stylistics of expression and stylistics of appeal on the one hand, and stylistics of phonetics and stylistics of phonology on the other. In the phonological description of a language one must take into account the stylistics of phonology (of both the expressive and the conative function). However, the proper object of such a description must remain the phonological study of the "plane of representation." In this way phonology need not be divided into a phonology of expression, a phonology of appeal, and a phonology of representation. The term "phonology," as before, can remain restricted to the study of sounds pertaining to the representational plane of the system of language, while "stylistics of phonology," which in itself is only part of "phonostylistics," takes care of the study of the expressive and conative phonic means of the system of language.

---

[1] Still earlier, in 1870, J. Baudouin de Courtenay had developed a similar concept in his Russian inaugural lecture. Although it was published, it remained inaccessible to most European linguists, primarily because it was written in Russian (see R. Jakobson, *Slav. Rundschau*, I, 810).

[2] Among those, in particular, the chairman of that circle, Vilém Mathesius, who as early as 1911 had published his notable treatise on the potentiality of linguistic phenomena ("O potenciálnosti jevů jazykových," in *Věstník Král. české společnosti nauk*), and R. Jakobson, whose phonologically oriented book on Czech verse as compared to Russian verse had appeared already in 1922 (Russian title: *O češskom stiche* [Berlin, 1923]; see N. S. Trubetzkoy, *Slavia*, II, 452 ff.).

[3] The papers given at that conference and the ensuing discussions are published in Volume IV of the *Travaux du Cercle linguistique de Prague* (*TCLP*).

[4] On the historical development of modern phonology, see V. Mathesius, "Ziele und Aufgaben der modernen Phonologie," in *Xenia Pragensia* (1929), pp. 432 ff.; Laziczius Gy., "Bevezetés a fonológiába," in *A Magyar Nyelvtudományi Társaság Kiadványai*, no. 33 (1932), pp. 109 ff.; N. S. Trubetzkoy, "La phonologie actuelle," in *Journal de psychologie*, XXX (1933), translated into Japanese by H. Kobayasi, "Gendai no oninron," in *Kaiho*, no. 43 (August 1936); and J. Vachek, "What is Phonology?" in *English Studies*, XV (1933).

[5] For more details, see E. Zwirner and K. Zwirner, *Grundfragen der Phonometrie* (Berlin, 1936). [2d revised and enlarged ed., Basel, 1966.]

[6] Cf. R. Jakobson, *TCLP*, II, 103.

[7] E. Otto, "Grundfragen der Linguistik," in *Indogerm. Forsch.*, LII, 177 ff.

[8] On the relationship between phonology and phonetics, cf. Karl Bühler, "Phonetik und Phonologie," in *TCLP*, IV, 22 ff.; Viggo Brøndal, "Sound and Phoneme," in *Proceedings of the Second International Congress of Phonetic Sciences*, pp. 40 ff.; J. Vachek, "Several Thoughts on Several Statements of the Phoneme Theory," in *American Speech*, X (1935); as well as the above book by Arvo Sotavalta, *Die Phonetik und ihre Beziehung zu den Grenzwissenschaften* (*Annales Academiae Scientiarum Fennicae*, XXXI, 3 [Helsinki, 1936]).

[9] Cf. Karl Bühler, "Axiomatik der Sprachwissenschaft," in *Kant-Studien*, XXXVIII, and *Sprachtheorie* (Jena, 1934).

[10] A. W. de Groot in his paper "Phonologie und Phonetik als Funktionswissenschaften," in *TCLP*, IV, 116 ff., in particular pp. 124 ff., still treats the relations of phonology and phonetics to the different planes of the speech sound in this sense. But by merely calling attention to the problem, de Groot already did a great service.

[11] J. v. Laziczius, "Probleme der Phonologie," in *Ungarische Jahrbücher*, XV (1935), and *Proceedings of the Second International Congress of Phonetic Sciences* (London, 1935), p. 57. Also cf. L. Ščerba, "O raznych stil'ach proiznošenija," in *Zapiski Neofilolog. obščestva pri SPBU*, VIII (1915), and R. Jakobson, *O češskom stiche* (Berlin, 1923), pp. 40 ff.

[12] On the function of folk costumes, cf. the excellent study by P. Bogatyrev, "Funkcie kroja na Moravskom Slovensku," in *Spisy Národopisného Odboru Matice Slovenskej*, I (1937).

[13] G. D. Sanže'ev, *Darxatskij govor i fol'klor* (Leningrad, Akad. Nauk SSSR, 1931), p. 17.

[14] In *Jazyki i pis'mennost' narodov Severa*, III, 13.

[15] *Ibid.*, III, 158.

[16] That this feature is purely conventional and not somehow physiologically conditioned, is also evident from the fact that for some women it occurs distinctly only in coquettish, affected speech, in other words, when they attempt to stress their femininity.

[17] In any event, a European will understand the emotions a good Japanese actor wishes "to express," even though he is not able to understand a word of what the actor is saying. His understanding will come not only from the actor's pantomime but in part also from his intonation.

[18] Conventionally determined means of appeal in any language must therefore be strictly distinguished from spontaneous expressions of emotions. In a dissertation by Elise Richter, titled "Das psychische Geschehen und die Artikulation," in *Archives néerlandaises de phonétique expérimentale*, XIII (1937), which contains a great amount of data, these concepts are unfortunately not kept apart.

[19] Cf. pp. 207 ff. and 254 with respect to the special phonic structure of those *words* that have no representative, but only an expressive and appeal function (interjections, commands to animals, etc.).

[20] This, of course, does not include conventionalized imitations of sound which frequently bear very little resemblance to the imitated sound of nature (e.g., boom! cockadoodledoo!), and which are often incorporated into the grammatical system, so that they can be used without any interruption of speech, Cf. J. M. Kořínek, "Studie z oblasti onomatopoje," in *Práce z vědeckých ústavů*, XXXVI (Prague, 1934).

PHONOLOGY

PRELIMINARY REMARKS

We have stated above that in the perception of human speech the individual properties of the sound impressions* are simultaneously projected onto three different planes, namely, the plane of expression, the plane of appeal, and the plane of representation. The attention of the hearer can be focused on any one of these three planes, to the exclusion of the other two. Thus it is possible to observe and consider sound impressions on the plane of representation quite independently of the plane of expression and the plane of appeal. But it would not be correct to assume that all sound impressions on the plane of representation fulfill the same function. It is true, of course, that they all serve to designate the lexical meaning of the sentence at hand, that is, they all relate to entities of the system of language having a specific lexical meaning. Nevertheless, it is possible to differentiate clearly three distinct functions on this plane. Some phonic properties have a *culminative* function, that is, they indicate how many "units" (words, combinations of words) are contained in a particular sentence. This includes, for example, primary stress in German. Other sound properties fulfill a *delimitative* function. They signal the boundary between two units (compounded words, words, morphemes). For German this includes, for example, initial glottal stop before vowels. Finally, still other sound properties have a meaning-differentiating or *distinctive* function, as they distinguish the individual units of meaning. For example: German "List"/"Mist"/"Mast"/"Macht" (list/junk/mast/might). Each

---

*Schalleindrücke.

27

unit of language must contain phonic properties having a distinctive function, or else it cannot be distinguished from the other units of language. Individual linguistic units are distinguished exclusively by phonic properties having a distinctive function. Yet the phonic properties having a culminative and delimitative function are not indispensable for the units of language. There are sentences in which individual words are not delimited by any special phonic properties, and many words are used within the context of a sentence without express culminative properties. The possibility of pausing between the individual words of a sentence always exists. The phonic properties with a delimitative and culminative function serve as a kind of substitution for such pauses. These two functions are therefore always convenient ancillary devices, while the distinctive function is not only convenient but absolutely necessary and indispensable for communication. It follows that of the three sound functions, which can be distinguished on the plane of representation, the distinctive function is by far the most important.

In accordance with the three functions of sound on the representational plane, synchronic (descriptive) phonology can be divided into three main parts. It is clear that the section that must deal with the distinctive function has to be much larger than the other two devoted to the culminative and delimitative functions respectively.

PART I

THE THEORY OF DISTINCTIVENESS

The Distinctive or Meaning-differentiating Function of Sound

I BASIC NOTIONS

1 THE PHONOLOGICAL (DISTINCTIVE) OPPOSITION

The concept of distinctiveness presupposes the concept of *opposition*. One thing can be distinguished only from another thing: it can be distinguished only insofar as it is contrasted with or opposed to something else, that is, insofar as a relationship of contrast or opposition exists between the two. A phonic property can therefore only be distinctive in function insofar as it is opposed to another phonic property, that is, insofar as it is a member of an opposition of sound. Oppositions of sound capable of differentiating the lexical meaning of two words in a particular language are *phonological* or *phonologically distinctive* or *distinctive oppositions*.[1] In contrast, those oppositions of sound that do not have this property are *phonologically irrelevant* or *nondistinctive*. In German the opposition *o-i*, as in "so"/"sie" (thus, so/she, they), "Rose"/"Riese" (rose/giant) is phonological (distinctive). The opposition alveolar *r* and uvular *r*, on the other hand, is nondistinctive since in German there does not exist a single word pair that is differentiated by this opposition.

Sounds are *interchangeable* or *noninterchangeable*. Interchangeable

31

sounds can occur in the same phonic environment in a given language (as, for instance, *o* and *i* in German in the foregoing examples). Sounds that are not interchangeable, on the other hand, can never occur in the same phonic environment in the particular language. The *ich* and *ach* sounds in German, for example, belong to this category. The latter occurs only after *u*, *o*, *a*, and *au*, while the former occurs in all other positions, but never after *u*, *o*, *a*, and *au*. It follows that noninterchangeable sounds in principle cannot form phonological (distinctive) oppositions. They never occur in the same phonic environment. Accordingly they can never function as the sole distinctive elements of two units. The German words "dich" and "doch" (you, acc.; yet) are not only distinguished by the two *ch* sounds but also by the vowels. While the distinction between *i* and *o* in many other German word pairs occurs as an independent and sole distinctive factor ("stillen"/ "Stollen" [to nurse/tunnel], "riss"/"Ross" [tore/horse], "Mitte"/ "Motte" [middle/moth], "bin"/"Bonn" [(I) am/Bonn], "Hirt"/"Hort" [shepherd/treasure]), the opposition of *ich* and *ach* sounds in German occurs only in the presence of an opposition in the preceding vowels. It cannot occur as the *sole* discriminative means between two words. This is true for all oppositions of noninterchangeable sounds (but see p. 33). Interchangeable sounds can form distinctive as well as nondistinctive oppositions. It depends entirely on the function such sounds fulfill in a given language. For example, in German the relative pitch of vowels in a word is irrelevant for its meaning (i.e., for its representative function). Differences in the relative pitch of vowels in German can, at most, be used for the function of appeal. But the lexical meaning of a disyllabic word remains quite unchanged irrespective of whether the relative pitch of the vowel in the second syllable is higher or lower than that of the vowel in the first syllable, or whether the vowels are pronounced with the same tone. If we consider the low-tone *u* and the high-tone *u* as two separate sounds, we can say that these two sounds are interchangeable in German but do not form a distinctive opposition. On the other hand, *r* and *l* are also interchangeable in German, but do form a distinctive opposition; compare, for example, such pairs as "Rand"/"Land" (rim/land), "führen"/ "fühlen" (lead/feel), "scharren"/"schallen" (to dig/to sound), "wirst"/ "willst" (will/want), where the difference in meaning is manifested only by the opposition *r–l*. Conversely, in Japanese, though *r* and *l* are interchangeable, they are incapable of forming a distinctive opposition. *r* can be substituted for *l* in any word and vice versa, without a change in meaning. The relative pitch of individual syllables, on the other hand, is phonologically distinctive in Japanese. Low-tone *u* and high-tone *u* are interchangeable and form a distinctive opposition. A word like "tsuru," for example, can thus have three distinct meanings, depending on the relative pitch of the two *u*'s: it means "climber" (bot.) when the tone of the first *u* is lower than that of the second; "crane" (zool.) when the tone of the first *u* is higher than that of the second; and "to fish" when both *u* vowels show the same tone.[2] Accordingly two types of interchangeable sounds can be distinguished: those that in a given language form distinctive oppositions and those that form nondistinctive oppositions only.

We have said above that noninterchangeable sounds do not form distinctive oppositions. This statement must, however, be qualified. Noninterchangeable sounds having no common phonic properties that would distinguish them from all other sounds of the same system do form distinctive oppositions. The opposition between the German *ich* and *ach* sounds is nondistinctive since these sounds are not interchangeable and their common phonic properties of voiceless dorsal spirants do not recur in any other sound of the German sound system. However, the opposition of the German *h* and *ŋ* ("ng") sounds, which are also noninterchangeable, is nevertheless distinctive (*h* occurs only before vowels except before unstressed *e* and *i*; while *ŋ* occurs only before unstressed *e* and *i* and consonants). The reason for this is that the only property these two sounds have in common, that is, their consonantal property, is by no means unique to them alone and does not distinguish them from the other consonants of German. To differentiate distinctive oppositions of this type from the usual oppositions existing between interchangeable sounds, we designate the former *indirectly distinctive* (or *indirectly phonological*) oppositions. For, while ordinary directly phonological oppositions (such as *o-i* and *r-l*) can be used directly to differentiate words, it is, of course, impossible to do so in the case of indirectly phonological oppositions. Members of indirectly phonological oppositions can, however, enter into a relationship of direct phonological opposition with any other sound, that is, with a sound that has the same property common to both. Accordingly German *h* and *ŋ* ("ng"), for example, are in a relationship of directly distinctive opposition with many German consonants: with *p* ("hacken"/"packen" [hack/pack], "Ringe"/"Rippe" [rings/rib]), with *l* ("heute"/"Leute" [today/people], "fange"/"falle" [catch/fall]), and with others.

2   THE PHONOLOGICAL (DISTINCTIVE) UNIT, PHONEME, AND VARIANT

By (directly or indirectly) phonological or distinctive opposition we thus understand any phonic opposition capable of differentiating lexical meaning in a given language. Each member of such an opposition is a *phono-*

logical (or *distinctive*) *unit*.[3] It follows from this definition that the scope
of the distinctive units can be quite varied. A word pair such as "bahne"/
"banne" (pave/expel) is differentiated only by syllable division (or by the
related difference in vowel and consonant length), while the difference in
sound in a word pair such as "tausend"/"Tischler" (thousand/carpenter)
extends over the entire word, with the exception of the initial sound. And
in a pair such as "Mann"/"Weib" (husband/wife) both words are different
in sound from beginning to end. The foregoing is evidence that there
are smaller and larger distinctive units, and that it is possible to group
the distinctive units of a given language according to their relative size.

There are distinctive units that can be analyzed into a successive number
of still smaller distinctive units. The units $[m\varepsilon]$ and $[by\!:]$ in German
"Mähne"/"Bühne" (mane/stage) are of this type: from the contrasts
"Mähne"/"gähne" (mane/yawn) and "Mähne"/"mahne" (mane/
admonish) the analysis of $[m\varepsilon\!:] = [m] + [\varepsilon\!:]$ results, and from "Bühne"/
"Sühne" (stage/expiation) and "Bühne"/"Bohne" (stage/bean) the
analysis of $[by\!:] = [b] + [y\!:]$ results. But the distinctive units m, b, $\varepsilon\!:$, and
$y\!:$ cannot be represented as sequences of still smaller successive distinctive
units. From a phonetic point of view, any b consists of a number of articulatory movements. First the lips are narrowed toward each other. Then
they are placed together so that the oral cavity is completely closed from
the front. The velum is raised simultaneously and pressed against the back
wall of the velic, so that the entrance from the velic chamber to the nasal
cavity is blocked. The vocal cords start vibrating immediately thereafter.
The air escaping from the lungs penetrates into the oral cavity and accumu-
lates behind the closed lips. Finally, the lip closure is ruptured by the air
pressure. Each of these consecutive movements corresponds to a specific
acoustic effect. However, none of these "acoustic atoms" can be considered a phonological unit since all of them always occur in unison, never in
isolation. The labial implosion is always followed by an explosion, which
again is always introduced by the implosion. The labial plosive between
implosion and explosion cannot occur without labial implosion and explosion. Thus b in its entirety is a phonological unit that cannot be analyzed
into successive components. The same can also be said of the other phonological units mentioned above. "Long" y ($\ddot{u}$) cannot be interpreted as a
sequence of "short" y's. From a phonetic point of view, $(y\!:)$ is, of course,
a span of time filled by y articulation. But if one would substitute another
vowel articulation for part of this span, the result would not be a new
German word ("Baüne," "Büane," "Biüne," "Buüne," etc. are not possible in German). Long $\ddot{u}$ from the point of view of the phonological system
of German is simply indivisible in time.

Phonological units that, from the standpoint of a given language, cannot be analyzed into still smaller successive distinctive units are phonemes.[4] Accordingly the phoneme is the smallest distinctive unit of a given language. The signifier aspect of every word in the system of language can be analyzed into phonemes, that is, it can be represented by a particular sequence of phonemes.

Of course, the matter should not be oversimplified. The phonemes should not be considered as building blocks out of which individual words are assembled. Rather, each word is a phonic entity, a *Gestalt*, and is also recognized as such by the hearer, just as an acquaintance is recognized on the street by his entire appearance. But the recognition of configurations presupposes that they are distinct. This is possible only if individual configurations are distinguished from each other by certain characteristics. The phonemes are then the *distinctive marks* of the configurations of words. Each word must contain as many phonemes, and in such a sequence, as to distinguish itself from any other word. The entire sequence of phonemes is characteristic of each individual word; but each single member of that sequence also occurs in other words as a distinctive mark. In every language the number of phonemes used as distinctive marks is much smaller than the number of words, so that individual words always represent only a specific combination of phonemes that also occur in other words. This is by no means in contradiction with the configurative character of the word. As a *Gestalt*, each word always contains something more than the sum of its constituents (or phonemes), namely, the principle of unity that holds the phoneme sequence together and lends individuality to a word. Yet in contrast with the individual phonemes it is not possible to localize this principle of unity within the word entity. Consequently one can say that each word can be *completely analyzed* into phonemes, that it *consists of* phonemes in the same way as a tune composed in major scale can be said to consist of the tones of that scale, although each tune will contain something that makes it a specific musical configuration.[5]

The same sound (*Lautgebilde*) can at the same time be a member of a distinctive and a nondistinctive opposition. Thus, the opposition of the *ach* and *ich* sounds is nondistinctive, but the opposition of both *ch* sounds to the *k* sounds is distinctive (e.g., "stechen"/"stecken" [stab/stick], "roch"/ "Rock" [smelled/skirt]. This is possible only because every sound contains several acoustic-articulatory properties and is differentiated from every other sound not by all but only by a few of these properties. The *k* sounds thus are distinguished from the *ch* sounds by forming a complete closure, while the latter only form a stricture between the dorsum and palate. But the difference between *ich* and *ach* sounds consists in the fact that the stricture in the former takes place at the center of the palate, in the latter at the soft palate. The circumstance that the opposition *ch-k* is distinctive, while the opposition of *ich* and *ach* sounds is nondistinctive, presents evidence that for *ch* the occurrence of a stricture between dorsum and palate is *phonologically relevant*, while the position of stricture in the back or central dorsal-palatal region is *phonologically irrelevant*. Sounds participate in phonological (distinctive) oppositions only by means of their phonologically relevant properties. And since every phoneme must be a member of a distinctive opposition, it follows that the phoneme is not identical with an actual sound but only with its phonologically relevant properties. One can say that the phoneme is *the sum of the phonologically relevant properties of a sound* (*Lautgebilde*).*[6]

Any sound perceived and produced in the concrete act of speech contains, in addition to the phonologically relevant properties, many others that are phonologically irrelevant. None of these sounds can therefore simply be considered a phoneme. But insofar as such a sound also contains the phonologically relevant properties of a specific phoneme, it can be considered the *realization* of this phoneme. Phonemes are realized by the sounds of language (more precisely, by speech sounds), of which every act of speech is constituted. These speech sounds are never phonemes in themselves since a phoneme cannot contain any phonologically irrelevant properties. This would be unavoidable for an actually produced speech sound. Rather, the actual sounds produced in speech are only material symbols of the phonemes.

The continuous sound flow of a speech event is realized or symbolized by a specific phoneme sequence. At specific points in the sound flow the distinctive phonic properties characteristic of the individual phonemes of the particular phoneme sequence can be recognized. Each of these points can be regarded as the realization of a specific phoneme. However, in

---

* *Translator's note:* The term "Lautgebilde" (also "Schallgebilde"), for want of a more appropriate term, is here rendered simply by "sound." This translation falls somewhat short of the German meaning which may be interpreted as referring to the internal structuring of the sound, possibly also to its "Gestalt."

Another term suggested by Roman Jakobson is "sound unit," which again does not exactly convey the meaning, and when translated back to German becomes "Laut-" or "Schalleinheit."

Of the above definition, which already implies the division of the phoneme into distinctive features, Vachek writes (*op. cit.*, p. 46): "This . . . definition . . . was in reality not Trubetzkoy's, but Jakobson's; he formulated it as early as 1932. [In translation] . . . by this term [the phoneme] we designate a set of those concurrent sound properties which are used in a given language to distinguish words of unlike meaning." Cf. also Trubetzkoy's own footnote 6.

addition to the distinctive phonic properties, there are still many other nondistinctive phonic properties that occur at the same point in the sound flow. We designate the sum of all distinctive as well as nondistinctive properties occurring at a specific point in the sound flow as *speech sound*. Each speech sound thus contains, on the one hand, phonologically relevant marks that make it the realization of a specific phoneme. On the other hand, it contains quite a number of phonologically irrelevant marks, the choice and occurrence of which depend on a number of things.

It follows that a phoneme can be realized by several different speech sounds. For example, for German g the following marks are phonologically relevant: complete closure between dorsum and palate, accompanied by raising of the velum, relaxation of the muscles of the tongue, and unaspirated plosive release of the closure. But the place where the dorsal-palatal closure must take place and the position of lips and vocal cords during closure are phonologically irrelevant. German consequently has quite a number of speech sounds that are regarded as the realization of a single phoneme g. There are voiced, semivoiced, and completely voiceless g sounds (even in those German-speaking regions where mediae are voiced as a rule), rounded velar g sounds (as in "gut" [good], "Glut" [embers]), closely rounded palatals (as in "Güte" [benevolence], "Glück" [luck]), unrounded velars (as in "ganz" [whole], "Wage" [scales], "tragen" [carry]), unrounded strongly palatal sounds (as in "Gift" [poison], "Gier" [greed]), moderately palatal sounds (as in "gelb" [yellow], "liege" [lie]), etc. We designate these various speech sounds, which are realizations of the same phoneme, as *variants* (or phonetic variants) of the particular phoneme.

3 DEFINITION OF THE PHONEME

Not all linguists accept the present definition of the terms "phoneme," "speech sound," and "variant"; and initially the definition was not formulated in this way.

Originally the phoneme was defined in psychologistic terms. J. Baudouin de Courtenay defined the phoneme as the "psychic equivalent of the speech sound." This definition was untenable since several speech sounds (as variants) can correspond to the same phoneme, each such sound having its own "psychic equivalent," namely, acoustic and motor images corresponding to it. Furthermore, this definition is based on the assumption that the speech sound itself is a concrete, positive given entity. But in reality this is not the case. Only the actual continuous sound flow of the speech event is a positive entity. When we extract individual "speech sounds" from this continuum we do so because the respective section of the sound continuum "corresponds" to a word made up of specific phonemes. The speech sound can only be defined in terms of its relation to the phoneme. But if, in the definition of the phoneme, one proceeds from the speech sound, one is caught in a vicious circle.

With reference to the phoneme, the present writer sometimes used the term "Lautvorstellung" (sound image) in his early phonological writings.[7] This expression was mistaken for the same reason as the above definition by Baudouin de Courtenay. Acoustic-motor images correspond to every phonetic variant inasmuch as the articulation is regulated and controlled by the speaker. Furthermore, there is no reason to consider some of these images "conscious" and others "subconscious." The degree of awareness of the process of articulation depends on practice. Through special training it is also possible to become conscious of nonphonological phonic properties. It is this fact that makes it possible to have what is known as auditory phonetics. The phoneme can thus be defined neither as "sound image" nor as "conscious sound image" and contrasted as such with the speech sound (phonetic variant). The expression "Lautabsicht" (sound intent), used by the present author in his paper to the Second International Congress of Linguists in Geneva,[8] was actually only an alternative phrasing of the designation of the phoneme as "sound image." Consequently it was also wrong. Whoever intends to utter the word "gib" (give) must by the same token intend also to make all necessary movements with his speech organs. In other words, he must intend to articulate a palatal *g*. This intent is not identical with the intent involved in the desire to utter the word "gab" (gave) which has a velar *g*. All these psychological ways of expression fail to do justice to the nature of the phoneme and must therefore be rejected lest they lead to an obliteration of the boundary between sound and phoneme, as could sometimes be actually observed with Baudouin de Courtenay and some representatives of his school.

Reference to psychology must be avoided in defining the phoneme since the latter is a linguistic and not a psychological concept.[9] Any reference to "linguistic consciousness" must be ignored in defining the phoneme, "linguistic consciousness" being either a metaphorical designation of the system of language or a rather vague concept, which itself must be defined and possibly cannot even be defined. The definition proposed by N. van Wijk (*De Nieuwe Taalgids* [1936], p. 323) can therefore also be challenged. According to Van Wijk, "the phonemes of a language form a category of linguistic elements which are present in the psyche of all members of the speech community." Phonemes "are the smallest units sensed as not

further divisible by linguistic consciousness."* The fact that the concept
"phoneme" is here linked with such vague and nondescript notions as
"psyche," "linguistic consciousness," or "sensory perception" cannot be
of help in clarifying the phoneme concept. If this definition were to be
accepted, one would never know in an actual case what to consider a
phoneme. For it is impossible to penetrate the "psyche of all members of
a speech community" (especially where extinct languages are involved). An
inquiry into the "sensory perception" by the "linguistic consciousness" is
also a ticklish and extremely difficult enterprise. The statement that "linguistic consciousness" is not capable of analyzing a phoneme into
successive parts and that all members of a speech community "are in command of" the same phonemes are two quite correct claims. But they can
by no means be considered a definition of the phoneme. The phoneme is,
above all, a functional concept that must be defined with respect to its
function. Such definition cannot be carried out with psychologistic
notions.

Other equally inadequate definitions proceed from the circumstance of
the existence of combinatory variants.† Daniel Jones defined the phoneme
as a family or group of acoustically or articulatorily related speech sounds
that never occur in the same phonic environment. This first definition by
Daniel Jones proceeded from the assumption that human speech consists of
phonemes and speech sounds, these not belonging to different planes but
coexisting side by side on the same level. In a word such as "Wiege"
(cradle) in German the v, $i:$, and $ə$ are speech sounds since they do not
show combinatory variants perceptible to the naked ear. g, on the other
hand, is a phoneme since its realization depends on its environment. It is
clear that this use of the terms speech sound and phoneme only makes
sense with reference to the letters of the alphabet. The term "phoneme"
would then apply to those letters that are pronounced differently depending
on their position within a word, while the term "speech sound" (or
"phone") would apply to those always pronounced in the same way. For
Jones the phoneme concept was originally also very closely related to the
problem of "phonetic transcription."[10] However, he very soon recognized

---

* *Translator's note:* The term *Sprachbewusstsein* is here translated literally by "linguistic consciousness," to distinguish it from *Sprachgefuehl*, "linguistic intuition,"
though that appears to be what is meant. Cf. J. Vachek, *The Linguistic School of Prague*,
p. 30: "There is another point [in addition to the inadmissibility of separation of levels]
in which the approaches of the two groups [transformationalists and Praguians] reveal
some similarity, and that is their attitude toward what the transformationalists call
intuition and to which the Prague group refers by the term . . . linguistic consciousness."
Cf. here pp. 64, 78, 85, 88, 301.

† *Translator's note:* The term *kombinatorische Variante* is here translated as "combinatory variant," instead of "allophone," in keeping with Prague School terminology.

that the "phoneme theory" in this form was untenable and required further refinement. The definition of the phoneme actually remained unchanged. However, it was not only applied to families or groups of such noninterchangeable sounds as could be perceived by the naked ear as different sounds, but also to those whose difference could not be perceived directly. And since experimental phonetics had supplied proof that it was impossible to produce exactly the same sound in different environments, in a word like the above "Wiege" (cradle) not only the *g* but also the *v*, *i*, and *ə* became phonemes in accordance with this new interpretation. In this first developmental period of the phoneme concept Jones also assumed "diaphones" in addition to phones and phonemes. By this term were understood families of sounds which could be substituted for each other without changing the meaning of the word. Now, since the methods of instrumental phonetics show that it is impossible to repeat exactly the same sound in the same environment, Jones should actually speak only of diaphones instead of speech sounds or phones, and define the phoneme as a family of nonsubstitutable diaphones. In the final state of development of his phoneme theory Jones in fact arrives at a similar view. In so doing he bases himself on the theory of "abstract sounds," developed by the Japanese professor Jimbo and the English linguist in Tokyo, Dr. Palmer. The actual sounds that we perceive are all different, and it is impossible to produce exactly the same sound twice. Yet some sounds have so many common features and resemble each other to such a degree that their common features can be summed up in one image (*Vorstellung*) and this image can be conceived of as such. This is the way in which "abstract sounds" come into existence, for example, a velar *g*, a palatal *g*, etc. But this is only an abstraction at the first level. A second level of abstraction is reached if one sums up into one general image a whole family of such abstract sounds which, while bearing a certain resemblance to each other, never occur in the same environment in a given language. Phonemes, then, are such abstract sounds at the second level. Objections must be raised against this definition, especially for the reason that every abstraction is based on that principle according to which it is made. A number of actual dogs can correspond to the abstract concepts of "big dog," "black dog," "faithful dog," "poodle," etc., depending on what is chosen as the principle for abstraction. Every one of these "abstract dogs" will include quite different "actual dogs." Jones speaks of abstract sounds without paying attention to the principle by which such abstracting takes place. At "the first level" abstracting takes place on the basis of acoustic-articulatory similarity; at "the second level," on the basis of the relation of the sounds to their environment. These two principles of abstracting are so different from each other that they should by no means be regarded as two levels of the same abstracting process. Further, the vagueness of the term "speech sound" ("actual sound") must again be stressed. Actual sounds exist only insofar as they are the realizations of phonemes. The first level of abstraction is, therefore, really the second. As long as Jones's phoneme concept was only coined for purposes of transcription, it had some practical value, but little relation to linguistics as such. But as soon as this concept was revamped to correspond to specific linguistic phenomena, the point of departure for the definition of the phoneme became invalid.

The phoneme can be defined satisfactorily neither on the basis of its psychological nature nor on the basis of its relation to the phonetic variants, but purely and solely on the basis of its function in the system of language. Whether it is considered as the smallest distinctive unit (L. Bloomfield) or as "Lautmal am Wortkörper" (vocal mark on the body of the word) (K. Bühler), the result is the same: every language presupposes distinctive (phonological) oppositions. The phoneme is a member of such an opposition that cannot be analyzed into still smaller distinctive (phonological) units. There is nothing to be changed in this quite clear and unequivocal definition. Any change can only lead to unnecessary complications.

Incidentally, the reasons for such complications are sometimes not only psychologically understandable but are also quite legitimate. For example, the extremely complicated definition of the phoneme advocated by the American phonologist W. Freeman Twaddell in his interesting monograph *On Defining the Phoneme* (Language Monographs, published by the Linguistic Society of America, XVI [1935]) seems to have arisen from the fear of a hypostasis of the phoneme, that is, from the fear of the conception of phonemes as objects that the speaker possesses and uses like building blocks to assemble words and sentences (see especially, p. 53). To guard against this danger, Twaddell wants to give special emphasis to the relational character of the phoneme (i.e., to its nature as an opposition member). With this end in mind he develops his phoneme theory which may be summed up as follows: An "utterance" (i.e., a concrete speech event) is a physical phenomenon (a sound) coupled with a specific meaning. An articulatory complex that recurs in various utterances and has the same meaning everywhere is called a "form." Two forms with different meaning are in principle also different in sound—apart from homonyms which are relatively rare in all languages.[11] The degree of difference in sound between two different forms may vary. The minimal difference in sound between two dissimilar forms corresponds to the fractions of the respective articulatory complexes. A group of forms that are minimally different form a "class." Such a class is characterized by the articulatory complex common to all its members. If the minimal difference constitutes the same fraction in all these members, for example, the initial or final fraction, the class is "ordered." Thus, for example, the words "nahm"/ "lahm"/"kam"/"Rahm"/"Scham"/"zahm" (took/lame/came/cream/ shame/tame) form an ordered class in German. The relations between the members of such a class are minimal phonological oppositions. Twaddell calls the members of such oppositions "micro-phonemes." Thus in our case *n-l-k-r-sch-ts* are "micro-phonemes" of the form class characterized by the following *am*. The phonetic equivalent of a micro-phoneme contains several articulatory properties. Two form classes are called "similarly ordered" if the relationship between their micro-phonemes is identical. For example, the classes *pill-till-kill-bill* and *nap-gnat-knack-nab* in English are similarly ordered. Although the phonetic makeup of the micro-phonemes in both cases is not quite the same—*p, t, k* are aspirated initially, unaspirated finally—the relation between these micro-phonemes is nevertheless identical. All micro-phonemes found in the same position in various similarly ordered form classes form a "macro-phoneme" which corresponds to our concept "phoneme." J. Vachek remarked quite correctly (*Proceedings of the Second International Congress of Phonetic Sciences*, pp. 33 ff.) that this definition of the phoneme fundamentally agrees with ours. W. Freeman Twaddell's micro-phonemes and macro-phonemes are opposition members that cannot be analyzed into smaller fractions. With regard to the macro-phoneme, it is expressly stated that it is the sum of the phonologically relevant phonic properties. By a complicated roundabout way Twaddell thus arrives at the same result as we had reached in a more direct way.* Yet this complicated detour offers no advantage. There is nothing in our definition that would presuppose or require a hypostasis of the phoneme. Karl Bühler's conception of the phoneme as a "vocal mark on the face of the word," which does justice to the conception of the word as a configuration, is wholly in accord with our definition. So is the "abstract

---

* *Translator's note:* With respect to his own phoneme definition and theory, Twaddell says of the Prague School: "It should be clear for what kinds of procedure in linguistic study a unit like the (macro-) phoneme is adopted. It is a procedure very much like the 'phonology' of the Cercle linguistique de Prague. That such a procedure is in order can scarcely be questioned. . . . The only limitation which the definition proposed above would impose upon such a procedure is the necessity for antecedent and concurrent phonetic (and articulatory) analysis. If the valuable and suggestive work of many members of the Cercle linguistique de Prague has not been wholly convincing to many students of language, it is (aside from its newness) because of the subjective mentalistic definition of units and a somewhat truculent denial of the relevance of phonetic analysis" (*On Defining the Phoneme* [1935], reprinted in M. Joos, ed., *Readings in Linguistics*, p. 77).

relevancy" which Bühler rightly considers the basis and logical prerequisite for our phoneme concept (see *TCLP*, IV, 22–53). The advantages that a distinction between micro-phonemes and macro-phonemes has to offer can just as easily be attained through our theory of neutralization of phonological oppositions, and of archiphonemes (see end Chap. III). In addition, our solution of the problem avoids the danger connected with the micro-phoneme theory, that of atomizing phonology. We therefore believe that Twaddell's complicated theory cannot replace our definition of the phoneme. Twaddell's great merit consists in putting an end to psychological and naturalistic prejudices that had arisen around the phoneme concept on the part of some proponents as well as opponents of phonology. It is true, of course, that his abstract way of expression and his philosophically trained thinking make rather high demands on the reader which some obstinate opponents of phonology are not able to meet. This can lead, and has already led, to misunderstandings. Thus, for example, B. Collinder and P. Meriggi eagerly took Twaddell's claim that the phoneme is no physical and mental reality but an "abstractional fictitious unit" as a flat rejection of the phoneme concept.[12] In reality, of course, Twaddell only meant the same as what Ferdinand de Saussure considered the essence of every linguistic value ("entités oppositives, relatives et négatives," *Cours de linguistique générale*, p. 164), which actually can be said of every value concept. Since the phoneme belongs to *langue*, and *langue* is a social institution, the phoneme also is a *value* and has the same kind of existence as all values. The value of a currency unit, for example, the dollar, is also neither a physical nor a psychic reality, but an abstract and "fictitious" value. But without this "fiction" a government cannot exist.

A. W. de Groot defined the phoneme as follows (*TCLP*, IV, 125): "The phoneme is thus a phonological symbolic sign which has a self-evident function. The essential function of the phoneme is the following: to make possible or facilitate, if need be, the recognition and identification of words or parts of words that have symbolic value by means of the fact that the phoneme itself is recognizable and identifiable. Phonemes may be defined as *the shortest fractions of sound sequences that have this function.*" Arvo Sotavalta (*Die Phonetik und ihre Beziehungen zu den Grenzwissenschaften*, p. 10) agrees with this definition, but formulates it more clearly. However, he does not speak of phonemes but of "speech sounds." By speech sound he understands "*the smallest fraction of a sequence of sounds* occurring in the speech flow which requires a more or less specific time for its production and which *can be recognized and identified*; it is further capable of forming recognizable, identifiable linguistic forms by combining with sounds of like nature." The question may be raised:

Why are "speech sounds" or "words" and "parts of words" recognized? What is meant by "recognition" and "identification"? Of course, only that which is distinguished from other things of like nature can be recognized at all. Recognizable, identifiable words are those that distinguish themselves from all other words by specific phonic discriminative marks. The word "Leber" (liver) is identified because it is differentiated by an *l* from the words "Weber" (weaver) and "Geber" (giver), by an *e* from the word "Lieber" (dear), by a *b* from the word "Leder" (leather), and by an *r* from the word "Leben" (life). A phonic element that is not capable of differentiating one sound sequence from another cannot be recognized either. Recognition is thus not the primary import but the logical consequence of differentiation. Further, "recognition" is a psychological process and it is not advisable to draw on psychological concepts in the definition of linguistic notions. Our definition of the phoneme must therefore be given preference.

[1] In "Projet de terminologie phonologique standardisée," in *TCLP*, IV, the term "phonologischer Gegensatz," "opposition phonologique," is proposed. This term may be retained for all those languages in which the word "phonological" cannot cause misunderstandings. For English, however, we would recommend the term "distinctive opposition" since both "phonological opposition" and "phonemic opposition" might give rise to misunderstandings.

[2] It is true, however, that the tone is sometimes shifted when individual words form compounds: "ása" (morning): "asá-meshí" (breakfast): "samúrai" (knight): "ináka-zámurai" (country squire), etc.

[3] Cf. "Projet de terminologie phonologique standardisée," in *TCLP*, IV, 311. For English the term "distinctive unit" is probably to be recommended.

[4] In 1912, L. V. Ščerba in *Russkije glasnyje* (St. Petersburg, 1912), p. 14, gave the following definition of the phoneme: "The shortest general sound image of a given language which is capable of associating with images of meaning and of differentiating words . . . is called phoneme." In this definition, which is still under the spell of association psychology, as in Ščerba's *Court exposé de la prononciation russe* (1911, p. 2), the differential function of the phoneme seems to have been clearly stressed for the first time. In 1928 N. F. Jakovlev, in an article titled "Matematičeskaja formula postrojenija alfavita" (in *Kul'tura i pis'mennost' Vostoka*, I, 46), gave a definition that had already been cleansed of psychologistic elements: "By Phonemes we understand those phonic properties that can be analyzed from the speech flow as the shortest elements serving to differentiate units of meaning." The definition of the phoneme which we quoted above was formulated for the first time in 1929 by R. Jakobson in his "Remarques sur l'évolution phonologique russe" (*TCLP*, II, 5): "Tous termes d'opposition phonologique non susceptibles d'être dissociés en sous-oppositions phonologiques plus menues sont appelés phonème." This is the definition that was incorporated

in somewhat altered form into the "Projet de terminologie phonologique standardisée" (*TCLP*, IV, 311): "... non susceptible d'être dissociée en unités phonologiques plus petites et plus simples."

⁵ Cf. Karl Bühler, "Psychologie der Phoneme," in *Proceedings of the Second International Congress of Phonetic Sciences*, pp. 162 ff., and N. S. Trubetzkoy, "Über eine neue Kritik des Phonembegriffes," in *Archiv für vergleichende Phonetik*, I, 129 ff., in particular pp. 147 ff.

⁶ For a similar definition, cf. R. Jakobson in the Czech encyclopedia *Ottův slovník naučný*, Dodatky II, I, 608 (see "fonéma").

⁷ N. S. Trubetzkoy, "Polabische Studien," in *Sitzb. Wien. Akad., Phil.-hist. Kl.*, CCXI, no. 4, p. 111, and "Versuch einer allgemeinen Theorie der phonologischen Vokalsysteme," in *TCLP*, I, 39. Incidentally, this term was never intended as an exact scientific definition. This writer was at that time not at all interested in the formulation of definitions, but only in the correct application of the phoneme concept. The phoneme concept was used in exactly the same way in the first-mentioned phonological articles by the present writer as it is used by him today (cf. e.g., "Polabische Studien," pp. 115–120).

⁸ Cf. *Actes du IIᵉ Congrès International de Linguistes*, pp. 120 ff.

⁹ Cf. *TCLP*, II, 103.

¹⁰ Also cf. J. Vachek in *Charisteria Guilelmo Mathesio*, pp. 25 ff., and the writings by D. Jones, cited there.

¹¹ Cf. B. Trnka, "Bemerkungen zur Homonymie," in *TCLP*, IV, 152 ff.

¹² Cf. P. Meriggi in *Indogerm. Forsch.*, LIV, 76, and B. Collinder in *Actes du IVᵉ Congrès International de Linguistes* (Copenhagen, 1938).

II RULES FOR THE DETERMINATION OF PHONEMES

1 DISTINCTION BETWEEN PHONEMES AND VARIANTS

After ascertaining the definition of the phoneme in the preceding chapter, we now must give the practical rules by which a phoneme can be distinguished from phonetic variants on the one hand, and from combinations of phonemes on the other.[1]

What are the conditions under which two speech sounds can be considered realizations of two different phonemes, and under what conditions can they be considered phonetic variants of a single phoneme? Four rules can be formulated.

RULE I.—*Two sounds of a given language are merely optional phonetic variants of a single phoneme if they occur in exactly the same environment and are interchangeable without a change in the lexical meaning of the word.*

Several subtypes can be distinguished. According to their relation to the speech norm, optional variants are divided into *general* and *individual* variants. The former are variants that are not regarded as speech defects or deviations from the norm and can therefore be used by the same speaker. For example, the lengthening of consonants before a stressed vowel in German is not considered a speech defect, and the same speaker may pronounce the same word sometimes with a short and sometimes with a long initial *s* and *sch* (phonem. |z, š|). The difference in pronunciation is here used for emotional coloration of speech ("ssoo?" "schschöön!"

46

North German "jja!"). Individual variants, on the other hand, are distributed among the various members of the speech community. Only a specific variant is considered "normal," "good," or "model" pronunciation, while the rest are regarded as regional, social, or pathological deviations from the norm. An example would be the uvular and alveolar r in various European languages. But the value of these two sounds differs depending on the language. In the Slavic languages, as well as in Italian, Spanish, Hungarian, and Modern Greek, alveolar r is regarded as the norm. The uvular r is treated as a pathological deviation or a sign of snobbish affectation. More rarely it is considered a regional peculiarity, as, for example, in Slovenian, where it occurs especially in certain dialects of Carinthia. Conversely, in German and French the uvular r (or, more precisely, different types of uvular r) are considered the norm, and the alveolar r is considered a regional deviation or an archaizing affectation, such as the r used by French actors. In all these cases, which certainly are not rare, the distribution of the variants is a "norm" in itself. It frequently also happens that two variants of a phoneme are general but that the frequency of their use is subject to individual fluctuations: a phoneme A is sometimes realized by all speakers as α' and sometimes as α''; but one speaker prefers its realization as α', another as α'', etc. Consequently there is a gradual transition between "general" and "individual" variants.

With respect to the function of the optional variants, they can be divided from this point of view into *stylistically relevant* and *stylistically irrelevant* variants. Stylistically relevant variants express differences between various styles of speech, as, for example, between an excited emotional and a careless familiar style. In German, for instance, lengthening of pretonic

47

consonants as well as the overlengthening of long vowels and spirantiza-
tion of intervocalic *b*, in a word such as "aber" (but) in careless, familiar,
or tired speech, are used for this function. Not only emotional but also
social styles of speech can be characterized by stylistic variants: it is possible to have an uneducated, a cultured, and a stylistically neutral variant of
the same phoneme coexist in one language. These variants reveal the degree
of education or the social class of the speaker. Stylistic variants on their
part can consequently be divided into emotional or pathognomic and
physiognomic variants. However, none of these aspects is important
with respect to stylistically irrelevant optional variants. The stylistically
irrelevant optional variants have no function whatever. They replace one
another quite arbitrarily, without any change in the expressive or the conative function of speech. In Kabardian, for example, the palatal occlusives
are sometimes pronounced as *k* sounds and sometimes as *tsch* sounds: one
and the same Kabardian pronounces the word "gane" (shirt) sometimes as
ǧane and sometimes as ǯane, without noticing any difference and without
thereby producing any stylistic or emotional coloration.[2]

As already stated above (Introduction, sec. 2), one of the tasks of phonostylistics is to differentiate and systematize the stylistic variants. From the
point of view of phonology in the narrower sense, that is, from the point
of view of the phonology of representation, both the stylistically relevant
and the stylistically irrelevant optional variants can be grouped under the
general concept of optional variants. It should be kept in mind that from
the point of view of representational phonology the "variant" is a purely
negative concept: a relation of variance exists between two sounds if they
cannot be used to differentiate lexical meaning. The question of whether
or not the difference between these two sounds has any other function, such
as an expressive function or an appeal function, is not part of phonology in
the narrower sense but belongs to phonostylistics. All optional phonetic
variants owe their existence to the fact that only part of the articulatory
properties of each speech sound is phonologically relevant. The remaining
articulatory properties of a speech sound are "free" with regard to distinctiveness, that is, they can *vary* from case to case. The question of whether
or not this variation is used for purposes of expression and response is of
no importance from the point of view of representational phonology,
especially from the standpoint of word phonology.

RULE II.—*If two sounds occur in exactly the same position and cannot be
interchanged without a change in the meaning of the words or without
rendering the word unrecognizable, the two sounds are phonetic realizations
of two different phonemes.*

Such a relationship exists, for example, between the German *i* and *a* sounds: in a word such as "Lippe" (lip) the substitution of *a* for *i* would result in a change in meaning: "Lappe" (Lapp). A word like "Fisch" (fish) would be rendered unrecognizable by such a substitution ("Fasch"). In Russian the sounds *ä* and *ö* occur exclusively between two palatalized consonants. Since their interchange would either change the lexical meaning ("t'ät'ɔ" [daddy]: "t'öt'ɔ" [aunt]) or render the words unrecognizable ("ĭd'öt'ĭ [you go]: "ĭd'ät'ĭ??"; "p'ät'" [five]: "p'öt'??), they are interpreted as realizations of different phonemes.

The degree to which words are "made unrecognizable" may vary considerably. By substituting *f* for *pf* initially in German, words usually do not become unrecognizable to the degree they would by a substitution of *a* and *i*. In a large part of Germany speakers of literary German systematically replace any initial *pf* by *f*. Nevertheless, they are understood without any difficulty by all other Germans. However, the occurrence of such pairs as "Pfeil"/"feil" (arrow/for sale), "Pfand"/"fand" (pawn/found), "Pfad"/"fad" (path/stale), "hüpfte"/"Hüfte" (jumped/hip), "Hopfen"/ "hoffen" (hop/hope) provides proof that in literary German *pf* and *f* must be regarded as different phonemes even in initial position; further, that those educated German speakers who replace initial *pf* by *f* actually do not speak correct literary German but a mixture of literary German and their native dialect.

RULE III.—*If two sounds of a given language, related acoustically or articulatorily, never occur in the same environment, they are to be considered combinatory variants of the same phoneme.*

Three typical cases can be distinguished:

a. A given language has, on the one hand, a whole class of sounds (α', α'', α'''. . .) which occur only in a specific position, and on the other, only one sound (α) which never occurs in just this position. In this case the sound α can only be in a relation of variance with that sound of class α', α'', and α''' to which it is most closely related acoustically or articulatorily. Example: In Korean *s* and *r* do not occur in final position, while *l* is found only in that position. Since *l* as a liquid is obviously more closely related to *r* than to *s*, *l* and *r* can here be regarded as combinatory variants of a single phoneme.

b. A given language has one series of sounds that occurs only in a specific position and another series that cannot occur in just that position. In this case a relation of combinatory variance exists between every sound of the first series and that sound of the second series which is most closely related to the former acoustically or articulatorily. Examples: In Russian the sounds ö and ä occur only between two palatalized consonants, while the sounds o and a are not found in this position. Since ö as a half-open, rounded vowel is more closely related to o than to a, and since, on the other hand, ä as a very open unrounded vowel is closer to a than to o, o and ö are regarded as combinatory variants of one phoneme ("O"), and a and ä as combinatory variants of another phoneme ("A"). In Japanese the sounds c (ts) and f occur only before u, while t and h are not permitted before u. Of these sounds t and c (ts) are the only voiceless dental occlusives, h and f the only voiceless spirants. t and c must therefore be regarded as combinatory variants of one phoneme, h and f as combinatory variants of another phoneme.

c. A given language has only *one* sound that occurs exclusively in a specific position, and *one* other sound that does not occur in that position. In this case the two sounds can only be considered combinatory variants of a single phoneme provided they do not form an indirect phonological opposition. Thus, for example, the German sounds h and ŋ ("ng") are not combinatory variants of a single phoneme but representatives of two different phonemes, although they never occur in the same position (see p. 33 above). In Japanese, on the other hand, g which is only found word-initially and ŋ which can never occur in that position are considered combinatory variants of a single phoneme: they are the only voiced gutturals of Japanese, that is, they have certain common properties that distinguish them from all other sounds in Japanese.[3]

RULE IV.—*Two sounds that otherwise meet the conditions of Rule III can still not be regarded as variants of the same phoneme if, in a given language, they can occur next to each other, that is, if they are part of a sound sequence in those positions where one of the sounds also occurs in isolation.*

For example, in English r can occur before vowels only, ə, on the other hand, does not occur before vowels. Since r is produced without any noise of friction or explosion, and ə is produced with a rather indeterminate degree of opening and timbre, one might be tempted to consider English r and ə as combinatory variants of the same phoneme. However, this becomes impossible due to the fact that in such words as "profession" (pron. "prəfešn") the r and ə sounds occur in succession and that there are other words in which ə occurs in isolation in the same environment; for example: "perfection" (pron. "pəfekšn").

The phonetic variants are therefore either optional or constant. In the latter case they can, of course, only be combinatory. But in addition there are also optional combinatory variants. For example, in Russian the phoneme "*j*" is realized as a nonsyllabic *i̯* after vowels, but after consonants sometimes as *i̯* and sometimes as a spirantal *j*. In this case the two variants are optional. In certain Central German dialects *t* and *d* coalesce phonologically, that is, only one phoneme is found in these dialects, which in most positions is optionally realized sometimes as a *t* and sometimes as a *d*. After nasals, however, only *d* occurs. For example: "tinde"/"dinde" = standard German "Tinte" (ink).

We have seen above that some of the optional variants, namely, the so-called "stylistic variants," fulfill specific functions on the plane of appeal or the plane of expression (see pp. 43 f.). The function of the combinatory variants lies entirely on the plane of representation. They are, so to speak, phonological auxiliary devices either signaling a word or morpheme boundary or the neighboring phoneme. We will discuss their function as boundary signals (*Grenzsignale*) in its appropriate place, when we examine the delimitative function of sound (see pp. 273 ff.). As regards the signaling of neighboring phonemes by combinatory variants, this is by no means a superfluous, though not necessarily an indispensable, function. In fast and unclear speech the realization of a phoneme can lose its identity completely. It is therefore always good if this identity finds additional expression through a special marking in the realization of the neighboring phoneme. But this can only be the case if the particular realization of the adjacent phoneme occurs not only in fast speech but whenever the two phonemes in question occur next to each other. Only then does such special realization leave an imprint on the consciousness and become an actual signal for the immediate proximity of the particular phoneme. For example, the articulation of Japanese *u* is not very distinctive in itself: the lips participate only slightly, and its duration is so short that in fast speech the vowel is not pronounced at all. Under these circumstances it is very welcome for communication that certain Japanese phonemes have special combinatory variants before *u*, namely, the variant *c* in the case of *t*, and the variant *φ* in the case of *h*. If the *u* should not be perceived, one would still be able to surmise from the realization of the preceding phoneme that a *u* was intended to follow.[4]

2   FALSE EVALUATION OF THE PHONEMES OF A FOREIGN LANGUAGE

The phonological system of a language is like a sieve through which everything that is said passes. Only those phonic marks that are relevant for the identity of the phoneme remain in it. The rest falls down into another sieve in which the phonic marks, relevant for the function of appeal, are retained. Still further down is yet another sieve in which those features are retained which are characteristic for the expression of the speaker, etc. Starting from childhood, each person becomes accustomed to analyzing what is said in this fashion. This analysis is carried out quite automatically and unconsciously. The system of "sieves," however, which makes such analysis possible, is structured differently in each language. Each person acquires the system of his mother tongue. But when he hears another language spoken he intuitively uses the familiar "phonological sieve" of his mother tongue to analyze what has been said. However, since this sieve is not suited for the foreign language, numerous mistakes and misinterpretations are the result. The sounds of the foreign language receive an incorrect phonological interpretation since they are strained through the "phonological sieve" of one's own mother tongue.

Here are some examples. In Russian all consonants are divided into two classes. They are either palatalized or nonpalatalized, the latter being velarized. For most consonants, membership in one or other of these classes is phonologically relevant. A Russian speaker immediately perceives which consonant in a Russian word is palatalized and which is not. The contrast between palatalized and nonpalatalized consonants is emphasized additionally by the fact that all vowels have specific combinatory variants depending on the class membership of the preceding or following consonants. The phoneme "i," for example, is realized as a pure i, that is, as a "high, tense front vowel" only when it occurs initially or after a palatalized consonant. Speakers of Russian also transfer this peculiarity to foreign languages. If a Russian hears a German word containing a long i, he assumes that he has "misheard" the palatalization of the preceding consonant: i for him is a signal of palatalization of the preceding consonant. Such palatalization must take place. If a Russian speaker does not hear it, he assumes this can only have been due to an acoustic delusion. When a Russian has to pronounce a German word that he has heard, he palatalizes the consonant before the i: "l'ige," "d'ip," "b'ibel," "z'iben," (lie down, thief, Bible, seven). He does this not only because he is convinced that it must be so, but also because he cannot pronounce a close, tense i after a nonpalatalized consonant. German short i is lax. There is no exact equivalent for this lax i among the Russian stressed vowels. Consequently a Russian speaker cannot associate this sound with the palatalization of the preceding consonant. A Russian hears that the initial consonants in German words, such as "Tisch," "Fisch" (table, fish) are not palatalized. But a nonpalatalized consonant is velarized for a Russian, and after a velarized consonant the Russian phoneme i is realized as ui, an unrounded

tense high central or back vowel. These words are consequently pronounced as *tuš* and *fuš* by a Russian speaker. What has been said is, of
course, true only of Russian speakers who have just started to learn
German. These difficulties are overcome in time, and the correct
German pronunciation is acquired. Something of a "Russian accent"
nevertheless remains, and even after long years of practice a Russian who
otherwise speaks correct German will palatalize his consonants somewhat
before a long *i* and will slightly back his articulation of short *i*.

Another example: standard Russian has a vowel *ə* that can be described
as an unrounded mid back (or back-central) vowel. This vowel occurs only
after consonants, that is, on the one hand in posttonic syllables, on the
other in pretonic syllables, with the exception of directly pretonic syllables.
For example: "dɔ:mɔ̃" (at home), "pɔ̆tɐmu:" (therefore). Since the vowel
ă in unstressed syllables occurs only in initial position (e.g., "ăd'ïnɔ:kɔ̃į"
[lonely]), after vowels (e.g., "vɔ̆ărŭžat'" [to arm]), or after consonants in
directly pretonic syllables (e.g., "dămɔį" [home]), a relation of combinatory variance exists between *ɔ̃* and unstressed *ă*. Bulgarian also has a vowel
ə with acoustic-articulatory properties approximately identical to those
of Russian *ə*. However, this vowel in Bulgarian not only occurs in unstressed but also in stressed syllables: "pət" (way), "kəštɔ̃" (house),
etc. Russians who learn Bulgarian find it extremely difficult to pronounce
the Bulgarian stressed *ə*. They substitute *a*, *uι*, and a mid *ě*. Only with great
effort and after long practice are they able to pronounce it halfway correctly. The fact that *ə* occurs in their own mother tongue does not facilitate
the correct pronunciation of the Bulgarian *ə*. On the contrary, it impedes
it. For although the Russian *ə* sounds almost like the Bulgarian *ə*, it has
a completely different function: the former calls attention to the relative
position of the stressed syllable. The fact that it is not stressed is therefore
not accidental but has a reason for existence, while the *ə* in Bulgarian may
be stressed. For this reason a Russian speaker is able to identify the stressed
Bulgarian *ə* with any vowel of his mother tongue except with *ɔ̃*.

The Russian stressed vowels are not only more forceful but also longer
than the unstressed vowels. One can say that in Russian all stressed syllables are long, all unstressed syllables are short. Quantity and stress
parallel each other and form an indivisible unity for speakers of Russian.
The stressed syllable can occur word-finally, initially, or medially. Its
position is frequently important for the meaning of the word "pàl'it'i"
(you ignite, pres. indic.), "pal'ìt'i" (ignite, imper.), "pal'it'ì" (fly). In
Czech quantity and stress are distributed quite differently. Stress always
occurs on the first syllable of a word and is hence nonsignificant for the
differentiation of lexical meaning: it merely signals the beginning of a word.

Quantity, on the other hand, is not bound to a particular syllable. It is free, and often serves to differentiate the meaning of words ("píti" [drink]: "pití" [the drinking]). This presents a source of great difficulty for Russians learning Czech and for Czech speakers studying Russian. A Russian will either stress every initial syllable of Czech words but then also lengthen it or he will shift the accent to the first long syllable. Thus he will pronounce instead of "kùkātko" (opera glasses) and "kàbāt" (skirt) either "kùkatko" and "kǎbat" or "kukàtko" and "kabǎt." He has difficulty separating quantity from accent because for him both are the same. Czech speakers who speak Russian usually interpret the Russian accent as a long quantity. They stress the first syllable of every word in Russian sentences and they pronounce etymologically stressed syllables with lengthening. A Russian sentence such as "pr'ĭn'ĭsit'ĭ mn'è stǎkàn vǎdù" (bring me a glass of water) in the mouth of a Czech becomes "priñesīti mñe stàkān vòdī." All this is, of course, only true as long as the student has not yet had sufficient practice. Gradually these rather gross mistakes disappear. But some characteristic features of a foreign accent remain: a Russian, even when he speaks Czech well, will always stress the first syllable somewhat, especially when the words are long and have the accent on one of the final syllables, such as "gosudàrstvo" (the state) or "konnozavòdstvo" (studs), and place the accent incorrectly. Czech and Russian speakers retain their differences of interpretation of quantity and stress even when they have a good command of both languages. This is demonstrated particularly clearly in the interpretation of foreign poetry.[5] Russian metrics are based on the regular alternation of stressed and unstressed syllables, stressed syllables, as already mentioned, being long, unstressed syllables short. Word boundaries can occur anywhere in the verse and the continuous irregular rearrangement of word boundaries serves to animate and vary the verse structure. Czech verse is based on a regular distribution of word boundaries. As was already mentioned, the beginning of each word is emphasized by an increased loudness of voice. Long and short syllables, on the other hand, are irregularly distributed in the verse and their free rearrangement serves to animate the verse. A Czech who hears a Russian poem will regard its meter as quantitative and the entire poem as rather monotonous. A Russian, on the other hand, who hears a Czech poem for the first time will be completely disoriented and will not be able at all to indicate in which meter it was composed. The rhythm of the stressed initial syllables intermingles with the irregular alternation of long and short syllables. Both sets of rhythm become confused and disturb and paralyze each other, so that the Russian does not gain any rhythmic impression at all. Upon better acquaintance with the language, these first impressions will be weakened. A Czech will nevertheless often remain incapable of really appreciating the aesthetic value of Russian verse; and the same can also be said of a Russian with respect to Czech poetry.

The number of such examples could easily be multiplied. They prove that the so-called foreign accent does not at all depend on the inability of a particular foreigner to pronounce some sound, but rather on his incorrect evaluation of this sound. And such incorrect evaluation of sounds in a foreign language is conditioned by the differences between the phonological structure of the foreign language and the mother tongue of the speaker. Mistakes in pronunciation are mostly not different from other typical mistakes in the speech of a foreigner. Any Hungarian is familiar with the opposition between male and female. But for him this difference belongs to the sphere of the lexicon, not to the sphere of grammar. When he speaks German, therefore, he confuses "der" (masc. def. art.) and "die" (fem. def. art.), "er" (he) and "sie" (she), etc. Likewise a Russian speaker is familiar with long, tense *i*, but for him it is a combinatory variant of the phoneme *i* which signals palatalization of the preceding consonant. Consequently, when he speaks German he palatalizes all consonants before the *i*.

3   INDIVIDUAL PHONEMES AND PHONEME COMBINATIONS

A   Monophonematic Evaluation

It is not always easy to distinguish between a single phoneme and a combination of phonemes. The sound flow of the concrete speech event is an uninterrupted movement. From a purely phonetic point of view, that is, ignoring the linguistic function of sound, it is not possible to say whether a particular segment of this sound continuum is to be considered "monophonematic," that is, a single phoneme, or "polyphonematic," that is, a combination of phonemes. Here, too, there are definite phonological rules that one must follow.[6]

In general one can say that in a given language only those combinations of sound *can* be interpreted as monophonematic whose constituent parts are not distributed over two syllables, and which are, further, produced by a homogeneous articulatory movement. Their duration must not exceed the normal duration of single sounds. A combination of sounds that fulfills these purely phonetic prerequisites is only "potentially monophonematic." However, it will also be interpreted as being *actually* monophonematic, that is, as the realization of a single phoneme, if in accordance with the rules of the particular language it is treated as a single phoneme, or if the

general structure of the phonemic system of that language calls for such
an evaluation. A monophonematic evaluation of a combination of sounds
is particularly *favored* when its constituent parts cannot be taken as the
realization of any other phonemes of the same language. Accordingly
the phonetic prerequisites and the phonological conditions governing the
monophonematic evaluation of a combination of sounds can be summarized
by the following six rules.

RULE I.—*Only those combinations of sound whose constituent parts in a
given language are not distributed over two syllables are to be regarded as the
realization of single phonemes.*

In Russian, Polish, Czech, etc., where both constituents of the sound
combination *ts* always belong to the same syllable, this combination of
sounds is interpreted as a single phoneme (*c*). Examples: Russian "ce-ləį"
(entire), Polish and Czech "co" (what); Russian "l'ĭ-co" (face), Polish
"pła-ce" (I pay), Czech "vī-ce" (more); Russian "ka-n'ec," Polish
"ko-n'ec," Czech "ko-nec" (end). In Finnish, however, where this sound
combination occurs only medially, with *t* closing the preceding syllable, *s*
beginning the following syllable ("it-se" [self], "seit-se-män" [seven],
etc.), it is regarded as the realization of the phoneme sequence *t + s*.
In Russian, Polish, and Czech, in cases where the combination "vowel
+ nonsyllabic *į*" occurs before a vowel, the *į* attaches to the following
vowel and forms the onset of the following syllable (Russian "zbru-jɔ̃"
[harness of horses], Czech "ku-pu-je" [he buys], etc.). In these languages
such combinations are consequently considered the realizations of the
phoneme sequence "vowel + *j*," even in cases where the entire sequence is
monosyllabic (e.g., Russian "daį" [give] = phonol. "daj"). In German,
on the other hand, where the *i* and *u* diphthongs are not distributed
over two syllables before vowels, for example, "Ei-er," "blau-e," "mistrau-
isch" (eggs, blue, distrustful), these diphthongs appear to be monophonematic.[7]

RULE II.—*A combination of sounds can be interpreted as the realization
of a single phoneme only if it is produced by a homogeneous articulatory
movement or by the progressive dissolution of an articulatory complex.*

Diphthongs are very often regarded as unitary phonemes. This is most
clearly illustrated in English, where, for example, *ei* and *ou* are regarded
as uniform phonemes: as is known, English speakers also pronounce the
long *e* and *o* of German as *ei* and *ou* because they confuse the German
monophthongs with their own diphthongal phonemes.[8] J. Vachek noted

(in "Über das phonologische Problem der Diphthonge," *Práce z vědeckých ústavů filosof. fakulty Karlovy university*, XXXIII [Prague, 1933]) that in English as well as in other languages only the so-called diphthongs of movement (*Bewegungsdiphthonge*) are regarded as monophonematic, that is, only those diphthongs that are produced during the change in position of the vocal organs. Neither the point of departure nor the end point of this change is important, only the general direction of movement. This proposition must not be inverted (as is done by Vachek, incorrectly in my opinion): not every diphthong of movement *has* to be evaluated as monophonematic. But if a diphthong is regarded as monophonematic, it must be a diphthong of movement. In other words, it must involve a homogeneous articulatory movement. A combination, such as *aia* or *aiu*, cannot be considered monophonematic in any language because it involves two differently oriented articulatory movements. The so-called transitional sounds between two consonants are "counted" as belonging to either the preceding or the following consonant, so that a "nuclear sound" together with its adjacent transitional sound is considered a unit. Yet in a combination such as "*s* + transitional sound from *s* to *k* + *s*" the transitional sound would be considered the realization of a specific phoneme, namely, "*k*" (even if a genuine *k* articulation would not be effected) because the articulatory movement in this case would not be homogeneous.

Looking at the typical cases of monophonematic interpretation of groups of consonants, one can easily see that this always involves the gradual dissolution of an articulatory complex. In the case of "affricates" an "occlusion" is first relaxed to form a stricture, and finally released completely. In the case of aspirates the oral closure is released with a plosive effect, but the larynx still remains for some time in the position it had during oral closure. The aspiration following the stop is the acoustic result. In the case of the "glottal occlusives" the glottal closure is formed simultaneously with the oral closure. After dissolution (plosive release) of the oral closure, the closure of the glottis at first still continues and is then also released with a plosive effect. The acoustic result is the sudden occurrence of a glottal stop, and so on. Those palatalized and labialized consonants that leave the acoustic impression of being combinations of consonants with a very short, incompletely formed *i* (*j*) or *u* (*w*) show the same kind of a not quite simultaneous dissolution of an articulatory complex. All these cases involve a homogeneous articulatory movement in the same direction, that is, in the direction of "dissolution," or of return to a neutral position. A sequence of sounds such as *st*, on the other hand, could never be considered monophonematic because it involves the progressive "movement" toward an occlusion that is subsequently "dissolved" (released with a plosive effect). Nor can a sequence such as *ks* be regarded as monophonematic because it requires two different articulatory movements.[9]

RULE III.—*A combination of sounds can be considered the realization of a single phoneme only if its duration does not exceed the duration of realization of the other phonemes that occur in a given language.*

From a practical point of view, this rule is less important than the two preceding rules. Nevertheless, it should be emphasized that the duration of the Russian affricates *c* and *č*, for example, normally does not exceed that of the other "short" consonants. In any case, it never reaches the normal duration of sequences such as *ks* and *kš*.[10] Further, the duration of Czech *ou* exceeds the duration of the normal long vowels of the Czech language. This seems to be important for the polyphonematic interpretation of this diphthong.

The following rules state when articulatory complexes that are potentially monophonematic *must* actually be evaluated as monophonematic.

RULE IV.—*A potentially monophonematic combination of sounds, that is, a combination of sounds corresponding to the conditions of Rules I to III, must be evaluated as the realization of a single phoneme, if it is treated as a single phoneme; that is, if it occurs in those positions in which phoneme clusters are not permitted in the corresponding language.*

For example, many languages do not permit initial consonant clusters. If, in such languages, combinations of sound such as *ph*, *th*, *kh*, or *pf*, *kx*, *ts*, *or tw*, *kw*, etc., can occur initially, it is clear that they must be regarded as the realization of single phonemes (aspirates, affricates, labialized consonants, etc.). This is true, for example, of the combinations *ts*, *dz*, *tš*, *dž* in Tlingit,[11] Japanese, the Mongolian, Turko-Tatar languages; of *ph*, *th*, *kh*, *tsh*, *tšh* in Chinese; of *ph*, *th*, *kh*, *ḳx̌*, *kx*, *ts*, *tš*, *t'*, *k'* in Avar,[12] and of many similar cases. German combines consonant plus *l* initially, as in "klar" (clear), "glatt" (smooth), "plump" (plump), "Blei " (lead), "fliegen" (fly), "schlau" (shrewd), or with *w*, as in "Qual" (torture), "schwimmen" (swim). But as regards combinations of "two consonants + *l* or *w*," only *špl* as in "Splitter" (splinter), *pfl* as in "Pflaume" (plum), "Pflicht" (duty), "Pflug" (plough), "Pflanze" (plant), and *tsw* as in "zwei" (two), "zwar" (although), "Zwerg" (dwarf), "Zwinger" (arena), are permitted in initial position. Since, apart from *štr*, *špl*, and *špr*, groups of three consonants are not permitted in initial position in German words, it becomes necessary to regard German *pf* and *ts* as single phonemes.[13]

RULE V.—*A combination of sounds fulfilling the conditions of Rules I to III must be considered the realization of a single phoneme, if this produces symmetry in the phonemic inventory.*

In languages such as Chechen,[14] Georgian, and Tsimshian,[15] which permit consonant sequences in all positions, the sequences *ts* and *tš* must nevertheless be considered unitary phonemes (affricates), and not realizations of phoneme clusters. This is required by the entire context of the phonemic system: in these languages all occlusives occur in two forms, either with or without a glottal catch, whereas this opposition is not found with respect to the fricatives in these same languages. Since, in addition to *ts* and *tš* without a glottal catch, there also occur *ts'* and *tš'* (or in American transcription *ts!* and *tc!*) with a glottal catch, the latter are grouped with the stops (*p-p' t-t', k-k'*), and the relation between *ts-s* or *tš-š* is completely parallel to that of *k-x*.

RULE VI.—*If a constituent part of a potentially monophonematic sound combination cannot be interpreted as a combinatory variant of any other phoneme of the same language, the entire sound combination must be considered the realization of a single phoneme.*

In Serbo-Croatian, and also in Bulgarian, the *r* is often found with a syllabic function. Usually this involves the combination of *r* plus a vocalic glide of indeterminate quality which sometimes occurs before and sometimes after the *r*, depending on the environment. In Serbo-Croatian such "indeterminate vowel" does not occur in any other position. The indeterminate vocalic glide that occurs before or after the *r* cannot be identified with any phoneme of the phonemic system, and the entire sequence of *r* plus (preceding or following) vocalic glide must be considered a single phoneme. Bulgarian, on the other hand, has an "indeterminate vowel" (usually transcribed by *ă*) which occurs also in other positions. For example: "*kăstă*" (house) = "*kə̀stə*"; "*păt*" (way) = "*pət*," etc. The transitional vowel to syllabic *r* in this case is considered a combinatory variant of the indeterminate vowel, and the entire sequence is regarded as polyphonematic (as *ăr* or *ră*).

As a consequence of Rule VI, a potentially monophonematic sound combination must be considered a single phoneme if the only phoneme sequence for which it could be considered is realized by another combination of sounds which does not follow Rules I to III. Polish *č* (written *cz*), for example, which does not exceed a normal consonant in duration, and which in intervocalic position belongs entirely to the next syllable, must be considered the realization of a single phoneme because the phoneme cluster

$t + š$ (written *dsz*, *tsz*, or *trz*) in Polish is realized by another sound combination. The duration of the latter exceeds that of a normal consonant, and in intervocalic position this sound sequence is occasionally distributed over two syllables. For example: "podszywać," pronounced *pot-šyvać*." In Russian, too, the phoneme clusters $t + s$ and $t + š$ are realized by sound combinations which in duration and relation to the syllable boundary are quite different from "*c*" and "*č*," which are interpreted as monophonematic. The glottalized palatal sibilant fricative of Western Adyghe ("Adyghe" or "Circassian"), for example, in such words as "ɣeŝ'aɣ̆°e" (peculiar), is realized quite differently from the combination "palatal sibilant constrictive + glottal stop" in such words as "ɣeŝʔaɣ(e)" (gave to recognize). The former can therefore only be considered monophonematic. Examples of this type can easily be multiplied.

B   Polyphonematic Evaluation

The polyphonematic evaluation of a single sound is exactly the opposite of a monophonematic evaluation of a sound combination. In almost all such cases a phoneme sequence consisting of a vowel plus a preceding or following consonant is realized either as the consonant alone or as the vowel alone. The former case can occur only when the "suppressed," that is, the unrealized vowel has a particularly slight degree of sonority in other positions and accordingly approximates a consonant from an acoustic and articulatory point of view. The second case, on the other hand, is possible only if the suppressed consonant in other positions is realized as particularly "open," that is, with as much sonority and as little friction as possible, and consequently approximates a vowel. The first case actually involves short or unstressed high or indeterminate vowels, the second sonorants (liquids, nasals, and *w* and *j*). These are the *phonetic prerequisites* for the polyphonematic evaluation of single sounds. The *phonological conditions* governing this phenomenon can all be summarized under the following rule.

RULE VII.—*If a single sound and a combination of sounds corresponding to the above phonetic prerequisites stand in a relation of optional or combinatory variance, in which the sound combination must be considered the realization of a phoneme sequence, the single sound must also be considered the realization of the same phoneme sequence.*

Three typical cases can be distinguished:

a. The particular single sound occurs only in those positions where the respective combination of sounds is not permitted. Examples: In

German syllabic *l*, *m*, and *n* occur only in unstressed syllables before consonants or in final position, while the sound sequences *el*, *em*, and, *en* occur only in unstressed syllables before vowels. These sound sequences cannot be considered monophonematic since the syllable boundary lies between the ə and the following sonorant (see Rule I*a*, above). Syllabic *l*, *m*, and *n* are therefore considered realizations of the phoneme sequences "ə*l*, ə*m*, and ə*n*." (This is, incidentally, often revealed in slow and clear speech.) In many Polish dialects, namely, those in which the "*ą*" of literary Polish initially corresponds to ǫ and ų or *om* and *um*, nasalized vowels occur only before constrictives. The combination "vowel + nasal," on the other hand, occurs before stops and vowels, and in final position. Since the sequence "vowel + nasal" does not fulfill any of the three requirements for monophonematic evaluation, and since its constituent segments represent independent phonemes in other positions, they are considered the realization of the phoneme sequence "vowel + nasal." Nasalized vowels in the respective dialects must therefore be considered realizations of the same phoneme sequence "vowel + nasal."

b. A particular single phone α only occurs in a specific sound combination (αβ or βα) in which it is considered a combinatory variant of a particular phoneme. It also occurs in another position in which the sound sequence αβ or βα is not allowed: in this position the single phone α must then be regarded as replacing the entire sound sequence αβ or βα and must consequently be regarded as the realization of the corresponding phoneme sequence. Examples: In the Russian sound sequence ǫ*l* the tense ǫ is considered a combinatory variant of the phoneme "*o*." In addition to its occurrence in this sound sequence (and in the position before unstressed *u*, as in "pǫ̇-ŭxŭ" [over the ear]), the only other occurrence of tense ǫ is in the word "sǫ̀ncɔ̆" (sun). But since the sequence ǫ*l*, as well as any sequence of "vowel + *l*," never occurs before "*n* + consonant," the ǫ in "sǫ̀ncɔ̆" is. interpreted as substitution for the sequence ǫ*l*. Phonologically the entire word is then regarded as *solncă*. The unstressed "ŭ" in Russian is realized as an *ü* after palatalized consonants and after *j*, in all other positions as a *u*. For example, "jül'ìt'" (to turn and twist) is phonemically *jŭl'it*'; "t'ül'èn'" (seal) is phonemically *t'ŭl'en*'. In cases where *ü* in unstressed syllables occurs after a vowel it is regarded as a substitution for the phoneme combination "*jŭ*," which in that position cannot be realized in any other way. For example, "znàüt" (they know) is phonemically *znajŭt*. In Czech the "*i*" after *j* and after the palatals *t*', *d*', and *ň* is realized as a tense vowel, after gutturals, dentals, and sibilants, on the other hand, as a lax vowel. In connected discourse the initial *j* of the sequence *ji* is suppressed, that is, it is not realized after a final consonant of the preceding word. In this way tense *i* comes to occur directly after gutturals, dentals, and sibilants and is then regarded in that position as the realization of the phoneme sequence "*ji*." For example: Czech spelled "něco k jídlu" (something to eat), pronounced approximately as *ňecokĭdlu*; spelled "vytah ji ven" (he pulled her out), pronounced approximately as *vitaxĭven*; spelled "už ji mám" (I already have her), pronounced approximately as *ušĭmām*, which is different from *ušimām*, spelled "uši mám" (I have ears), having a lax *i*.

c. In many languages where sequences of consonants are not permitted at all, or are only permitted in a certain position, for example, initially or finally, the high vowels may optionally be suppressed. The consonant preceding another consonant then is considered the realization of the sequence of "consonant + high vowel." In Uzbek, which does not permit consonant sequences in initial position, the *i* in unstressed initial syllable is usually suppressed. For example, the word "to cook" is pronounced *pširmoq*, but is evaluated as *piširmoq*.[16] Japanese does not have any consonant sequences, with the exception of "nasal + consonant." Nor are consonants permitted in final position. However, in fast speech, especially after voiceless consonants, the vowel *u* is often suppressed. The preceding consonant then represents the combination "consonant + *u*." For example, "desu" (is) is pronounced *des*.

4   ERRORS IN MONOPHONEMATIC AND POLYPHONEMATIC EVALUATION OF THE SOUNDS OF A FOREIGN LANGUAGE

The rules governing monophonematic and polyphonematic evaluation refer to the structure of a given system and to the special role of the particular sound in this system. Sounds or combinations of sounds that are evaluated as monophonematic or polyphonematic in one language need not be considered such in other languages. But in the perception of a foreign language the "naive" observer transfers to the foreign language the phonic values that are the result of the relations existing in his own mother tongue. This, of course, leaves him with a quite incorrect impression of that language.

Evgenij L. Polivanov, in his article "La perception des sons d'une langue étrangère" (*TCLP*, IV, 79 ff.), gives a number of instructive examples. Japanese does not have any consonant sequences at all. Its high vowels are very short and can optionally be suppressed. Japanese speakers think that they also hear short high vowels between consonants and in final position in foreign languages. Polivanov illustrates this by the Japanese pronunciation of the Russian words "tak" (so), "put'" (way), "dar" (gift), "kor'" (measles), as *taku, puč'i, daru, kor'i*. The point may be illustrated further by the Japanese pronunciation of such English words as club *kurabu*, film *hurumu*, cream *kurimu*, ski *suki*, spoon *supun*, etc. The Japanese *Kirisuto* for "Christ" and many other cases may be cited. (Also compare Henri Frei, "Monosyllabisme et polysyllabisme dans les emprunts linguistiques," in *Bulletin de la Maison franco-japonaise*, VIII [1936].) As a consequence of this interpolation between consonants and after final consonants of *u* and *i* (and of *o* after *t* and *d*), as well as of the confusion of *r* and *l*, it is very difficult to understand a Japanese trying to speak a European language. Only after long practice is a Japanese able to break away from such pronunciation. But he then often goes to the opposite extreme and suppresses the foreign *u*'s and *i*'s that are etymological: consonants followed by a *u* or *i* and consonants without following vowels are for a Japanese simply optional variants of a phoneme sequence. He finds it extremely difficult to get accustomed not only to relating a distinctive function to these supposed optional variants, but also to regarding them as single phonemes and not as realizations of a phoneme sequence. Another example given by Polivanov is the Korean treatment of the sequence "*s* + consonant." Contrary to Japanese, Korean permits certain consonant combinations, though only medially. The combination "*s* + consonant," however, is foreign to Korean as it is spoken today. When a Korean hears such a sequence in a foreign language, he interprets the *s* as a special kind of pronunciation of the following consonant which he is not able to imitate; and when he wants to pronounce the respective word, he omits the *s*: Russian "starik skazal" (the old man said) becomes *tarik kazal*. Edward Sapir (*Journal de psychologie*, XXX, 262) tells us that American students, who in phonetic studies became acquainted with the existence of glottal plosives, tend to hear this sound after every short, stressed final vowel of the foreign language. The reason for this "acoustic" delusion lies in the fact that in English all final stressed vowels are long and that persons whose mother tongue is English can conceive of a short vowel only before a consonant.

Whenever we hear a sound in a foreign language which does not occur in our mother tongue, we tend to interpret it as a sound sequence and to regard it as the realization of a combination of phonemes of our mother tongue. Very often the sound perceived gives reason for doing this since every sound is a sequence of "sound atoms." The aspirates actually consist of occlusion, plosion, and aspiration; the affricates, of occlusion and friction. It is therefore not surprising if a foreigner in whose mother tongue these sounds are not present, or where they are not considered monophonematic, regards them as realizations of phoneme sequences. Likewise, it is quite natural that speakers of Russian and Czech consider the English long vowels, regarded as clearly monophonematic by English speakers, as diphthongs, that is, as combinations of two vowel phonemes. For these vowels are actually "diphthongs of movement." But the polyphonematic interpretation of foreign sounds is very often based on a delusion: different articulatory properties, which in reality occur simultaneously, are perceived as occurring in succession. Speakers of Bulgarian interpret German *ü* as *ju* ("juber" = "über" [over]), etc. They perceive the frontal position of the tongue and the protraction of the lips, which in German occur simultaneously, as separate stages. Ukrainians, to whom the *f* sound is unfamiliar, reproduce the unfamiliar *f* by *xv* (*Xvylyp* = *Philip*). They interpret the simultaneous properties of *f*, that is, voiceless friction and labiodental position of articulation, as two successive stages. Many foreigners perceive Czech *ř*, an absolutely homogeneous sound, as the sound sequence *rž*. (This interpretation even found its way into the Czech grammar by the Parisian Slavicist A. Mazon!)[17] In reality *ř* is only an *r* with less amplitude in vibration of the tip of the tongue, so that a frictionlike noise resembling a *ž* is audible between the trills of the *r*.[18] In some North Caucasian languages, such as Circassian, Kabardian, Artshi, and Avar, and in all languages of Western Daghestan, as well as in some American Indian languages and in some African languages such as Zulu, Suto, and Pedi, so-called voiced as well as voiceless "lateral spirants" occur. Foreign observers perceive the voiceless variety as *tl*, *kl*, *θl*, *xl*, *sl*, that is, voicelessness and lateral articulation are perceived as two successive phonemes.[19] Examples of this kind can easily be multiplied. From a psychological point of view, these examples can be explained by the fact that the phonemes are not symbolized by sounds but by specific distinctive *sound properties*, and that a combination of such sound properties is interpreted as a combination of phonemes. However, since two phonemes cannot occur simultaneously, they must be interpreted as occurring in succession.

When learning a foreign language, one must fend against all these difficulties. It is not enough to get one's vocal organs accustomed to a new articulation. One must also get one's phonological consciousness accustomed to interpreting such new articulations correctly as either monophonematic or polyphonematic.

---

[1] Cf. N. S. Trubetzkoy, *Anleitung zu phonologischen Beschreibungen* (Brno, 1935).

[2] Cf. N. F. Jakovlev, "Tablicy fonetiki kabardinskogo jazyka," in *Trudy podrazrjada issledovanija severnokavkazskich jazykov pri Institute vostokovedenija v Moskve*, I (Moscow, 1923).

[3] A fourth case can be mentioned. Sometimes a sound (α) occurs only in those positions in which two other sounds (α' and α'') are never found, α being closely related to α' as well as to α'', so that α must be considered a combinatory variant of both α' and α''. This is a case of neutralization of a phonological opposition. We will discuss this in detail later in its appropriate place (cf. pp. 77 ff.).

[4] This special function of signaling the neighboring phoneme can be termed *associative* or *ancillary-associative*.

[5] Cf. R. Jakobson, *O češskom stiche*.

[6] In this connection, cf. N. S. Trubetzkoy's *Anleitung zu phonologischen Beschreibungen*, pars. 7–16, mentioned above.

[7] It is, of course, true that in such German words as "Eier" (eggs), "blaue" (blue) transitional sounds may develop between the diphthong and the following vowel, which belong to the following syllables (so, for example, "æe̯-i̯ər," etc.). However, what is important is that the diphthong still belongs entirely to the first syllable.

[8] Cf. A. C. Lawrenson in *Proceedings of the Second International Congress of Phonetic Sciences*, p. 132.

[9] What has here been said must not be misunderstood. Each phenomenon pertaining to speech sounds has two aspects, an articulatory and an acoustic one. The fact that "Rule II" is only expressed in articulatory terms is due only to the circumstance that there are not enough means in present-day scientific terminology to describe acoustic impressions with precision. However, there is no doubt that there is a precise acoustic equivalent for the distinction between homogeneous articulatory movements, just as these exist for the movements for the dissolution of a sound and the movements for the formation of a sound; so that it is possible to determine, without knowing the requirements of articulation simply on the basis of the acoustic impression, whether a combination of sounds is "potentially monophonematic" or not.

[10] Cf. L. Ščerba, "Quelques mots sur les phonèmes consonnes composés," in *Mémoires de la Soc. de Ling. de Paris*, XV, 237 ff.

[11] Cf. John R. Swanton in *Bulletin of the Smithsonian Institution, Bureau of Ethnology*, XL.

[12] Cf. P. K. Uslar, *Etnografija Kavkaza*, I, "Jazykoznanije," III (*Avarskij jazyk*) (Tiflis, 1889).

[13] Furthermore, in native German words combinations of the type "occlusive + constrictive" are not permitted initially. (Words such as "Psalm" (psalm), "Xanthippe" (proper name) clearly bear the mark of foreign origin.) This also influences the monophonematic interpretation of *pf* and *ts* (*z*).

[14] Cf. P. K. Uslar, *Etnografija Kavkaza*, I, "Jazykoznanije," II (*Čečenskij jazyk*) (Tiflis, 1888).

[15] Cf. Franz Boas in *Bulletin of the Smithsonian Institution, Bureau of Ethnology*, XL.

[16] Cf. E. L. Polivanov in *TCLP*, IV, 83.

[17] *Grammaire de la langue tchèque* (Paris, 1931), p. 14.

[18] Cf. J. Chlumský, "Une variété peu connue de l'*r* lingual," in *Revue de phonétique* (1911).

[19] N. S. Trubetzkoy, "Les consonnes latérales des langues caucasiques-septentrionales," in *BSL*, XXIII, 3, 184 ff.

III LOGICAL CLASSIFICATION OF DISTINCTIVE OPPOSITIONS

1 PHONEMIC CONTENT AND PHONEMIC SYSTEM

If all the above-stated rules are applied correctly, a complete inventory of all phonemes of a given language can be established. But the *phonemic content* of each individual phoneme must be determined as well. By phonemic content we understand all phonologically distinctive properties of a phoneme, that is, those properties which are common to all variants of a phoneme and which distinguish it from all other phonemes of the same language, especially from those that are most closely related. German "*k*" cannot be defined as "velar" because only some of its variants possess this property. Before *i* and *ü*, for example, "*k*" is realized as palatal. A definition of German "*k*" as "dorsal" (a sound produced with the dorsum of the tongue), on the other hand, would also be inadequate since "*g*" as well as "*ch*" are "dorsal." The phonemic content of the German phoneme *k* can only be formulated as follows: "tense nonnasalized dorsal occlusive." In other words, only the following properties are distinctive for the German phoneme *k*: (1) complete occlusion (as opposed to "*ch*"); (2) blocking of the entrance to the nasal cavity (as opposed to "*ng*"); (3) tightening of the muscles of the tongue and simultaneous relaxation of the muscles of the larynx (as opposed to "*g*"); (4) participation of the dorsum (as opposed to "t" and "p"). *k* shares the first of these four characteristics with *t, p, tz, pf, d, b, g, m, n,* and *ng*; the second with *g, t, d, p,* and *b*; the

66

third with *p*, *t*, *ss*, and *f*; and the fourth with *g*, *ch*, and *ng*. Only the sum of all four marks is characteristic for *k* alone. From what has been said it is evident that the determination of the phonemic content of a phoneme pre-supposes its prior classification in the system of distinctive oppositions existing in the language in question. The definition of the content of a pho-neme depends on what position this phoneme takes in the given phonemic system, that is, in final analysis, with which other phonemes it is in oppo-sition. A phoneme can therefore sometimes be defined in purely negative terms. For example, if one considers all the optional and combinatory variants of the German phoneme *r*, the only way in which this phoneme can be defined is as a "nonlateral liquid." This is a purely negative definition since a "liquid" itself is a "nonnasal sonorant," and a "sono-rant" is a "nonobstruent."

2   CLASSIFICATION OF OPPOSITIONS

A   On the Basis of Their Relationship to the Entire System of Oppositions: Multilateral and Bilateral, Isolated and Proportional Oppositions; and the Structure of the Phonemic Systems Based Thereon

The phonemic inventory of a language is actually only a corollary of the system of distinctive oppositions. It should always be remembered that in phonology the major role is played, not by the phonemes, but by the distinctive oppositions. Each phoneme has a definable phonemic content only because the system of distinctive oppositions shows a definite order or structure. In order to understand this structure, various types of distinctive oppositions must be studied.

Above all, certain notions must be introduced which are of decisive importance, not only for phonological systems of oppositions but for any other kind as well.[1]

An opposition not only presupposes those properties by which the opposition members are distinguished from each other, but also those properties that are common to both opposition members. The latter properties may be termed "the basis for comparison." Two things that have no basis for comparison, that do not have a single property in common, as, for example, an inkpot and free will, do not form an opposition. In a system of oppositions such as the phonological system of a language, two types of oppositions are to be distinguished: *bilateral* and *multilateral*. In the case of *bilateral* oppositions the basis for comparison, that is, the sum of the properties common to both opposition members, is common to these two opposition members alone. It does not recur in any other member of the same system. The basis for comparison of a multilateral opposition, on the other hand, is not limited exclusively to the two respective opposition members. It also extends to other members of the same system. The difference between bilateral and multilateral oppositions can be illustrated by examples from the Latin alphabet. The opposition of the letters *E* and *F* is bilateral because the sum of the features common to these two letters—a vertical bar and two horizontal lines extending to the right, the one extending from the upper end of the bar, the other from its middle—does not recur in any other letter of the Latin alphabet. The opposition of the letters *P* and *R*, on the other hand, is multilateral, because the sum of the features that both letters have in common, that is, a loop toward the right on the upper end of a vertical bar, in addition to its occurrence in these two letters, also occurs in the letter *B*.

The distinction between bilateral and multilateral oppositions is extremely important for the general theory of oppositions. It can be made in any system of oppositions and so, of course, also in systems of distinctive oppositions (or phoneme inventories). For example, the opposition *t-d* is bilateral in German because *t* and *d* are the only dental occlusives of the German phonemic system. The opposition *d-b*, on the other hand, is multilateral in German because the weak occlusion that the two phonemes have in common also recurs in another German phoneme, namely *g*. Consequently, every distinctive opposition can be recognized quite accurately and clearly as being bilateral or multilateral. Of course, only the phonologically distinctive properties are to be considered. However, some nondistinctive properties may be taken into consideration as well if, on the basis of these properties, the members of the opposition in question are placed in opposition with other phonemes of the same system. For example, the opposition *d-n* (as in French) is to be considered bilateral because its members are the only voiced dental occlusives. Yet neither voicing nor occlusion is distinctive for *n*, as neither voiceless nor spirantal *n* occur as independent phonemes in the respective system.

In every system of oppositions the multilateral oppositions outnumber the bilateral ones. The consonantal system of stage German, for example, contains twenty consonant phonemes (*b, ch, d, f, g, h, k, l, m, n, ng, p, pf, r, ss, s, sch, t, w,* and *tz*)* and consequently one hundred and ninety possible oppositions. Of these, only thirteen are bilateral (*b-p, d-t, g-k, b-m, d-n, g-ng, pf-f, k-ch, tz-ss, f-w, ss-s, ss-sch,* and *r-l*). All the others, that is, 93 percent of the entire system, are multilateral. There are phonemes that do not take part in any bilateral oppositions: among the German consonants, *h* is such a phoneme. But every phoneme must take part in multilateral oppositions. Among the oppositions in which a specific phoneme participates, the multilateral oppositions are always more numerous than the bilateral ones. Every German consonant phoneme participates in nineteen oppositions. At the most, only two of these are bilateral. But it is precisely the bilateral oppositions that are the most important for the determination of the phonemic content of a phoneme. Consequently, despite their relatively low number, bilateral oppositions play an important role in the structure of phonological systems.

Within the multilateral oppositions *homogeneous* and *heterogeneous* oppositions are to be distinguished. *Homogeneous* oppositions are those multilateral oppositions whose members can be conceived of as the outermost points in a "chain."[2] For example, in German the opposition *u-e* is multilateral: both phonemes have only in common that they are vowels. This property is not limited to them alone, but is also shared by a whole number of other German phonemes, namely, by all vowels. The members of the opposition *u-e* are nevertheless to be conceived of as the outermost points of the chain *u-o, o-ö, ö-e,* consisting entirely of bilateral oppositions: in the German vowel system *u* and *o* are the only back rounded vowels, *o*

---

* *Translator's note:* The letters of the alphabet rather than phonetic symbols are used—which is slightly confusing (*ch* = phonetic symbol "x," *ng* = "ŋ," *ss* = "s," *s* = "z," *sch* = "š," *w* = "v"). The German consonant phonemes in phonetic transcription thus are: *p, t, k, b, d, g, p̆, c, f, š, s, x, h, v, z, (ž), m, n, ŋ, l,* and *r.* As regards "*j*," see footnote 3. *ž,* not mentioned above, occurs in loanwords.

and *ö* the only rounded vowels with a mid-degree of aperture, and *ö* and *e* the only front vowels with a mid-degree of aperture. The opposition *u-e* is therefore homogeneous. Also homogeneous is the multilateral opposition *x-ŋ* ("ch-ng") of the German consonant system: it can be analyzed into a chain of the following bilateral oppositions: *x-k*, *k-g*, *g-ŋ*. The multilateral opposition *p-t*, on the other hand, is heterogeneous since there are no phonemes between *p* and *t* that could be conceived of as standing in a relation of bilateral opposition to these two phonemes as well as to each other. It is clear that with respect to the total phonemic system of a language, the heterogeneous multilateral oppositions must always be more numerous than the homogeneous ones. But homogeneous oppositions are very important for the determination of the phonemic content of a phoneme and consequently also for the entire structure of a given phonemic system.

Two types of homogeneous multilateral oppositions can be distinguished, depending on whether the opposition members can be related to each other by means of one or several "chains" of bilateral oppositions. These are the *linear* and the *nonlinear* oppositions. Of the two examples given above, the opposition *x-ŋ* is linear because the "chain" *x-k-g-ŋ* is the only possible one in the framework of the German phonemic system. The opposition *u-e*, on the other hand, is nonlinear because the "path" from *u* to *e* within the German phonemic system can be conceived of via several "chains" of bilateral oppositions (*u-o-ö-e*, *u-ü-ö-e*, *u-ü-i-e*, or *u-o-a-ä-e*).

Of no less importance than the distinction between bilateral and multilateral oppositions is the distinction between *proportional* and *isolated* oppositions. An opposition is proportional if the relation between its members is identical with the relation between the members of another opposition or several other oppositions of the same system. For example, the opposition *p-b* in German is proportional because the relation between *p* and *b* is identical with that between *t* and *d* or between *k* and *g*. The opposition *p-š*, on the other hand, is isolated because the German phonemic system does not have any other pair of phonemes whose members would be related to each other in the same way as *p* is related to *š*. The distinction between proportional and isolated oppositions can exist in the case of bilateral as well as multilateral oppositions: in German, for example, the opposition *p-b* is bilateral and proportional, *r-l* bilateral and isolated, *p-t* multilateral and proportional (see *b-d*, *m-n*), and *p-š* multilateral and isolated.

In every system the isolated oppositions are more numerous than the proportional ones. In the German consonant system, for example, only

40 oppositions are proportional and 150 (i.e., 80 percent) are isolated. They are distributed as follows:

bilateral proportional	11 (6%)
bilateral isolated	2 (1%)
multilateral proportional	29 (15%)
multilateral isolated	148 (78%).

This means that the bilateral oppositions are predominantly proportional, the multilateral oppositions predominantly isolated.

The absolute figures, of course, vary from language to language. In principle, however, the ratio remains the same everywhere: the largest group is formed by isolated multilateral oppositions, the smallest by isolated bilateral oppositions. The proportional oppositions are found between these extreme points, with multilateral oppositions always outnumbering the bilateral ones. What is important for the characterization of a given system is not so much the numerical ratio between the various opposition classes, as the percentage of phonemes participating in each of these classes. The German consonant phonemes include only a single phoneme, *h*, which participates exclusively in an isolated multilateral opposition; three phonemes participate only in an isolated bilateral opposition, namely, *š*, *r*, and *l*; all the rest (i.e., 80 percent of all consonant phonemes) participate simultaneously in bilateral and multilateral proportional oppositions. In Russian the consonants that take part in proportional oppositions constitute 88 percent, in Burmese as much as 97 percent. Even more important is the ratio of the number of bilateral proportional oppositions to the number of phonemes participating in these oppositions. While 16 phonemes take part in 11 bilateral proportional oppositions in the German consonant system, 30 consonant phonemes participate in 27 of these oppositions in Russian, and 60 consonant phonemes in 79 such oppositions in Burmese.* If the number of bilateral proportional oppositions is divided by the number of participant phonemes, one obtains 0.69 for the German consonant system, 0.90 for the Russian, and 1.32 for the Burmese.

These different types of oppositions determine the inner order or structure of the phonemic inventory as a system of distinctive oppositions. All proportional oppositions that show identical relations between their members can be combined into a "proportion," hence the term "proportional." For example, in German b-d = p-t = m-n, or u-o = $ü$-$ö$ = i-e.

---

* *Translator's note:* In "Outline of Burmese Grammar" by W. S. Cornyn, Lang. Diss. No. 38, published by the Linguistic Society of America, 1944, the total number of phonemes in Burmese is given as 29 consonants, 9 vowels, and 4 tones.

On the other hand, we have already mentioned those "chains" of bilateral oppositions which can be interpolated between the members of the homogeneous, and in particular of the linear-homogeneous, multilateral oppositions: in German, for example, x-k-g-$ŋ$ or u-$ü$-i. If one of the oppositions of such a "chain" is proportional, the "chain" intersects with a "proportion." If a phoneme participates simultaneously in several proportional oppositions, several "proportions" intersect. A phonemic system can therefore be represented in the form of a series of intersecting parallels. In the German consonant system the proportions b-d = p-t = m-n, b-p = d-t, and b-m = d-n form an intersection that can be represented in the form of two parallel chains: p-b-m and t-d-n. The proportions p-b = t-d = k-g and b-m = d-n = g-$ŋ$ result in the parallelism of the chains p-b-m and t-d-n with k-g-$ŋ$. However, the last chain can be augmented by an additional member. It then takes on the shape x-k-g-$ŋ$. The relation x-k (stricture/occlusion) is identical in essence with the relations f-$p̆$ and s-c which themselves are only a section of the parallel chains v-f-$p̆$ and z-s-c. Finally, s is simultaneously a member of the bilateral isolated opposition s-$š$. Thus the following picture emerges:

$$
\begin{array}{cccc}
 & v & z & \\
 & x \quad f & s & š \\
p & t \quad k & p̆ & c \\
b & d \quad g & & \\
m & n \quad ŋ & &
\end{array}
$$

This comprises seventeen phonemes, that is 85 percent of the entire consonant system of German. Outside this scheme are the phonemes r and l which, as the only liquids of German, form an isolated bilateral opposition; and, too, the phoneme h, which stands exclusively in a relation of multilateral isolated opposition to all the other consonants.[3]

The order achieved by dividing phonemes into parallel rows does not exist only on paper and is not only a matter of graphics. It corresponds to phonological reality. Due to the fact that a specific relation between two phonemes obtains in several proportional oppositions, the relation itself can now be thought of and used phonologically independently of individual phonemes. As a result, the particular properties of the respective phonemes are recognized as such with particular clarity and the phonemes can be more readily dissolved into their phonological features.

It is a basic fact of phonology that the phonemic content of a phoneme depends on the position of this phoneme in the phonemic system and consequently on the structure of that system. Since the systems of distinctive oppositions differ from language to language and from dialect to dialect, the phonemic content of the phonemes also varies according to language and dialect. This difference can also affect the realization of the phonemes.

The phoneme *r* in the various languages may serve as an illustration. As we have seen, German *r* stands in a relation of bilateral opposition only to *l*. Its phonemic content is very poor, actually purely negative: it is not a vowel, not a specific obstruent, not a nasal, nor an *l*. Consequently, it also varies greatly with respect to its realization. Before vowels it is a dental vibrant for some speakers of German, a uvular vibrant for others. For still others it is some sort of almost noiseless guttural spirant. In positions other than before vowels it is generally pronounced either as a nonsyllabic vowel of indeterminate quality, or as an incompletely articulated guttural, only rarely as a weak vibrant. Czech *r* has a much richer phonemic content, as it stands in a relation of bilateral opposition not only to *l* but also to a special Czech phoneme *ř*: *r* and *l* are the only liquids, *r* and *ř* the only two vibrants of Czech. *r* is distinguished from *ř* in that it is not an obstruent but a liquid; from *l* in that it is a vibrant. For this reason, Czech *r* is always, and in all positions, pronounced as a clear and energetically trilled sonorant. In contrast with the German *r*, it cannot be "slurred over." A uvular pronunciation is unpopular for Czech *r* since the opposition *r-ř* would thereby lose some of its distinctness. Czech *r* is normally dental (i.e., it is an alveolar *r*). A uvular *r* only occurs as an extremely rare individual variant and is considered incorrect.[4] The *r* phoneme of Gilyak, a language that is spoken in Eastern Siberia at the mouth of the Amur and in the northern part of Sakhalin Island, presents quite a different picture.[5] In addition to voiced *r*, this language also has a voiceless ɹ with clear friction. Since this ɹ is considered a voiceless spirant, the opposition *r-ɹ* is not only bilateral but also proportional, and forms a proportion with the oppositions *v-f*, *z-s*, *γ-x*, *ǰ-x̌*. Consequently *r* in this case is regarded as a voiced spirant. When the *r* in Gilyak is articulated energetically, especially when it occurs in gemination, a *ž*-type friction can clearly be heard. This can never be the case with Czech *r* since it might then be confused with *ř*. Furthermore, the oppositions *v-f*, *z-s*, *γ-x*, *ǰ-x̌* are linked with the chains *b-p-p'*, *ž-ć-ć'*, *g-k-k'*, *ǧ-ḳ-ḳ'*. In parallel manner *r-ɹ* are also linked with *d-t-t'*. Thus, the following diagram emerges:

$$
\begin{array}{ccccc}
d & b & \dot{z} & g & \check{g} \\
t & p & ć & k & ḳ \\
t' & p' & ć' & k' & ḳ' \\
r & v & z & γ & \check{γ} \\
ɹ & f & s & x & \check{x}
\end{array}
$$

A uvular pronunciation of Gilyak r is therefore completely out of the question. It is always realized as a dental. The phonemic content of Gilyak r is thus "a voiced continuant of the dental series." Since Gilyak also has an l, r must be pronounced as a distinct vibrant. Last in this series of examples, the Japanese r may be discussed. This is the only liquid of the Japanese phonemic system. It stands in a relation of bilateral opposition with only one phoneme, namely, palatalized r'. But since all Japanese consonants have palatalized equivalents, palatalization cannot be considered a specific peculiarity of r. Japanese r must therefore be defined as a "nonpalatal liquid." (The term liquid refers to a consonant phoneme that is neither an obstruent nor a nasal.) The realization of this phoneme is therefore rather indeterminate. l sometimes occurs as an optional variant, but even when this is not the case, r cannot be vigorously trilled since by so doing it would acquire too distinct a character, r is mostly realized as a single "flap of the tongue." A uvular articulation is impossible, as this might place in jeopardy the proportionality of the opposition r-r'.

The number of examples could be increased ad infinitum, and illustrations could be taken from many other languages to show the dependence of the phonemic content of the phoneme r on its position in the phonemic system and, therefore, on the structure of this system. And in most cases the phonetic realization of r, the number of its variants, etc., can be deduced from its phonemic content. Any other phoneme could be chosen instead of r. The result would remain unchanged. In summary, one can say that the phonemic content of a phoneme depends on the structure of the corresponding phonemic system. And since phonemic systems are structured differently in every language and even in every dialect, it is relatively rare to find a phoneme with exactly the same phonemic content in two different languages. One must not be misguided by the use of common international symbols of transcription. These symbols are only useful expedients. If the same letters should only be used for phonemes with fully equivalent phonemic content, a separate alphabet would have to be used for every language.

B   Classification of Oppositions on the Basis of the Relation
      between Opposition Members: Privative, Gradual, and
      Equipollent Oppositions

The structure of a phonemic system depends on the distribution of the bilateral, multilateral, proportional, and isolated oppositions. The division of oppositions into these four classes is therefore of importance. The principles of classification then relate to the phonemic system: whether

an opposition is bilateral or multilateral depends on whether the properties
shared by the opposition members in question are common to these members alone or recur in still other members of the same system. Whether an
opposition is proportional or isolated depends on whether or not the same
relation of opposition recurs in still other oppositions of the same system.
But the different types of phonological oppositions can also be classified
without consideration of the respective system by establishing a principle
of classification based on the purely logical relations obtaining between two
opposition members. Such a classification is of no importance for the
purely external structure of the phonemic inventory. It becomes very
important, however, from the standpoint of the function of the phonemic
systems.

In regard to the relation existing between opposition members, phonological oppositions can be divided into three types:

a. Privative oppositions are oppositions in which one member is characterized by the presence, the other by the absence, of a mark. For example:
"voiced"/"voiceless," "nasalized"/"nonnasalized," "rounded"/"unrounded." The opposition member that is characterized by the presence
of the mark is called "marked," the member characterized by its absence
"unmarked." This type of opposition is extremely important for
phonology.

b. Gradual oppositions are oppositions in which the members are
characterized by various degrees or gradations of the same property. For
example: the opposition between two different degrees of aperture in
vowels, as in German *u-o, ü-ö, i-e*, or between various degrees of tonality.
The member of a gradual opposition that possesses an extreme (either
minimal or maximal) degree of the particular property is the *extreme* or
external member, while the other member is the *mid* member. Gradual
oppositions are relatively rare and not as important as privative
oppositions.

c. Equipollent oppositions are oppositions in which both members are
logically equivalent, that is, they are neither considered as two degrees
of one property nor as the absence or presence of a property. For example:
German *p-t* and *f-k*. Equipollent oppositions are the most frequent in
any system.

A phonic opposition, taken out of the context of the phonemic system
and its functioning and considered in isolation, is always at once equipollent
and gradual. As an example, let us study the opposition between voiced
and voiceless obstruents. Instrumental phonetics teaches that consonants
are only rarely absolutely voiced or absolutely voiceless: most cases merely
involve various degrees of voice participation. Further, the voicing of

an obstruent is connected with the relaxation of the muscles of the vocal organs. Voicelessness, on the other hand, is related to their tensing. The relation between *d* and *t*, as, for example, in Russian or French, is ambiguous from a purely phonetic point of view. In order to interpret their relation as privative, it is first of all important to focus attention on a single discriminative property alone (for example, only on voice or only on tensing of the muscles of the tongue). All others must be disregarded. In the second place, the lesser degree of the particular property must be "equated with zero." For example, the relation between *u* and *o* is privative as well if one regards these two vowels as the two extreme degrees of opening or closure, and if one interprets one of the degrees of aperture or closure as "zero degree": *u* is then the "unopen," *o* the "open" vowel, or, vice versa, *u* is the "close" and *o* the "unclose" rounded (or back) vowel phoneme. But the same relation of *u-o* becomes one of gradual opposition if the same vowel system has still another vowel with a degree of aperture exceeding that of *o*: *u* is then the extreme, and *o* the mid, member of a gradual opposition.

The interpretation of a distinctive opposition as equipollent, gradual, or privative thus depends on the standpoint from which it is viewed. Yet, one should not assume that its interpretation is purely subjective and arbitrary. The structure and the functioning of the phonemic system in most cases indicates quite unequivocally and clearly how each opposition is to be evaluated. In a language that in addition to *u* and *o* has still other back, or back and rounded, vowels with a degree of opening greater than that of *o*, for example, ɔ or *a*, the opposition *u-o* must be evaluated as gradual. On the other hand, in a language where *u* and *o* are the only back vowels, there is no reason to regard the opposition *u-o* as gradual. The opposition *t-d*, which was given as an example above, would only have to be evaluated as gradual in the case where the respective phonemic system contains still a third "dental" occlusive with a degree of voicelessness (and tensing of the muscles of the tongue) greater and more complete than that of *t*, or, vice versa, smaller than that of *d*. In cases where this condition does not prevail, there is no reason to interpret the opposition *t-d* as gradual. If the functioning of the phonemic system points to *t* as the unmarked member of the opposition *t-d*, the opposition *t-d* must be considered privative. The tensing of the muscles of the tongue must then be considered an irrelevant side phenomenon, the degree of voicing of *t* being "zero," so that *t* is to be regarded as "voiceless" and *d* as "voiced." But if, on the other hand, in accordance with the functioning of the phonemic system, not *t* but *d* is the unmarked member, voicing becomes an irrelevant side phenomenon, and the tensing of the muscles of the tongue the discriminative mark of the opposition. *t* must then be considered "tense" and *d* as "lax." Finally, if from the standpoint of the functioning of the phonemic system neither *d* nor *t* can be considered unmarked, the opposition *t-d* must be regarded as equipollent.[7]

The classification of concrete oppositions into gradual or privative oppositions thus depends partly on the structure and partly on the functioning of the phonemic system. But in addition, the opposition itself must contain something that makes its evaluation as either gradual or privative possible. An opposition such as *k-l* can be neither privative nor gradual under any circumstances because its members can be conceived of neither as the presence and absence, nor as two different degrees, of the same property. The opposition *u-o*, on the other hand, can be conceived of as privative ("close"/"unclose" or "open"/"unopen") as well as gradual. Whether it actually must be regarded as privative, gradual, or equipollent depends on the structure and functioning of the respective phonemic system. It is therefore possible to distinguish *potentially* or *logically* privative or gradual oppositions from oppositions that are *actually* privative or gradual, and *logically* equipollent oppositions from those *actually* equipollent. Logically equipollent oppositions are always actually equipollent as well. Actually equipollent oppositions, on the other hand, are not always logically equipollent but are sometimes logically privative or logically gradual. Presented in a diagram, they are as follows:

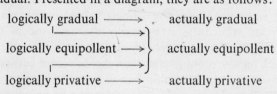

C   Classification of Oppositions on the Basis of the Extent of
     Their Distinctive Force: Constant and Neutralizable Oppositions

By the functioning of a phonemic system we understand the combinations of phonemes permissible in a given language, as well as the rules governing the distinctive force of the individual oppositions.

So far we have spoken of phonemes, distinctive oppositions, and systems of oppositions, without consideration of the actual distribution of the phonological units in the formation of words and forms. The role of the individual oppositions in a given language is rather varied, depending on the extent to which they actually possess distinctive force in all positions.[8] In Danish *æ* and *e* occur in all conceivable positions: they form a *constant* distinctive opposition whose members are independent phonemes. In Russian *e* occurs only before *j* and before palatalized consonants, while ε occurs in all other positions: here *e* and ε are noninterchangeable phones that cannot be considered two independent phonemes but are two combinatory variants of a single phoneme. In French, however, *e* and ε occur only finally in open syllable as members of a distinctive opposition "les"/ "lait," "allez"/"allait". In all other positions the occurrence of *e* and ε is predictable: ε occurs in closed syllable, *e* in open. These two vowels must thus be considered two phonemes only in final open syllable and combinatory variants of a single phoneme in all other positions. The distinctive opposition in French is thus *neutralized* in certain positions. We call such oppositions *neutralizable* oppositions, the positions in which the neutralization takes place, *positions of neutralization*, and those positions where the opposition is relevant, *positions of relevance*.

The psychological difference between constant and neutralizable distinctive oppositions is very great. Constant distinctive oppositions are perceived clearly even by those members of the speech community who have had no phonetic training. The terms of such an opposition are considered two distinct "phonic entities." In neutralizable distinctive oppositions perception fluctuates: in positions of relevance both opposition members are clearly distinguished; in positions of neutralization, on the other hand, it is often not possible to indicate which of the two had just been produced or perceived. However, even in the position of relevance, members of a neutralizable opposition are often felt only as two meaning-differentiating nuances, that is, as two distinct yet closely related phonic entities. This sense of intimate relatedness is especially characteristic of opposition members of this type. From a purely phonetic point of view, the difference between French *i* and *e* is not greater than the difference between *e* and ε. But the closeness of the relationship between *e* and ε is apparent to any Frenchman, while in the case of *i* and *e* there can be no question of any particular closeness: the reason for this phenomenon is, of course, that the opposition between ε and *e* is neutralizable, while the opposition between *i* and *e* is constant.

Still, it should not be assumed that the distinction between neutralizable and constant distinctive oppositions is meaningful only from a psychological point of view. This distinction is of extreme importance for the functioning of phonemic systems, as was first stressed by N. Durnovo. It must be considered one of the basic principles of the theory of phonemic systems. Neutralization and neutralizability of distinctive oppositions therefore deserve a detailed discussion.

Above all, the term itself must be clearly delineated. Not every type of distinctive opposition can be "neutralized." In those positions in which a neutralizable opposition is actually neutralized, the specific marks of an opposition member lose their distinctive force. Only those features which are common to both opposition members, that is, which serve as the basis for comparison for the respective opposition, remain relevant. One member of the opposition thus becomes the representative of the "archiphoneme" of the respective opposition in the position of neutralization. By the term "archiphoneme" we understand the sum of distinctive properties that two phonemes have in common.[9] It follows that only bilateral oppositions can be neutralized. In effect, only those oppositions that can be contrasted with all other phonological units of a given system have archiphonemes. And it is this contrastive capacity that is the basic prerequisite for phonological existence in general. In German the bilateral opposition *d-t* is neutralized in final position. The opposition member, which occurs in the position of neutralization, from a phonological point of view is neither a voiced stop nor a voiceless stop but "the nonnasal dental occlusive in general." As such it can be placed in opposition with the dental nasal *n*, as well as with the nonnasal labial and velar stops. However, the fact that German *t* and *d* cannot occur before *l* in word-initial position, while *b* and *p* do occur in that position, cannot effect a neutralization of the oppositions *d-b* and *p-t*: in a word such as "Blatt" (leaf) *b* retains all its properties, that is, it remains a voiced labial stop. It cannot be considered the representative of the archiphoneme of the opposition *d-b* because the phonological content of such an archiphoneme could only be a "voiced stop in general." But the *b* in "Blatt" cannot be interpreted as such because the *g* in "glatt" (smooth) is also a voiced stop. Actual neutralization, by which an opposition member becomes the representative of an archiphoneme, is therefore only possible in cases of distinctive bilateral oppositions. But this by no means implies that all bilateral oppositions are in effect neutralizable: constant bilateral oppositions probably exist in almost any language. But, whenever a language has a neutralizable opposition, it is always bilateral.

How is the archiphoneme representative of a neutralizable opposition to be realized? There are four possible cases:

CASE I.—The representative of the archiphoneme of a neutralizable opposition occurring in the position of neutralization is not identical with either of the opposition members.

a. It is realized by a sound phonetically related to both opposition members but not identical with either one. In Russian the opposition between palatalized and nonpalatalized labials is neutralized before palatalized dentals. A special type of "semipalatalized" labial occurs in the position of neutralization: in English, where the opposition between voiced lenes *b*, *d*, *g*, and voiceless fortes *p*, *t*, *k*, is neutralized after *s*, a special type of voiceless lenes consonant occurs in that position; in certain Bavaro-Austrian dialects, in which the opposition between fortes and lenes is neutralized initially, special "semifortes" or "semilenes" sounds occur in that position, and so on. The number of examples could easily be multiplied. In all these cases the archiphoneme is represented by a phone *intermediary* to the two opposition members.

b. Somewhat different are those cases in which the representative of the archiphoneme, in addition to the features that it shares with one or the other opposition member, has still other specific features proper to it alone. Features of the latter category are then a result of assimilation to the phoneme next to which the opposition is neutralized. In the Peking dialect of Chinese, for example, the opposition *k-c* is neutralized before *i* and *ü* and a palatal *č'* appears as the representative of the archiphoneme.[10] In Yami, a language spoken on Tobago Island, palatalized *l*, occurs before *i* as the archiphoneme of the opposition "dental *l*"/"retroflex *l*," etc.[11]

In all these cases, that is, in the cases discussed under (*a*) as well as (*b*), the phone that occurs in the position of neutralization is some kind of combinatory variant of the one as well as the other opposition member. Cases in which the archiphoneme is represented by a phone not fully identical with either of the opposition members are rather numerous. However, they are still less frequent than cases in which the sound occurring in the position of neutralization is more or less identical with the realization of a specific opposition member in the position of relevance.

CASE II.—The representative of the archiphoneme is identical with the realization of one of the opposition members, the choice of the archiphoneme representative being conditioned *externally*. This is possible only in cases where the neutralization of a neutralizable opposition depends on the proximity of some particular phoneme. The opposition member that "bears a closer resemblance or relation" to such a neighboring phoneme, or is even identical with it, becomes the representative of the archiphoneme. In many languages where the opposition between *voiced* and *voiceless* (or fortes and lenes) obstruents is neutralized before other obstruents of the same type of articulation, only voiced obstruents can occur before voiced (or lenes) obstruents, and only voiceless obstruents before voiceless (or fortes) obstruents. In Russian, where the opposition between palatalized and nonpalatalized consonants is neutralized before nonpalatalized dentals, only nonpalatalized consonants can occur in that position, and so on. In cases of this type which are relatively rare, the choice of an opposition member as the representative of the respective archiphoneme is conditioned purely externally by the nature of the position of neutralization.

CASE III.—The choice of an opposition member as the archiphoneme representative is conditioned *internally*.

a. In cases of this type one of the opposition members occurs in the position of neutralization, and its choice is in no way related to the nature of the position of neutralization. However, due to the fact that one of the opposition members occurs in that position as the representative of the respective archiphoneme, its specific features become nonrelevant, while the specific features of its partner receive full phonological relevance: the former opposition member is thus considered "archiphoneme + zero," while the latter is considered "archiphoneme + a specific mark." In other words, the opposition member that is permitted in the position of neutralization is *unmarked* from the standpoint of the respective phonemic system, while the opposing member is *marked*. This, of course, can only be the case where the neutralizable opposition is logically privative. However, most neutralizable distinctive oppositions belong to this category, that is, they are regarded as oppositions between unmarked and marked members, the member in the position of neutralization being regarded as unmarked.

b. If, however, the neutralizable opposition is not privative but gradual, as, for example, the opposition between the different degrees of aperture in vowels, or between the various levels of tone, it is always the *external* or *extreme* opposition member that occurs in the position of neutralization. In the dialects of Bulgarian and Modern Greek, in which the oppositions *u-o* and *i-e* are neutralized in unstressed syllables, the maximally close (actually minimally open) *u* and *i* serve as representatives of the respective archiphonemes in the position of neutralization. In Russian, where the opposition *o-a* is neutralized in unstressed syllables, the maximally open (actually minimally close) *a* represents the respective archiphoneme in the immediately pretonic syllable. In Lamba, a Bantu language of N. Rhodesia, where the opposition between low and mid tone is neutralized in final position, the position of neutralization, that is, in final syllables, permits only low tone.[12] Examples could easily be multiplied. The reason for this phenomenon is not always clear. As we have already emphasized, a gradual opposition can be regarded as gradual only if the same phonemic system contains still another element that shows a different degree of the same property. But such degree must always be higher than that of the "mid" opposition member: *i-e* forms a gradual opposition provided that the same vowel system contains still another vowel with a greater degree of aperture than *e*, etc. The "extreme" member of a gradual opposition always represents the minimal degree of the particular property, while the mid member of the same opposition exceeds this minimum, that is, it can be represented as "minimum + something more of the same property." And since the archiphoneme can only contain that which is common to both opposition members, it can only be represented by the extreme opposition member.[13] If the neutralizable opposition is logically equipollent, an internally conditioned choice of the representative of the archiphoneme is, of course, impossible. But it should be noted that the neutralization of a logically equipollent opposition is a rare phenomenon in any event.

CASE IV.—Both opposition members represent the archiphoneme: one member in one, the other in another, environment of the position of neutralization. This case is logically opposed to the first, in which neither of the two opposition members is the representative of the archiphoneme. In its pure form it is rather rare. In most instances this fourth possibility is only a combination of the second and the third case. Thus, for example, in Japanese the opposition between palatalized (*i*- and *j*-colored) consonants and unpalatalized consonants is neutralized before *e*. It is clear that the choice of the representative of the archiphoneme before *i* was here conditioned externally, and before *e* internally. But there are cases that do not permit such interpretation. In German the opposition *s-š* is neutralized before consonants. The archiphoneme is represented root-initially by *š* root-medially and finally by *s*. Here there can be no question of an externally conditioned choice of the archiphoneme representative nor of an internally conditioned choice, particularly since an equipollent opposition is involved. In other cases the various positions of neutralization are not quite equivalent from a phonological standpoint. The two representatives of the archiphoneme cannot therefore be considered in entirely equivalent terms either. For example, in German the opposition between "sharp" *s* and "soft" *z* is neutralized root-initially as well as morpheme-finally, the archiphoneme being represented by "soft" *z* initially, and "sharp" *s* finally. However, in German, final position is also the position of the least phonemic distinction: the oppositions *p-b, k-g, t-d, s-z, f-v*, as well as the oppositions of vowel quantity, are neutralized in that position. Only eighteen out of the total of thirty-nine phonemes in the German language can occur in that position, while thirty-six phonemes can occur initially (*a, ah, äh, au, b, ch, d, e, eh, ei, eu, f, g, h, i* or *j* respectively, *ih, k, l, m, n, o, ö, öh, oh, p, pf, r, s, sch, t, u, ü, üh, uh, w, z*).* It is clear that the representative of the archiphoneme which occurs in initial position must under

---

* *Translator's note:* In phonetic transcription: *a, a:, æ:, au, b, x, d, ɛ, e:, ei, eu, f, g h, I or j, i:, k, l, m, n, ɔ, ö, ö:, o:, p, p̆, r, z, š, t, v, ü, ü:, u:, v, c.*

these circumstances be regarded as "the more genuine." And since the opposition "sharp" s/"soft" z is logically privative, one can probably regard it as actually privative, and the "soft" z as its unmarked member.

Thus there are cases in which the neutralization of a privative opposition clearly and objectively indicates which member of that opposition is unmarked and which is marked: in CASE III the unmarked member of the neutralized opposition serves as the only representative of the archiphoneme; in CASE IV it serves as the archiphoneme representative in the position of maximal phonemic differentiation.

The neutralization of an opposition sometimes points to the marked character of the member of another opposition. That is to say, a neutralizable opposition in the vicinity of the marked member of a related opposition is frequently neutralized. For example, in Artshi, an East Caucasian language, the opposition between rounded and unrounded consonants is neutralized before o and u, whereby o and u are proved to be the marked members of the opposition o-e and u-i.

Logically privative oppositions thus become actually privative by neutralization, and the distinction between unmarked and marked opposition members obtains an objective basis.

3   CORRELATIONS

Two phonemes that are in a relation of bilateral opposition to each other are by that very fact closely related to each other: what is common to both of them does not recur in any other phoneme of the same system. They are therefore *the only ones of their kind*. In placing them in opposition with each other, that which is unique to each of them is clearly brought into relief with that which links them to each other. Two phonemes that are in a relation of multilateral opposition with each other, on the other hand, appear as indivisible units. In the case of phonemes that participate in a proportional opposition, it is easy to separate the discriminative property from the other properties since the discriminative property recurs as such in several phoneme pairs of the same system. Consequently it can be easily abstracted or thought of as independent from all other properties. In contrast, in the case of phonemes that participate in an isolated opposition, the discriminative property cannot be abstracted as easily, simply because it occurs only once in such a system, namely, together with the other properties of those phonemes to which it pertains. Of all possible relations between two phonemes, it is the privative relation that most clearly shows the presence or absence of certain properties of the particular phonemes. The analysis of the phonemic content of phonemes that are in a relation of privative opposition with each other is therefore easiest. In contrast, the phonemic content of phonemes that are in an equipollent relation to each other is the most difficult to analyze. Two phonemes that participate in a neutralizable opposition are considered as closely related even in the position of relevance. Each of them is regarded as a special variety of the archiphoneme in question, and the reality of the latter is guaranteed by means of its occurrence in the position of neutralization. The appurtenance to one archiphoneme, on the other hand, is much less evident for two phonemes that are in a relation of constant, nonneutralizable opposition.

The following conclusion can be drawn from what has been said: the participation of two phonemes in a bilateral, proportional, privative, and thus neutralizable, opposition has as a result, first that the phonemic content of such phonemes can be analyzed most clearly since the discriminative property is clearly brought into relief with what constitutes the basis for comparison; and second, that the two phonemes are considered as particularly closely related to each other. In contrast, two phonemes that are in a relation of isolated, multilateral (and consequently nonneutralizable) opposition with each other are maximally opaque with respect to their phonemic content, and maximally distant from each other in relatedness. (These features are particularly prominent in the case of a heterogeneous opposition.)

If one considers the neutralizable, privative, proportional, bilateral oppositions and the isolated, heterogeneous, multilateral oppositions as two extremes, all remaining types of opposition can be classified between these two extreme points. The more neutralizable, privative, proportional, bilateral, and homogeneous oppositions there are in a system, the greater its cohesion. On the other hand, the more logically equipollent, isolated, multilateral, and heterogeneous oppositions there are in a system, the greater the noncohesion of that system. It therefore seems appropriate to distinguish the privative, proportional, bilateral oppositions from all other oppositions by a special term. In phonemic literature the term *correlation* is used for this purpose. But the definition that is given for the term "correlation" and some other related notions in the "Projet de terminologie phonologique standardisée" (*TCLP*, IV, 1930) must be changed to some degree since it was formulated at a time when the theory of oppositions had not as yet completely developed. We now propose the following definitions.

By *correlation pair* we understand two phonemes that are in a relation of logically privative, proportional, bilateral opposition with each other.

A *correlation mark* is a phonological property whose presence or absence characterizes a series of correlation pairs, as, for example, the nasality of nasals which in French distinguishes between the correlation pairs *an-a*, *on-o*, *in-e*, *un-eu*. By *correlation* is to be understood the sum of all correlation pairs characterized by the same correlation mark. A *paired phoneme* is a phoneme that participates in a correlation pair, while an *unpaired phoneme* is one that does not participate in any correlative pair.

The notion "correlation" is certainly a very fruitful one for the development of phonology, though its importance had been somewhat overestimated during the first period after its discovery. All oppositions whose members did not form correlative pairs were thrown together and designated by the general term "disjunction," so that two types of relations were recognized between phonological units: they either formed a correlation or a disjunction. But a closer examination revealed that in fact several types of distinctive oppositions had to be distinguished, and that the term "disjunction" was unproductive in its original, too general formulation. Furthermore, the fundamental difference between neutralizable and nonneutralizable correlations had to be uncovered. A nonneutralizable correlation, incidentally, also retains its importance for the cohesion of the phonemic system. Subject to this reservation, the theory of correlations may take the place it deserves in phonology.[14]

Depending on the correlation mark, different types of correlations are distinguished: for example, the correlation of voice (French *d-t*, *b-p*, *g-k*, *z-s*, etc.) or the correlation of quantity (*ā-a*, *ī-i*, etc.). These various correlation types are related to each other in varying degrees and can be classified in related groups. The relation of the correlation mark to the other properties of the respective phonemes serves as the basis for comparison. For example, the correlation of voice (French *d-t*, *b-p*) and the correlation of aspiration (Sanskrit *t-th*, *p-ph*) belong to the same related class because their correlation marks represent different types of work performed by the larynx and different types of tensing in the oral cavity, independent of the place of articulation in the oral cavity.

The classification of correlations in related groups is not merely a theoretical artifice. It corresponds to concrete reality. Even naive linguistic consciousness "feels" quite clearly that the oppositions *u-ü* and *ö-e* in German, though different, are still on the same plane, while the opposition between long and short *a* lies on quite a different plane. The projection of distinctive oppositions (and thus also of correlations) sometimes onto the same and sometimes onto different planes is the psychological consequence of just those kin relationships between the correlation marks on which the classification of correlations into related classes is based.

4   CORRELATION BUNDLES

In cases where a phoneme participates in several correlations of the same related class, all phonemes taking part in the same correlative pairs unite to form a multimember *correlation bundle*. The structure of such a bundle is quite varied. It depends not only on the number of participant correlations but also on their mutual relationship.

Bundles of two related correlations are the most frequent. Here two possibilities exist: both members of the one correlation may also participate in the other correlation, or both correlations have only one member in common. In the first case the result is a *four-member*, in the second a *three-member*, correlational bundle. These two cases can best be illustrated by Sanskrit and Classical Greek. In both languages stops participated simultaneously in the correlations of voice and of aspiration. In Sanskrit the result was a four-member bundle:

$$p\text{-}ph \quad k\text{-}kh \quad t\text{-}th$$
$$b\text{-}bh \quad g\text{-}gh \quad d\text{-}dh, \text{etc.}$$

In Classical Greek it was a three-member bundle:

By linking three correlations that are related in type it is theoretically possible to havè bundles of four to eight members. In fact many of these types can be attested by examples from different languages. In most languages of the Caucasus the correlation of voice and the correlation based on type of expiration combine with the correlation of occlusiveness. The latter term refers to the opposition of stops or affricates with spirants. In Chechen, for example, four-member bundles result as follows:[15]

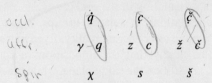

Here the opposition of occlusiveness is relevant only in the case of voicelessness ("z" and "$\check{z}$" are realized as affricates initially, and as spirants medially and finally), the opposition of expiration only in the case of occlusives (and affricates). In Georgian the same correlations yield five-member bundles because the correlation of occlusiveness extends to both members of the correlation of voice:

$$
\begin{array}{cccc}
 & \underset{\textstyle\varsigma}{} & & \underset{\textstyle\check{c}}{} \\
3 & c & \check{3} & \check{c} \\
z & s & \check{z} & \check{s}
\end{array}
$$

Finally, in Circassian the same correlations make up a six-member bundle because in the latter case the correlation based on type of expiration extends to both members of the correlation of occlusiveness:

$$
\begin{array}{ccc}
\hat{3} & \hat{c} & \hat{\varsigma} \\
\hat{z} & \hat{s} & \hat{\underset{.}{s}}
\end{array}
$$

The tie between members of a correlation bundle becomes particularly close when the entire bundle can be neutralized. Such neutralizable bundles are not rare. The above-mentioned four-member bundles of Sanskrit were neutralizable before obstruents and in final position (the unaspirated tenuis occurring as the only archiphoneme in absolutely final position). In Korean, where the occlusives form three-member bundles (lenis–fortis–aspirate), these bundles are neutralized in final position. The corresponding archiphonemes are represented by implosives. But the Korean consonants also form a three-member correlation bundle with respect to timbre (neutral–palatalized–labialized). These bundles are neutralized in final position. Their archiphonemes are represented by consonants of neutral timbre. But in addition, the correlation of palatalization is neutralized before i, the representative of the archiphoneme being conditioned externally; the correlation of labialization is neutralized before u and y, the representative of the archiphoneme being conditioned internally.[16] In Artshi, a language of the Eastern Caucasus group, the acute sibilants form a six-member correlation bundle (media–voiceless affricates without glottal occlusion–weak affricates without glottal occlusion–strong affricates with glottal occlusion–weak voiceless spirants–and strong voiceless spirants) which is neutralized before t and d. The archiphoneme in this case is represented by the (weak?) spirant. Examples can easily be multiplied.

As a result of the projection of all members of a correlation bundle onto the same plane, and as a result of the close interrelatedness of these members, it is sometimes rather difficult to analyze the bundle into individual correlations. For example, in cases where different prosodic correlations combine into a bundle, the members of such a bundle are sometimes conceived of as different "accents," with little attention given to differences of quantity or differences of type of tone close. Sometimes they are conceived of as different degrees in quantity without regard to differences in tone movement. Mistakes of this type are made not only by laymen and untutored speakers. They are also made by theoreticians and sometimes even by professional phoneticians. Cases of this type are proof of the psychological reality of the classification of correlations into related groups. They are possible only where a correlation bundle is actually present, that is, where a phoneme participates in several correlations of the *same related group*.

If a phoneme participates simultaneously in several correlations of *different* related groups, such correlations do not combine into "bundles": they are not projected on the same plane but *superimposed* on one another. German stressed long *i* participates simultaneously in several correlations, namely, in the correlation of accent, the correlation of quantity, and the correlation of rounding. But while the former two form a bundle (the prosodic correlation bundle), the correlation of rounding (*i-ü, e-ö*) clearly belongs to another "plane." It can happen, of course, that two correlation bundles belonging to different "planes" are superimposed on each other and that both are neutralized in certain positions. We have already mentioned Korean, in which occlusives form a correlation bundle consisting of lenes–fortes–aspirates, and in which, further, all consonants, including the occlusives, form bundles of timbre consisting of a neutral, a palatalized, and a labialized member. Both correlation bundles are neutralized in final position. Consequently in word-final position in Korean, the guttural implosive *K* represents an archiphoneme that corresponds to nine phonemes medially—$g, k, k'; g', k', k''; g°, k°, k°'$. Still, the bundles g-k-k' and g-g'-$g°$ obviously belong to quite different planes.

[1] In this connection cf. N. S. Trubetzkoy, "Essai d'une théorie des oppositions phonologiques," in *Journal de psychologie*, XXXIII, 5–18.

[2] The term was first used by N. Durnovo.

[3] The "phoneme *j*" is nonexistent in stage German. Stage German *j* should be regarded as a combinatory variant of the vowel *i*. Accordingly it does not belong to the consonant system.

[4] Cf. Fr. Trávníček, Správná česká výslovnost (Brno, 1935), p. 24.

[5] In this regard cf. E. A. Krejnovič, "Nivchskij (giljackij) jazyk," in *Jazyki i pis'mennost' narodov Severa*, III (1934), 188 ff.

[6] As for the division of multilateral oppositions into heterogeneous and homogeneous oppositions, and the division of homogeneous oppositions into linear and nonlinear oppositions, they are ultimately also based on the same principles.

[7] In this connection, see under C.

[8] On this point, cf. our essay "Die Aufhebung der phonologischen Gegensätze," in *TCLP*, VI, 29 ff., as well as A. Martinet, "Neutralisation et archiphonème," in *ibid.*, pp. 46 ff.

[9] Cf. R. Jakobson in *TCLP*, II, 8 f.

[10] Cf. Henri Frei in *Bulletin de la Maison franco-japonaise*, VIII (1936), no. 1, 130.

[11] Cf. Erin Assai, "A study of Yami Language, an Indonesian Language spoken on Botel Tobago Island" (Leiden, 1935), p. 15.

[12] Cf. Clement M. Doke, "A Study of Lamba Phonetics," in *Bantu Studies* (July 1928).

[13] What has been said applies, of course, only to those neutralizable gradual oppositions in which one member is "extreme." In cases where both members show different "mid" degrees of the same property, either the one or the other member can represent the archiphoneme. It depends on how the particular property is treated from the viewpoint of the given language. Most cases actually involve the opposition between two types of *e* or *o* vowels. In some languages close *e* and *o* are considered unmarked, in others open *e* and *o*. This can be seen from their occurrence in the position of neutralization. Accordingly the opposition in such cases ceases to be gradual from a phonological point of view.

[14] With respect to what follows, cf. (subject to the above reservation) N. S. Trubetzkoy, "Die phonologischen Systeme," in *TCLP*, IV, 96 ff. The term "correlation," proposed and defined by R. Jakobson, was used for the first time with reference to a proportional bilateral opposition in his proposal to the Congress of Linguists in The Hague, cosigned by S. Karcevskij and the present writer. See *Ier Congrès International de Linguistes* (La Haye, 1928), "Propositions," pp. 36 ff., and *Actes du Ier Congrès International de Linguistes*, pp. 36 ff., and *TCLP*, II, 6 f.

[15] Cf. N. S. Trubetzkoy, "Die Konsonantensysteme der ostkaukasischen Sprachen," in *Caucasica*, VIII (1931).

[16] Cf. A. Cholodovič, "O latinizacii korejskogo pis'ma," in *Sovetskoje jazykoznanije*, I, 144 ff.

IV PHONOLOGICAL CLASSES OF DISTINC-
TIVE OPPOSITIONS

1 PRELIMINARY REMARKS

So far we have considered the various types of distinctive oppositions thus: (a) from the point of view of their relation to other oppositions in the same system; (b) from the point of view of the logical relations between the opposition members themselves; and (c) from the point of view of the extent of their distinctive force. These three viewpoints resulted in three different classifications: (a) bilateral and multilateral, proportional and isolated oppositions; (b) privative, gradual, and equipollent oppositions; and (c) neutralizable and constant oppositions. All these standpoints and principles of classification are valid not only for phonological systems but for any other system of oppositions as well. They contain nothing that is specifically phonological. In order to be applied successfully in the analysis of concrete phonological opposition systems, they must still be supplemented by specifically phonological principles of classification.

The specific character of a phonological opposition consists in the latter's being a *distinctive opposition of sound*. "Distinctiveness" in the phonological sense, that is, the capacity of differentiating meaning, is something that requires no further classification. Phonological oppositions can, nevertheless, from this point of view be divided into oppositions *differentiating words* (lexical oppositions) and oppositions *differentiating sentences* (syntactic oppositions). For the meanings that can be distinguished by phonological oppositions are either the meanings of words, including the meanings of individual grammatical word forms, or the meanings of sentences. This division is certainly of importance for the phonemic systems of the individual languages. It is less important for the general classification of distinctive oppositions, for all distinctive oppositions that appear with a syntactic function in one language may occur with a lexical function in another language. There are actually no specific phonological oppositions for differentiating sentences: an opposition that in one language serves to differentiate sentences in another serves to differentiate words.

Much more important for the general classification of phonological oppositions is the fact that these oppositions are *phonic* oppositions. Neither gesticulations with one's hands nor flag signals, but specific phonic properties, are placed in opposition with each other in phonological oppositions. It is presumed common knowledge that the purpose of contrasting sounds with each other is to differentiate meaning. The problem as to *how* phonic properties are placed in opposition with each other, that is, what types of opposition result, was discussed in Chapter III. The question now is to examine what phonic properties form phonological (distinctive) oppositions in the various languages of the world.

In Chapter III we operated with purely logical concepts. We must now combine these logical concepts with acoustic and articulatory, that is, with *phonetic*, concepts. For no other discipline except phonetics can teach us about individual sound properties. But we must not forget what has been said in the Introduction about the relationship of phonology to phonetics. Already in view of the fact that they are made part of the system of opposition categories that were discussed in Chapter III, the phonetic concepts with which the phonologist operates appear of necessity somewhat

91

schematized and simplified. Thus actually very little remains of phonetics in the following exposition. But this should not disappoint the phonetician. The object of the present chapter is not a classification of the sounds that can be produced by the human vocal apparatus, but a systematic survey of the phonic properties that are in effect utilized for the differentiation of meaning in the various languages of the world.

It is therefore also rather unimportant for the phonologist whether he uses acoustic or sound-physiological phonetic terminology. Important is only the unambiguous designation of phonic properties, which in phonetic literature are studied and investigated from various points of view, and which all phoneticians, despite existing differences of opinion, should be familiar with at least as *objects of study*. In modern instrumental phonetics, especially by means of sound film and X rays, it has become increasingly evident that the same sound effects can be produced by quite different movements of the vocal organs (Paul Menzerath, G. Oscar Russel). Such terms as "front vowel" or "occlusive" are therefore rejected from the standpoint of the modern methods. However, these terms have the advantage of being understood correctly by anyone familiar with traditional phonetics. Even the most accurate phonetician, provided he is not pedantic, can accept such terms, for lack of better and more accurate ones, as conventional designations for familiar objects of study. Acoustic terminology unfortunately is still very sparse. Consequently it is unavoidable in most cases to use physiological terms coined by traditional phonetics, although modern phonetics ascribes more consistency and uniformity to the acoustic effect than to the articulatory movements producing it. The phonologist, who is for the most part only interested in making reference to generally known phonetic concepts, is able to overcome these terminological difficulties.

2   CLASSIFICATION OF DISTINCTIVE PHONIC PROPERTIES

The phonic properties that form distinctive oppositions in the various languages can be divided into three classes: *vocalic, consonantal,* and *prosodic.* Vowel phonemes consist of distinctive vocalic properties, consonantal phonemes of distinctive consonantal properties; but there are no phonemes that consist exclusively of prosodic properties. Depending on the language, prosodic properties may combine with a single vowel phoneme, a single consonantal phoneme, or an entire sequence of phonemes.

Before defining the various classes of distinctive phonic properties, the term "vowel" and "consonant" must therefore be examined.

L. Hjelmslev attempted to define these terms without reference to any phonetic concepts: vowels are to be those phonemes, or in Hjelmslev's terminology, "cenemes" or "cenematemes," which have the faculty of forming a notional unit or a word by themselves, while all other phonemes or "cenemes" or "cenematemes" respectively are consonants.[1] Hjelmslev subsequently refined this definition which obviously restricted the application of the vowel concept too much. (For example, in German only three vowel phonemes would remain: *Oh! Au!* and *Ei!*) He added the following supplement: "Nous comprenons par voyelle un cénème susceptible de constituer à lui seul un énoncé . . . ou bien admettant à l'intérieur d'une syllabe les mêmes combinaisons qu'un tel cénème."[2] But even in this second, expanded version the definition is untenable. Again, in German, of the pure vowels only the *o* and of the diphthongs only *æe̯* and *ao̯* are used as interjections, only *Au* and *Ei* as words. These three vowel phonemes, among others, can also occur word-finally ("froh," "Frau," "frei" [glad, woman, free]), but they are not found before *ŋ*. Short vowels, on the other hand, cannot occur in final position, but some, namely *i*, *u*, *ü*, *a*, and *e*, occur before *ŋ*. If one regards interjections such as *Oh! Ai!* and *Au!* as independent notional units (énoncés), one must also recognize as such the interjection *ssh!* (a plea for silence). In keeping with Hjelmslev's definition, German short *u̯*, *ü*, *i*, *a*, and *e* would accordingly have to be regarded as consonants, while German *š* and all phonemes participating in the same combinations, that is, practically all consonants, would have to be regarded as vowels.

The untenability of the definition proposed by Hjelmslev is even more apparent in other languages. In addition to the interjection *š!* Russian also has the interjections *s!* and *c!* In certain other languages the number of isolated "syllabic consonants" used as interjections or command words for animals is even more numerous.[3] On the other hand, there are many languages in which vowels cannot occur initially, and where it is consequently impossible to have words consisting of a single vowel.

The untenability of the definition given by Hjelmslev is not an accident. "Vowel" and "consonant" are *phonic* or acoustic terms, and can only be defined as such. Any attempt to eliminate or circumvent acoustic-articulatory concepts in the definition of vowels and consonants must necessarily fail.

The process of phonation of human speech can best be illustrated by the following scheme: somebody whistles or sings a melody into the mouthpiece of a tube and alternately opens and covers the other end of that tube with his hand. It is clear that three types of elements can be distinguished acoustically in the course of this process: first, the segments between closing and opening the orifice; second, the segments between opening and closing it; and third, the segments of the melody whistled or sung into the tube. Elements of the first type correspond to consonants, elements of the second type to vowels, and those of the third type to prosodic units.

Important for a consonant is, in the words of Paul Menzerath, "a closure–aperture movement, with an articulatory maximum between these two points," for a vowel "a movement of aperture–closure, with an articulatory minimum in the interspace." [4] In other words, what characterizes a consonant is the *production of an obstruction and the overcoming of such an obstruction*. A vowel, on the other hand, is characterized by the *absence of any obstruction*.[5]

It follows from what has been said that properties that are specifically consonantal can refer only to various types of obstructions or to the ways of overcoming these obstructions. They may therefore be called *properties based on the manner of overcoming an obstruction* (*Ueberwindungsarteigenschaften*). Properties that are specifically vocalic, on the other hand, can only refer to the various types of absence of an obstruction, that is, practically speaking, to the various degrees of aperture. They may therefore be called *properties based on degree of aperture* (*Oeffnungsgradeeigenschaften*).

In addition to these properties, which are specifically consonantal or vocalic, consonantal and vowel phonemes may have certain other properties. Let us suppose that in the presented scheme of the phonation process the length of the tube changes continually, or the position of its orifice varies continually. It follows that with respect to the consonants the different types of obstruction or the different modes of overcoming these obstructions, and with respect to the vowels, the different degrees of aperture, must be localized in different positions. As a result, special *properties of localization* are produced for the consonants as well as for the vowels. These form, so to speak, a second coordinate to consonant or vowel quality, respectively.

For some vowel and consonant phonemes still a third quality coordinate can be established. To stay with our phonation scheme, let us suppose that our tube is connected with another resonator, and during phonation this connection is alternately established and disrupted. This, of course, must affect the character of the sound produced. The specific acoustic properties that the phonation of consonants and vowels produces by means of establishing and disrupting the connection with the second resonator can be termed *properties of resonance*.

A distinctive property exists only by virtue of being a member of a distinctive opposition. German *d*, when placed in opposition with *t*

("Seide"/"Seite" [silk/side]), has the property "lenis" based on the manner of overcoming an obstruction; when placed in opposition with *b* ("dir"/"Bier" [you/beer]) or with *g* ("dir"/"Gier" [you/greed]), the property of localization "dental" or "apical"; and the property of resonance "nonnasal" when placed in opposition with *n* ("doch"/"noch" [yet/ still]). Similarly, French *o* has a specific property based on degree of aperture in opposition with *u* ("dos"/"doux"), a specific property of localization in opposition with *ö* ("dos"/"deux"), and a specific property of resonance in opposition with *õ* ("dos"/"don"). In contrast, German *o* does not have any property of resonance because a distinctive opposition between nasalized and nonnasalized or between pharyngealized and nonpharyngealized vowels is alien to standard German. The "three coordinates" to vowel or consonantal quality need not, therefore, be present in every vowel or consonant phoneme. But each one of the properties that make up a vowel or a consonant phoneme must belong to one of the "three coordinates" mentioned.

As regards the prosodic units, our phonation scheme shows that they are rhythmic-melodic units—"musical" in the broadest sense of the word. Even from a purely phonetic point of view, the "syllable" is basically something quite different from a combination of vowels and consonants.[6] The phonological prosodic unit is, of course, not simply identical with the "syllable" (in the phonetic sense). However, it always relates to the syllable because, depending on the language, it is either a specific segment of the syllable or an entire sequence of syllables. It is quite clear that its properties cannot be identical with the vocalic and consonantal properties discussed above. Since the prosodic unit must be conceived of as "musical" (rhythmic-melodic), or better, as a segment of a "musical" unit, it follows that "prosodic properties" refer either to the specific marks of each constituent segment of a melody (intensity, tone) or to the type of segmentation of the melody in the phonation process of human speech. The former type of properties effectuates the rhythmic-melodic differentiation of prosodic units. The latter characterizes the contact of a given prosodic unit with an immediately adjacent unit. Prosodic properties can therefore be divided into *properties based on type of differentiation* and *properties based on type of contact.*

3 VOCALIC PROPERTIES

A Terminology

As already discussed, vocalic properties are divided into properties based on degree of aperture, properties of localization, and properties of resonance. The first two types of properties are much more closely related to each other than to the properties of resonance, so that they may be combined into a special group or bundle.[7]

Among all speech sounds, vowels can most easily be analyzed acoustically. The degrees of aperture correspond acoustically to "degrees of saturation or sonority." In principle the more the lower jaw is lowered, that is, the wider the mouth is opened, the higher the degree of saturation. But this principle appears to be fully valid only in the case of isolated vowels when they are sung. In spontaneous connected speech the same acoustic effects can also be achieved with the articulating organs in a different position. The parallelism between degree of saturation of the vowel and degree of lowering of the lower jaw (vertical movement) is therefore not always complete.[8] Since the linguist, after all, is ultimately interested in the acoustic effect, it would perhaps be advisable to replace the term *properties based on degree of aperture* by *properties based on degree of sonority* or *properties based on degree of saturation*. The properties of localization correspond acoustically to various gaps in the series of partial tones: the "front vowels" show an increase of the higher and a suppression of the lower partial tones; conversely the higher partial tones are the ones that are suppressed in the case of the "back vowels." In general, the stronger or higher the partial tones, the shorter the "front resonator," that is, in terms of the human vocal apparatus, the shorter is the distance between the rims of the lips and the highest point of the mass of the tongue. But since the same acoustic effect can also be achieved by other positions of the vocal organs, the parallelism between tongue and lip movement ("horizontal movement") is not always present in this case either. The term *properties of localization* with reference to the vowels may therefore be replaced by *properties of timbre*. In the following discussion the "inexact" terms "properties pertaining to degree of aperture" and "properties of localization" are used in addition to the acoustic terms.

Languages having only one vowel phoneme do not seem to exist in the world. If such a "one-vowel" language should ever have existed, it must have permitted numerous consonant combinations. For only under this condition would a single vowel phoneme be able to exist at all, since it could be placed in opposition with the absence of a vowel (zero vowel) between the members of a consonant combination or after consonants in final position. A "one-vowel" language without consonant combinations, on the other hand, would be vowelless from a phonological point of view, since the obligatory vowel after every consonant would have to be evaluated as a matter-of-fact component in the realization of the consonant and would not have any distinctive force.[9] The languages with which we are familiar have several vowel phonemes which form specific *vowel systems*.

From the point of view of degrees of aperture (degrees of sonority) and vocalic localization series (classes of timbre), three basic types of vowel system can be set up:[10] (a) *linear systems*, in which the vowel phonemes possess specific degrees of sonority but no distinctively relevant properties of timbre (properties of vocalic localization); (b) *quadrangular systems*, in which all vowel phonemes not only possess distinctive properties based on degree of sonority but also distinctive properties of timbre; and (c) *triangular systems*, in which all vowel phonemes possess distinctive properties based on degree of sonority. Distinctive properties of timbre are found with all vowels except the maximally open vowel phoneme. The latter phoneme is outside the oppositions of localization. Within these basic types, subtypes can be set up depending on how many degrees of sonority and classes of localization there are, and depending on the relations of logical opposition between the individual types of distinctive property.

B Properties of Localization or Timbre

There are languages in which these vowel properties are not distinctive, because they are automatically conditioned by the phonic environment. This is the case in Adyghe, where three vowel phonemes are distinguished: the maximally close "ə" which is realized as *u* in the neighborhood of labialized velars, as *ü* between two labials and after labialized sibilants, as *ɯ* after nonlabialized back velars, as *i* after palatals, and in all other positions as a close indeterminate vowel *ə*; mid-open "*e*" which is realized after labialized velars as *o*, after labialized sibilants and between labials as *ö*, after laryngeals and nonlabialized back velars as *a*, in the remaining positions as *e* or as indeterminate open vowel *ë*; and the maximally open "*a*" which is realized between two labials as slightly rounded, between two palatals as *ä*, and elsewhere as a long *ā*. The duration of these vowels is in accord with their sonority: "*a*" is the longest, "*e*" somewhat shorter (after laryngeals and nonlabialized back velars this difference in quantity is clearly noticeable), "ə" the shortest, with a tendency to be reduced. Long, *ū*, *ō*, *ē*, and *ī* do occur, but only as optional variants of diphthongs ("*ew*," "*əw*," "*ej*," "*əj*"). Similar conditions hold true for Abkhas, but there the realization of the mid-open vowel is more uniform: it occurs as an *e* only in the vicinity of *j*, as an *o* only before a *w* in closed syllable, elsewhere always as *a* which is distinguished from the maximally sonorous vowel mainly by its shorter duration. The vowel system of Ubyk is in all probability based on the same principle. Vowel phonemes with a phonologically specific degree of sonority and phonologically irrelevant timbre would thus appear to be a peculiarity of the West Caucasian languages. Whether such "linear" vowel systems also occur elsewhere is hard to say at the present state of phonological studies in the world. As far as we know, linear systems do occur in certain languages as partial systems, in particular in certain Finno-Ugric and Turkic languages, in which the vocalism of the first syllable is richer than the vocalism of all other syllables. (On this point see further below.)

In the overwhelming majority of languages, the properties of timbre of the vowel phonemes are distinctive. The only difference between triangular systems and quadrangular systems is that in the former distinctive oppositions of timbre exist only with respect to the vowels of nonmaximal degree of aperture, while in the latter type they are found in vowel phonemes of all degrees of aperture. Actually there are only two oppositions of timbre: one opposition between rounded and unrounded vowels (opposition of lip rounding), and another between back and front vowels (opposition of tongue position).[11] These oppositions can occur with distinctive force either independently or in combination, thus producing different *classes of timbre*. The following eight classes of timbre are conceivable: rounded, unrounded, front, back, front rounded, back rounded, front unrounded, back unrounded. All eight of these classes do in fact occur in different languages. But in a single system only four classes of timbre can exist at the most. The triangular and quadrangular systems can accordingly be divided into *two-class*, *three-class*, and *four-class* systems. Acoustically, the rounded vowels are darker than the unrounded, and the front vowels clearer than the back vowels. Every multiclass vowel system must therefore have a *maximally dark* and a *maximally clear* class of timbre, which may be designated as *extreme* classes since there may be one or two *medial* classes between them.

Three possibilities exist for *two-class systems*: either the opposition of tongue position alone is distinctive, or the opposition of lip rounding alone is distinctive, or both oppositions occur in combination. In the first case the back and front vowels are placed in opposition with each other, and lip participation is phonologically irrelevant. In the second case rounded and unrounded vowels are opposed to each other, and the position of the tongue is phonologically irrelevant. Finally, the third case involves a distinctive opposition between back rounded and front unrounded vowels. In this case the properties of timbre of the vowel phonemes cannot be divided. Thus one should actually not speak of back rounded and front unrounded vowels, but only of maximally dark and maximally clear vowels. It is evident that the first and second cases involve logically privative oppositions, while the third case involves a logically equipollent opposition.

In quadrangular two-class systems, cases one and two are the ones usually found, that is, the correlation of tongue position or the correlation of lip rounding is found in its pure form. It all depends here on the makeup of the two vowel phonemes with the maximal degree of aperture. If both are unrounded, one must be a back vowel, the other a front vowel. As a result, the opposition of tongue position also becomes a bilateral proportional opposition in the other vowel pairs of the same system. On the other hand, the fact that back vowels of nonmaximal degree of aperture are rounded is nonsignificant from the point of view of the total system. As an example of such a two-class quadrangular system, the vowel system of those archaic Montenegran dialects may be cited in which the Proto-Slavic "semivowels" did not develop into an *a*, as they did in Serbo-Croatian, but into a particularly open *æ* sound (a "sound intermediary between *a* and *e*"):[12]

$$a \quad æ$$
$$o \quad e$$
$$u \quad i$$

If, however, the "dark" vowel of maximal degree of aperture is rounded, and its "partner" is an unrounded nonfront vowel, the lip position alone is phonologically relevant for such a vowel pair. As a result, the opposition of lip rounding becomes exclusively distinctive for all other vowels of the same system as well, while the frontal character of the unrounded vowels is considered merely an insignificant secondary phenomenon. The vowel system of the Płaza dialect of Polish (in Western Little Poland) will serve as an example of such a quadrangular system:

$$å \quad a$$
$$o \quad e$$
$$ů \quad y$$
$$u \quad i \quad [13]$$

Quadrangular two-class systems, in which the maximally open vowel pair is represented by a back rounded vowel and a front unrounded vowel phoneme, are extremely rare. In systems of this kind individual properties of localization cannot be isolated: the vowels are divided into two classes of timbre, a maximally dark and a maximally clear class. These stand in a relationship of logically equipollent opposition to each other. The vowel system of the Uzbek dialect of Tashkent may serve as an example:[14]

$$ɔ \quad æ$$
$$o \quad e$$
$$u \quad i$$

This relation of logically equipollent opposition between the two classes of timbre, which as indicated is extremely rare in quadrangular systems, predominates in triangular two-class systems. In systems of the latter type back rounded (maximally dark) vowels are contrasted with front unrounded (maximally clear) vowels as "polar" members of an equipollent opposition; and the maximally open vowel phoneme *a*, which stands outside this opposition, is a back unrounded vowel, that is, it belongs to neither of the two classes of timbre as the remaining phonemes of the respective vowel system. The well-known vowel system of Latin may serve as a classical example:

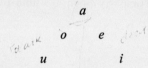

a

o   *e*

u   *i*

Similar triangular systems, only sometimes with a different number of degrees of aperture, occur in the most diverse languages in all parts of the world.

Only rarely does it happen that the correlation of lip rounding or the correlation of tongue position alone has distinctive force in a two-class triangular system, so that the relation between the two classes of timbre would be logically privative. This may be deduced either from the realization of the vowel phonemes or from the circumstances surrounding the neutralization of the various oppositions. The vowel systems of Russian, Artshi, and Ostyak may be cited as examples of such triangular two-class systems in which only the correlation of lip rounding is distinctive. In Russian the front or back position of the tongue is contextually conditioned in the realization of the vowel phonemes: between two palatalized consonants "*ü*," "*ä*," "*e*," and "*i*" are pronounced as front vowels (*o*, *ä*, *ė*, and *i*). *u* is also fronted in that position, though not as much as the other vowels. On the other hand, after nonpalatalized (phonetically velarized) consonants "*u*," "*o*," and "*a*" are realized as vowels of the back series, "*i*" as a vowel of the back-central series (*ш*). "*e*," too, is pronounced by some Russians as a vowel of the central series in this position. Back or front position of the tongue is therefore phonologically irrelevant for Russian vowels: the correlation of lip rounding of the vowel phonemes alone has distinctive force.[15] Artshi, an East Caucasian language of Central Daghestan, has a "correlation of consonantal rounding," that is, certain consonants are divided into a rounded and an unrounded variety. This correlation is neutralized before and after the rounded vowels *u* and *o*.[16] As a result, these vowels are placed in opposition with the remaining vowels of the Artshi system, namely, with unrounded *a*, *e*, and *i*. This means that all vowels are divided into rounded and unrounded vowels, while the back or front position of the tongue proves irrelevant for the classification of vowel phonemes, and consequently also for the phonemic content of these phonemes.[17]

Ostyak, or more precisely, the Kasym dialect of Northern Ostyak, now elevated to the rank of a standard written language, has a two-class triangular system in word-initial syllables:

Only unrounded vowels (*i*, *e*, *ε*, and *a*) occur in all other syllables.[18] In other words, the *correlation of timbre* is here neutralized in noninitial syllables, the unrounded vowels representing the archiphonemes of the corresponding oppositions (*u-i*, *o-e*, *ɔ-ε*). Since the choice of the representative of the archiphoneme in this case is obviously internally conditioned, unrounded *i*, *e*, and *ε* in the pairs *u-i*, *o-e*, and *ɔ-ε* must be considered the unmarked opposition members. Lip rounding must therefore be regarded as the phonologically relevant correlation mark.

As an example of such two-class triangular systems, in which only the correlation of tongue position is distinctive, the Japanese vowel system may be cited. In this system, the correlation of palatalization of consonants, that is, the opposition between palatalized and nonpalatalized consonants, is neutralized before the front vowels *e* and *i*, but retained before the back vowels *u*, *o*, and *a*. As a result, *i* and *e* are put in opposition with the remaining vowels, that is, all vowels are divided into front and back vowels, lip rounding being irrelevant for the classification of the vowel phonemes, and hence for their phonemic content.[19] The vowel system of Japanese and that of Artshi (*u*, *o*, *a*, *e*, *i*), already referred to, are therefore quite different phonologically, despite their apparent similarity. The correlation of tongue position alone is the phonological basis of the one, the correlation of lip rounding of the other.

In addition to the two "extreme" classes of timbre, three-class vowel systems further contain a "medial" class which is phonetically realized either by unrounded back or central vowels, or by rounded front or central vowels. The medial class of timbre is most frequently represented by front rounded vowels. The relationship of the medial class of timbre to the extreme classes is not identical in all languages. The presence of the medial class of timbre partly facilitates and partly complicates the analysis of complexes of properties that occur in the extreme classes.

In a three-class vowel system a medial class of timbre that consists of front rounded vowels may be related more closely to the one or the other extreme class of timbre of the same vowel system, depending on the language involved. The closeness of the relationship is primarily expressed in the neutralization of the corresponding oppositions. Thus, for example, the oppositions $y(=\ddot{u})$-u, $\ddot{o}$-o, and $\ddot{a}$-a are neutralizable in Finnish. y, $\ddot{o}$, and $\ddot{a}$ cannot occur after a syllable containing u, o, or a. Conversely u, o, and a cannot occur after a syllable containing y, $\ddot{o}$, and $\ddot{a}$. The oppositions u-i, y-i, o-ϱ, and $\ddot{o}$-e, on the other hand, cannot be neutralized. In other words, only oppositions between front and back vowels (of the same degree of aperture) are neutralizable, while oppositions between rounded and unrounded vowels (of the same degree of aperture) are constant. After a syllable containing u, y, o, $\ddot{o}$, a, or $\ddot{a}$, therefore, only five vowels are possible in each case; that is, after u, o, and a, the vowels

$$a$$
$$o \qquad e$$
$$u \qquad\qquad i$$

and after y, $\ddot{o}$, and $\ddot{a}$, the vowels

$$\ddot{a}$$
$$\ddot{o} \qquad e$$
$$y \qquad\qquad i$$

Quite a different distribution of classes of timbre is seen in a three-class vowel system, such as that of Polabian.[20] In Polabian the correlation of palatalization was present in consonants. However, it was neutralized before all front vowels and before the maximally open vowel a which stood outside the classes of timbre. As a result, the back vowels u, o, and a acquired a special position in the system. The oppositions between the back and front vowels of the same degree of aperture were constant (non-neutralizable), while the oppositions between rounded and unrounded vowels of the same degree of aperture ($\ddot{u}$-i, $\ddot{o}$-e) were neutralizable after v and j, the archiphoneme being represented by unrounded i and e. As a result, the medial class of timbre was more closely linked to the front class.

A certain hierarchy existed with respect to the correlation of tongue position and the correlation of lip rounding:

$$\text{back vowels—front vowels}\begin{cases}\text{rounded}\\[1.2em]\text{unrounded}\end{cases}$$

The properties of lip participation were phonologically irrelevant for the back vowels.[21] Graphically this may be represented as follows:

$$a$$

$$\alpha \qquad e$$

$$o \qquad \ddot{o}, \hat{e}$$

$$u \qquad \ddot{u}, i$$

It seems that three-class vowel systems are comparatively rare, such as those of Finnish and Polabian, in which the medial class of timbre is more closely related to one of the extreme classes, thereby creating a certain hierarchy between the correlations of tongue positions and lip rounding. In most three-class systems that have front rounded vowels in the medial class of timbre, it is not possible to establish a closer relationship between that class of timbre and one of the extreme classes. For example, in standard German, Dutch, French, Norwegian, Swedish, and Danish the three classes of timbre are opposed to each other as equidistant opposition members. As far as we know, there is also no reason to assume a closer relationship between the medial class of timbre and one of the extreme classes in Northern Albanian, Estonian, Ziryene,[22] and Annamese.[23] In K'üri, now Lezghian, in which the oppositions *a-e* and *u-i* are not neutralizable, while both the oppositions *ü-u* and *ü-i* are neutralized in certain positions (stressed *ü* cannot occur in a syllable after *u* or *i*, and stressed *u* and *i* in turn cannot occur in a syllable containing *ü*), the medial class of timbre is also equally closely related to both extreme classes.[24]

In the three-class vowel systems discussed so far, the medial class of timbre was represented by front rounded vowels. Systems in which the medial class of timbre contains back (or central) unrounded vowels are found much more rarely. As examples Romanian, Siamese,[25] and Votyak ("Udmurt")[26] may be mentioned. In systems of this type, too, there is sometimes a closer relationship between the medial class and one of the extreme classes of timbre. For example, in the East Sorbian (East Lusatian-Wendic) dialect of Muskau,[27] described by Ščerba, the opposition between vowels of the medial and front class of timbre is neutralized after nonguttural lingual consonants, that is, after dentals, palatals, sibilants, and *r* and *l* sounds: the unrounded central vowels *ï* (Ščerba's *ë*) and *ë* (Ščerba's *æ*) occur after *d, t, n, l, r, s, z, c*; the front vowels *i* and *ε*, on the other hand, occur after *ʒ', c', z', s', n, l, r*, and *j* (while, for example, after labials, *i* and *e* as well as *ï* and *ë* may occur with distinctive function). The vowels of the medial class of timbre in this case are therefore more closely related to the vowels of the front (maximally clear) class.

As for *four-class* vowel systems, they are found much more rarely than three-class systems. The vowel system found in many Turkic languages may be cited as an example:

$$o \quad a \quad ö \quad ä$$
$$u \quad ɯ \quad ü \quad i$$

In those Turkic languages in which the so-called vowel harmony is carried through consistently, the vowel system cited exists only in word-initial syllable in the above form, that is, with full phonological validity. In all other syllables the oppositions of timbre are neutralized. The realization of the vocalic properties of timbre in noninitial syllables is conditioned by the vowel of the preceding syllable. In the four-class vowel systems such a system as that of Eastern Cheremis[28] must also be counted, in which the vowels with the minimal degree of aperture have four, with the mid-degree of aperture three, and with the maximal degree of aperture two, classes of timbre, so that the entire system contains nine vowel phonemes. The correlation of tongue position is neutralizable in all vowel pairs, while the correlation of lip rounding is neutralizable only in the vowels with the minimal degree of aperture.[29] The particular vowel system could therefore be represented in about the following diagram (using the transcription as it appeared in *Anthropos*):

$$a \quad ä$$
$$o \quad ö \quad e$$
$$u \quad ü \quad ə̂ \quad i$$

But there are also those four-class vowel systems in which the oppositions of timbre cannot be neutralized at all, so that all four classes of timbre coexist fully autonomously and with full equality. The vowel system of Ostyak-Samoyed (now Selkup),[30] in which not a single opposition is neutralizable, appears to belong to this type:

$$a$$
$$å \quad æ$$
$$o \quad з \quad ɵ \quad e$$
$$u \quad ɯ \quad y \quad i$$

C   Properties Based on Degree of Aperture or Sonority

Above we discussed the so-called linear vowel systems whose members only possessed properties based on degree of aperture but no properties of localization or timbre. The question now is whether there are also vowel systems whose members, conversely, possess only properties of timbre but no properties based on degree of aperture. J. van Ginneken believes that he can answer this question in the affirmative. As an example he cites the vowel systems of Lak, an East Caucasian language of Central Daghestan, and of "Assyro-Babylonian[31] of the Achaemenid inscriptions." With respect to the latter, no opinion can be ventured at all since it is an extinct language. With respect to Lak, it can be positively shown that the vowel phonemes of this language contain not only properties of timbre but also properties based on degree of aperture. It is true, of course, that the three vowels of Lak are realized as *u*, *a*, and *i* in most phonic positions. It is this circumstance that leads van Ginneken to assume that the *u* involved a "back rounded vowel in general," the *i* a "front unrounded vowel in general," and the *a* a "back unrounded vowel in general," so that the degree of aperture of these three vowels was phonologically irrelevant. However, in the neighborhood of strongly palatalized consonants the realization of all three Lak vowel phonemes changes: "*u*" in this position is realized as *ö*, "*i*" as *e*, and "*a*" as *ä*.[32] Thus no opposition of timbre, but an opposition of degree of aperture, exists in this position between "*i*" and "*a*." A comparison of the two variants of each vowel phoneme of Lak shows that with respect to "*a*" the maximal degree of aperture alone is important, while for "*u*" and "*i*," first, the minimal degree of aperture, and, second, a specific property of timbre, that is, for "*u*" the property of being rounded, for "*i*" the property of being unrounded, are phonologically relevant. Lak can therefore by no means be used as proof for the existence of vowel systems without properties based on degrees of aperture. The same is also true of other languages with three-member vowel systems of the type "*u*," "*a*," "*i*."[33] In Arabic a clear opposition based on degree of aperture exists between "*i*" and "*a*" since "*a*" is mostly realized as a front vowel (unless it occurs in the vicinity of "emphatic consonants"). But after emphatic consonants the "*a*" sounds "dark," so that in that position it rather stands in opposition to "*u*" with respect to degree of aperture. Arabic "*a*" before "emphatic consonants" is realized as a back or back-central vowel (like the "*a*" in English "father"). But short "*i*" in this position is also pronounced as back-central *i̇*. Therefore, in this case too, an opposition based on degree of aperture is found between "*a*" and "*i*."[34] The same phonological properties as for the three vowel phonemes

of Lak discussed above must therefore also be assumed for Arabic "*u*,"
"*a*," and "*i*." In Modern Persian long "*a*" is normally pronounced with
rounding, while short "*a*" has changed to "*ä*." Long *a* in this case thus
stands in an opposition based on degree of aperture with the corresponding
maximally dark vowel (*u*), and short *ä* with the corresponding maximally
clear vowel (*e*).[35] In other languages with only one "maximally dark,"
one "maximally clear," and, with respect to timbre, one "neutral," vowel
phoneme the "neutral" vowel phoneme is also much more open than the
other two. While there actually exists only an opposition of timbre between
the "maximally dark" and the "maximally clear" vowel, both vowels
stand in an opposition based on degree of aperture with the "neutral"
vowel phoneme. In certain phonic positions this is particularly apparent.

Accordingly there are no vowel systems without distinctive oppositions
based on degree of aperture. This is of course only true with respect to
"total systems": in "partial systems," that is, in those systems that exist
only in a specific phonic position in a given language, it happens that
oppositions based on degree of aperture are excluded. For example, in
Russian only two vowel phonemes, that is, *ĭ* and *ŭ*, occur in pretonic syllables after palatalized consonants as well as after *č*, *š*, and *ž*. The phonemic
content of these vowel phonemes in this particular position consists only
of their properties of timbre (*ĭ* unrounded, *ŭ* rounded). But this partial
system does not have an independent existence. It exists only in connection
with the partial system of the remaining unaccented syllables (*ŭ*, *ă*, and *ĭ*)
and with the partial system of the accented syllables (*u*, *o*, *a*, *e*, and *i*)
which have oppositions based not only on classes of timbre but also on
degrees of aperture.

Every language has thus a vowel system with oppositions based on
degrees of aperture. And just as all vowel phonemes with the same property
of timbre form a "class of timbre" within a given vowel system, all vowel
phonemes with the same degree of aperture (= degree of sonority) can
be comprised under one "degree of sonority" within the same system.
Vowel systems can accordingly be divided not only into "one-class" (=
linear), "two-class," "three-class," and "four-class" systems, but also
into "two-degree," "three-degree," "four-degree" systems, etc.

Two-degree vowel systems are not rare. The systems of Lak, Arabic, and
Modern Persian have already been cited above. These are two-degree
(and two-class) triangular systems. Schematically:

$$a$$

$$u \qquad i$$

Certain other vowel systems also belong to the same type, for example, the system of Tlingit and Haida (in North America)[36] and Old Persian. But there are also two-degree *quadrangular* systems, for example, the vowel system of Tonkawa, in Texas,[37] which has a back and a front class of timbre, the vowels of the back class being realized more openly than the corresponding front vowels. Thus there is no symmetry from a phonetic point of view:

$$a \quad e$$
$$o \quad i$$

A two-degree, three-class quadrangular system, for example, is present in K'üri (Lezghian):[38]

$$a \quad e$$
$$u \quad ü \quad i$$

As an example of a four-class, two-degree quadrangular system, the afore-mentioned vowel system of many Turkic languages can be cited:

$$o \quad a \quad ö \quad ä$$
$$u \quad ɯ \quad ü \quad i$$

It is clear that in all two-degree vowel systems the opposition based on degree of aperture can be conceived of as a logically privative opposition— "low"/"nonlow" or "high"/"nonhigh." But since, as far as we know, the opposition based on degree of aperture does not seem to be neutralizable, it has not become an actually privative opposition anywhere.[39]

By far the majority of languages has *three-degree* vowel systems. A two-class, three-degree *triangular* system is found with varying realization in numerous languages in all parts of the world: for Europe, let us mention Modern Greek, Serbo-Croatian, Czech, (standard) Polish; for the Soviet Union, (standard) Russian, Erza-Mordvin, Georgian, Avar, Andi, Artshi, Tavgy-Samoyed ("Ngasan"); for Asia, Japanese and Tamil; for Africa, Lamba, Shona, Zulu, Ganda, and Chichewa; for America, Maya, etc.:

$$a$$
$$o \quad e$$
$$u \quad i$$

But three-class, three-degree triangular systems are not rare. Of the three-degree *quadrangular systems* the already-mentioned vowel system of the Montenegran dialects may be cited:

$$a \quad ä$$
$$o \quad e$$
$$u \quad i$$

In all three-degree vowel systems the individual degrees of sonority stand in a relation of gradual opposition with each other. The neutralizability of a phonic opposition within such a system conforms to the rules that govern the neutralization of gradual oppositions, that is, either the "extreme" opposition member functions as the representative of the archiphoneme or its choice is conditioned externally.

Considerably rarer than three-degree vowel systems are *four-degree* systems. Still, they do occur in quite a number of languages in various parts of the world. As examples, the triangular system of Italian:

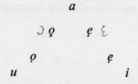

and the above-mentioned quadrangular system of many Polish dialects may be cited:

$$å \quad a$$
$$o \quad e$$
$$ů \quad y$$
$$u \quad i$$

(in the traditional transcription of Polish dialectologists). Here, as in all vowel systems of more than two degrees, the individual oppositions based on degree of aperture are gradual oppositions. Special relations result where some of these oppositions are neutralizable. For, if the opposition between the two medial degrees of sonority is neutralizable, this opposition loses its gradual character and becomes a privative opposition. The opposition "mark" is then either the "closeness" or "openness," depending on which opposition member represents the archiphoneme. For example, in the Scottish dialect of Barra Island (Hebrides)[40] a four-degree vowel

system exists, but only in word-initial syllable. The medial oppositions
o-ɔ and *e-æ* are neutralized in the remaining syllables, so that in that
position there occur only the open vowels *ɔ* and *æ*. These vowels may thus
be considered the unmarked opposition members. The correlation *o-ɔ, e-æ*
must then be designated as a "correlation of closeness." However, where
the neutralizable opposition of sonority contains one of the "extreme"
degrees of sonority, that is, either the maximal or minimal degree, the
gradual character of the opposition is not changed. In Danish the oppositions *u-o, y-ø,* and *i-e* are neutralized before a preconsonantal nasal (and
before *ŋ*). There is also a clear tendency to neutralize the same oppositions
before *r*.[41] Nevertheless, Danish *o, ö,* and *e* cannot be considered open *u, y,
i*. The situation is somewhat different where this type of neutralization
affects the entire vowel system. This is the case in Ibo, Southern Nigeria.[42]
This language has a two-class, four-degree vowel system, in which, on the
one hand, the oppositions based on degree of aperture between the vowels
of the first and second degree of sonority are neutralizable. On the other
hand, the vowels of the third and fourth degree of sonority are neutralizable in such a way that there exists a proportion "1:2 = 3:4." A word can
only contain vowels of the first and third degree or of the second and fourth
degree of aperture. All affixes (prefixes and suffixes) follow the vocalism
of the stem in this regard. Accordingly all oppositions based on the degree
of aperture are equipollent in this system:[43]

low $\begin{cases} \text{open} \quad . \quad . \quad . \quad . \quad . \quad \textit{ɔ-a} \quad . \quad . \quad . \quad . \quad \text{4th degree of aperture} \\ \text{close} \quad . \quad . \quad . \quad . \quad . \quad \textit{o-ɛ} \quad . \quad . \quad . \quad . \quad \text{3rd degree of aperture} \end{cases}$

high $\begin{cases} \text{open} \quad . \quad . \quad . \quad . \quad . \quad \textit{ʊ-e} \quad . \quad . \quad . \quad . \quad \text{2nd degree of aperture} \\ \text{close} \quad . \quad . \quad . \quad . \quad . \quad \textit{u-i} \quad . \quad . \quad . \quad . \quad \text{1st degree of aperture} \end{cases}$

One can divide the words, or stems, or roots of this language into an
"open vowel" category and a "close vowel" category, and the affixes into
a "low vowel" category and a "high vowel" category. But none of these
classes can be considered unmarked or marked.

As already mentioned, four-degree vowel systems are much rarer than
three-degree systems. Five-degree vowel systems may be considered
special rarities. In Europe such systems exist in Switzerland, for example,
in the Kerenz dialect of the Canton Glarus.[44] In Africa, Fante on the Gold
Coast seems to have a five-degree (two-class) triangular system: *u, ʊ, o, ɔ,
a, ɛ, e, ɪ, i*.[45] Gweabo, in Liberia, seems to have a *six-degree* (two-class)
triangular system, if the opposition between "bright" and "muffled"
vowels of this system can be evaluated as an opposition based on the
degree of sonority.[46] In Gweabo there exists a type of "vowel harmony"

that presupposes the neutralizability of the oppositions between the first
and second, the third and fourth, and the fifth and sixth, degrees of sonority.
The rules for vowel harmony are here much more complicated than in
Ibo. In any event they presuppose the following division of the entire
system (we leave E. Sapir's transcription unchanged):

low	"bright" . . . . . *a*	. . . . .	6th degree of aperture
	"muffled" . . . *O*	*E*	5th degree of aperture
mid	"bright" . . *ɔ*	*ɛ*	4th degree of aperture
	"muffled" . . *o*	*e*	3rd degree of aperture
high	"bright" . *ǫ*	*ẹ*	2nd degree of aperture
	"muffled" . *u*	*i*	1st degree of aperture

In every vowel system the maximally dark and the maximally clear class
of timbre always contains the same number of degrees of sonority. This is
valid without reservation for quadrangular systems. In triangular systems
the vowel with the maximal degree of sonority, which is outside the classes
of timbre, is to be added. A four-degree quadrangular system, for example,
must therefore contain four vowels of the maximally dark, and four vowels
of the maximally clear, class of timbre, while a four-degree triangular system contains only three dark and three clear vowels and in addition a
maximally open vowel. In quadrangular systems individual oppositions
based on degree of aperture are usually neutralized in both the maximally
dark and the maximally clear class of timbre. The result of such neutralization is then always another "quadrangular" partial system (with fewer
degrees of sonority). In triangular systems the neutralization of a particular
degree of aperture may take place in the two "extreme" classes of timbre,
which again creates a "triangular" partial system; or it may take place
only in one of the two extreme classes of timbre, in which case the partial
system is quadrangular. For example, in certain dialects of Modern Greek
the opposition between the first and second degree of sonority of a three-
degree, two-class triangular system is neutralized in unstressed syllables,[47]
resulting in a two-degree triangular system in that position:

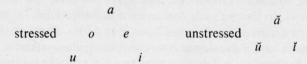

In the North Great Russian dialects, on the other hand, where stressed
syllables also possess a three-degree, two-class triangular system, the
opposition *a-e* is neutralized in unstressed syllables. The representative of

the archiphoneme is conditioned externally (*e* after palatalized consonants, *a* after nonpalatalized consonants). This gives rise to a two-degree quadrangular system:[48]

a

stressed   *o*   *e*   unstressed   *ŏ ă*
                                            ŭ ĭ
        u   *i*

Examples can easily be multiplied.

In three-class vowel systems the medial class of timbre cannot contain more vowel phonemes than either of the extreme classes. An equal number of vowels in all three classes is found primarily in triangular systems, for example, in the Mongolian system:[49]

a

o ö e

u   ü   i

In three-class quadrangular systems, on the other hand, the medial class of timbre almost always contains fewer vowel phonemes than either of the extreme classes. (See, for example, the above-cited vowel systems of Finnish and K'üri or Lezghian.) The same relation is not rare for triangular systems either. See, for example, the Norwegian vowel system:[50]

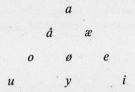

a

å   æ

o   ø   e

u   y   i

as well as the analogously structured, but differently realized, vowel systems of Polabian, Annamese, the Scottish dialect of Barra Island, and (with an unrounded central series) the East Sorbian dialect of Muskau, referred to above and described by Ščerba. When the medial class of timbre contains fewer degrees of sonority than either of the extreme classes, it usually lacks the equivalent to the most sonorous vowels of the extreme classes of timbre. At any rate, the minimal degree of sonority always appears to be fully represented in three-class systems, that is, by three vowel phonemes.

It follows from what has just been said that the medial class of timbre of a three-class system can sometimes also be represented by a single vowel phoneme. In this case such a phoneme must have the same degree of aperture as the minimally sonorous vowels of the extreme classes of timbre. Examples of this type are indeed not lacking. The vowel system of K'üri (Lezghian), which was already mentioned, may be cited:

$$a \qquad e$$

$$u \quad ü \quad i$$

Middle Greek had a three-degree triangular system, in which the medial series was represented by *ü* alone:

$$a$$

$$o \qquad e$$

$$u \qquad ü \qquad i$$

In Tübatulabal, an Indian language of the Shoshonean group of the Uto-Aztecan family, an analogous system still exists today, with the difference that an unrounded *ï* occurs instead of an *ü*.[51] These are by no means the only examples of this type.

Neutralization of individual oppositions based on degree of aperture in the three-class vowel systems follows the same rules as in the two-class systems, but the medial class of timbre may not contain any more phonemes in the partial system than in either of the extreme classes of timbre. Since oppositions of timbre are sometimes also neutralizable, it often happens that a two-class (or even a linear), two-degree partial system exists besides a three-class, multidegree total system. For example, the already-cited three-class, three-degree vowel system of Mongolian occurs only as such in first syllables:

$$a$$

$$o \quad ö \quad e$$

$$u \qquad ü \qquad i$$

In noninitial syllables following a syllable containing an *i*, the opposition *ü-ö* is neutralized, and the following partial system results:

$$a$$

$$o \qquad e$$

$$u \qquad ü \qquad i$$

Finally, after a syllable with any other vowel (except *i*) the oppositions of timbre *u-ü*, *o-ö*, *ö-e*, and *o-e*, on the one hand, and the oppositions based on degree of aperture *o-a*, *ö-a*, *e-a*, on the other, are neutralized. As a result, the following partial system arises:

$$A$$

$$\text{U} \qquad \text{I}^{52}$$

All this is valid only for the long vowels of Mongolian. In short vowels all oppositions of timbre are neutralized after a syllable containing an *i*, so that a three-degree linear system results:

$$a$$

$$e$$

$$i$$

After a syllable containing any other vowel the system shrinks even more, and only two short vowels, "*i*" and "*e*," remain. The latter takes on the quality of the vowel of the preceding syllable.

The statement was made above that where the medial class of timbre of a three-class vowel system was represented by a single vowel phoneme, this phoneme had the minimal degree of sonority, and in this respect formed a group with the minimally sonorous vowels of the extreme series of timbre *u* and *i*. This rule applies without exception where a rounded front vowel is involved: if the vowel system contains only one such phoneme, it is always *ü*, never *ö*. But there are cases where in addition to the vowels of the extreme classes of timbre a multidegree vowel system contains still another, unrounded vowel phoneme which does not belong to any of these classes of timbre, and which has neither the maximal nor the minimal degree of sonority. Since such a vowel phoneme can therefore be characterized only negatively, it may be designated as an "indeterminate vowel."[53] This phoneme must not be confused with the sole representative of the (unrounded) medial class of timbre: the latter stands in a relation of pure (isolated bilateral) opposition of timbre with *u* and *i*, while the "indeterminate vowel" does not stand in a bilateral opposition relation with any other phoneme of the vowel system. In any event, it does not participate in any pure opposition of timbre.

Many languages in various parts of the world have an indeterminate vowel in the above-defined sense in stressed as well as in unstressed syllables. The vowel may be long or short: the vowel in the English word *bird* (in standard Southern English) may be regarded as a long indeterminate vowel. But in many languages the indeterminate vowel only appears in partial systems in those phonic positions where several oppositions based on degree of aperture and oppositions of timbre are neutralized.

It follows from what has been said that the indeterminate vowel must be considered not as the sole representative of a specific medial class of timbre but as a vowel phoneme that lies outside any class of timbre. As a result thereof the indeterminate vowel may enter into a special relation to that vowel of maximal degree of sonority which characterizes triangular systems and which also lies outside any class of timbre. Under certain circumstances an "indeterminate" vowel in a triangular system can thus become a "specific" vowel by entering into a relation of bilateral opposition with "a." Such a case is present, for example, in Bulgarian. The Bulgarian indeterminate vowel has approximately the same degree of aperture as o and e, but it is neither rounded nor palatal. It would hardly be possible to assume a pure opposition of timbre between Bulgarian $ə$ and o, or between Bulgarian $ə$ and e. But the proportions $o:a = u:ə, e:a = i:ə$, and the proportion $u:o = i:e = ə:a$ deduced therefrom may well be established. The conditions in unstressed syllables (at least in a part of the local types of pronunciation) are proof that this proportion corresponds to a reality. For in these syllables o, e, and a are not permitted, only u, i, and $ə$ are. In other words, the oppositions based on degree of aperture u-o, i-e, and $ə$-a are neutralized, while the triangular character of the vowel system is preserved. Graphically, this may be represented as follows:

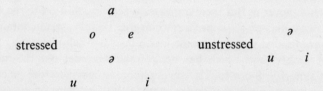

The Bulgarian vocalism is thus a three-class triangular system, in which the medial class of timbre is characterized by its neutral character and by an increase in the degree of aperture of its members.[54]

The Bulgarian vowel system appears to be a rather rare case. In the other languages with which we are familiar no special bilateral relation can be ascertained between this vowel and the "a." There is accordingly no reason to include the indeterminate vowel and the "a" in a special medial class of timbre.

Not much can be said about the number of degrees of sonority in four-class vowel systems since vowel systems of this type are in general extremely rare. According to our knowledge, in such systems none of the medial classes of timbre can contain more degrees of sonority than either of the extreme classes. (The total number of vowel phonemes of the two medial classes of timbre cannot therefore exceed the total number of vowel phonemes of the two extreme classes.) In the above-cited vowel system of Eastern Cheremis the lowest degree of sonority is represented in all four classes of timbre. This system is proof that the two medial classes of timbre of a four-class system need not necessarily contain the same number of degrees of sonority.

Also very closely related to the study of the properties based on degree of aperture is the difficult problem of the position in the vowel system of monophonematically evaluated diphthongs. The situation is simplest in such cases as the vowel systems of the archaic Great Russian and North Ukrainian dialects, where the phonemes that are represented by ω and ě in Russian dialectology are realized as diphthongs of movement with an increasing degree of aperture (approximately like ûo, ie). These diphthongs begin somewhat lower than the maximally high vowels of the same system, but they do not end with as great a degree of aperture as that found in undiphthongized o and e of the same system. The position of these phonemes in the vowel system can therefore evoke no doubts: such vowel systems are four-degree triangular systems in which "ω" and "ě" represent the second degree of sonority (u, ω, o, a, e, ě, and i). The oppositions ω-o and ě-e are neutralizable in the dialects in question. In unstressed syllables where these oppositions are neutralized, the respective archiphonemes are represented by o and e. (This is true, at least, of the North Great Russian and the North Ukrainian dialects which have an "ω" and an "ě".) It follows that in this case diphthongization or, more precisely, the decrease in vowel height must be regarded as the correlation mark. Equally clear is the position of the diphthongs "oa" and "ea" in Daco-Romanian, where they obviously stand between o and e, on the one hand, and a, on the other: [55]

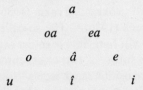

In the Slovenian dialect of Carinthia, north of the Drau (in the dialect of the so-called Drauci), the diphthongs uə and iə, which end less high than they start, are obviously to be classed between u and i, and o and e, whereas oa and ea evidently lie between o, e, and the maximally open å, and a. Accordingly there exists a five-degree quadrangular system: [56]

$$
\begin{array}{cc}
\mathring{a} & a \\
oa & ea \\
o & e \\
u\mathschwa & i\mathschwa \\
u & i
\end{array}
$$

More difficult is the classification of those monophonematically evaluated diphthongs in which one part is more open and the other higher than the neighboring vowels of mid-degree of aperture. German and Dutch present a case of this type. The three German diphthongs "*au*," "*eu*," and "*ei*" can be grouped into the three classes of timbre of the German vowel system, but it is impossible to accommodate them within the system constituted by degrees of sonority. The fluctuation and indeterminacy of the degree of aperture of these phonemes, which is due to flexibility in articulation, may well be considered their specific mark. It distinguishes them from all other long (i.e., unchecked) vowel phonemes of the German language. The long vowel phonemes must therefore first be divided into two categories: those with a "stable" and those with a "movable" degree of aperture. Further classification according to the three classes of timbre can then be carried out in both categories. Classification according to the three degrees of sonority, on the other hand, can only be carried out in the category of vowels with a stable degree of aperture.[57]

The diphthongs of English present particularly complicated problems, even if one limits oneself to the form of the modern language as codified by Daniel Jones.[58]

Recently several attempts have been made to interpret the vowel system of this form of English phonemically; in chronological sequence these were by Josef Vachek (1933),[59] Bohumil Trnka (1935),[60] A. C. Lawrenson (1935),[61] and Kemp Malone (1936).[62] The so-called short vowels appear to offer no difficulties: all four investigators agree that in technical terminology these vowels form "a two-class, three-degree quadrangular system." In English the opposition mark seems to be tongue position rather than lip rounding. Difficulties appear in regard to the so-called long vowels and diphthongs (or triphthongs). However, these difficulties seem to have arisen primarily because the English vowel system had been treated without considering the peculiarities of the English prosodic system. In English "quantity" is a *prosodic opposition based on type of contact*. A vowel is "short" if its pronunciation is *interrupted* by the beginning of the following consonant, "long" if its pronunciation is undisturbed and displays its full extent. The description by Daniel Jones indicates that of the "unchecked" vowel phonemes in English only *a*: and *ǝ*: have no diphthongal variants. All remaining unchecked vowel phonemes have diphthongal variants, in other words, they have variants that are characterized by a movable degree of aperture. Such variants are only optional for *ɛ*: and *ɔ*:, and they are used much more rarely than in the case of *i*: and *u*:. Still, they do exist, and this is sufficient. In the variety of modern English described by Jones no fundamental difference can be recognized between the "true" diphthongs and the "long monophthongs" (with the exception of *a*: and *ǝ*:). Both are *unchecked vowel phonemes with a movable degree of aperture.* The *only unchecked vowel phonemes with a stable degree of aperture* are maximally open *a*: and indeterminate *ǝ*:, that is, those unchecked vowel phonemes that stand outside the classes of timbre. The flexibility in degree of aperture in the variety of English studied is thus related to "uncheckedness" as well as to membership in a specific class of timbre.

On the basis of the preceding, a principle of classification can be established for the vowel phonemes with a movable degree of aperture, namely, the *direction of articulatory movement* (*Ablaufsrichtung*). Some unchecked vowels have a centripetal, others a centrifugal, direction of articulatory movement. I.e., some move back to a (neutral) center position[63] from a point characterized by the marks of a specific class of timbre, while others move in the direction of the extreme representative of the specific class of timbre. In German we can designate the former as vowels with an articulatory movement toward the center (*hineinablaufende Vokale*), the latter as vowels with an articulatory movement away from the center (*hinausablaufende Vokale*). It is significant that *a*: and *ǝ*:, which stand outside the system of timbre, in the center so to speak, have an immovable degree of aperture. In the remaining unchecked phonemes in English it is possible to determine the relative degree of aperture of the starting point. Both classes of timbre[64] have three degrees of sonority. In the case of the vowel phonemes with an articulatory movement away from the center, these are *uw* (= *u*:), *ou*, and *au* in the dark class of timbre, and *ij* (= *i*:), *ei*, and *ai* in the clear class of timbre. In the case of the vowel phonemes with an articulatory movement toward the center, the first degree of sonority is evidently represented by *vǝ* and *ιǝ*. To the second we assign *ǝ*: and *ɛ*:, which actually also have the optional variants *ɔǝ* and *ɛǝ* and which, on the basis of their phonological content, should rather be considered the realization of the vowels moving toward a neutral center ("*ǝ*"). The phonemes that Jones designates as triphthongs *auǝ* and *aiǝ*, and for which he lists the optional variants *aǝ*, *aǝ* and *a*:, *a*: respectively, should probably be considered as having the third degree of sonority.[65] Since the maximally open *a* stands outside the classes of timbre, the entire English system of unchecked vowel phonemes must be regarded as a "four-degree, two-class triangular system containing an indeterminate vowel." However, due to the fact that the two directions of articulatory movement are distinguished in every class of timbre, the total number of unchecked vowel phonemes is not eight but fourteen:

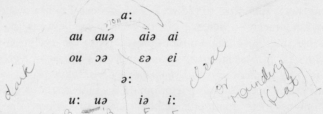

$$
\begin{array}{cccc}
 & a: & & \\
au & au\partial & ai\partial & ai \\
ou & \partial\partial & \varepsilon\partial & ei \\
 & \partial: & & \\
u: & u\partial & i\partial & i: \\
\end{array}
$$

As to the diphthong *oi*, it is considered a phoneme combination by all the above investigators, except A. C. Lawrenson. But the positive arguments Lawrenson raises in favor of his monophonematic interpretation do not seem to carry much weight (see Kemp Malone, *op. cit.*, p. 160, no. 4).[66]

While in standard German and Dutch there are only few unchecked vowels that have a movable degree of aperture and are always "articulated away from the center," most unchecked vowel phonemes in English are characterized by the movability of their degree of aperture and, in addition, present an opposition based on the direction of articulatory movement. It is possible that similar conditions also exist in certain other languages or dialects, in particular in those languages that have a prosodic structure based on the same principle as that of English. In any event, all languages that have a large number of diphthongs of movement must always be examined as to the question whether differences in direction of articulatory movement similar to those found in English are not significant for them.

D   Resonance Properties

While the properties of localization and the properties based on degree of aperture of the vowels are so closely linked with each other as to form a kind of "bundle," the resonance properties belong on quite a different plane. By the term "oppositions of resonance" we understand all "distinctive oppositions" between "pure" vowels and vowels that are somehow "impure."

a. The correlation of nasalization

The *correlation of nasalization* is the most common.[67] In many languages it exists for all vowels. The nasalized vowels, of course, need not be fully identical with the corresponding nonnasalized vowels with respect to tongue, lip, and jaw positions. Only sameness of position in the system is important. For example, in Burmese the long nasalized vowel phonemes with the second and third degree of sonority are realized as diphthongs, while the corresponding nonnasalized vowels are realized as monophthongs:[68]

	a			*ã*			
	ɔ	ɛ			ãu	ãɩ	
nonnasalized			nasalized				
o		*e*		õu		ẽɩ	
u	*i*			*ũ*		*ĩ*	

In many languages the correlation of nasalization extends only to part of the vowel system. Often one of the mid degrees of sonority remains unaffected by this correlation. This is true, for example, of the variety of Scottish spoken on Barra Island:[69]

	a				*ã*		
	ɔ	æ			ɔ̃	æ̃	
nonnasalized				nasalized			
o	*ø*	*e*			*ũ*	*ỹ*	*ĩ*
u	*y*	*i*					

or of Northern Albanian:[70]

	a	ɛ		*ã*	ɛ̃	
nonnasalized	*o*	*ø*	*e*	nasalized		
u	*y*	*i*		*ũ*	*ỹ*	*ĩ*

Sometimes not the mid, but the maximally high, vowels are exempted from nasalization, as, for example, in French:

	a a					
	ɔ	ɛ			*ã*	
nonnasalized			nasalized			
o	*ø*	*e*		õ	ø̃	ẽ
u	*y*	*i*				

In all of these cases all classes of timbre are represented in the nasalized vowels. There are languages with two-class vowel systems which have only two nasalized vowels. This is the case, for example, in the Jauntal dialect of Slovenian spoken in Carinthia (nasalized vowels õ and ã),[71] and in the

Kashub dialects ($\tilde{o}$ and $\tilde{a}$).[72] In other languages no specific degrees of aperture, but certain classes of timbre, are excluded from nasalization.

In the Central Chinese dialect of Siang-tang (Honan Province) only unrounded vowels are nasalized:

$$a \qquad\qquad \tilde{a}$$

nonnasalized o e nasalized $\tilde{e}$

$$u \quad v \quad \ddot{v} \quad i \qquad\qquad \tilde{\iota}^{73}$$

In the dialect of Marchfeld the vowels of the medial class of timbre as well as the vowels of the second mid degree of aperture are exempted from nasalization:[74]

$$a \qquad\qquad\qquad\qquad\qquad \tilde{a}$$

$$au \;\; \ddot{a}\ddot{u} \;\; \ddot{a}i \qquad\qquad\qquad \tilde{a}u \quad \tilde{a}\iota$$

nonnasalized ϱ $\ddot{\varrho}$ ε nasalized $\tilde{o}$ $\tilde{e}$

$$o \qquad \ddot{o} \qquad e \qquad\qquad \tilde{u} \qquad\qquad\qquad \tilde{\iota}$$

$$u \qquad \ddot{u} \qquad i$$

The number of nasalized vowels is thus never greater than the number of nonnasalized vowels.

It may happen that a language contains only a single "nasalized vowel." For such a vowel neither a particular class of timbre nor a particular degree of aperture is relevant. These could only become relevant in contrast with other nasalized vowels. The coloration of such a single nasalized vowel is therefore determined by its consonantal environment alone. Its aperture is not present at all. In other words, such an "indeterminate" nasal vowel is nothing but a syllabic nasal that is assimilated to the following consonant. In sketches on African languages where such phonemes occur, they are usually represented by the letters m, n, η, etc. But it is very questionable whether this phoneme can really be identified with m, n, etc. It must be kept in mind that in most such languages consonant combinations do not occur at all (or that only the combinations "obstruent + liquid" are permitted). The phonemes in question can therefore only form distinctive oppositions with the vowel phonemes, while m, n, etc., stand in a relation of direct, distinctive opposition only to the other consonants. Furthermore, the "syllabic nasal" in the particular African languages shows the same distinctive differences of tone (differences of tonal register) as the vowels. All this favors the view that in cases such as Ibo "mbε" (bisyllabic, high-tone m, low-tone ε [turtle]) the "syllabic nasal" may be considered an "indeterminate nasalized vowel."

However, even with this interpretation certain difficulties remain. For in languages such as Ibo, Efik, Lamba, Ganda, etc., which do not have any nasalized vowels nor a nonnasalized indeterminate vowel, the "syllabic nasal" stands in a relation of distinctive opposition to the vowels only, but this relation is always multilateral. In such a case, the "syllabic nasal" can probably be regarded as an "indeterminate vowel in general." Its nasalization, however, is a purely phonetic, phonologically irrelevant property. In languages such as Ewe, Yoruba, Fante, etc., on the other hand, where the correlation of nasalization comprises the entire vowel system, this "syllabic nasal" would have to be grouped with the category of nasalized vowels. A curious situation would result: the system of nasalized vowels would then contain one phoneme more than the system of nonnasalized vowels, which would contradict everything we know about the correlation of nasalization.

b. The correlation of muffling

The correlation of nasalization is probably the most common, but by no means the only, correlation of resonance. Whether there exists only one or several other additional types of oppositions of resonance is very difficult to say at the present stage of investigation. The languages in which distinctive oppositions between "pure" and somewhat "muffled" vowels exist are "exotic" languages. The notations that one finds about them by observers, usually better trained and more interested in ethnology than in linguistics, are, for the most part, rather unclear.[75] Subject to this reservation, we continue to use the term "correlation of muffling" (or opposition of muffling), without taking up the question of whether this always involves the same or different correlations in the various languages.

Recently the phonetic aspect of the problem has been considerably advanced, at least for Africa. Dr. A. N. Tucker, who had studied and mastered the pronunciation of the "pure" and "muffled" vowels in the Nilotic languages, was himself subjected to an instrumental phonetic study by Panconcelli-Calzia in Hamburg. The results showed that in the case of the "squeezed" vowels the faucal pillars are compressed and the velum is lowered, without, however, enabling the flow of air to escape through the nose. In the case of the "breathy" vowels the velum is raised, the fauces retracted, and the larynx clearly lowered, so that quite a large cavity is formed behind the oral cavity proper. The glottis appears to be in the position of whispering.[76] Dr. Ida C. Ward made the same observations for the Abua language of Southern Nigeria: this language also involves the opposition of vowels with a compressed pharynx and vowels with a wide-open pharynx, resulting in a "flat" sound.[77] It seems that in certain dialects of Modern Indic the same phonetic basis for the "correlation of muffling" can be determined. In any event, J. R. Firth here also speaks of an opposition between "tight" and "breathy phonation." [78] The phonetic nature of vowel muffling in certain East Caucasian languages, on the other hand, remains unclear from the description by A. Dirr. Of the corresponding vowels of Tabarasan it is claimed that they have laryngeal friction and that, in comparison with other vowels, they have an energetic expiration.[79] Of the corresponding vowels of Aghul it is said that the larynx is compressed in their articulation. This produces a slight noise of laryngeal friction.[80]

The "correlation of muffling," like the correlation of nasalization, also extends either to the entire vowel system or only to a specific part thereof. The former seems to be the case in Nuer, a Nilotic language of the Egyptian Sudan,[81] possibly also in other Nilotic languages, while in Abua, according to Ida C. Ward, the correlation of muffling is present only in the vowels *e* and *o*; in Tabarasan, according to A. Dirr, only in *u* and *a*, and probably also in Aghul, where "muffled" *u* is realized as a type of *o*. (Unmuffled *o* does not occur as an independent phoneme in words of native origin.) The above-mentioned languages with two nasalized vowels can be compared with these cases.

In all types of "oppositions of resonance" the rules for monophonematic and polyphonematic interpretation must be observed with particular stringency. Phonetically nasalized vowels are very often only the realization of the phoneme sequence "vowel + nasal," and the vowels accompanied by a noise of laryngeal friction are only the realization of a combination of a vowel phoneme with a laryngeal consonantal phoneme.

4   CONSONANTAL PROPERTIES

A   Properties of Localization (*Lokalisierungseigenschaften*)

There is no language in which the properties of localization of the consonantal phonemes would be phonologically irrelevant. There are, of course, individual consonantal phonemes without distinctive properties of localization in every language. But these always take some special position in the system because they deviate from the "norm." Several consonantal phonemes of a given language may be equivalent to each other with regard to the distinctive properties of localization (and distinguish themselves from each other only by the properties based on the manner of overcoming an obstruction or the properties of resonance). By *series of localization* is meant the sum of all consonants with the same distinctive properties of localization, regardless of whether such a series consists of several consonants or only of a single one. Within a system of consonants the individual classes of localization stand in various relations of opposition to each other.

   a. The basic series. Those consonantal series of localization that stand in a relation of heterogeneous multilateral opposition to each other, we call "basic series." Some of these basic series occur in almost all languages of the world. They are the gutturals ("dorsals"), the apicals ("dentals"), and the labials. We do not know of any languages that do not have apicals. Gutturals do not occur, for example, in some Slovenian dialects of Carinthia. Labials are absent in Tlingit (Alaska). But these are extremely rare cases. Except for these, the three mentioned series of localization occur in all languages of the world. This certainly cannot be an accident. It must have some basis in the makeup of these three series. It is probably easiest to seek an explanation in the fact that the lips, the tip of the tongue, and dorsum of the tongue are movable organs that are best suited for obstructing the oral cavity. Thus for the labial series the bringing together of the lips is relevant; for the apical series the participation of the tip of the tongue, the tongue itself being extended, and a frontal position of articulation; and, finally, for the guttural series the participation of the back of the tongue, the tongue being contracted, and a back position of articulation.[82] These three positions of the vocal organs may be considered the "most natural," but by no means in the sense of being "innate." It is well known that children must first acquire these positions laboriously. The sounds that are spontaneously produced by children in the babbling stage for the most part only remotely resemble labials, apicals, and gutturals. The three types of consonants mentioned are "natural" only in the sense that they solve most easily and naturally, with the aid of the movable parts of the oral cavity, the task of producing different sounds that have their own individual character and that are clearly discriminated from each other. This may also explain their universal (or near universal) presence in the world.

   Just as universal as the labials, apicals, and gutturals are the sibilants. The only language known to this author in which an "s" is almost completely absent is Eastern Nuer in the Egyptian Sudan. The grooved shape of the tongue surface distinguishes sibilants from the apicals which are produced with the tongue flatly extended, and from the gutturals which are produced with the tongue arched and contracted. The grooved shape of the tongue surface gives special direction to the airstream, creating a specific acoustic effect. But since the upper and back portion of the resonating cavity is approximately the same for sibilants and apicals, these two series of localization show a certain relatedness, and in some languages they unite into a single series under certain circumstances.

In addition to the four series of localization commonly found and referred to above, there are some languages that have still other basic series.
One of these is particularly the *lateral* series, which occurs as a special
series of localization in many North American and some African languages
(Zulu, Pedi, Herero, Sandawe, etc.).[83] A type of intermediary series of
localization between the guttural and the labial series is represented by the
series of localization that is usually called "labiovelar." As far as we know,
it exists in the above form only in the so-called Sudan languages, and, it
seems, in certain Japanese dialects. This series is characterized by simultaneous labial and guttural occlusion. We would prefer to call it "gutturolabial." A type of intermediary series between the guttural and the apical
is represented by the *palatal* series of localization, which occurs in very
many languages in all parts of the world. In many languages it can be considered a basic series, but in some languages it enters into a bilateral
relation with the guttural or the apical series. The phonetic realization of
the palatal series, too, differs from language to language.[84] Lastly, the
laryngeal series of localization must be regarded as a basic series on a par
with the others, at least for a part of the many languages in which it occurs.
In addition to the four universal (or near-universal) basic series, that is, the
labial, guttural, apical, and sibilant, there thus exist four less common
series, namely, the lateral, the gutturolabial (= labiovelar), the palatal,
and the laryngeal.

However, the phonological concept of series of localization must not
be confused with the phonetic one of position of articulation. For example,
in Czech a relation of neutralizable opposition exists between voiced
laryngeal h and voiceless guttural x ("ch"), which is fully analogous to the
relation "voiced"/"voiceless." x and k, however, stand in a bilateral
proportional relation to each other $(x:k = s:c = š:č)$. The h in Czech
thus does not belong to a special laryngeal series, which does not even
exist in that language. It belongs to the guttural series, for which, from the
standpoint of the Czech phonological system, only the fact that lips and
tip of tongue do not participate is relevant.[85] In Greenlandic Eskimo[86] all
spirants have occlusives as "partners." These belong to the same series of
localization: s-c, x-k, $š$-q, f-p. The lateral spirant $λ$ alone has no "occlusive partner." Since, however, there is no closer spirantal equivalent of the
apical occlusive t, the t is evaluated as the "occlusive partner" of $λ$, that
is, the lateral egress of air in $λ$ is irrelevant for Greenlandic. Its apical
articulation alone is relevant. Examples of this type can easily be multiplied.
One can speak of a particular lateral, palatal, or laryngeal series in the
phonological sense only if the phonemes in question do not stand in a
relation of proportional bilateral opposition to any phoneme of another

localization series. In cases where, as in the examples cited above, there exists a bilateral opposition between consonants of different positions of articulation, and that opposition is proportional to analogous relations between phonemes of the same series of localization (Czech and Slovak h-$x = z$-$s = \check{z}$-$\check{s}$, Greenlandic t-$\lambda = p$-$f = k$-$x = q$-$\check{x} = c$-s), both members of the opposition in question must be assigned to one series of localization. Cases in which two series of localization stand in a relation of bilateral opposition to each other are not to be confused with the above.

   b. *Equipollent related series.* Each of the above basic series stands in a relation of multilateral opposition to the other basic series. In certain languages, however, two series occur for some of these basic series, and these stand in a relation of *bilateral equipollent* opposition to each other. Instead of a single labial series, characterized by the participation of the lower lip, a labial and a labiodental series may occur. Both are labial, but at the same time they remain distinct from each other. This is the case, for example, in standard German, where the labial series is represented by *b*, *p*, and *m*, the labiodental series by *v*, *f*, and *p̌*. It is even more pronounced in Shona, a language spoken in Rhodesia, where the occlusives *p* and *b* are contrasted with the spirant *β* in the bilabial series, and the occlusives (affricates) *p̌* and *ḅ* with the spirant *v* in the labiodental series.[87] Many languages have two apical series, one characterized by the tip of the tongue pointed upward, the other by the tip of the tongue pointed downward, instead of a single series characterized by the participation of the tip of the tongue. Depending on the language, this relation can be expressed as opposition between "retroflex" and "plain" apicals,[88] or as opposition between "alveolars" and "interdentals,"[89] or, finally, as opposition between "dentals" and "prepalatals."[90] The relation itself remains identical in all cases: the tip of the tongue is always relatively higher in the realization of the one series than in the realization of the other. Instead of a single "guttural" series, characterized by participation of the dorsum, many languages have two distinct dorsal series: a postdorsal series and a predorsal series. This is the case in many North American languages, for example, in Kwakiutl, Tlingit, and Haida; in Eskimo and Aleut; also in the so-called Paleo-Asiatic languages (Chukchi, Koryak, Kamchadal, Gilyak, Kettic); and in all Caucasian idioms. Or rounded and unrounded gutturals stand in opposition to each other, as in Tigre, in Ethiopia.[91] Instead of a single sibilant series, an *s* and an *š* series occur. Such a "split" in the sibilant series is very common among European languages: English, French, German, Italian, Hungarian, Albanian, Romanian, all Slavic languages, and Lithuanian and Latvian. This phenomenon is rather common in other parts of the world also. Finally, the laryngeal series, which is characterized by the passivity of all mouth organs, may also be replaced by two series: a purely laryngeal series and a pharyngeal series, as found, for example, in Somali, in the Semitic languages, and in some North Caucasian languages.

As for the palatal series, in some systems it stands in a relationship of bilateral opposition to the apical or the dorsal series and must then be evaluated either as "a series with the tip of the tongue lowered," or as a "predorsal series." The bilateral nature of an opposition is proved objectively by its neutralizability. In Czech, Slovak, Hungarian, and Serbo-Croatian, where the opposition between dentals and palatals is neutralizable, these two series of phonemes can be considered "a split" in the apical series. In the Central Chinese dialect of Siang-tang (Honan Province), where the opposition between velar and palatal consonants is neutralizable in certain positions (before u, a, i, $\tilde{a}$, and $\tilde{\imath}$),[92] these two series must be considered "splits" in the dorsal series.

All cases discussed above thus involve a "split" of a basic series into two "related series" which stand in a relation of bilateral opposition to each other, but in a relation of multilateral opposition to all other series of localization in the same system. It must be stressed, however, that there can be a question of such a split in a basic series only if the context of the entire system requires it. Spirants frequently do not have the same position of articulation as occlusives. For example, in Modern Greek there exist, on the one hand, bilabial, postdental, dorsal, and sibilant occlusives (π, τ, κ, $\tau\sigma$), on the other, labiodental, interdental, dorsal, and rill spirants (φ, θ, χ, σ or β, δ, γ, ζ respectively). Occlusives and spirants thus agree in position of articulation with respect to the dorsal and the sibilant series only. However, since the relation $\kappa:\chi$ and $\tau\sigma:\sigma$ is parallel to the relation $\pi:\varphi$ and $\tau:\theta$, the fact that the position of articulation of the spirants φ, θ is not in complete agreement with the position of articulation of the corresponding occlusives π, τ is considered phonologically irrelevant. This case does not involve the "split of a series." The concept of localization is merely slightly extended: instead of "bilabial" and "labiodental" it is here simply "labial," that is, it is "characterized by participation of the lower lip." Instead of "postdental" and "interdental" it is simply "apical," that is, it is "characterized by participation of the tip of the tongue." In French, however, where the labiodental spirants f and v and the bilabial occlusives p and b are pronounced from a purely phonetic point of view approximately like Modern Greek φ, β, π, $\mu\pi$, it is nevertheless not possible to speak of a single labial series. For in the entire French consonant system there is not a single phoneme pair in which the relation "spirant: occlusive" would occur in its pure form (as, for example, in Modern

Greek $\chi:\kappa$, $\sigma:\tau\sigma$). Two separate series of localization, bilabial and labio-dental, will therefore have to be posited here. Though these series stand in a relation of bilateral opposition to each other, they still remain distinct from each other.[93]

According to what principle does the split of the basic series into related series take place? Is there one articulatory or acoustic mark that in such cases serves to distinguish between two related series, or does each pair of related series involve a different discriminative mark? According to the classification by Jakobson, several such series involve a split into a "strident" and a "mellow" series. This opposition is especially evident for the spirants of the particular series. The strident spirants are at the same time also more audible than the corresponding mellow spirants. For example, the labiodental f is strident and more audible than the mellow bilabial φ. The strident pharyngeal $\hbar$ is more audible than the mellow laryngeal h. The strident postvelar $\check{x}$ (as it occurs in snoring) is more audible than the mellow prevelar x, and strident $\check{s}$ is more audible than mellow s (although the latter is itself much more audible than the remaining mellow spirants mentioned above).[94] However, not all splits of basic series into related series can be explained by this principle. The differentiation within the apicals is a result of the modification in the volume and shape of the two resonating cavities, the one located in front, the other in back of the position of articulation. The split of the guttural series into velar and palatal is based on the difference in length of the anterior resonator, as is the split of the guttural series into simple velar and labiovelar. Insofar as the elongation of a resonating cavity can acoustically be converted into a lowering in timbre, and its reduction into a rise in timbre, one might be inclined to consider the relative height of timbre as the discriminative mark. But this would hold true only for the splits in the guttural series which we have just mentioned. In the case of the apicals the matter is not quite so simple since these involve two resonating cavities, anterior and posterior. In these, elongation or reduction does not take place in a parallel manner. Further, in addition to the relative volume, the shape of the resonating cavities plays a role here acoustically. Perhaps one comes closest to a solution by looking at the extreme case of the so-called retroflexes, also called "cerebrals" and "cacuminals," with respect to their relation to the alveolars or postdentals. The acoustic impression left by the retroflexes can best be designated as "flat timbre" (*hohler Klang*), in contrast with the "plain timbre" (*flacher Klang*) of ordinary "dentals."* The same

---

* *Translator's note:* Trubetzkoy's opposition flat–plain is for the most part identical with Jakobson's dichotomy flat–plain (now flat–nonflat). Trubetzkoy does not make the distinction, however, as does Jakobson, between flat–plain and plain–sharp. Instead he

relation between "flat" and "plain" timbre exists also between labiovelar and simple velar consonants (in addition to the above-mentioned height of timbre). The opposition between velars and palatals ("back palatals"), and between "dentals" and "dentopalatals," can also be attributed to this discriminative mark, although not as clearly. The same could perhaps also be said of the opposition between alveolars and interdentals.

It thus seems that in all cases where a basic series is split into two related series, the discriminative mark of these two related series is either the opposition "strident"/"mellow," or the opposition "flat"/"plain." Both oppositions are equipollent.

The relationship between the labial, apical, dorsal, sibilant, laryngeal, lateral, palatal, and labiovelar series represents a relationship of multi-lateral (and heterogeneous) opposition. The "split" of these basic series, discussed above, produces two series each, which form a bilateral opposition: labiodental/bilabial, postdorsal/predorsal, etc. But there are cases in which a basic series is not split into two but three series, and these series stand in a relation of *gradual* opposition to each other. Cases of this type are extremely rare. We know only of the following examples: (*a*) three guttural series are found in three North American Indian languages, in Tsimshian (Nass dialect), Chinook, and Hupa: a postvelar series, a pre-velar series, and a (back) palatal series;[95] (*b*) three sibilant series occur in two North Caucasian languages, Kabardian[96] and Udi:[97] an *s* series, an *š* series, and an *ŝ* series, the latter being phonetically intermediary between the *s* and *š* sounds. Low Sorbian (Low Lusatian-Wendic) probably also belongs to this type, where in addition to *s* and *š* sounds special *ŝ* sounds occur which take an intermediary position.[98] The slight *i* coloring of the intermediary sibilant series in Kabardian and Low Sorbian can probably be considered a phonologically irrelevant secondary phenomenon. Accordingly Tabarasan[99] (in Daghestan in the Eastern Caucasus) and Shona (in Rhodesia, South Africa)[100] may also be considered as belonging to the same class, although the intermediary sibilant series here shows a *u* or *ü* coloring.[101] The number of examples is thus very small. The picture would of course change completely if yet another third group of languages should be included, namely, the languages with a gradual split into three of the apical series. Many languages that have the phonological opposition between retroflex and plain apicals, or between alveolar and interdental apicals, also have a palatal series. Considering the ambiguous character of

considers these two binary oppositions, where simultaneously present, as belonging to the opposition flat–plain, which then takes on a gradual character.

Trubetzkoy's opposition further does not extend to include the vowels. (Cf. Jakobson–Fant–Halle, *Preliminaries to Speech Analysis* [Cambridge, Mass., 1952], pp. 31–36; Jakobson–Halle, *Fundamentals of Language*, pp. 31, 32.)

the palatals, it is not impossible that the three series (retroflex, plain, and palatal, or alveolar, interdental, and palatal respectively) may be interpreted as three different degrees of rising or lowering the tip of the tongue. This could be proven objectively only in those cases where the opposition between the palatals and one of the apical series is neutralizable and would therefore be bilateral. However, this seems to be the case neither in the particular African languages (Herero, Nuer, and Dinka) nor in the modern Indian or Dravidian languages. With respect to Old Indic (Sanskrit), where the opposition between "palatals," "dentals," and "cerebrals" was neutralizable, it must be noted that this opposition existed not only in the case of the apicals but also in that of the sibilant phonemes. It should thus be interpreted rather as a bundle of correlations of timbre (see p. 132). The domain of gradual splits may therefore be considered very limited.

   c. *The secondary series* (*Nebenarbeitsreihen*). Finally, in many languages the basic and the related series are split into two series each, which stand in a relation of privative opposition. Insofar as such oppositive relation is not only privative but also proportional, it gives rise to correlations. From an articulatory point of view, this always means that in the one, namely, the unmarked series of localization, the vocal organs are always in a position considered normal for the corresponding basic or related series, whereas in the other (marked) series the same position of the vocal organs is associated with still another specific *secondary task* to be performed by the vocal organs (or any part thereof) not involved directly in the basic task. The acoustic result is either a specific coloration, that is, a kind of vocalic timbre, or a click sound. Correlations that arise out of placing the *secondary series* in opposition with their corresponding pure basic or related series may therefore be grouped into "correlations of timbre" and "click correlations."

   α) From an acoustic point of view, the *correlations of consonantal timbre* involve the combining of a series of localization, which may be either a basic or a related series, with two opposed "colorations." One of these is evaluated as "neutral" (i.e., as unmarked). Insofar as this combination takes place in several, sometimes even in all, series of localization, the corresponding "colorations" are abstracted from the individual series of localization and conceived of as independent thereof. Various types of correlations of timbre are distinguished, depending on which colorations serve as correlation marks.

   The *correlation of palatalization*, that is, the opposition between neutral and *i*- (or *j*-) colored consonants, is probably the most common. For example, it occurs as the only correlation of timbre in Gaelic, Polish, Lithuanian, Russian, Ukrainian, the Moldavian dialect of Romanian,

Mordvin, and Japanese.[102] But its scope within the consonantal system is not the same everywhere: in Japanese and Lithuanian it comprises all series of localization, whereas in Ukrainian and Mordvin it only comprises the apical and the s-sibilant series. Individual languages that have this correlation also differ rather strongly with respect to the phonetic realization of the palatalized consonants. Still, the principle remains the same everywhere: the "palatalized" consonant has an i- or j-like coloration which combines with its other phonetic properties, while the corresponding "nonpalatalized" consonant does not have any i or j coloring. The i coloring of palatalized consonants is the result of raising the central part of the tongue against the hard palate. In order to stress this opposition even more, the back part of the tongue is often raised toward the soft palate in the case of the nonpalatalized consonants.[103]

These shifts in tongue position very often bring about secondary modifications of articulation as well. In some cases palatalized consonants are thus not only distinguished from nonpalatalized consonants by their "coloration" but also by specific articulatory marks. But from the point of view of the phonemic system of the particular language, such secondary articulatory differences are irrelevant, though frequently these marks are the ones most noticed by a foreign observer. The opposition between palatalized and nonpalatalized consonants also strongly influences the realization of the neighboring vowels. A foreign observer will sometimes notice only the combinatory variants of the vowels without being aware of the differences in timbre in the consonants. But this is an acoustic deception, which is frequently also found with regard to other correlations of consonantal timbre. In a language with a correlation of palatalization the "coloration" ("timbre") of the consonant is always the most important. Of all other articulatory properties, only those properties are observed which are shared by the particular consonant and its "partner." One of the conclusions to be drawn is that in a language of this type the palatal series is hardly possible as an autonomous series of localization: it is always interpreted as a "palatalized apical" or "palatalized guttural" series. In *Polabische Studien* we posited for Polabian a correlation of palatalization as well as an autonomous palatal series. This was an error: the opposition between the gutturals k, g and the palatals ħ, ɓ was neutralizable in Polabian (k and g did not occur before front vowels, and "ħ" and "ɓ" were not permitted before consonants or in final position). Since the correlation of palatalization was found in the other series of localization, the Polabian palatals might also be considered "palatalized gutturals." (Phonemically, the Polabian word for *gums* should therefore be transcribed as "g'uNsna," for *work* as "g'olü," for *dough* as "k'ostü," for *darkness* as "k'ɑmă," for *man* as "k'arl," for *where* as "k'edž," for *mountain* as "g'öra," for *horse* as "k'ün," etc.)

The *correlation of emphatic palatalization*, which is found in certain languages of the Eastern Caucasus, namely, in Chechen, Ingush, Bats, Lak, and Udi, must be distinguished from the correlation of simple palatalization.[104] It seems that in emphatic palatalization a reduction of the resonator orifice is produced mainly by an upward shift of the larynx by which the mass of the tongue also moves toward the front. The special position of the larynx in the production of emphatic-palatalized consonants produces a specific "hoarse" fricative noise which extends to the neighboring vowels as well. Due to the particular shift of the tongue, the neighboring vowels also receive a clearer coloration and seem to be pronounced more openly: *i* tends toward *e*, *a* toward *æ*, and *u* toward *ö*. A foreign observer tends to notice these concomitant phenomena only: he hears the hoarse laryngeal glide after the consonant as well as the hoarse, clearer, and more open pronunciation of the surrounding vowels. But these concomitant phenomena are irrelevant for the phonemic system of the particular language. Only the specific consonantal coloring is important, which a foreign observer learns to notice only after prolonged practice.

Just as the palatal series cannot exist as an autonomous series of localization in languages with simple palatalization, because it is inevitably interpreted as a "palatalized apical" or "palatalized guttural" series, so the "glottal" (or "pharyngeal") series must be interpreted as a "palatalized laryngeal" series in languages with a correlation of emphatic palatalization.

From the correlation of emphatic palatalization it is necessary to distinguish the *correlation of emphatic velarization* that plays an important role in the Semitic languages, especially in Arabic. The Arabic "emphatic" consonants are characterized by a thickening of the root of the tongue, which at the same time causes a shift of the larynx. The opposition between "emphatic" and "nonemphatic" consonants is found in the apical, guttural, sibilant, and laryngeal series. It is accompanied in all series by specific shifts in the position of articulation: the "emphatic" apicals are not only velarized (in the above-defined sense), but are also alveolar in contrast with the postdental nonemphatic apicals. Likewise in the case of the emphatic sibilants, the tip of the tongue is raised higher than in their nonemphatic equivalents. The emphatic gutturals are postdorsal or even uvular, while nonemphatic *k* is predorsal or palatal. In certain dialects of the Egyptian Sudan the voiced equivalent of nonemphatic *k* is almost marginally palatal. Finally, the emphatic laryngeals are closer to being pharyngeal, while the nonemphatic laryngeals are pure laryngeal sounds.[105] However, these concomitant differences in the position of articulation must be ignored. For in the phonemic system of Arabic the emphatic velarized consonants form a closed category, which is placed in opposition to the category of the nonemphatic consonants. What makes the correlation of emphatic velarization in Arabic somewhat opaque is the fact that it does not comprise all consonants of the respective series, and further that it cannot be neutralized:

nonemphatic

$$t \quad d \quad \theta \quad \delta \quad n \quad k \quad g \quad - \quad s \quad z \quad \check{s} \quad \check{z} \quad \Omega \quad h \quad - \quad b \quad f \quad m \quad r \quad l$$

emphatic

$$t^{\alpha} \quad d^{\alpha} \quad - \quad \delta^{\alpha} \quad - \quad q \quad \gamma \quad x \quad s^{\alpha} \quad z^{\alpha} \quad - \quad - \quad - \quad \hbar \quad \hbar \quad - \quad - \quad - \quad - \quad -.$$

Consequently, whether the phonemes q, γ, and x are to be interpreted as "emphatic gutturals." or as a special postvelar (uvular) series, and whether $\hbar$ and $\hbar$ are "emphatic laryngeals" or whether they form a special pharyngeal series, is subject to debate. But since similar questions do not arise with regard to the apicals and sibilants, one may probably assume the correlation of emphatic velarization in the case of the gutturals and laryngeals as well, and accordingly designate x, q, γ, $\hbar$, $\hbar$, as x^{α}, k^{α}, g^{α}, h^{α}, and $\hbar^{\alpha}$. In languages that have a correlation of consonantal timbre, all bilateral oppositions between series of localization which permit such an interpretation are considered privative with respect to the particular correlation of timbre.

The case is much simpler and clearer for the *correlation of rounding* or *labialization*. It occurs as the sole correlation of timbre in some languages of the Northern Caucasus (Kabardian, Ch'ak'ur, Rutulian, Lezghian, Aghul, Artshi, and Kubachi), in Kwakiutl (North America),[106] and possibly also in some African (in particular Bantu) languages. In Kwakiutl this correlation extends only to the two guttural series. In the languages of the Northern Caucasus, in which this correlation is found, it occurs also mainly with respect to front and back gutturals but is not limited to this series. In Kabardian and Lezghian it includes also the apical series; in Ch'ak'ur, Rutulian, and Aghul, the apical series and both sibilant series; and in Artshi the lateral series as well.

The various correlations of timbre tend to combine into *bundles*. We are only familiar with bundles that are produced by the combination of the correlation of palatalization with the correlation of rounding. They are found in Circassian, Ubyk, Abkhas, Dungan Chinese, Korean, and Burmese. The bundles do not occur in all series. For example, in Adyghe, the s series alone has three types of timbre (s, s', s°), the $\check{s}$ series has only the correlation of palatalization, the two guttural series and the apical series only the correlation of rounding. (The labial, lateral, and laryngeal series do not have any differences of timbre.)[107] In standard Abkhas three types of timbre occur in both guttural series and in the š series, while the s series occurs only with the correlation of palatalization, the apical and the laryngeal series only with the correlation of labialization, and the labial series with no differences of timbre at all.[108] In Burmese the labial series alone has three series of timbre (p, p', and $p°$), while the remaining series, that is, the two apical, the guttural, the sibilant, and the palatal ones, have only the correlation of labialization.[109] But in Korean all series of localization appear to participate in both correlations of timbre. The transparency of the system is increased here by the fact that the entire correlation bundle can be neutralized.[110] In all cases discussed so far, the combination of the correlation of palatalization and labialization results at the most in three-member bundles. In the Bsyb dialect of Abkhas, however, the š sounds indicate four classes of timbre (neutral, simple-palatalized, simple-labialized, and "ü-colored" palatalized-rounded). A similar case seems to be on hand in Kinyarwanda, a Bantu language described by P. P. Schumacher (*Anthropos*, XXVI): four classes of timbre are distinguished in the bilabial series and, it seems, also in the š series (only three in the apical and in the s series; only two, i.e., f-$f°$ and v-$v°$ in the labiodental series).[111]

A different type of correlational bundle of timbre should probably be posited for Sanskrit. Since any reduction in the front resonator results acoustically in a reinforcement of the higher partial tones, and consequently in a clearer timbre, it is evident that the timbre of the "dental" occlusives and sibilants of Sanskrit must have been higher than that of the "cerebrals" and lower than that of the "palatals." However, not only the opposition between "dentals" and "palatals" but also the opposition between "dentals" and "cerebrals" was neutralizable and consequently bilateral. It is therefore possible that in this case a correlation bundle existed. The opposition between "dental" and "palatal" occlusives (t-c, th-ch, d-j, dh-jh) and between s and $ç$ could then be interpreted as a correlation of palatalization (similarly as in Ukrainian or Mordvin, for example). The opposition between "dental" and "cerebral" occlusives (t-$ṭ$, th-$ṭh$, d-$ḍ$, dh-$ḍh$), nasals (n-$ṇ$), and s-$ṣ$, on the other hand, would have to be considered a special "correlation of retroflexion." The characteristic feature of the "cerebral" phonemes would then consist of the elongation of the front resonator of the mouth (i.e., of the space between the highest point of the tongue and the orifice of the mouth), resulting from the retraction and retroflexion of the tongue, and the corresponding lowering of timbre of the respective consonants. The entire bundle has, of course,

a certain gradual character. The question as to what extent the bundle of
timbre which existed in Sanskrit can also be posited for other languages,
must remain unanswered for the present. Much depends on whether the
opposition between "dentals" and "palatals" is bilateral in the language
in question. This can be proven objectively only by its neutralizability.

β) The _click correlation_ is geographically much more limited in scope.
Even in those areas where it is found it extends only to a few languages.
It occurs only in a few Southern Bantu languages. Of these, Zulu is the
most important. It is found further in the genetically isolated Hottentot and
Bushman languages, which are also spoken in South Africa; and, finally,
it occurs in Sandawe in the Kilimatinde district of East Africa, which again
is geographically and genetically isolated.

The phonetic aspect of click sounds is well studied at the present. Good
instrumental phonetic recordings and detailed descriptions are available.
Recently a whole monograph appeared in which the "click problem" was
discussed from various points of view.[112] Roman Stopa, the author, discusses the phonetic nature of the click sounds in detail. He develops hypoth-
eses as to the origin of these sounds and the origin of language in general.
But he does not even raise the question of the position of the click phonemes
in the phonemic system of the respective languages. The small essay by
P. de V. Pienaar is very valuable.[113] Although it does not clarify the phonemic problem, it at least contributes new reliable and essential phonetic
material. A recently published study by D. M. Beach,[114] in which the
phonetic, and in part also the phonemic, character of the clicks is placed
in a new light, is very commendable. Thanks to this excellent study, we
now have at our disposal an absolutely reliable description of Hottentot,
that is, of all its main dialects: Nama, Damara, Griqua, and Korana. Of
the other languages concerned, Zulu has been studied most completely
from the point of view of phonetics. The basic work on the sounds of
this language by Clement M. Doke,[115] though itself not phonological in
our sense, nevertheless makes it possible to work out the phonemic system
without great difficulties. For Sandawe, too, the phonemic system can be
worked out in its general outline (at least with respect to the consonants).[116]
The same may also be said for the description by A. N. Tucker of the
phonetics of the Suto-Chuana group.[117] The situation is somewhat more
difficult with respect to Bushman, which is generally regarded as "the
click language par excellence." The copious notations by Wilhelm Heinrich
Bleek[118] are an extremely important source for the study of Bushman.
But the fluctuating and inconsistent transcription of the sounds of the
Bushman language makes it extremely difficult, if not impossible, to infer
its phonemic system, at least without the commentary of the collaborator

of this deserving Bushman scholar. Although P. Meriggi succeeded in bringing a certain order to this confusion,[119] complete clarity has by no means been achieved.

The problem the phonologist encounters with regard to the click sounds of the African languages is the following: Is the opposition between click phonemes and nonclick phonemes in these languages an opposition of localization or an opposition based on the manner of overcoming an obstruction? Phoneticians who studied the physiological nature of click sounds have interpreted and treated the specific properties of these sounds as properties based on type of articulation. The "clicking" (avulsive) type of articulation of these sounds was compared with other types of articulation (ingressive, implosive, ejective, etc.). The comparison was a general one, without regard to the consonantal system of a particular language. The phonologist, however, must study the position of the click phonemes in the consonantal system of individual languages. Such a study leads to the following results. In Zulu, which has apical, palatal, and lateral clicks, there also exist nonclick apicals, palatals, and laterals. Disregarding the clicks for a moment, one will find that in every series of localization, including the apical, palatal, and lateral, there exists a voiced consonant, a recursive occlusive, a voiceless aspirated occlusive, and a nasal.[120] *Mutatis mutandis*, the same oppositions also exist with respect to the three "click" series: each of these has a click with a voiced (soft) vowel onset, another in which the vowel has a "hard" onset (glottal plosion), a third in which the vowel has an aspirated onset, and, finally, a nasalized click. All oppositions between these various types of clicks are distinctive. Accordingly the apical clicks, the palatal clicks, and the lateral clicks in Zulu form a special series, which represents a parallel with the respective nonclick series. In Bushman, where the same four types of clicks occur (i.e., with a voiced soft, a voiceless hard onset, an aspirated vowel onset, and nasalization), the same four types of articulation are found for the corresponding nonclick consonants as well. Accordingly here too a relation of parallel series exists between the apical and palatal clicks and nonclicks. A similar relationship can also be shown for Sandawe, as will be demonstrated further below. The relation of the "click series" to the "nonclick series," which was noted for Zulu, therefore seems to be characteristic also for "click" languages in general. If the distinction between "click" and "nonclick" articulation would consist only in the relation between ingress and egress of air, it would, of course, be impossible to classify this distinction according to oppositions of localization. But more recent phonetic studies have shown that "click sounds" always require a specific shape of the tongue. In addition to the basic closure that is formed either

by the lips or by the anterior parts of the tongue, and which produces the
various types of clicks (labials, dentals, retroflexes, palatals, and laterals),
each click has still another, so-called supplemental closure which is always
velar (i.e., it is produced by raising the posterior part of the dorsum against
the soft palate). The presence of two closures, of which one must be velar
and the other somewhere in the anterior part of the oral cavity, is part of
the nature of click sounds. A suction act rarefies the air in the space between these two closures. Upon release of the anterior closure, outside air
rushes into this air-starved space. But immediately thereafter the posterior
velar closure is released. From a phonetic point of view, all these properties
of the click sounds are equally important. However, from a phonological
point of view, the presence of the velar occlusion, in addition to another
closure (labial, apical, palatal, etc.), and the resultant specific modification
of the shape of the tongue, and hence the configuration of the entire oral
resonating cavity, are most important. This circumstance makes it possible to interpret the difference between click and nonclick articulation as an
opposition of localization, more specifically, as an opposition between
basic and secondary series. Since this opposition is logically privative and
occurs in several series of localization of the same system, it may be
designated as "click correlation."

The presence of a velar "supplemental closure" quite naturally produces a shift in the position of articulation of the front part of the tongue.
It is therefore at times very difficult to pair a click series with a particular
nonclick series. In Bushman nonclick consonants have a labial, an apical,
a dorsal, a palatal, a sibilant, and a laryngeal series. The click consonants,
on the other hand, have a plain-apical, a "cerebral," a palatal, and a lateral
series. A click correlation can therefore be determined here at first glance
only for the apical and the palatal series. However, what has been said by
D. M. Beach (op. cit., pp. 81 ff.) about the corresponding phonemes of
Hottentot, namely, that retroflexion of the tip of the tongue is optional
and not essential, can probably be repeated for the "cerebral" clicks of
Bushman. Important for cerebral clicks is solely that in comparison with
the "dentals" and "palatals" they are shifted further backward, so that a
comparatively large "empty" space, that is, a space not filled by the tongue,
is formed in the front part of the mouth. The relationship that thus exists
between "dental" and "cerebral" clicks may be compared with the
relationship between apical and guttural nonclicks. The "cerebral" clicks
may be considered a secondary series of the guttural series. The system of
clicks in Hottentot, as described by Beach, pages 75 to 82, can be summarized as follows: There are two series of plosive clicks. In one, which is
the "dentialveolar series," according to Beach, and the "palatal series,"

according to earlier observers, the tongue fills the anterior part of the oral cavity up to the teeth. In the other, which is the "alveolar series," according to Beach, and the "cerebral series," according to earlier observers, an empty cavity remains in the anterior part of the mouth. In addition to these two "plosive" series, two "affricate" series are found which stand in exactly the same relationship to each other as the "plosives." In other words, in the one, namely, the "dental" series, the front part of the oral cavity is filled by the tongue, while in the other, namely, the lateral series, it is not. In releasing the anterior closure in the case of the "plosive" series, the tongue is simply torn away from the palate, while in the case of the "affricate" series it permits the air to penetrate gradually: from the front in the "dental" series, from the sides in the lateral series. It is clear that the opposition between "affricate" and "plosive" series is not an opposition of localization. Accordingly there are actually only two click series of localization in Hottentot, one characterized by a completely filled-out anterior part of the mouth (by the tongue), the other by an empty anterior part of the mouth. The nonclick consonants of Hottentot are divided into labials, apicals (including sibilants), gutturals, and laryngeals. The labials and laryngeals obviously stand outside the click correlation. In the remaining series the apical nonclicks correspond to the "clicks with a filled-out anterior cavity," and the guttural nonclicks to the "clicks with an empty anterior cavity." Thus there exists in Hottentot a correlative relation between the click and nonclick series of localization as well.

In connection with the click correlation, a type of secondary series must still be discussed, namely, the "correlation of full gutturalization"* and the "correlation of labiovelarization." These correlations are found in certain Bantu languages, namely, in the Shona group, and in the neighboring Venda.[121] A correlation of full or pure gutturalization exists in the opposition between nonvelarized consonants and consonants in which, in addition to the basic articulation, a secondary guttural articulation takes place, which consists of raising the dorsum of the tongue against the soft palate. The tongue can be raised high enough so as to practically form a velar closure. (This is usually the case in the Zezuru dialect of Central Shona.) Or it may be raised somewhat lower so that it results only in a velar stricture. (This is characteristic for the other dialects of Eastern and Central Shona, especially for the Karanga subgroup.) In the Zezuru dialect this correlation is found in the bilabials and palatals. The correlation of

---

* *Translator's note:* The term gutturalization instead of velarization is used here in view of N. S. Trubetzkoy's apparent preference for this term.

labiovelarization is a combination of the correlation of full gutturalization and the correlation of labialization. It occurs independently of the correlation of full gutturalization in all dialects of Eastern and Central Shona, in the apicals, palatals, and the two sibilant series. The acoustic impression of the fully gutturalized and labiovelarized consonants on a foreign observer is that of combinations of consonants (*pk*, *ck*, *tkw*, *ckw*, or *px*, *cx*, *txw*, *cxw* respectively). They must nevertheless be evaluated as monophonematic since the languages in which they occur do not permit any other consonantal clusters. If one compares the clicks and the fully gutturalized (or labiovelarized) consonants, one arrives at the conclusion that the difference is only phonetic, not phonological. The suction element, which, at first glance, seems to be characteristic of clicks, is only a special way of releasing the anterior oral closure. For the position of the click sounds in the phonemic system it is much less important than the presence of the velar "supplemental closure." But the latter is also present in the pure gutturalized and labiovelarized consonants of Zezuru and the other dialects of Eastern and Central Shona, though perhaps not in quite as energetic a form.

In summary, it can be said that the localization properties may form rather complicated systems of oppositions. The basic series stand in a relation of multilateral (heterogeneous) opposition. But in many languages some of these basic series are split into two related series each. These stand in a relation of bilateral equipollent opposition to each other, and in a relation of multilateral opposition to the other (basic or related) series of the same system. Finally, each series of localization can be split into series that stand in a relation of (actually or logically) privative opposition to each other. If such a split comprises several series of localization in the same consonantal system, it represents a correlation, which may be either a correlation of consonantal timbre or a click correlation.

d Consonantal phonemes outside the series of localization. In many, and possibly in most, languages there are consonantal phonemes that stand outside the localization series (or at least outside the noncorrelative series of localization). The "liquids" and "*h*" are *usually* among these consonantal phonemes. But one should not generalize this statement. The liquids and the *h* can sometimes also be incorporated into the series of localization. Above we have already mentioned Gilyak, where the *r* must be considered a voiced continuant of the apical series.[122] In Eskimo, where the *r* is always realized as a uvular and without a trill, it takes the same position in the postdorsal series as the *w* takes in the labial series and the *y* in the predorsal series. In the apical series this position is taken by *l*, which has a voiceless spirant λ as its counterpart, so that the following system results:[123]

$$p \quad t \quad k \quad q \quad c$$
$$\varphi \quad \lambda \quad x \quad \breve{x} \quad s$$
$$w \quad l \quad y \quad r$$
$$(m) \quad (n) \quad (\eta) \quad (\breve{\eta})$$

In languages that have only one liquid and that have a palatal series of localization, the w can be interpreted as the labial, the y as the palatal, and the sole liquid as the apical sonorant. But whether such an interpretation is correct can be established only where it is substantiated by the way the system functions or by grammatical alternation. For example, in Mende (Sierra Leone), where the l is the only liquid, t and l are in grammatical alternation. This alternation takes place under the same conditions as the alternation $p - w$. Accordingly a proportion $t:l = p:w$ may be set up.[124] In Chichewa, where the only liquid is realized sometimes as an r and sometimes as an l, it becomes d following the prefix m or n. Under the same conditions y is replaced by $\tilde{j}$ and w by b.[125] In these instances there exists objective proof that the "sole liquid" belongs to the apical series. But in cases where similar proof does not exist the classification of single liquids into a particular localization series is always subject to doubt. In languages that have more than two liquids, it is not uncommon that at least one or two liquids belong to specific series of localization. For example, in Serbo-Croatian (Štokavian) the relationship between l and l is obviously analogous to the relationship between $n:\acute{n}$, $t:\acute{c}$, and $d:d$. This justifies grouping l with the "dental," and l with the "palatal" series. Thus only the r remains outside the series of localization. The case of Tamil will be discussed later (pp. 141 f.).

Most languages of the world have only two liquids. Only in extremely rare cases can these be grouped with any localization series.[126] They generally stand outside these series. They form a bilateral opposition which can be interpreted as logically privative. The relation r-l can then be considered either "trilled"/ "untrilled" or "nonlateral"/ "lateral." In a language such as Italian, where the r is always a trilled vibrant, the first interpretation is probably the more suitable one, while in German, where the "untrilled" varieties of the r sound are very frequently realizations of the r phoneme, the second interpretation would be the only one possible. But insofar as the opposition r-l cannot be neutralized in a given language, it remains only logically privative. The opposition between r and l is then at any rate not an opposition of localization but an opposition based on the manner of overcoming an obstruction. This is true even for languages such as German, where r is the "nonlateral" and l the "lateral" liquid. From a phonological point of view, the lateral articulation can be considered a localization property only if it is shared by several phonemes whose remaining distinctive marks are the same as the properties based on the manner of overcoming an obstruction of the phonemes of other basic (or related) series of the same system (as is the case, for example, in Pedi, Sandawe, Tlingit, Chinook, Adyghe, Avar, etc.). However, in languages that have only a single lateral phoneme, and in which that phoneme stands in a relation of bilateral opposition to the *r* that lies outside the localization series, the lateral articulation (i.e., the unimpeded frictionless passage of egressing air between the side of the tongue and the "side wall" of the oral cavity) must be considered a special manner of overcoming an obstruction. The ambiguous character of lateral articulation, which causes such difficulties in *phonetic* systemization, is something that can quite easily be resolved in *phonological* systemization, the more so since the important thing here is only to establish to which other phoneme the particular "lateral" phoneme stands in a relation of opposition, and to determine the nature of such an oppositive relationship.

As for *h*, in many languages it is the "indeterminate consonantal phoneme in general." In many others, however, it is grouped with a particular series of localization. This may be either the "guttural series," which in such a case is characterized by the fact that the tip of the tongue and the lips are not involved in articulation, or it may be a particular laryngeal series. The latter is the case primarily where the same system contains a laryngeal plosive (glottal stop) that stands in a relation of bilateral opposition to *h*. In Danish, where *h* occurs only in those phonic positions in which (voiceless) unaspirated lenes *b, d,* and *g* are in opposition with the aspirated fortes *p, t,* and *k, h* obviously stands in the same oppositive relationship to the unaspirated vowel onset as *p, t,* and *k* stand to *b, d,* and *g*.[127] A laryngeal series could, therefore, be posited here, in which *h* would be the "aspirate" (or "fortis"). In German, on the other hand, where the relationship between *h* and unaspirated vowel onset is not paralleled by the relationship between *p, t, k* and *b, d, g, h* must be considered an "indeterminate" phoneme which stands outside any series of localization (*h* is voiced intervocalically, while *p, t,* and *k* are voiceless in that position; *h* does not occur in final position, while *p, t,* and *k* in that position represent the archiphonemes of the neutralized oppositions *p-b, t-d, k-g,* etc.). The same is also true of many other languages.

B   Properties Based on the Manner of Overcoming an Obstruction
(*Überwindungsarteigenschaften*)

a. Degrees of obstruction and the correlations based on the manner of overcoming an obstruction of the first degree. It has been stated above (p. 94) that the creation of an obstruction and the overcoming of such an obstruction constituted the nature of a consonant. Considered from this point of view, the traditional classification of consonants into occlusives, fricatives (or spirants), and sonorants must be considered a classification based on *degrees of obstruction*. The *occlusives* have the highest degree of obstruction, the *fricatives* a medial degree, and the *sonorants* the lowest degree (which may already come close to an "absence of any obstruction" characteristic of vowels, without, however, wholly reaching that point). Occlusives are *momentary sounds* (*Momentanlaute*), while the fricatives and sonorants are *continuants*. But the occlusives and the fricatives may also be designated as *obstruents* in contrast to the sonorants. Accordingly five bilateral oppositions can exist between the three degrees of obstruction: (*a*) sonorant/obstruent, (*b*) momentary sound*/continuant, (*c*) occlusive/ fricative, (*d*) fricative/sonorant, (*e*) occlusive/sonorant. All five of these are logically privative. If, in a given system, they are proportional, that is, if they occur in several localization series, each of these oppositions produces a special correlation. Such a correlation may be designated *correlation based on the manner of overcoming an obstruction of the first degree* (*Überwindungsartkorrelation ersten Grades*).

The *correlation of sonants*, that is, a bilateral and proportional opposition between sonorants and obstruents, is, of course, only possible in those languages in which the opposition between occlusives and fricatives is phonologically irrelevant. A very clear case of this type exists in Tamil,[128] which has five obstruent phonemes. These are realized differently, depending on their environment: they occur as aspirated occlusives (p^h, t^h, t^h, k^h, and $\hat{c}^h$) initially. Medially after vowels they occur as spirants (i.e., β, δ, $\underset{.}{\delta}$ as voiced, x and $\hat{s}$ mainly as unvoiced). After nasals they are realized as voiced occlusives (b, d, $\underset{.}{d}$, g, $\hat{3}$), and after r as voiceless unaspirated occlusives (p, t, $\underset{.}{t}$, k, $\hat{c}$). The oppositions between voiced and voiceless aspirated and unaspirated obstruents, as well as between occlusives and spirants, are therefore here determined by their phonic environment, and are phonologically irrelevant. The phonological nature of the above-mentioned five phonemes of Tamil consists, on the one hand, in their membership in specific localization series, on the other, in their being obstruents. These

---

* *Translator's note:* The term *Momentanlaut* (momentary sound) will henceforth be rendered by the familiar term "stop." The author uses this term only to distinguish between *Momentanlaut* and *Dauerlaut* (continuant). Momentanlaut becomes "occlusive" in relation to the fricative/sonorant division within continuants.

It seems that Trubetzkoy's division cannot be completely equated with Jakobson's interrupted/continuant opposition (cf. *Preliminaries*, p. 21). In Trubetzkoy's terminology both *r* and *l* are included in the sonorants and hence, according to his classification, in the continuants, while Jakobson contrasts them as being interrupted and continuant respectively. Cf. Jakobson–Fant–Halle, *Preliminaries to Speech Analysis*, pp. 19, 21, 22.

five obstruents in Tamil are opposed to five sonorants: the labial P phoneme is opposed to a w, plain-apical T to an l, retroflex apical T to a retroflex l, and palatal sibilant $\hat{C}$ to a y. The guttural K phoneme in Tamil seems to correspond to the sonorant R (transcribed as "$ɹ$" by J. Firth). Firth describes its realization as follows: "It is a frictionless continuant with an indeterminate back vowel coloring. It is produced by retracting the entire body of the tongue toward the back, spreading the seam of the tongue toward both sides so that the tongue so to speak becomes short, thick, and blunt, and approaches the center of the hard palate" (XVI). Only Tamil r lies completely outside any localization series and does not stand in a relation of bilateral opposition to any other phoneme.[129] A *correlation of sonants* is thus present in Tamil (or a *correlation of liquids*, if one makes the decision to consider w and y as liquids as well). This correlation comprises the entire consonantal system (with the exception of r). We do not know of any other examples of this type. Sonorants generally either stand outside all localization series and form a phoneme class by themselves. In this case they stand in a relation of bilateral opposition to each other, but in a relation of multilateral opposition to all other phonemes. Or only a few, but not all, sonorant phonemes are incorporated into the system of localization series and enter into a relation of bilateral opposition to a particular class of obstruents.

The bilateral opposition between stops and continuants presupposes that the opposition between fricatives and sonorants is phonologically irrelevant. In its pure form it seems to occur very rarely. At least we do not know of any consonantal system that is structured in accordance with this principle. There are languages, however, in which the (oral) sonorants together with the spirants form a class of continuant phonemes, which is opposed to the class of stop phonemes in all or in several series of localization. But this correlation does not occur by itself, at least not in the cases known to us. It occurs only in connection with other correlations, and in such a way that either the stops or the continuants, or both categories, are divided into voiceless and voiced lenes and fortes. Compare, for example, the consonantal systems of Eskimo (p. 138) and Gilyak (pp. 73 ff.) cited above. This correlation (which may be termed *correlation of stops* or *correlation of continuants*) is therefore always only a member of a correlation bundle.

The correlation of sonorants and the correlation of stops are rare phenomena in general. More often, the three degrees of obstruction (occlusives, spirants, and sonorants) are put into opposition with each other in pairs. In most cases oppositions of this type extend only to part of the consonantal system.

We use the term *correlation of constriction* or *correlation of occlusiveness* for the opposition between occlusives and spirants simultaneously existing in several localization series. In German this correlation is found in the dorsal, labiodental, and *s*-sibilant series (*k-x, p̆-f, c-s*). In Polish, Czech, Slovak, and Ukrainian this correlation comprises the guttural and all sibilant series. In Serbo-Croatian and Hungarian it is limited to the two sibilant series (Serbo-Croatian *c-s, ǧ-ž, č-š*; Hungarian *cs-s, dzs-zs, c-sz, dz-z*). In Albanian, in addition to the two sibilant series (*c-s,* "*x*"-*z*, "*ç*"-"*sh*," "*xh*"-"*zh*"), it also comprises the labial (*p-f, b-v*) and apical series (*t*-"*th*," *d*-"*dh*"). In Modern Greek it includes all series of localization (*π-φ, τ-θ, κ-χ, τσ-σ*). In English the opposition between occlusive and constrictive quite evidently exists in the case of the *š* sounds (*č-š, ǯ-ž*). However, in the case of the English apicals and labials the matter is not quite clear: English *t* and *d* are realized with the tip of the tongue raised rather high. In the case of energetic, affricated aspiration of initial *t* an *š*-like "off-glide" is audible, while the plain-apical spirants *θ* and *δ* in English are realized with the tip of the tongue in a rather low position ("interdental"). Likewise *p* and *b* are "bilabial," while *f* and *v* are "labiodental." It is true, of course, that in Modern Greek and Albanian the labial and dental spirants do not correspond exactly to the respective occlusives with regard to position of articulation either. But such an exact correspondence is found here in two other localization series (the Albanian *s* and *š* series, and the Modern Greek *χ* and *σ* series), thus creating a "systemic constraint." Further, the oppositions *p-f, t-θ*; and *k-x* are neutralizable in Modern Greek, and a grammatical alternation exists between its members. Since these conditions are absent in English (and the affricated aspiration of initial *t* and *p* clearly underlines the phonetic difference of localization which exists between these sounds and *θ* and *f*), it is doubtful whether the oppositions *t, d*—*θ, δ* and *p, b*—*f, v* should be interpreted as "oppositions of constriction" in English.[130] Similar doubts also arise with respect to certain other languages. It can nevertheless be said that in most cases the situation is quite clear, and that the correlation of constriction, though it is only rarely found in all localization series, is one of the most common correlations in the languages of all parts of the world.

A bilateral relation of opposition between a sonorant and a fricative, on the other hand, is a rather rare phonological phenomenon. In Czech such a relation is found between *r* and *ř*, in Zulu and in the language of the Pueblo Indians of Taos (New Mexico)[131] between l and *l̦*. In several languages a similar relation seems to exist between *w* and *β* (or *v*), but in each of these cases one must check out whether the *w* is actually a consonant and not rather a combinatory variant of the vowel *u*. Discounting such doubtful cases, there remain only very few languages that have the opposition "labial sonorant"/"voiced labial spirant." (Examples are K'üri, Pedi, Chichewa, and a few others.) Relative to the opposition between a palatal sonorant and a voiced palatal spirant, we do not know of a single example.[132] Cases in which two consonantal phonemes are actually distinguished only by the presence or absence of friction are thus extremely rare. This opposition does not seem to form a correlation that extends over several series of localization in any language.

As regards the opposition between sonorants and occlusives, it occurs particularly in those languages that do not have any spirants, for example, in the Eastern dialect of Nuer in the Egyptian Sudan. In this language all five voiced occlusives b, d, interdental $ḍ$, g, and j are in contrast with an equal number of sonorants, w, l, r, γ, and y.[133] Of the latter, w, γ, and y obviously stand in a relation of bilateral opposition with b, g, and j. r and l should perhaps also be grouped with the two apical related series. Bilateral oppositions between sonorants and occlusives are also found in other languages. In Serbo-Croatian (Štokavian) we find the proportion $b:v = d:l = d:l$ (lj). In those Montenegran dialects where Proto-Slavic x has become a voiced velar continuant without any perceptible friction,[134] the same proportion appears to have been expanded to include the pair $g:\breve{\gamma}$. In Danish, in particular in the standard language, a proportional opposition occurs between lenis b, d, and g, on the one hand, and the continuants v, δ, and γ, on the other. Since in Danish v, δ, and γ are realized almost without friction, and since their combination with a preceding vowel is prosodically equivalent to a long syllabic nucleus (as is the combination vowel $+ r$ or l, or vowel $+ m$ or n), they may be considered sonorants from the point of view of the Danish phonemic system.[135] Accordingly here too a correlation is present which includes all lenis occlusives and part of the sonorants. Since from an acoustic and articulatory point of view occlusives and sonorants involve maximally different types of articulation, this correlation might well be termed the (consonantal) *correlation of contrast*. It is to be noted that in all cases discussed above the (phonetic) intermediary degrees between occlusives and sonorants, namely, the voiced or lenis spirants, are absent: Eastern Nuer does not have any spirants at all. In Serbo-Croatian and Danish spirants are absent, at least in those series of localization which participate in the "correlation of contrast." This is quite understandable, of course, since only under this condition can the opposition between occlusive and sonorant be bilateral.

b. Correlations based on the manner of overcoming an obstruction of the second degree (Überwindungsartkorrelationen zweiten Grades). From the above survey it should be apparent that the correlations that arise from bilateral oppositions between the different degrees of obstruction comprise the entire consonantal system only relatively seldom. Usually a few consonantal phonemes remain unaffected by such correlations; but these enter into specific relations of bilateral opposition to other phonemes of the same degree of obstruction. Bilateral oppositions between phonemes having the same degree of obstruction (and belonging to the same series of localization) give rise to a specific set of correlations which may be termed *correlations based on the manner of overcoming an obstruction of the second degree*, in contrast with the primary correlations which are the result of the opposition between three degrees of obstruction.

In each correlative pair of a correlation based on the manner of overcoming an obstruction of the second degree, both members of the opposition must belong to the same degree of obstruction. But a correlation based on the manner of overcoming an obstruction of the second degree is theoretically not bound by any specific degree of obstruction. It can occur in different degrees of obstruction, depending on the language.

We distinguish the following six typical correlations based on the manner of overcoming an obstruction of the second degree:

The *correlation of tension*, or the opposition between "fortes" and "lenes"—an opposition in which the size of the obstruction and that of the means of overcoming the obstruction (air pressure) are adapted to each other: if the obstruction is reinforced by a tensing of the buccal muscles, the air pressure increases accordingly. On the other hand, if there is a slackening of the muscles of the buccal organs, the air pressure decreases as well.

The *correlation of intensity (or pressure)*, which shows a somewhat different type of relation between resistance and air pressure: when the muscles of the buccal organs are being relaxed, the air pressure is too strong. Hence the short duration and possible aspiration of the "weak" opposition members. When the buccal muscles are being tensed, the air pressure seems just about able to accomplish its task. Hence the relative length, the lack of aspiration, and the fact that the obstruction is overcome with great effort in the case of the "strong" opposition members.

The *correlation of voice*, or the opposition between voiced and voiceless consonants.

The *correlation of aspiration*, or the opposition between aspirated and unaspirated consonants (insofar as only aspiration and no other articulatory properties are phonologically relevant).

The *correlation of recursion*, or the opposition between consonants produced by air flowing from the lungs and consonants that are only produced by the air accumulated above the closed glottis and expelled by means of a pistonlike thrust of the closed glottis.[136]

The *correlation of release*, the opposition between occlusives in which the oral closure is released with plosion and those in which it is released normally.[137]

The *correlation of preaspiration* could, perhaps, be mentioned as a seventh correlation based on the manner of overcoming an obstruction of the second degree, that is, the opposition between consonants with aspirated implosion and those without such implosion. This opposition is found in some American languages, for example, in Fox and Hopi. But it is not clear whether the "preaspirated" consonants in these languages should be considered monophonematic or polyphonematic (i.e., as h + consonant).[138]

All correlations based on the manner of overcoming an obstruction of the second degree involve the opposition between a "stronger" and a "weaker" consonant.

Correlation	Strong Opposition Member	Weak Opposition Member
Correlation of Tension	fortis	lenis
Correlation of Intensity	heavy	light
Correlation of Voice	voiceless	voiced
Correlation of Aspiration	aspirated	unaspirated
Correlation of Recursion	infraglottal	recursive
Correlation of Release	explosive	injective

The question whether the "strong" or the "weak" opposition member of a correlation based on the manner of overcoming an obstruction of the second degree is unmarked can, in the final analysis, be determined objectively only from the functioning of the particular phonemic system. However, in any correlation based on the manner of overcoming an obstruction a "natural" absence of marking is attributable to that opposition member whose production requires the least deviation from normal breathing. The opposing member is then of course the marked member. From this general or "natural" point of view the marked member in the correlation of tension is the fortis consonant, in the correlation of intensity the heavy consonant, in the correlation of aspiration the aspirated member, in the correlation of recursion the recursive member, and in the correlation of release the injective member. By looking at it in this way it is possible to determine the phonological nature of a correlation based on the manner of overcoming an obstruction of the second degree in some doubtful cases. In a language in which voiced lenis consonants form a neutralizable opposition with voiceless fortis consonants, and in which the archiphoneme in the positions of neutralization is represented by a voiceless fortis consonant, the correlation of voice is present. This means that in this case the opposition between voiced and voiceless consonants alone is phonologically relevant, while the difference in the tension or relaxation of the buccal muscles is a secondary phenomenon which is phonologically irrelevant. In a language where a recursive lenis is opposed to an aspirated fortis consonant, the correlation of recursion is present, provided that the archiphoneme is represented by an aspirated fortis consonant in the position of neutralization. Only in those cases where the given phonemic system contains direct proof for another ("unnatural") distribution of markedness or unmarkedness of the opposition members can this "natural" way of evaluation be ignored.

On the basis of these general considerations it may be concluded, for example, that the correlation of voice is present in Russian, Polish, Lithuanian, Czech, Slovak, etc., where the voiceless fortis consonant functions as the archiphoneme in the position of neutralization. In Lapp, on the other hand, where the archiphonemes of the neutralized correlation based on the manner of overcoming an obstruction of the second degree are represented by lenis consonants initially, the correlation of tension is obviously present. This correlation is also present in High German, where obstruents are neither voiced nor aspirated, and where tensing of the buccal organs is the only means of differentiation. But in cases where several principles of differentiation combine, and where the particular correlation cannot be neutralized, or where the way in which it is neutralized does not contain any indication as to the markedness or unmarkedness of the opposition members, it is actually impossible to determine precisely the nature of a correlation based on the manner of overcoming an obstruction of the second degree. English *t*, *p*, and *k* are aspirated voiceless fortes before stressed vowels, but unaspirated voiceless fortes elsewhere; *b*, *d*, and *g*, on the other hand, are always voiced lenes. The correlation is neutralized, on the one hand, before obstruents, the representative of the archiphoneme being conditioned externally, and on the other, after *s*, the archiphonemes being represented by voiceless lenes, that is, by sounds that are phonetically intermediary between the two opposition members. Consequently it is impossible to say whether in English a correlation of tension or a correlation of voice is present. *Mutatis mutandis*, the same is also true for standard German, French, Hungarian, Serbo-Croatian, etc., where voiceless fortes are found in opposition to voiced lenes. The type of neutralization of this opposition does not give any clues to its nature. In

Danish the situation is equally unclear, though here the correlation of voice is not involved. All obstruents are voiceless in Danish. But since aspirated fortes in Danish are in opposition to unaspirated lenes, and the latter represent the archiphonemes in the positions of neutralization, it is not clear whether a correlation of aspiration or a correlation of tension is here to be posited. According to H. J. Uldall (*International Journal of American Linguistics*, VIII [1933], 74), two classes of occlusives are presumably in opposition to each other in Achumawi. One of these is realized by aspirated voiceless consonants, while the other is realized optionally by voiced or voiceless lenes or by recursive consonants. A similar situation is found in many languages. In cases of this type it seems advisable to designate the correlation simply as a correlation based on the manner of overcoming an obstruction of the second degree, and the opposition members simply as "strong" and "weak." The situation is usually much clearer in those cases where more than two manners of overcoming an obstruction are differentiated phonologically within one degree of obstruction. However, even those cases do not preclude a certain indeterminacy, at least with regard to one component of the correlation bundle. In principle the differentiation of the phonemes within one degree of obstruction by second degree correlations based on the manner of overcoming an obstruction is the greater the higher the degree of obstruction. This means that the occlusives usually show more classes based on the manner of overcoming an obstruction than the fricatives, and the fricatives more classes than the sonorants. However, this is no law, only a general tendency.

α) In a two-degree consonantal system such as, for example, the above-mentioned system of Eastern Nuer, the occlusives are divided into two classes by means of a correlation based on the manner of overcoming an obstruction of the second degree (b-p, d-t, $d̦$-$ț$, g-k, $j̦$-c), whereas the sonorants form only one such class (w, r, l, γ, y, and m, n, η, $n̦$ respectively). In many languages in which three degrees of obstructions are represented, the occlusives are divided into two classes with respect to the manner of overcoming an obstruction, whereas the fricatives and the sonorants form only one class each. This is the case, for example, in Danish (occlusives b-p, d-t, g-k, fricatives f, s, sonorants r, l, j, v, δ, γ, and m, n, η respectively); in the language of the Mayas of Yucatan (occlusives p-p', t-t', c-c', $č$-$č'$, k-k', $d̦$, fricatives s, $š$, h, sonorants m, n, w, l, j);[139] in Yurak-Samoyed (occlusives b-p, d-t, g-k, c, $d̦$, fricatives s, h, sonorants m, n, η, $n̦$, w, l, r, j);[140] and in Lamba (occlusives b-p, d-t, g-k, $d̦$-$ț$, fricatives f, s, $ș$, and sonorants m, n, η, $n̦$, r, l, v).[141] In other languages fricatives are divided into the same two classes as the occlusives with regard to the manner of overcoming an obstruction, while the sonorants are not differentiated in this way. This probably represents the most common type of consonantal system: in Europe it is found in English, French, Dutch, Russian, German, Lithuanian, Latvian, Polish, White Russian, Ukrainian, Slovak, Czech, Hungarian, Romanian, Serbo-Croatian, Bulgarian, Italian, etc.[142] In other parts of the world it is by no means rare either. On the other hand, it is difficult to find a language in which not only the occlusives and fricatives but also the sonorants are differentiated by *the same* correlation based on the manner of overcoming an obstruction of the second degree. In those languages in which each of the three degrees of obstruction is divided into two classes, each relative to overcoming an obstruction, we find either a different correlation based on the manner of overcoming an obstruction of the second degree for each degree of obstruction (as, for example, in the Scottish-Gaelic dialect of Barra Island where, with respect to manner of overcoming an obstruction, the occlusives are divided into two classes by the correlation of aspiration, the fricatives by the correlation of voice, and the sonorants by the correlation of intensity),[143] or at least the sonorants do not involve the same correlation as the occlusives and the fricatives. (This is the case, for example, in the North Albanian dialect of Skutari, where occlusives and fricatives are differentiated by the correlation of voice, and sonorants by the correlation of intensity.)[144] Of all the languages with which we are familiar only Irish has a single correlation based on the manner of overcoming an obstruction, namely, that of voice, in all three degrees of obstruction. In addition, it is peculiar in that its sonorants participate not only in this correlation but also in the correlation of intensity. Thus a greater number of classes based on the manner of overcoming an obstruction is found here for the sonorants than for the obstruents.[145]

Consonantal systems in which the occlusives and fricatives are divided into two classes each with regard to the manner of overcoming an obstruction should theoretically have four obstruents in each series of localization containing both occlusives and fricatives. In some languages this is actually the case, as, for example, in the North Albanian dialect of Skutari, mentioned above. However, series of localization which involve the correlation of constriction frequently do not have four but only three obstruent phonemes. This is the case, for example, in Czech, where *dz*, *dž*, and *g* occur only in loanwords: *p-b, t-d, t'-d', f-v, k-ch-h, c-s-z, č-š-ž*.[146] The same relations are found in the Čakavian dialect of Serbo-Croatian (*p-b, t-d, ṭ-ḍ, f-v, k-x-γ, c-s-z, č-š-ž*), in Erza-Mordvin (*p-b, t-d, t'-d', k-g, c-s-z, c'-s'-z', č-š-ž*), in Upper Sorbian (*p-b, t-d, ć-dź, k-x-h, c-s-z, č-š-ž*), and in Kinyarwanda (*p-b, t-d, k-g, c-s-z, č-š-ž, p̌-f-v*).[147] This, then, is a phenomenon that repeats itself in several genetically unrelated languages and must consequently have a deeper reason. Also to be mentioned here is Dutch, where the only series of localization that involves the correlation of constriction, namely, the dorsal series, is also the only series in which a weak occlusive is absent.[148] It may well be assumed that in all these cases, the correlation of constriction combines with a correlation based on the manner of overcoming an obstruction of the second degree to form a "three-member bundle." The strong fricative is then the phoneme that so to speak "keeps" the entire bundle "together." But there are also bundles of a different type which consist of the correlation of constriction and a correlation based on the manner of overcoming an obstruction of the second degree. A correlation of constriction clearly existed in Late Avestan: *p-f, t-θ, k-x, č-š*. However, Avestan also had a correlation based on the manner of overcoming an obstruction of the second degree, which cannot be determined more closely. It probably was the correlation of voice. Be that as it may, the formation of an occlusion or constriction was phonologically irrelevant for the weak opposition members of this correlation since they were realized as occlusives in initial position, but as fricatives intervocalically. Accordingly they could be considered the "weak" partners of *p, t, k*, and *č* as well as of *f, θ, x*, and *š*, and therefore had to "keep together" the bundle. (The relation *s-z* was unambiguous only in the *s* series since in that series no corresponding strong occlusive occurred.) In Cheremis, three-member bundles (*c-s-z, č-š-ž*, and *č-š-ž*) are found in the sibilant series of localization. In the other series pairs of phonemes are found, consisting of a strong occlusive and a weak fricative (*p-β, t-δ, k-γ*). After nasals, all of these oppositions are neutralized in all series. Weak occlusives function as the archiphoneme representatives in this position. In initial position the opposition *p-β* is maintained, while the oppositions *t-δ* and *k-γ* are neutralized and represented by the archiphonemes *t* and *k*. However, the sibilant series are represented initially by strong occlusives and strong fricatives (*c-s, č-š, č-š*). Thus it seems that an actual correlation of constriction is present only in the sibilant series of localization, while in the remaining series the occlusiveness of the strong and the constrictiveness of the weak opposition member must be considered secondary; these series of localization, that is, the labial, apical, and dorsal series, would thus involve "obstruents in general," which are differentiated by a single correlation based on the manner of overcoming an obstruction of the second degree. In addition to the three-member bundles *c-s-z, č-š-ž*, and *k-x-γ*, certain Slovenian dialects have phoneme pairs consisting of a voiceless occlusive and a voiced fricative (*p-β, t-δ*) in the remaining series of localization. Here voiced fricatives are replaced by voiceless fricatives in final position. The correlation of constriction thus appears in all series in its pure form: p-f, t-θ, k-x, c-s, $\check{c}$-$\check{s}$. Accordingly only the correlation of constriction is here phonologically relevant for the labial and dental obstruents, the correlation of voice, on the other hand, only for the fricatives of the two sibilant series and the dorsal series of localization. This means that we would have here the rare case in which the fricatives have more classes with regard to the manner of overcoming an obstruction than the occlusives.

All these phenomena point toward the conclusion that, although the correlation of constriction is a correlation based on the manner of overcoming an obstruction of the first degree, in many languages it is related especially closely to the correlations based on the manner of overcoming an obstruction of the second degree. The necessary prerequisite for the "formation of a bundle" thus appears to be provided.

Consonantal systems in which the individual degrees of obstruction are differentiated by several correlations based on the manner of overcoming an obstruction are not a rare phenomenon in the world. It is true, of course, that the European languages, with the exception of a few dialects, in principle have at the most only one correlation based on the manner of overcoming an obstruction of the second degree for each degree of obstruction. Often it is difficult to determine what should be regarded as the correlation mark. But in many languages in other parts of the world, as well as in some European dialects, an additional correlation based on the manner of overcoming an obstruction of the second degree is found. But here, too, the tendency toward greater differentiation with respect to the "higher degrees of obstruction" is maintained.

β) Languages that have two correlations based on the manner of overcoming an obstruction of the second degree in the case of the occlusives and no such correlations in the case of the fricatives and sonorants are represented in all parts of the world. Mentioned here are, for example, the Chinese dialect of Siang-tang (Honan Province) (occlusives b-p-p^h, d-t-t^h, g-k-k^h, $\hat{g}$-$\underaccent{.}{k}$-$\underaccent{.}{k}^h$, $\mathit{з}$-c-c^h, fricatives x, $\underaccent{.}{x}$, s, sonorants m, n, η, $\underaccent{.}{n}$)[149] and Haida (occlusives b-p, d-t-t', g-k-k', $\check{g}$-$\underaccent{.}{k}$-$\underaccent{.}{k}$', $\mathit{з}$-c-c', λ-λ-λ', fricatives x, $\check{x}$, s, l, h, sonorants m, n, η, w, l, j).[150] Classical Greek also belonged to this type (π-β-ϕ, τ-δ-θ, κ-γ-χ on the one hand, and σ, ρ, λ, μ, ν on the other). In another series of languages the occlusives have two correlations, the fricatives only one, based on the manner of overcoming an obstruction, while the sonorants are not differentiated by any such correlation. As examples of this type the Tsaconian dialect of Modern Greek, in which geminated occlusives have become aspirates, may be mentioned here. Thus the following systems resulted: b-p-p^h, d-t-t^h, g-k-k^h, $\mathit{з}$-c; v-f, δ-θ, γ-x, z-s, $\check{z}$-$\check{s}$; r, l, $\underaccent{.}{r}$, $\underaccent{.}{l}$, m, n, $\underaccent{.}{n}$;[151] Georgian (b-p-p', d-t-t', g-k-k', $\mathit{з}$-c-c', $\check{\mathit{з}}$-$\check{c}$-$\check{c}$', $\underaccent{.}{k}$; γ-x, z-s, $\check{z}$-$\check{s}$; v, r, l, m, n); Tibetan (b-p-p^h, d-t-t^h, g-k-k^h, $\mathit{з}$-c-c^h, $\hat{\mathit{з}}$-$\hat{c}$-$\hat{c}^h$, $\int$-h, z-s, *ź-ṣ̌*; *m, n, ŋ, ṇ, v, j, r, l*);[152] Amharic (*b-p-p'*, *d-t-t'*, *g-k-k'*, *g̈-ḳ-ḳ'*, *ž-č-č'*; *z-s*, *ž-š*; *m, n, ṇ, r, l, w, y*);[153] Chichewa in Northeast Rhodesia (*b-p-pʰ*, *d-t-tʰ*, *g-k-kʰ*, *ž-č-šʰ*, *з-c*, *ḅ-p̌*; *z-s, v-f*; *m, n, ŋ, ṇ, w, l, γ*), etc.[154]

Still other languages involve two correlations based on the manner of overcoming an obstruction of the second degree for occlusives and fricatives, while the sonorants do not participate in any such correlation: Kabardian, for example, belongs to this type: *b-p-p'*, *d-t-t'*, *g-k-k'*, *з-c-c'*, *ḳ-ḳ'*, *ƀ-h*; *ź-š-š'*, *v-f-f'*, *l-l-l'* (+ *γ-x*, * γ̈-x̣*, *z-s*, *ž-š*, *ḥ*).[155] In Burmese both the occlusives and the fricatives show two correlations based on the manner of overcoming an obstruction of the second degree. The sonorants, on the other hand, have only one such correlation: *b-p-pʰ*, *d-t-tʰ*, *g-k-kʰ*, *j-ḳ-ḳʰ*; *z-s-sʰ* (+ δ-θ); *m-mʿ*, *n-nʿ*, *ŋ-ŋʿ*, *l-lʿ*, *y-yʿ* (+w).[156] All these cases confirm the rule according to which higher degrees of obstruction tend toward greater differentiation by means of secondary correlations. However, an exception to this rule is found in Tsimshian, where the same two correlations based on the manner of overcoming an obstruction as are present in the occlusives also occur in the sonorants, while the fricatives are not differentiated by any such correlation: *b-p-p'*, *d-t-t'*, *g-k-k'*, *g̈-ḳ-ḳ'*, *ğ-ḳ-ḳ'*, *з-c-c'*; *x*, *x̣*, *x̌*, *s*, *h*; *l-lʿ-l'*, *w-w'*, *y-y'*, *m-m'*, *n-n'*, *r*.[157]

The above examples, which can easily be multiplied in number, seem to point to the conclusion that in those systems in which the occlusives (or the obstruents) are differentiated by two correlations based on the manner of overcoming an obstruction of the second degree, one of these correlations is either the correlation of aspiration or the correlation of recursion. The other, on the other hand, is either the correlation of tension in its pure form or a "merger" of the correlation of tension with the correlation of voice ("voiceless fortis"/"voiced lenis"). If one considers that the unmarked members of the correlation of recursion are usually realized as aspirates (in order to bring out more clearly the contrast to the recursives, which are produced with a closed glottis and hence with very little air), one must become aware of the close relation between the correlation of aspiration and the correlation of recursion: they are distinguished from each other only in that in the one the "strong," in the other the "weak," member of the opposition is marked. Phonetically this is expressed by an exaggeration of its "strength" (through energetic air pressure, that is, aspiration) or of its "weakness" (through lessening of the air pressure by means of glottal closure). By combining with the correlation of tension (or the correlation of voice), a three-member bundle is produced whose members form a gradational series. If one component of this correlational bundle is the correlation of aspiration, the "mid" member of the gradational series is an unaspirated voiceless fortis consonant (*d-t-tʰ*). If, on the other hand, the correlation of recursion is one component of the correlation bundle, the "mid" member of the gradational series is a (voiced or voiceless) lenis with infraglottal expiration (t-d-t'). In all languages in which such three-member bundles are only common to occlusives, and in which the other degrees of obstruction are differentiated only by a second-degree correlation, the latter (generally the correlation of voice merged with the correlation of tension) is one of those correlations that occur in the occlusives as well.[158]

γ) Languages with more than two second-degree correlations based on the manner of overcoming an obstruction within one degree of obstruction are very rare. The East Caucasian languages of Daghestan, on the one hand, and the Western dialects of Circassian, on the other, present a combination of the correlation of tension and voice respectively with the correlation of recursion and with the correlation of intensity. All three correlations occur with respect to the occlusives and, depending on the language, produce different "bundles": in Avar five-member bundles are produced (although not in all series, for example: g-k-K-k'-K', but d-t-t'), in Lak four-member bundles (d-t-T-t'), and so on. The correlation of intensity with respect to the fricatives occurs in all languages of Daghestan, with the exception of K'üri and Rutulian. As far as the correlation of voice is concerned, the opposition between occlusives and fricatives is here usually irrelevant, and the correlation of recursion is completely alien to fricatives.[159] A four-member bundle (d-t-t'-T) is present with respect to the occlusives in the Western dialects of Adyghe. In the case of the fricatives the correlation of voice as well as the correlation of recursion (and in the sibilant series, it seems, also the correlation of intensity) are phonologically relevant.[160] What characterizes all these languages is the fact that the sonorants do not participate in any of the three mentioned correlations based on the manner of overcoming an obstruction of the second degree.[161] The languages of the Northern Caucasus thus show the tendency, referred to above, to gradate the number of classes with respect to the manner of overcoming an obstruction in accordance with degrees of obstruction. A combination between the correlation of voice (or tension) and the correlation of aspiration presumably exists in Dakota (of the Sioux language family in North America).[162] In the case of the occlusives these three correlations form a four-member bundle (b-p-p^h-p', d-t-t^h-t', g-k-k^h-k', and the defective bundle $č$-$č^h$-$č$' = ʒ-$č$-$č^h$-$č$, in the Ponka dialect). However, the correlation of aspiration is foreign to the spirants (z-s-s', $ž$-$š$-$š$', $γ$-x), and the sonorants (m, n, w, y, l) do not participate in any correlation based on the manner of overcoming an obstruction at all. In Sindhi the correlations of voice, aspiration, and release are combined to form a five-member bundle with regard to the occlusives (p-p^h-b-b^h-b', t-t^h-d-d^h-d', k-k^h-g-g^h-g', c-c^h-j-j^h-j', and the defective t-t^h-d-d^h). The spirants show only the correlation of voice (f-v, s-z, and defective s, h, x), and the sonorants do not present any correlation based on the manner of overcoming an obstruction of the second degree.[163] The number of examples for combinations of three (or even four) correlations based on the manner of overcoming an obstruction of the second degree within a single degree of obstruction can probably be increased considerably. There is, however, no doubt that such cases are extremely rare.

In order to conclude the section about correlations based on the manner of overcoming an obstruction of the second degree, we are going to give some interesting examples which will show that the nature of a correlation can sometimes be altered to such a degree by the context of the system to which it belongs that completely new correlations are produced.

In East Bengali the correlation of voice, the correlation of aspiration, and the correlation of recursion are found (at least word-initially). The correlation of aspiration is limited to occlusives only, and the correlation of voice to obstruents only, while the correlation of recursion is present in all degrees of obstruction: p-b-p'-b'-p^h, t-d-t'-d'-t^h, t-d-t'-d'-t^h, k-g-k'-g'-k^h, defective c-$з$-c'-$з$'; f-v-f', x-$γ$, $š$-$š$', s; m-m', n-n', r-r', l-l'.[164] In this case the sibilant series of localization is thus the only one in which an aspirated occlusive is absent. If one considers that s (in contrast with f and $š$) does not have a "recursive partner," one may well assume that s is the aspirated phoneme of the sibilant series. Accordingly, as far as the sibilant series of localization is concerned, the correlation of aspiration in East Bengali is replaced by the correlation of constriction (which, incidentally, is in fact the case from a diachronic point of view).

While in the case of East Bengali one can only speak of a possible interpretation, there are other languages in which the parallelism between the opposition of aspirated and unaspirated consonants and the opposition between spirants and occlusives is clearly apparent. For example, the Tiva language of the Pueblo Indians of Taos (N.M.) belongs among these.[165] Tiva has the correlation of voice (b-p, d-t, g-k, l-lʻ) and the correlation of recursion (but only for occlusives, p-p', t-t', k-k', c-c'), and in addition the correlation of constriction and the correlation of aspiration. The last two, however, are mutually exclusive, so that the opposition of aspiration is found only in the labial and apical series (p-p', t-t'), while the opposition of constriction is present only in the guttural, the labiovelar, and the sibilant series (k-x, $k̦$-$x̦$, c-s). It may probably be assumed that cases of this type involve not two distinct but one single correlation. The one member of such a correlation is characterized by an energetic occlusion followed by a plosive release that requires all the egressive air, while the other member presents only a light obstruction to the egressive airstream. Depending on the series of localization, it may be either a loose occlusion or a stricture. This correlation could therefore be most readily identified with the correlation of intensity, and it could then be assumed that the language of the Pueblo of Taos probably contains a correlation of voice, a correlation of recursion, and a correlation of intensity.

The consonantal system of Sandawe in East Africa provides a very peculiar and instructive illustration. Otto Dempfwolff, to whom we owe the description of this language,[166] lists the following consonants: (a) voiced lenes b, d, g, ȝ, λ (lateral affricate); (b) "semivoiced lenes," which presumably are identical with "'b'", "'d'," etc., of Ful, and must consequently be considered injectives (b$^{\cup}$, d$^{\cup}$, g$^{\cup}$); (c) unaspirated fortes p, t, k, c, λ (lateral affricates); (d) aspirated fortes p^h, t^h, k^h (the latter only in a single word); (e) recursive fortes k', c', λ'; (f) recursive fortes with a "squeezed" offset k^3, λ^3 (which, incidentally, may only be variants of k' and λ'); (g) voiceless spirants f, x, s, l, h; (h) nasals m, n, ŋ; and (i) liquids r, l, w, y. In addition, Sandawe has clicks which need not be considered here. An examination of this list reveals that the opposition between the fortes consonants of types (c) and (d) occurs only in the labial and dental series, while the opposition between types (e) and (c) is found only in the sibilant and lateral series. It is not difficult to see that both oppositions are analogous. In both cases a sound with a lesser amount of egressive air is opposed to a sound with a greater amount: in the case of the pairs p-p^h and t-t^h this is accomplished by only a slight opening of the glottis for one opposition member, but by opening it wide for the other; in the case of the pairs c-c' and λ-λ' it is accomplished by keeping the glottis completely closed with respect to one member, but not with respect to the other. In the guttural series the opposition k-k' belongs to the same correlation. If k^h and k^3 are really independent phonemes, which is by no means evident from Dempfwolff's material, k^h is an intensification of k, k^3 an intensification of k'. As for λ^3, it must obviously be interpreted in the same way as k^3. Turning to the lenis sounds, we see that b, d, and g are produced by an egress of air, while b$^{\cup}$, d$^{\cup}$, and g$^{\cup}$ are not. This opposition may again be attributed to the same rule as the oppositions t-t^h, p-p^h, and k-k', c-c', λ-λ': complete, unrestricted egress of air on the one hand, restriction of egress or *absence of complete egress* on the other. Accordingly a special correlation exists in Sandawe with regard to lenis and fortis consonants. Its nature resides in the opposition of occlusives with complete (unrestricted) egress of air and occlusives with incomplete (restricted) egress.

Spirants, nasals, and liquids participate neither in this correlation nor in any other correlation based on the manner of overcoming an obstruction of the second degree. As for the clicks, they are divided into voiced, voiceless-aspirated, voiceless with a "hard" onset, and nasalized. At least in the case of voicelessness they show the above opposition between complete and restricted egress of air.[167] The clicks in Sandawe, as described by Dempfwolff, are divided into a "lateral," a "dental," and a "cerebral" series, in accordance with the localization series. Grouping the lateral click phonemes with lateral λ, λ, λ' is a matter that needs no further discussion. According to Dempfwolff, the "dental" click with a hard onset seems very similar to ts' acoustically. Further, it is presumably also difficult to distinguish the "cerebral" recursive click acoustically from $k\tilde{s}$ (op. cit., p. 10). The "dental" click phonemes may therefore be grouped with the sibilant series, the "cerebral" clicks with the guttural series. The latter presupposes that for the "gutturals" of Sandawe it is not a particular part or a specific shape of the tongue which is phonologically relevant, but merely the contact of a particular part of the palate and the dorsum or retroflected tip of the tongue. The consonantal system of Sandawe may therefore be represented by the chart which follows.[168] (The transcription used by Dempfwolff is retained.)

Finally, the consonantal system of Hottentot may be discussed. Thanks to the excellent work done by D. M. Beach,[169] we now have reliable data on the number of phonemes in Hottentot and the essential characteristics of their phonetic realization. The only question is to determine the relation of these phonemes to each other. Hottentot, or more precisely the Nama dialect, has only one occlusive and one nasal in the labial series, and only one occlusive and one spirant in the laryngeal series. At first glance the apical series seems to show the same structure as the labial series ($t:n = p:m$), and the sibilant series the same structure as the laryngeal series ($c:s = \acute{c}:h$). However, this impression is contradicted first by the fact that the sibilant occlusive (affricate) c is strongly aspirated, while the other occlusives of Nama are voiceless lenes without, or almost without, aspiration. Second, the guttural series of Nama stands in a certain contradistinction with the above interpretation of the other series of localization. This guttural series has not only plosive k (realized as a voiceless lenis without aspiration) and a spirant x, but also a strongly aspirated affricate kx. It is clear that the relation $kx:x$ is identical with the relation $c:s$. But how then should the relation $k:kx$ be interpreted? Is it the opposition between plosives and affricates that is phonologically relevant for this pair of phonemes, or is it the opposition between unaspirated and aspirated occlusives? Aspiration cannot be explained as a phonetic consequence of

Consonants			Labials	Apicals	Gutturals		Sibilants		Laterals		Laryngeals	Without localization
					Simple	Click	Simple	Click	Simple	Click		
Occlusives	Voiced	Full expiration	b	d	g	ǃˤ	dz	/ˤ	d̰	//ˤ	ˤ	
		Restricted expiration	ɓ	ɗ	g̃							
	Voiceless	Full expiration	ph	th	k, kh	ǃh	ts	/h	t̰	//h	(h)	
		Restricted expiration	p	t	k', k³	ǃˤ	ts'	/ˤ	t'̰, t³̰	//ˤ	ˀ	
Fricatives			f	–	x		s		s̰		h	
Nasals			m	–	ṅ	ǃn	n[170]	/n	–	//n	–	
Liquids			w	–	–		–		l		–	y, r

affrication. Conversely, however, affrication may be interpreted as a phonetic consequence of strong aspiration. Consequently it would probably be advisable to consider Nama kx (or more precisely kxh) an aspirated fortis consonant, and the affrication an irrelevant phonetic phenomenon. But since the relation "kx":x in Nama must clearly be equated with the relation "c" (= tsh): s, the affrication of c (= tsh) must also be considered irrelevant. In other words, "c" (= tsh) is a strongly aspirated fortis consonant which stands in the same relation to the lenis t as the "kx" stands to k. Accordingly there is no reason to posit a special sibilant series for Nama: instead there exists only one apical series in which aspirates and spirants are realized as sibilants, the unaspirated tenuis consonant and the nasal, on the other hand, as nonsibilant occlusives. Accordingly in a phonemic transcription "kx" and "ts" must be rendered as k^h and t^h. From a phonological point of view, with respect to these phonemes there is no difference between Nama and Korana, where they are actually realized as unaffricated aspirated plosives. The results at which we have arrived so far may be summed up as follows: Nama shows the following correlations with respect to nonclicks: (a) the correlation of aspiration, (b) the correlation of constriction, and (c) the correlation of nasals. Neither the correlation of aspiration nor the correlation of constriction are present in the labial series. They coalesce in the laryngeal series. (h may therefore be designated with equal justification as a laryngeal aspirate or a laryngeal spirant.) The correlation of nasals, on the other hand, is found only in the labial and apical series. The "sole liquid" r stands outside the system of correlations. This may be presented in a diagram as follows:

p	t	k	$\acute{c}$		
$\cdot$	t^h	k^h	h	$+ r$
$-$	s	x		
m	n	$-$	$-$		

As regards the click series, we have already seen above, when we discussed the click correlation, that in Hottentot only the apical and the guttural series participate in that correlation.[171] We further mentioned that the clicks are divided into "plosive" and "affricative" clicks. Let us disregard this opposition for the present and occupy ourselves with the various manners of overcoming an obstruction which exist in each of the click series of Nama. According to D. M. Beach, there are five such manners or types: (a) "the weak unvoiced velar plosive type" (pp. 82 f.); (b) "the strong unvoiced velar affricative type" (pp. 83 f.); (c) "the glottal plosive type" (pp. 84 ff.); (d) "the glottal fricative type" (pp. 86 f.); and (e) "the nasal type" (pp. 87 f.). It is clear that the nasal clicks correspond to the nasal nonclicks, though one can at the most only speak of an exact correspondence in the prelingual series. The guttural series in Nama does not contain any nasal. However, similar symmetrical phenomena are not rare in the phonemic system of Nama, in which the click phonemes show great differentiation in general. It is also not difficult to interpret the other "types." Types (c) and (d) are characterized by the fact that the anterior as well as the posterior lingual closure (i.e., the "basic closure" and the "supplemental closure") are released first. Only then does the egress of air necessary for the articulation of the vowel begin, i.e., with a hard onset ($\acute{c}$) in the case of (c), with an aspirated onset (h) in the case of (d). It is clear that type (c) corresponds to the unaspirated occlusives, while type (d) corresponds to the aspirated occlusives. Types (a) and (b) are characterized by the fact that the egress of air sets in after the basic closure is released but prior to the release of the supplemental closure. Thus after the specific suction or click sound a k is audible in type (a), a kx in type (b). These sound approximately like normal k and kx. "kx," as we already know, is an aspirate. Therefore, exactly the same relation as between (c) and (d) holds between types (a) and (b). How then should the relation (a):(c) and (b):(d) be construed? The description by Beach shows that in the "glottal types" [(c) and (d)] both closures are released more quickly and the onset of the egress of air is delayed longer than is the case in the "velar types" [(a) and (b)]. The total duration of the clicks of type (a) is presumably shorter than that of the clicks of type (c) (op. cit., p. 117). Thus ultimately the delay in onset of the egress of air is decisive for the acoustic result.[172] Accordingly the relation between types (a) [or (b)] and (c) [or (d) respectively] could perhaps be designated as a correlation of intensity. The types with an accelerated onset of the egress of air [(a) and (b)] would then have to be considered the "weak" members of this correlation, the types with a delayed onset in the egress of air [(c) and (d)] the "strong" members.[173] The phonological interpretation of the opposition between the "plosive" and the "affricative" click series is the most difficult. We have already seen that in the nonclick series the affricates are only a phonetic realization of the aspirates. The opposition between k and "kx" (or t and "ts" respectively) in the click sounds thus corresponds to the opposition between types (a) and (b) [or between (c) and (d) respectively]. The opposition between plosive and affricative clicks has nothing to do with this because types (a), (b), (c), and (d) exist in the plosive as well as the affricative series. The question, however, remains whether the opposition between the plosive and the affricative click series could not be compared with the correlation of constriction in the nonclick series. The parallelism is certainly not complete. An actual "constrictive" or "spirant" cannot be produced under the phonetic conditions that are prerequisite to click production. Each click must of necessity begin with an occlusion, and this is part of its very nature. What remains then is the opposition between sudden (plosionlike) and frictionlike release, which is certainly not dissimilar to the opposition between occlusion and constriction. The "dental" affricative clicks have something "ts-like" and may therefore be considered click equivalents of s. The relation between the "lateral" affricative clicks and x is less evident, as is the relation between the plosive "alveolar" (or "cerebral") clicks and k. But since a real velar click is in general impossible, there can here be a question of relative similarity only. And if one considers that the position of friction is located much farther back for lateral clicks than for dental clicks, this relation can probably be compared with that between s and x.[174] But even if the interpretation of the Hottentot affricative click series proposed by us is accepted, a certain asymmetry remains in the phonemic system: while the nonclick lingual series have only one "fricative" each (s or x), the corresponding click series indicate five affricates or fricatives each. These are differentiated by the correlation of nasals and by a bundle consisting of the correlation of aspiration and the correlation of intensity. The chart opposite may illustrate our interpretation of the consonantal system of Nama. We are using the transcription in the Latin alphabet suggested by D. M. Beach, in which the various clicks are expressed by ligatures. As one can see by the chart, the category of "affricates" is ambiguous.[175]

These examples should suffice to give a picture of the variety of consonantal systems that are the result of a combination of various correlations based on the manner of overcoming an obstruction of the second degree.

c. *The opposition of gemination as a correlation of overcoming an obstruction of the third degree (Überwindungsartkorrelation dritten Grades).* Correlations based on the manner of overcoming an obstruction of the second degree may, of course, be considered as such only if both opposition members are evaluated as monophonematic. In a language such as Ukrainian a combination between a voiced consonant and a voiced aspirate occurs very frequently. However, since this combination always exceeds the duration of a single consonant and is either distributed over two syl-

Consonants			Labials	Prelingual		Postlingual		Laryngeals
				Simple	Click	Simple	Click	
Occlusives	Unaspirated	Light	p	t	$\neq k$	k	!k	(Not designated)
		Heavy			$\neq$		!	
	Aspirated	Light		ts	$\neq \chi$	$^k\chi$	!χ	
		Heavy			$\neq h$		!h	
Fricatives	Unaspirated	Light	–	δ	/k	χ	//k	h
		Heavy			/		//	
	Aspirated	Light			/χ		//χ	
		Heavy			/h		//h	
Nasals	Plosive		m	n	$\neq n$	–	!n	–
	Affricative				/n		//n	

+r

lables (as in "pid horoju" [at the foot of the mountain], "vid-horodyty" [delimit]) or can be divided etymologically ("z-hodyty s'a" [to unite, fit together]), it cannot be interpreted as the realization of a single phoneme but only as the realization of a phoneme sequence ($d + h$, $z + h$, etc.). Accordingly there can be no question of a correlation of aspiration in Ukrainian. However, many languages have so-called geminated consonants. These are distinguished from "simple" or "nongeminated" consonants by a longer duration, and in most cases also by a more energetic articulation that is reminiscent of the correlation of intensity. In intervocalic position geminated consonants are distributed over two syllables, their "on-glide" being grouped with the preceding syllable, their "off-glide" with the following syllable. Furthermore, these geminated consonantal combinations are found in those positions where consonantal combinations are permitted by the particular language. They have the same effect on their environment as consonant clusters and are generally treated in the same way as combinations of consonants. All these features point to a poly-phonematic interpretation, that is, they call for an interpretation of "geminated" consonants (or "geminates") as a combination of two identical consonants.[176] This becomes immediately clear in those languages where geminated consonants occur only at the morpheme boundary, as, for example, in Russian or Polish (with the exception of loanwords). However, in those languages where geminated consonants *do not occur only* in that position (as, for example, in Sanskrit), and particularly in those languages where they *never* occur at a morpheme boundary (as, for example, in Japanese), geminated consonants take an intermediary position between single phonemes and phoneme clusters. From the point of view of those languages, geminates are special consonantal phonemes which are distinguished from other consonantal phonemes in that their beginning and end exist phonologically as two separate points, while the beginning and end of all other consonantal phonemes coalesce phonologically into one point.

Accordingly a special *correlation of consonantal gemination* is present in some languages. Its correlation mark is the separate existence of the beginning and end of a consonantal phoneme, as opposed to the coalescence of beginning and end. It is evident that this correlation cannot be counted among the correlations based on the manner of overcoming an obstruction of the second degree. Its mark is fundamentally different from those of the six correlations enumerated above (Chap. IV, 4*Bb*). The correlation of gemination must therefore be termed a *third-degree* correlation based on the manner of overcoming an obstruction.

While oppositions based on the manner of overcoming an obstruction of the second degree exist within the individual degrees of obstruction, the correlation of gemination is basically found within the resultant classes. It is true, of course, that in some languages this correlation extends to all classes based on the manner of overcoming an obstruction, but in very many languages it is limited to only a few particular classes. For example, the opposition between geminated and nongeminated consonants is found only in sonorants in some languages of Daghestan (Tabarasan, Aghul, Lak, Darghinian, Kubachi, Artshi, and Andi),[177] only in nasals and voiceless obstruents in Japanese,[178] in all consonants except the "mediae" in Classical Greek (Ionic-Attic), and only in sonorants and lenis occlusives in Korean.[179]

There are languages that do not have any second-degree correlations based on the manner of overcoming an obstruction, but only oppositions based on the manner of overcoming an obstruction of the first degree on the one hand, and the correlation of gemination on the other. To these languages belong, for example, the above-mentioned Tamil, in which the correlation of gemination comprises all sonorants (except *r* and *R*) and all obstruents;[180] also Vogul ("Mansi"),[181] Ostyak [182] ("Hanti"), and a few others. Finnish should actually also be considered as belonging to the same type. Finnish *g* occurs only in the combination "*ng*," which from the point of view of the Finnish phonemic system must be considered the realization of a geminated dorsal nasal, that is, as *ŋŋ* (e.g., "hanko" [fork], gen. sing. "hangon"; "lintu" [bird], gen. sing. "linnun,"; "kampa" [comb], gen. sing. "kamman"). The opposition *t-d*, though bilateral, is thus isolated. (Incidentally, Finnish "*d*" is not a real occlusive.) Accordingly Finnish does not have any second-degree correlation based on the manner of overcoming an obstruction at all. But at the same time all Finnish consonants participate in the correlation of gemination (with the exception of *j*, *v*, *d*, and *h*, which are not permitted syllable-finally).[183]

The relationship between the correlation of gemination and the correlation of intensity takes on a different form, depending on the language. The marked members of the correlation of intensity are very often longer than the unmarked members. (In some languages this difference in length is even obligatory.) Thus there is a great similarity between the correlation of intensity and the correlation of gemination.[184] The difference between the two correlations lies mainly in the fact that geminated consonants occur *only* in those positions where consonantal clusters are also permitted in the particular language, while the "heavy" consonants (that is, the marked members of the correlation of intensity) do *not* occur *only* in those positions. For example, in Lak, *ll* and *mm* occur only between vowels. Various consonantal groups are permitted in this position as well, in particular "liquid + consonant," "consonant + liquid," "nasal + consonant," "consonant + nasal." The "heavy" *p·*, *t·*, *k·*, *ķ·*, *c·*, *č·*, *x·*, *x̌·*, *s·*, *š·*, on the other hand, occur not only in this position but are also found initially, where consonantal clusters are not permitted.[185] There are also complicated cases in which the correlation of intensity and the correlation of gemination form a correlation bundle that is difficult to analyze. This is the case in Lapp, for example, where consonantal combinations are permissible only intervocalically. The "long" consonants are also found only in this position. Consequently, these "long" consonants show different degrees of length, and their degrees of length are distinctive. In the maritime Lapp dialect of Maattivuono [186] geminated consonants show two distinctive degrees of length. But the same two degrees of length are found in consonantal clusters as well: in the case of the greater degree of length the first member of the consonant cluster is very long and forceful, with increasing syllable intensity. Conversely, in the case of the lesser degree of length the syllable intensity is level or falling, and the first member of the consonantal cluster is short and weak. It is clear that the opposition between longer and shorter first members of a consonantal cluster can only be an opposition of intensity, and not an opposition of gemination. The relations between intensity and length in the case of geminated consonants in the particular Lapp dialects are exactly the same as for consonantal combinations. The "longer" geminates must therefore be interpreted as "heavy," and the "shorter" ones as "light": the relationship between Maativuono Lapp nom. sing. "boTtu" (bush) and gen. acc. "bottu" is exactly equivalent to the relationship between nom. sing. "luNtu" (stopper in a cartridge) and gen. acc. "luntu" (the "heavy" consonants are transcribed by capital letters). There are other Lapp dialects that phonemically distinguish not just two but three types of consonantal clusters: combinations in which the first component is "heavy," combinations in which the second component is "heavy," and those in which both components are "light." Before combinations of the first type only quite short vowels are permitted. Short and semilong vowels are distinguished before the second type, and semilong and long vowels before combinations of the third type. Accordingly three types of geminates are also distinguished in these Lapp dialects. They exert the same influence on the quantity of the preceding vowels and must therefore be interpreted as Tt, tT, and tt (Pp, pP, pp, etc.).[187] Thus the intensity of a geminated consonant does not remain unchanged in these and similar cases: an opposition of intensity exists between the beginning and end of the particular consonant. In Lapp these differences in intensity are accompanied by a gradation in the total duration of the geminated consonants (Tt is longer than tT, which in turn is longer than tt). However, from a phonological point of view this is unimportant and unnecessary. There seem to be languages in which the differences in intensity between the beginning and end of a geminated consonant do not influence the total duration of a particular consonant. This seems to be the case in Gweabo, a language of Liberia which has been mentioned already.[188] Here three types of geminates are distinguished: the first type is set apart from the other two by its somewhat shorter duration, but above all by its "lighter," that is, less forceful articulation (E. Sapir transcribes this type by 'b, 'd, 'm, 'n̩, 'n, 'ñ, 'w, 'y); the second type (according to Sapir, 'B, 'D, 'G, 'GW, 'GB, 'DJ, 'V, 'Z, 'M, 'N, 'Ñ) is also distinguished from the third (according to Sapir, "B, "D, "DJ, "W, "Y, etc.) by the distribution of intensity (pressure) which also affects the following vowel. The present case, as well as Lapp, thus involves a combination of the correlation of gemination with the correlation of intensity.

Accordingly it is not difficult to delimit the correlation of gemination from the correlation of intensity. It is sometimes more difficult to decide whether the correlation of consonantal gemination or the so-called correlation of close contact is present in a given language. But this problem has to be discussed in its proper place in connection with the prosodic properties. [See esp. pp. 199 ff.]

C   Resonance Properties

Actually only the opposition between nasal and "oral" consonants belongs to the consonantal resonance properties.

Ordinary nasals are characterized by an oral closure with a lowered velum. Accordingly they stand in a relation of bilateral opposition to the occlusives. In most languages of the world the opposition "occlusive–nasal" is not only bilateral but also proportional, because it exists in at least two series of localization, the labial and the apical (d-n = b-m). In the few languages that do not have any labial obstruents, the dorsal (guttural) nasal usually exists as an independent phoneme, thus again creating a proportion (t-n = k-η). This is true, for example, in Aleut (Unangan),[189] in Hupa,[190] and in Chasta Costa.[191] Among the languages with which we are familiar only Tlingit indicates an isolated relation of opposition "occlusive/nasal" (d-n). The n here is the only nasal, and the labial class of localization is nonexistent altogether.[192]

The opposition between occlusives and nasals is bilateral and proportional in all languages (with very few exceptions), and may be conceived of as privative. It can therefore be regarded as a correlation. This *consonantal correlation of nasals* occurs in all languages, but it is only rarely neutralizable. A clear example of the neutralization of this correlation in final position is found in Ostyak-Samoyed (or Selkup):[193] here the opposition between occlusive and nasal is phonologically irrelevant in final position. This means that one and the same word in final position sometimes has a voiceless oral occlusive and sometimes the corresponding nasal. Accordingly m and p (or n and t, or η and k respectively) in that position are optional variants of one archiphoneme, while in all other positions m, n, and η on the one hand, and p, t, and k on the other, are distinguished as independent phonemes.

Any localization series with the exception of the laryngeal series may, in principle, have its own nasal. A distinction between the nasal of the apical series and the nasal of the sibilant series is, of course, only possible if the articulatory difference between these two series exists and is distinctly marked not only by the shape of the tongue but also by the point of contact at the roof of the mouth. Gweabo may be cited as an example in which the nasals are broken down into five localization series each, a labial, an apical, a palatal, a labiovelar, and a sibilant. The nasal "$ŋ$" probably corresponds to the apical series, and the nasal "n" to the sibilant series.[194] Normally, however, the sibilant series remains without its own nasal, insofar as it should not rather be designated as the palatal-sibilant or sibilant-palatal series. The number of languages in which each series of localization, except the pure sibilant and the laryngeal series, has its own nasal, is rather large. Such languages are found in Africa (Nuer, etc.) and Asia (Tamil, Central Chinese, Korean, etc.), as well as in America (Eskimo). However, there also exist those languages, and again in all parts of the world, in which the nasals occur only in part of the localization series. Particularly noteworthy is the circumstance that in very many of these languages the correlation of nasals is, so to speak, not compatible with the correlation of constriction within one localization series. In other words, these two correlations are mutually exclusive within the same localization series. This is true of Czech and Slovak, where the correlation of nasals is found in the labial, the apical, and the palatal series (p-m, t-n, t'-$ñ$), while the correlation of constriction occurs in the guttural and both sibilant series (k-ch, c-s, $č$-$š$). The same relation between these two correlations in Europe is also found in Upper Sorbian (p-m, t-n, $ć$-$ń$ ~ k-ch, c-s, $č$-$š$), and in Čakavian-Croatian; in Africa, for example, in Chichewa (p-m, t-n, k-$ŋ$, $ć$-$ņ$ ~ c-s, $p̌$-f),[195] in America, for example, in Tsimshian (Nass dialect: p-m, t-n ~ k-x, $ḳ$-$x̣$, $ḳ$-$x̣$, c-s),[196] in Chinook (p-m, t-n ~ k-x, $ḳ$-$x̣$, $ḳ$-$x̣$, c-s, $č$-$š$, $λ$-l),[197] in Kwakiutl (p-m, t-n ~ k-x, $ḳ$-$x̣$, c-s, $λ$-l),[198] and in Tonkawa (b-m, d-n ~ g-x, $ǧ$-$ẋ̣$, c-s, $ƛ$-h),[199] in the Caucasus, for example, in Avar (p-m, t-n ~ k-x, $ḳ$-$x̣$, $č$-$š$, $λ$-l),[200] and in Lak.[201] It seems as if there exists in all localization series an opposition between stops and continuants, which is realized in the one series by the correlation of constriction, in the other by the correlation of nasals. For the nasals are sonorants and accordingly continuants. In some of these languages a peculiar merger of the correlation of constriction with a second-degree correlation based on the manner of overcoming an obstruction may be observed, of which we already spoke above (pp. 154 f.). This is the case, for example, in Czech and Upper Sorbian (p-b-m ~ k-x-$γ$). In Chichewa the correlation of aspiration is found only in those series that also have the correlation of constriction. The same phenomenon also appears in the language of the Pueblo Indians of Taos (p-p^h-m, t-t^h-n ~ k-x, $k°$-$x°$, c-s).[202] All these observations are not sufficient to formulate any laws, or even to posit structural types. We must also forgo for the time being an explanation of the aforementioned phenomena.

In any event it may be emphatically stated that the relationship of mutual exclusion between the correlation of nasals and the correlation of constriction is by no means a general phenomenon. It is only valid for a small number of languages. In most languages the two correlations are either compatible in the same localization series (as, for example, k-x-η, t-θ-n, etc.), or neither one nor the other correlation is present in the individual localization series. (This is the case in Lithuanian, where the guttural series contains the two occlusives k and g, without a nasal and without a fricative.)

A nasal does not always stand in a relationship of bilateral opposition to a particular oral occlusive. In Hupa, Chasta-Costa, and Aleut,[203] m is the only labial phoneme. There are languages with a palatal nasal and without palatal occlusives, for example, Slovenian and French. In Slovenian that is, in the standard language, the palatal nasal ("nj") could stand in a relationship of bilateral and proportional opposition to the palatal l sound ("lj"): ($\underset{.}{n}$:$\underset{.}{l}$ = n:l, perhaps also = m:v). In French, however, the situation is different. Here the palatal nasal (written gn) could only stand in a relationship of bilateral opposition to j (written i, y, hi, ill). The opposition $\underset{.}{n}$-j seems to be isolated in the French phonemic system (insofar as one does not wish to relate it to the opposition m-v).[204] In any event, such cases are proof that the nasals can form correlations not only with occlusives but also with oral sonorants.

In languages that have only two nasals (usually an m and an n), a bilateral opposition exists between them. The parallelism of this opposition to b-d and p-t is not very marked because of its bilateral character. For, while m and n are the only nasals, p and t are not the only tenues, and b and d not the only mediae, etc. This relaxes the relation between the phoneme pair m-n and the phoneme pair p-t (or b-d, etc.). The relation m-n sometimes indicates a tendency to be evaluated as privative, m being considered as the marked, n as the unmarked opposition member. The neutralization of the opposition m-n in final position, where the archiphoneme is represented by n, is a phenomenon which is found in many languages. Examples are Classical Greek, Čakavian-Croatian, Italian, Finnish, Avar,[205] Lak,[206] Japanese, etc. These languages neutralize the opposition m-n in medial position before consonants as well. The representative of the archiphoneme is here conditioned externally, that is, it assimilates to the localization series of the following consonants. In this way a nasal phoneme of indeterminate localization, that is, a phoneme that is phonologically characterized exclusively by its minimal degree of obstruction, is produced in some languages in certain positions.

As a result of the neutralization of an opposition in final position or before consonants, such nasal consonant phonemes without any property of localization occur also in those languages that in other positions distinguish not only between m and n but between other nasals as well, and in which the individual nasals thus stand in a relation of multilateral opposition to each other. For example, Tamil differentiates five nasal phonemes before vowels (m, n, $ṇ$, $ŋ$, and $ñ$). It does not have these contrasts before obstruents, however, since the nasal always assimilates to the localization property of the obstruent (mb-nd, $ṇḍ$, $ŋg$, $n3$). Similarly, in some dialects of Central China four nasals (m, n, $ŋ$, and $ñ$) are phonologically differentiated before vowels, but in final position these oppositions are neutralized. The nasal phoneme found in that position is realized as an $ŋ$ after back vowels, and as an n after front vowels, etc. All these cases thus involve the neutralization of multilateral oppositions between *all* nasals, and only in this way is neutralization possible, that is, viewed only in this fashion is it possible to speak of a resultant archiphoneme that can be distinguished by specific phonological properties from all other phonemes that occur in this position.

As already mentioned, the specific properties of the "indeterminate" nasal (or of the nasal archiphoneme) are its nasal resonance and its sonorant character (i.e., the minimal degree of obstruction). That is why this archiphoneme comes close to the nasalized vowels. A rather close relation is indeed often found between the "indeterminate" nasal and the nasalized vowels. The nasalized vowels are frequently not independent phonemes, but only combinatory variants of the combination "vowel + indeterminate nasal." This is the case, for example, in the overwhelming majority of Polish dialects, where the indeterminate nasal (with an externally conditioned realization) occurs only before occlusives, while the nasalized vowels occur only before fricatives. But these vowels ("ę," "ą," i.e., $ẽ$ and $õ$) seem to be independent phonemes in standard Polish (as well as in Portuguese), where the nasalized vowels occur not only before fricatives but also in final position. Before occlusives the combinations "e, o + indeterminate (homorganic) nasal" may be considered their combinatory variants. In cases where the syllabic nasals assimilate in their realization to the localization property of the following consonant, as is the case in numerous African and in some South American languages, one may with equal justification speak of an indeterminate syllabic nasal or of an indeterminate nasalized vowel.

Nasals are always sonorants, that is, they are consonants with a minimal degree of obstruction, even though the oral cavity is completely closed in their articulation: the egress of air through the nose, which is made possible by lowering the velum, renders the oral closure ineffective so to speak. But there are languages in which nasals with complete oral closure are distinguished from nasals with incomplete oral closure. As is well known, this is assumed for Old Irish, which is presumed to have distinguished m and n with complete oral closure from the "lenis" m and n with incomplete oral closure.[207] In any event, such languages are rare. However, in certain other languages a genuine correlation of nasals must be distinguished from a *correlation of seminasals* or a correlation of consonantal nasalization. In languages of this kind normal occlusives are in opposition to normal nasals on the one hand, and to occlusives with nasalized implosion and nonnasalized plosive release on the other. Such seminasalized occlusives give the impression acoustically of being combinations of a very short nasal and an occlusive. They can exist as separate phonemes only if in the given language they are phonologically distinguished from normal (nonnasalized) occlusives on the one hand, and from combinations of "nasal + occlusive" on the other. A case of this type is present, for example, in Ful, where besides the nonnasalized d, b, g, and j the seminasalized $ḍ$, $ḅ$, $g̃$, and $f̃$ as independent phonemes are in opposition to the genuine nasals n, m, $ŋ$, and $ṇ$ and the nasal combinations nd, mb, $ŋg$, and $ṇj$.[208] While the true nasals are sonorants and consequently continuants, the "seminasals" may be considered stops. The relation $ḅ:m$, etc., may be equated with the relation "stop:continuant." In a language in which this relation is found, m, n, $ŋ$, and $ṇ$ must be termed "nasal continuants," and $ḅ$, $ḍ$, $g̃$, and $f̃$ "nasal stops." The phonologically nasal character of these stops is just as little affected by their nonnasalized plosive release as the occlusive character of the affricates is affected by their fricative off-glide. In Chichewa not only are the voiced seminasals $ḅ$, $ḍ$, $g̃$, $ʒ$, and $ʒ̃$ found, but also voiceless $p̃$, $ṭ$, $ḳ$, $ç$, and $č̣$, and the seminasal fricatives $v̰$, f, $z̰$, and $s̰$. Thus here all degrees of obstruction and all manners of overcoming an obstruction occur in nasalized and nonnasalized form. Similar relations are also assumed for some other African languages. But inasmuch as the "seminasalized" consonants are not in phonological opposition to the respective combinations of normal nasals and nonnasalized consonants, one cannot speak of a correlation of consonantal nasalization.

The correlation of nasals or of nasalization respectively seems to be the only consonantal correlation of resonance. In descriptions of languages with various vocalic "correlations of muffling" it is often claimed that differences in vocal quality exist not only in the case of vowels but also in the case of consonants. But from what can be gleaned from these descriptions, it appears that what is really involved are combinatory variants of the consonantal phonemes in the environment of the particular muffled vowels.

5 PROSODIC PROPERTIES

A Syllabic Nuclei

In the overwhelming majority of languages distinctive prosodic properties are found only with respect to vowels. One may therefore be inclined to count these properties among the vocalic properties and to discuss them together with the degrees of sonority and classes of timbre. In fact, the present writer did just this in an earlier article.[209] This was an error, however. Prosodic properties do not belong to the vowels as such but to the *syllables*. Part of the phonemes that constitute a syllable may be prosodically irrelevant. Usually such phonemes are consonants. But they can also be vowels which in this case are "nonsyllabic." On the other hand, certain languages have syllables that do not contain any vowel phoneme. The prosodically relevant part is then occupied by a consonantal phoneme. In such a case one speaks of a "syllabic" consonant. Finally, it is possible that certain prosodic properties belong to an entire polyphonematic phoneme combination (either "vowel + vowel" or "vowel + consonant"). Prosodic properties cannot therefore be considered vocalic properties, as, for example, degree of aperture or class of timbre, but must be considered properties of a specific portion of the syllable, and this syllable portion must be defined differently for the various languages.[210]

We term that portion of a syllable which, in accordance with the laws of the particular language, carries the distinctive prosodic properties, *syllabic nucleus* (*Silbenträger*). Depending on the language, a syllabic nucleus may consist of (*a*) a vowel, (*b*) a polyphonematic vowel combination, (*c*) a consonant, or (*d*) a polyphonematic combination of "vowel + consonant." *There is no language in which the vowels would not function as syllabic nuclei.* In most languages of the world the vowels are the only possible syllabic nuclei. For example, in languages such as Classical Greek, polyphonematic vowel combinations (αι, οι, ει, αυ, ου, ευ, υι) also occur as syllabic nuclei in addition to the vowels. In Serbo-Croatian, vowels and the liquid *r* occur; in many African languages, for example, in Lamba, Efik, and Ibo, vowels and the "homorganic nasal" occur, in Zulu, vowels and the nasal *m* (except before labials), and in the Hanakian dialect of Czech, vowels and the liquids *r* and *l*. Vowels, polyphonematic vowel combinations, and the liquids *l* and *r* occur as nuclei in Slovak (less distinctly in Czech). The combinations of "vowel + sonorant" seem to occur as syllabic nuclei only in those languages in which polyphonematic vowel combinations also occur with the same function, as, for example, in Danish, Lithuanian, Latvian, and Siamese. All four possible types of nuclei (vowels, consonants, polyphonematic vowel combinations, and combinations of "vowel + consonant") occur in certain Chinese dialects, as, for example, in the Peking dialect.

It should be noted that in the case of the consonants only the so-called sonorants, that is, the nasals and liquids, are considered independent syllabic nuclei or members of the nucleic combination "vowel + consonant." Whether a phonetically "syllabic" consonant is interpreted as a monophonematic nucleus depends primarily on whether the particular language has an indeterminate vowel that can be considered the realization of the vocalic element that is almost inevitably connected with the "syllabic" consonant. We have already mentioned that this is the basis for the difference between "r" in Serbo-Croatian (as in "srce"), which is regarded as monophonematic, and "ăr" in Bulgarian ("sărce" [heart]), which is regarded as polyphonematic. Languages that employ "syllabic" consonants as monophonematic nuclei have no "indeterminate" vowels in their phonological system. This rule applies to all languages enumerated above, and we do not know of any exceptions.

While the syllabic nucleus of such words as "l^4" (two) in the Peking dialect of Chinese, for example, is probably a liquid (which may well be interpreted l, as is done by Henri Frei),[211] the syllable nucleus of such words as s^4 (four), $š^2$ (stone), $ž^4$ (day), s^2 (ten), etc., causes certain difficulties. Phonetically, if pronounced clearly, it is a type of vowel with a much lesser degree of aperture and with a much more fronted position of articulation than, for example, i, so that a frictionlike noise resembling a humming is audible in its production. Syllabic z or $ž$ occur as optional variants in its place. Sometimes, particularly in unstressed final position, this phoneme is not realized at all. In Pekingese it occurs only after sibilants (c, c^h, s, $č$, $č^h$, $š$, and $ž$). Frei designates this phoneme, which is usually transcribed by an $ï$, as a "zero vowel" (voyelle zéro, p. 128), and one might be tempted to posit a syllabic s in a word like $sï$ (four). However, since in Pekingese a combination of sibilants with a normal i does not occur, the $ï$ should probably be interpreted rather as a combinatory variant of i after sibilants. In other Chinese dialects the "humming" ("gingival") vowel does not occur only after sibilants. (Some dialects, as, for example, the dialect of Hsiang-Hsiang, Honan Province, even distinguish two such vowels, a back and a front.) But its realization always depends on the preceding consonant. In these dialects the vowel may be designated as "indeterminate." Characteristically such dialects do not seem to have syllabic liquids.

One and the same phoneme may sometimes function as a syllable nucleus and sometimes as "nonsyllabic" in the same language. Generally these two functions are contextually conditioned. For example, in Czech *l* and *r* are syllabic when they occur after a consonant and are not followed by any vowel. In all other positions they are nonsyllabic. However, there are languages in which "syllabicity" becomes a distinctive property, that is, in which it is not completely conditioned by environment. This is true, for example, of standard Serbo-Croatian, in which *r* and *l* between a consonant and a vowel are syllabic in some words and nonsyllabic in others: for example, "gȑoce" ([trisyllabic] little throat), "gròza" ([bisyllabic] horror), "pìem" ([written *pijem*] I drink), "piȅna" ([written *pjena*] foam). The same phenomenon may also be observed between a vowel and a consonant; but in this case it depends entirely on whether there is a morpheme boundary between the vowel and the *r*: "zařd ati" (to rust), "varnica" (spark), "zaimati" (borrow), "zàjmiti" (lend). In Old Czech *r* and *l* were syllabic between two consonants in some words, nonsyllabic in others: in verse, words such as "mrtvý" (dead), "plný" (full) were treated as bisyllabic, words such as "krvi" (blood), "slza" (tear) as monosyllabic. In such instances one may speak of a special *correlation of syllabicity*. However, cases of this type are extremely rare. In most cases the syllabicity or nonsyllabicity of a phoneme is determined automatically by its environment.

In cases in which the syllabicity or nonsyllabicity of phonemes is conditioned externally, different special relations result. In standard German *i* does not occur before vowels; *j* on the other hand occurs exclusively before vowels. Accordingly *i* and *j* are here not two distinct phonemes but only combinatory variants of a single phoneme.[212] But standard German has a short as well as a long *i*, and this opposition is distinctive ("Mitte"/ "Miete" [middle/rent], "wirr"/"wir" [disarranged/we], "Riss"/"Ries" [rent/giant], etc.), while *j* is always short. Hence the opposition of quantity is neutralized for *i* before vowels. The same phenomenon is also found in other languages with externally determined syllabicity of the phonemes: these have only prosodic properties in those positions in which they occur as syllabic nuclei. A more complicated case is found in Bulgarian. Here syllabic *i* is impossible between two vowels, while *j* is possible; *j* does not occur after consonants, but *i* does, and it may be either stressed or unstressed. (For example: "žìvoto" [the living]: "živòtăt" [life]; "nìe" [we]: "čèrnitat" [the black one]; "vărvì" [it is all right]: "kràvi" [cows].) In initial position before vowels only *j* is permitted, but *i* is not; before consonants only *i* is permitted, either stressed or unstressed, but *j* is not (e.g., "ìmam" [I have]: "imàne" [worldly possession]). However, after a vowel in final position, or between a vowel and a consonant, either *j* or *stressed i* may occur. Unstressed *i* is not permitted in this position (e.g., "moj" [my, sing.]: "moì" [my, plur.]; "dvòjka" [pair]: "dvoìca" [dual]).

In this position the opposition of stress is thus replaced by the opposition of syllabicity. Bulgarian *i* and *j* must therefore be considered two phonemes that stand in a relation of neutralizable opposition to each other.[213]

B   Syllable and Mora: Phonological Conception of Quantity

The above summary of the possible syllabic nuclei shows that these may be either monophonematic or polyphonematic. There are languages that have only monophonematic syllable nuclei, while there are others that, in addition to monophonematic nuclei, have polyphonematic nuclei. But the question may be raised whether the so-called long syllable nuclei should not be considered geminates. A standard answer cannot be given for all languages; the problem must be studied separately for each language. However, it is possible to set up certain types.[214]

a. In languages where a morpheme boundary can fall between the beginning and the end of such a syllable nucleus, "long" syllable nuclei must definitely be considered polyphonematic, that is, geminated nuclei. For example, in Finnish the so-called partitive has the ending *a* or *ä* respectively: "talo" (house): "taloa." In words that end in *a* or *ä*, the final vowel is lengthened instead: "kukka" (flower): "kukkaa"; "leipä" (bread): "leipää." The so-called illative usually ends in an *n* with lengthening of the stem-final vowel: "talo" (house): "taloon" (in the house); "kylä" (village): "kylään" (into the village). In Lak, "maγi" (roof) forms the plural "maγiu," but "zunttu" (mountain) has plural "zuntū." The perfect, with an object of the first and third class, of the verb "itan" (let) is "iutra," of "qaqan" (to dry) "qauqra," but of "utan" (put) the equivalent form is "ūtra." In all cases of this kind the long vowels must be considered the sum of two homophonous short vowels. This interpretation may then also be extended to all long vowels of the same language.

b. The interpretation of long nuclei as a "monosyllabic combination of two like syllable nuclei" also holds for those languages in which the long nuclei are treated in the same way as the polyphonematic diphthongs in the functioning of the system. In certain Central Slovak dialects and in standard Slovak the so-called law of rhythm is found, according to which long nuclei in the position immediately after a long syllable are shortened. However, long nuclei are not only shortened after syllables containing long vowels or long liquids but also after syllables with the positional diphthongs (*Stellungsdiphthonge*) *ie, uo* (written *ô*), *ia*, and *iu*. After a syllable containing a long nucleus (or diphthong) these diphthongs are themselves replaced by monophthongal short vowels.[215] Accordingly long vowels and the polyphonematic diphthongs *ie, uo, ia*, and *iu* are treated alike. It follows that long nuclei are interpreted as monosyllabic combinations of two like vowels.

c. The same interpretation is also given to long nuclei in those languages where length in the delimitation of words is treated according to the formula "one long unit = two short units" (see further below). Classical Latin may be cited as a generally known example, where the accent delimiting words could not fall on the word-final syllable. It always occurred on the penultimate "mora" before the last syllable, that is, either on the penultimate syllable, if the latter was long, or on the antepenultimate, if the penultimate was short. A syllable with a final consonant was considered long. A long vowel was thus comparable to two short vowels or to a "short vowel + consonant."

Similar rules also exist for Middle Indic, but they are not restricted to word-final syllables. The final syllable of a word is always unstressed, and the accent falls on the "long" syllable closest to the end of the word. Not only syllables with long nuclei but also syllables with the combination "(short) vowel + consonant" are regarded as long. In colloquial Arabic the accent only occurs on the final syllable if the syllable ends in a long vowel + consonant or a short vowel + two consonants. It follows that the long vowel is prosodically equivalent to the combination of a short vowel plus a consonant.[216] In Polabian the accent fell on the syllable that contained the "penultimate mora" of the word; in other words, it fell either on the word-final syllable, if the latter was long, or on the penultimate, if the final syllable was short. Only those syllables that contained a long syllable nucleus or a biphonematic diphthong, such as *ou, au, ai,* or *ai,* were considered long.[217] In Southern Paiute, of the Shoshonean Group of the Uto-Aztecan family, the primary stress occurs on the second mora of the word, provided this mora is not part of the final syllable. Secondary stress occurs on all even morae of the word, that is, on the fourth mora, sixth mora, etc. Long vowels and diphthongs are regarded as syllable nuclei having two morae, and short vowels as nuclei having one mora.[218] In Tübatulabal of the Uto-Aztecan family the primary stress falls on the word-final mora, and a secondary stress on the penultimate, the fourth mora from the end, etc., in iambic rhythm.[219] In the Northeastern dialect of Maidu, of the California group of the Penutian family, the primary stress always seems to fall on the second mora of the word. Syllables containing a long vowel or diphthong, and closed syllables with a short vowel, are here considered bimoric, while open syllables with a short vowel are considered as having one mora.[220] In all these cases a long syllable nucleus is equated with two short syllable nuclei.

d. The evaluation of the length of the syllable nuclei as biphonematic is also clearly recognizable in those languages that make a phonemic distinction between two types of accent with regard to long nuclei. The phonetic nature of these accent types is unimportant. What is important, however, is that the beginning and the end of a long syllable nucleus be treated differently prosodically, the difference in treatment being distinctive, regardless of whether it involves the musical or expiratory prominence or absence of prominence of the beginning in one type of accent and of the end in the other. Lithuanian and Slovenian, for example, belong to this type. In languages of this kind the same two types of accent very often also occur with respect to the polyphonematic nuclei (diphthongs or combinations of vowels with sonorants). The long syllable nuclei are accordingly explicitly identified with the combinations of two phonemes, as, for example, in Lithuanian, Siamese, and Japanese. Long nuclei of course need not always be equated with biphonematic syllable nuclei. In Northern Chinese shorter and longer syllables are distinguished: the shorter syllables are either high or low, while the longer syllables are either rising or falling. Monophthongs and diphthongs are here treated alike not only in the longer syllables but also in the shorter ones. If one regards the longer syllables of Northern Chinese as bimoric, and the shorter syllables as having "one mora," one must conclude that this phonological system also contains polyphonematic diphthongs consisting of a single mora. Accordingly a certain discrepancy between the prosodic and the phonematic analysis of the syllable is present here.[221] As regards Burmese, which also has diphthongs in "one-mora" syllables, the situation is not quite clear, insofar as the polyphonematic character of the diphthongs cannot be proven.

e. What has here been said about languages with two types of accent for the long nuclei can also be repeated with respect to those languages in which the long syllable nuclei have the so-called stød (as in Danish). Whether this stød consists of a complete closure of the glottis or only of a strong constriction is not essential. What is important is that through this articulation the long syllable nucleus is divided into two parts.[222] The fact that in the languages in question the long syllable nuclei are divided into nuclei with an interruption and nuclei without such an interruption between their beginning and end, while no such contrast is found in short nuclei, clearly indicates that the existence of beginning and end as two separate moments in these languages is significant only for the long nuclei. In languages that have the contrast "with stød/without stød" for long nuclei, the same contrast also appears in the case of diphthongs and combinations of "vowel + sonorant." This is especially clear proof for the biphonematic nature of the long nuclei. For example, Danish and Latvian belong to this type.

In all languages discussed so far the long syllable nuclei may therefore be considered "geminated." Their length, or more particularly, their stretchability, in contrast with the unstretchability of the "short" syllable nuclei, is the external expression of their bipartite nature, i.e., of the circumstance that their beginning and end do not coalesce in one point but are evaluated as two separate moments in time.* According to R. Jakobson, who summarized the conditions for this divisibility, such an interpretation of the long nuclei is generally to be assumed for all languages in which long positional diphthongs are present. It does not matter if these languages cannot be subsumed under the five types enumerated above. The existence of biphonematically interpreted monosyllabic positional diphthongs, in addition to the long nuclei, would be the sixth criterion for establishing a biphonematic evaluation of the "long nuclei."[223] This assumption seems somewhat questionable to us. The mere presence of polyphonematic positional diphthongs is not sufficient proof that the long monophthongs are also evaluated as monosyllabic combinations of two like short vowels. Such an evaluation can be considered objectively demonstrated only if in a given language the long monophthongs are actually treated in the same way as the polyphonematic diphthongs (our type b). Where this is not the case there exists no objective reason to interpret long syllable nuclei as geminated. In colloquial Czech (middle Bohemian) long vowels are not permitted in initial position, while the positional diphthong ou can occur in this position (e.g., "ouřad" [authority]: "oučet" [invoice]). In standard Czech, on the other hand, long vowels are permitted in initial position, but diphthongs are not (e.g., "úl" [beehive]). Nothing in the phonological system of Czech seems to point to the need of equating ou with long vowels.

Thus there are languages in which long syllable nuclei are regarded as monosyllabic combinations of two qualitatively like short nuclei. The stretchability of the long syllable nuclei in such languages is merely an expression of their bipartite nature. But this same bipartite, or composite, nature in general can also be expressed in different terms. In many African and American languages several tones are used distinctively. Generally speaking, each syllable has one specific tone. But in some cases the beginning of a syllable does not have the same pitch as its end. The pitch may change within the syllable, resulting in (musically) rising, falling, falling-rising syllables. All of these prosodic types are distinctive. For some languages with such a prosodic system observers state expressly that

---

* *Translator's note:* Roman Jakobson, with respect to the intersyllabic variety of quantity features, for the length feature, contrasts "a normal, short, *unstretchable* phoneme, with the long, *sustained* phonemes of the other syllables in the same sequence" (*Fundamentals of Language*, p. 24. Cf. also Jakobson–Fant–Halle, *Preliminaries to Speech Analysis*, pp. 14, 59).

syllables, in which the pitch does not remain level with regard to beginning and end, are longer than syllables with a single "level" tone, as, for example, Efik.[224] In most cases investigators do not indicate this, however, and it seems impossible to ascribe their silence to carelessness alone. Rather, it should be assumed that in many languages that have a developed "tonal system" the prosodic multimember constituency of a syllable nucleus is not expressed through length but exclusively through change of pitch within the syllable nucleus itself. It may even be that in a language of this type both kinds of phonetic realization of "multimember constituency" exist side by side: bipartite nuclei that have the same tone on both parts are realized as long vowels (or syllabic sonorants) with "level tone"; bipartite nuclei that have a different tone on both parts, on the other hand, are realized as short vowels or syllabic sonorants with "nonlevel tone" (i.e., falling or rising).[225]

The interpretation of long syllable nuclei as geminated, or in terms of multimember constituency in general, may be regarded as an "arithmetic conception of quantity." Languages in which this conception finds expression are "mora-counting" languages since in these languages the smallest prosodic unit does not always coincide with the syllable.

Opposed to these languages are "syllable-counting" languages, in which the prosodic units always coincide with the syllables. Long nuclei, should these exist at all, are here evaluated as independent units and not as the sum of several smaller units. Here belong, particularly, languages that have exclusively monophonematic nuclei, as, for example, Hungarian, the Hanakian dialects of Czech, and Chechen. In Chechen the diphthongs are in part monophonematic. However, in part they are to be regarded as "vowel + *j* or *w*," where only the vowel occurs as the syllable nucleus, and *j* or *w* respectively is phonematically differentiated from *i* and *u*. Here belong also those languages in which polyphonematic diphthongs do exist, but where they do not get the same treatment as the long nuclei, as, for example, in standard, literary Czech. Finally, languages such as German, English, and Dutch must also be considered as belonging to the syllable-counting languages (see further below).

The relationship of opposition between long and short nuclei is always logically privative. Should this relationship become actually privative by neutralization, the short nuclei will always prove unmarked in mora-counting languages, while the long nuclei will be marked. In Slovak, or more precisely in standard Slovak, and in certain Central Slovak dialects, only *short nuclei* can occur after long and diphthongal nuclei; in Finnish only *short vowels* can occur before vowels (e.g., sing., "puu" [tree]: part. plur., "puita"). In Latin only *short vowels* could occur before final consonants, except before *s*. In Prākrit, that is, in Middle Indic, only *short vowels* could occur in closed syllables. In the Čakavian-Croatian dialect of Novi only *short vowels* can occur before a syllable with a long falling accent. In Slovenian (and in colloquial Egyptian Arabic) only *short vowels* occur in unaccented syllables. In Lamba, a Bantu language of N. Rhodesia, and in Ganda, in East Africa, only *short vowels* can occur in final position. The gemination of the nucleus may therefore here be considered as the correlation mark.

Syllable-counting languages are not as uniform in this respect. In Czech, especially in the Central Bohemian colloquial language, where only short vowels occur in initial position, the short syllable nuclei should probably be regarded as unmarked. In this case length (or stretchability) of the long nuclei may be regarded as the correlation mark. However, if one considers that length is an "intensity feature," and that no other intensity features are distinctive for Czech or for any other languages of this type, as, for example, Hungarian or Chechen,[226] one may be more inclined to consider intensity as the correlation mark, length or stretchability, on the other hand, only as a type of realization of intensity.*

Languages such as German, Dutch, and English, however, present quite a different picture. Intensity is here realized by the free expiratory ("dynamic") accent. The opposition of quantity is neutralized in final open syllable. Only *long* vowel phonemes are permitted in stressed final open syllable. The long, not the short, syllable nuclei must therefore be considered the unmarked correlation members. What is involved here can therefore only be an opposition between normal unchecked vowel phonemes on the one hand, and vowel phonemes whose articulation is interrupted or checked by the beginning of the following consonant on the other. "Close contact" (*scharfer Silbenschnitt*) is here the correlation mark. For this *correlation of close contact* length is only the expression of unimpeded, fully developed vowel articulation, and shortness is nothing but the expression of the interruption of vowel articulation by the following consonant.†

---

* *Translator's note:* As regards the relationship between intensity and quantity, cf. Jakobson–Halle, *Fundamentals of Language*, pp. 24–25:

"Languages where both length and stress appear as distinctive features are quite exceptional, and if the stress is distinctive the latter is mostly supplemented by a redundant length.

"The observation of force and quantity features in their intersyllabic variety seems to indicate that the prosodic distinctive features utilizing intensity and those utilizing time tend to merge."

† *Translator's note:* For *Silbenschnittkorrelation* the term "correlation of close contact" is used here rather than "correlation of contact" to distinguish that term more clearly from "oppositions based on type of contact" (*Anschlussartgegensätze*) which

Incidentally, a language that has a correlation of close contact need not necessarily be a language that "counts syllables." A very peculiar type of combination of this correlation with the correlation of prosodic gemination is found in Hopi, a language of the Uto-Aztecan family, more specifically in the dialect of the village of Mishongnovi in Arizona. The information on this language stems from a private letter from Benjamin L. Whorf, to whom we would here like to express our sincere gratitude. Hopi has neither diphthongs nor polysyllabic vowel combinations nor distinctive differences of tone movement (*Tonverlaufunterschiede*). Its long vowels cannot be divided on the basis of morphology. The rule by which primary stress must fall on the second mora of a word (provided this mora is not part of the final syllable) is now only of historical significance since it is no longer valid for all grammatical categories. Unstressed syllables that originally contained one mora or several morae are now no longer differentiated. From the standpoint of the present system of Hopi, prosodic relations must be construed quite differently. The peculiarity of this language lies in the existence of three distinctive degrees of quantity for the vowels, which are the only syllable nuclei. For example: "păs" (very): "pas" (field): "pās" (quiet). Likewise "tĕva" (nut): "teva" (to throw something); "qăla" (edge): "qāla" (rat); "sive" (container): "sīve" (charcoal). In the positions where the oppositions of quantity are neutralized (namely, before the so-called preaspirated occlusives ^hp, ^ht, ^hk, $^h\underline{k}$, ^hq, ^hc) neither the short nor the long but the medial degree of quantity occurs as the archiphoneme representative. It follows that opposition series, such as ă-a-ā, do not involve two gradual but two privative oppositions. Their unmarked member is the vowel of "medial length." This is also confirmed by those cases in which only one opposition, not both, is neutralized. The opposition ă-a is neutralized in open stressed final syllables, more precisely in final syllables with secondary stress. ă is not permitted in this position. In other words, in Hopi, just as in German, Dutch, and English, short vowels can only occur before consonants. This seems to point to the conclusion that vowel shortness in Hopi is only an expression of close contact, and that the pairs ă-a, ĕ-e, etc., in Hopi form a correlation of close contact.[227] As for the oppositions a-ā, e-ē,

---

also include the "correlation of stød" (*Stosskorrelation*). J. Vachek uses the term "correlation of contact" for what is here called "correlation of close contact." His discussion does not make mention of the correlation of stød, however, so that this further distinction within the oppositions based on type of contact there does not appear necessary. (See J. Vachek, *The Linguistic School of Prague*, p. 63.) Also cf. Jakobson's use of the terms *scharf geschnittener Akzent* (close contact) and *schwach geschnittener Akzent* (open contact) for what Trubetzkoy calls *fester* or *scharfer* and *loser Silbenschnitt* (cf. *Fundamentals of Language*, p. 24). See here pp. 197 ff.

etc., they occur only in polysyllabic words in open syllables word-medially and also, though only rarely, word-finally.[228] In contrast, this opposition is neutralized in closed syllables in polysyllabic words, and the archiphoneme in such syllables is represented by "medium-length" vowels. A restriction of this type is otherwise known to us only from mora-counting languages (Japanese, Middle Indic, etc.). It appears to be based on the equation of a syllable-final consonant with a prosodic "mora" ($\bar{a} = at$), and on the establishment of the maximum number of morae that cannot be exceeded in a syllable.[229] The opposition between a "medium-length" and a "long" vowel must therefore be regarded as a correlation of prosodic gemination. From a phonological point of view, "long" vowels in this language contain two morae and "medium-length" vowels one mora, so that a difference in the number of morae exists between $\bar{a}$ and a (or $\bar{\imath}$ and i, etc.). In contrast, the difference between "short" and "medium-length" vowels in Hopi does not consist in the number of morae (since both types of vowels contain one mora), but in the fact that one is checked, in other words, in the type of contact with the following consonant. Hopi thus shows a peculiar combination of the correlation of close contact and the correlation of prosodic gemination.[230]

Three (or even more!) distinctive degrees of quantity for the syllable nuclei are also indicated for some other languages, but not rightly so. In most of these cases quantity was confused with tone movement (*Tonverlauf*). For example, at the beginning of the nineteenth century the Croatian grammarian Š. Starčevič claimed that his native language contained three degrees of quantity for accented syllables: in addition to a "short accent," Illyrian, as Croatian was called at that time, was said to have also had a "somewhat lengthened" and a "completely lengthened" accent. But if one examines the examples given by Starčevič, it becomes clear that by a "somewhat lengthened" accent he meant a long falling accent and by a "completely lengthened" one the long rising accent of Serbo-Croatian.[231] He had interpreted the opposition of tone movement (falling–rising) as an opposition of quantity (shorter–longer), or better, he had regarded a phonologically unimportant side phenomenon, that is, the somewhat greater length of a rising accented syllable, as distinctive.[232] A similar situation seems to exist in Northern Albanian (Geg), for which usually three quantities are posited for stressed vowels—short, long, and over-long[233]—and where in reality an opposition of tone movement exists between "length and overlength" which should probably be regarded as phonologically distinctive.[234] In Estonian four quantities are found with respect to the vowels of the first syllable. The stem syllable of many nouns, such as "piim" (milk), "tuul" (wind), etc., shows the second degree of quantity in the genitive, the third in the partitive, and the fourth in the illative. Closer examination reveals, however, that the tone movement of the syllable nucleus also changes in parallel manner with the degree of quantity: the second degree of quantity shows a clearly falling tone movement, the third a level tone (followed by an abruptly falling tone of the following syllable), the fourth a falling–rising tone movement, in which the rising part is prominent. And since the corresponding forms of the diph-thongal stem syllables, such as "poeg" (son), do not show any differences in quantity but only the associated differences in tone movement (falling, level, falling–rising),[235] it may well be assumed that these differences of tone movement are phonologically distinctive, while the differences of quantity are merely phonetic side phenomena.[236] More than two degrees of quantity are also found in the descriptions of different investigators for the syllable nuclei in some Lapp dialects. In reality Lapp is a "moric language" since long vowels occur only in the same environments as clearly biphonematic diphthongs. It only has the phonological contrast between syllable nuclei with one mora and syllable nuclei with two morae. But, as we already indicated (p. 164), Lapp has a bundlelike combination of the correlation of consonantal gemination and the correlation of con-sonantal intensity, geminated consonants being longer than nongeminated consonants, heavy consonants longer than light consonants (and, dialec-tally, falling geminated consonants longer than rising geminated conso-nants). Since the phonetic length of vowels stands in an inverse relation to the phonetic length of the following consonants, five to eight different degrees of length result for vowels in the various Lapp dialects. But this is only a phonetic phenomenon. Phonemically, only two distinctive types of syllable nuclei occur before each type of consonant, namely, those with one mora and those with two morae. (In some dialects this opposition is neutralized before heavy geminated consonants.)

Apart from the completely isolated case of Hopi, where a peculiar combination of the correlation of prosodic gemination and the correlation of close contact is present, all cases in which allegedly three or more degrees of quantity are distinguished for syllable nuclei thus prove er-roneous. Some mora-counting languages that have distinctive differences of tone also have three- and four-mora nuclei in addition to syllable nuclei with one and two morae. The number of morae is then expressed primarily by means of the distribution of tones within the syllables. But it may also be that in some such languages the greater number of morae of a syllable is characterized by a greater length of that syllable. This can, of course, only be regarded as a phonologically irrelevant side phenomenon.

C   Prosodic Differential Properties

a. Classification. An examination of the prosodic relations of quantity thus brings us to the conclusion that the *syllable*, or more precisely the syllable nucleus, is the smallest prosodic unit for some languages, while for others it is the *mora*. Accordingly languages can be divided into languages counting syllables and languages counting morae. The smallest prosodic unit of a given language, in other words, the syllable in syllable-counting languages and the mora in mora-counting languages, we call a *prosodeme*.

Prosodic properties can be divided into differential properties and properties based on the type of contact (*Differenzierungs- und Anschlussart-eigenschaften*). Differential properties distinguish among the prosodemes themselves, while the properties based on type of contact do not characterize the prosodemes themselves but merely their type of contact with the following phonological element.

In syllable-counting languages the prosodemes are differentiated by intensity, in mora-counting languages by pitch. In cases where the differentiation of the prosodemes has only a distinctive function, each prosodeme has its own differential property. In a word that contains several prosodemes, all prosodemes may thus either be identical in this regard, or non-identical prosodemes may follow each other in different order. This means that in a syllable-counting language of this type all syllables in a poly-syllabic word can be intensive (e.g., Czech "říkání" [talk]), or they can all be unintensive (e.g., Czech "lopata" [shovel]), or intensive and unin-tensive in different sequence (e.g., Czech "kabátek" [dress coat], "zásada" [principle], "znamení" [sign], "mámení" [deception], "pořádný" [orderly], "bídáci" [the miserable ones]). Similarly, in a mora-counting language of this type morae with different pitch may occur within a word in different sequences: for example, Ibo "‾o‾si‾si" (stick), "‾n‾ke-ta" (dog), "‾i-ɉi-ɉi" (fly), "‾n˷ka‾ta" (conversation), "˷o˷lo‾ma" (orange), "‾‾an‾wen˷ta"(mosquito), "‾n˷ne˷ne"(bird), "˷o˷to˷bo"(rhinoceros), "˷n‾de‾de" (scrape), "˷ε‾ti˷ti" (middle one), "˷u‾do-do" (spider).[237] However, in those languages where the differentiation of prosodemes does not only have a distinctive function (i.e., a function-differentiating mean-ing), the prosodemes are distributed in such a way that each word has only a single prosodeme which by virtue of its differential property stands out among all others. The remaining prosodemes of the same word show the opposite differential property. For example, in a syllable-counting language such as Russian only the third syllable in a word such as "sămăvar" (samovar) is intensive, only the second in "bŭmagă" (paper), and only the first in "patăkă" (syrup). All other syllables in these words are unintensive. In a mora-counting language, such as Lithuanian, only the first mora of the first syllable is "high" in a word such as "lóva" (ˈlo.ova [bed]), only the second mora of the first syllable in "lõstas" (.loˈostas [type]), only the first mora of the second syllable in "lošéjas" (.looˈše.ejas [gambler]), only the second mora of the second syllable in "lovŷs" (.looviˈis [trough]). The remaining morae of the same words are "low." Prosodemes in such cases are basically differentiated by a lengthening of the culminative syllable in syllable-counting languages, and by a rise in pitch of the culminative mora in mora-counting languages. But other factors also play a role, especially the expiratory increase in force of the culminative prosodeme. This is very frequently also accompanied by a rise in pitch of the culminative syllable or a lengthening of the culminative mora respectively. What is phonologically important here is only a general prominence of the culminative prosodeme, that is, the fact that this prosodeme stands out among all others. The means for achieving this prominence, on the other hand, belong to the realm of phonetics. Culminative prominence is commonly called "accentuation" or "accent." There is no reason to replace this term. We designate the correlative opposition between "accented" and "unaccented" prosodemes as *correlation of accent*. The correlative opposition that is created through the accentuation or non-accentuation of a mora in a bimoric syllable nucleus in the mora-counting languages (e.g., the opposition between "acute accent" and "circumflex accent" in Lithuanian), this we designate as *correlation of tone movement*.

Distinctive prosodic oppositions can accordingly be divided into culminative and nonculminative oppositions. The correlation of accent and, as a subclass, the correlation of tone movement belong to the culminative type. Among the nonculminative distinctive oppositions belongs the correlation of prosodic intensity in the syllable-counting languages and the correlation of tone or register in the mora-counting languages. This entire classification is based on the concept of the prosodeme. In syllable-counting languages, where the prosodeme is equal to the syllable nucleus, the differentiation of the prosodemes can, of course, only occur in the two forms of accent and lengthening. But in the mora-counting languages still another distinctive opposition occurs in addition to the correlation of accent, the correlation of tone movement, and the correlation of tone register. This is the correlation of prosodic gemination, that is, the difference between syllable nuclei embracing one and two morae. This correlation is an essential characteristic of mora-counting languages and can combine with the other differential properties. In cases where it occurs alone, that is, without the correlation of tone register, accent, and tone movement, it can easily be confused with the correlation of prosodic intensity. This, incidentally, is also true of the correlation of consonantal gemination, which sometimes can only be distinguished with difficulty from the correlation of consonantal intensity.

b. *The correlation of prosodic intensity and gemination.* The correlations of prosodic intensity and gemination were already discussed above (pp. 173 ff.). Five criteria were listed which presented proof for the evaluation of long syllable nuclei as bimoric, and consequently for the evaluation of the opposition between long and short syllable nuclei as a correlation of prosodic gemination. Where these criteria are absent there is no reason to interpret the long syllable nuclei as bimoric. The opposition between long and short syllable nuclei must then be interpreted as correlation of intensity. It may be noted that the (nonculminative) correlation of intensity is a comparatively rare phenomenon. In any event, the correlation of prosodic gemination occurs much more frequently. (Incidentally, the same relationship also exists between the correlation of consonantal intensity and the correlation of consonantal gemination.)

Further, we have already noted that length is not the only possible phonetic expression of prosodic gemination (presence of two morae) and that in certain languages the number of morae in a syllable nucleus is not expressed by length but by change of pitch within the nucleus.

c. *The correlation of tone register.* Distinctive oppositions of tone register are a prosodic phenomenon that is completely foreign to the languages of Europe. This phenomenon is rather widespread, however, in non-European languages. Distinctive oppositions of tone register must not be confused with the so-called musical accent. In languages that have such distinctive oppositions, each syllable, or more precisely each mora—since all these languages are mora-counting—is characterized not only by its phonemes but also by a specific relative tone or register. In languages with a so-called musical accent each word must contain a musical peak. This is not at all necessary, however, in languages with distinctive oppositions of tone register: a polysyllabic word may consist entirely of musically high morae or musically low morae, or of high and low morae in any sequence. The tone of each mora depends only on the meaning. For example, in Lonkundo, a language of the Congo: "_bɔ_kɔ_ŋgɔ" (back) ~ "_bɔ_kɔ⁻ŋgɔ" (sand) ~ "_bɔ⁻kɔ⁻ŋgɔ" (a proper name); "_lo_ko_lo" (palm fruit) ~ "_lo⁻ko⁻lo" (exorcism).[238] Just as in other languages various grammatical forms of the same word can be distinguished by a change in phonemes (e.g., German "sieh" ~ "sah" [see, saw]; "verbinden" ~ "verbanden" ~ "verbunden" [connect, connected, connected]; French "allez" ~ "allait" ~ "alla"; Russian "vĭno" [wine] ~ "vĭna" ~ "vi-nu" ∼ "vĭne"; "l'ak" [lie down] ∼ "l'ok" [he lay down]; "kărovĭ" [the cows] ∼ "kărov'ĭ" [to the cow]), so in languages that have distinctive tonal variation the grammatical distinction often depends only on the tone of the individual morae. For example, Lonkundo: "_a⁻ta_o_ma" (you have not killed today) ∼ "_a⁻ta_o⁻ma" (you did not kill yesterday). In Efik[239] verbal roots always have two morae. These are either both high or both low, or the first is low and the second high. For example, aorist first person singular: "⁻N⁻ke⁻re" (I think), "⁻N_do_ri" (I lay), "⁻N_fe⁻he" (I run). In the subjunctive, however, all roots receive high tone on the first mora and low tone on the second: first person singular ⁻N⁻ke_re, ⁻N⁻do_ri, ⁻N⁻fe_he. In Ibo[240] the relationship between determinatum and determinator, such as between noun and adjective, verb and object, etc., is expressed by means of a rise in pitch of the final mora of the determinatum and the first mora of the determinator, and so on.

If one examines languages with distinctive tonal variation more closely, one finds that these languages distinguish either two or three tones phonologically. Lonkundo, in the Congo, and Achumawi, in North America,[241] for example, have only two tones, while Efik, Ibo, Lamba,[242] etc., have three.

Where more than three tone registers are indicated, this proves upon closer examination to be erroneous, at least from a phonological point of view. For example, Ethel G. Aginsky claims that Mende, a language she described, has four tones.[243] She admits, however, that the lowest of these tones (indicated by a 1) can be lowered arbitrarily, depending on the degree of emphasis desired. However, a closer look at the data offered by Mrs. Aginsky reveals that the "first" or lowest tone occurs in verb forms but not in nouns, pronouns, and adjectives, while the "fourth" or highest tone appears very frequently in nouns, pronouns, and adjectives, but never in verb forms. The solution to this puzzle is given by the text printed at the end of the grammar: the "first" tone occurs nine times, and in all nine cases at the end of the sentence before a period: (38) ve$_3$la$_1$. (61) li$_2$la$_3$ a$_1$. (77) ye$_3$e$_1$. (167) na$_1$. (there), compare (81) na$_2$ (there) sentence internally, (176) gbe$_3$e$_2$ŋga$_1$. (189) = (224) hũ$_1$. (in), compare (87) hũ$_2$ (142) hũ$_2$ (175) hũ$_2$ (197) hũ$_2$ (203) hũ$_2$ (214) hũ$_2$ (in, inside) sentence-internally. It can therefore be assumed that, as in Ewe, Efik, Ibo, etc., only three distinctive tones exist in Mende, but that sentence-finally the pitch of all words is lowered, so that in this position all tones are shifted by one level (without, however, changing their relative pitch within the word), and the lowest tone attains an otherwise unusual depth. This low tone affects the verb forms since, as a rule, they occur sentence-finally.[244] Clement

M. Doke, the meritorious student of South African languages, lists nine tones for Zulu.[245] It seems, however, that the tone of the syllable nuclei is frequently affected by the consonantal environment as well as by the tone of the neighboring syllables. It is very difficult to isolate these external influences and to determine the number of distinctive tones in each position. Doke himself unfortunately neglected to do so; and since he did not include a word list in his study, it is also impossible for the reader to do this work. The data supplied by Doke nevertheless shows that the number of distinctive tones in Zulu must in all probability be reduced from nine to three. Doke distinguishes among different "tone types" (nuclei) of words. For example, trisyllabic words are divided into six such tone types. Types I, II, III, and VI are characterized by low tone ("9") on the final syllable. Types IV and V, on the other hand, show a middle tone in the final syllable. In Type I the first syllable is lower than the second syllable—the first may be falling, the second rising—but both are higher than the third syllable. In Type II the second syllable is either as low as the third or it is only slightly higher in its onset (i.e., falling from tone "8" to "9"). The first syllable, on the other hand, is much higher than the other two. Type III is characterized by an abruptly falling (or possibly rising-falling) change of pitch in the second syllable. The first syllable is relatively high. In Type VI the first syllable is higher than the second syllable, but both are much higher than the third. In Type IV the first and the third syllable have approximately the same middle tone, while the second is falling ("2"–"4" or "3"–"5"). In Type V the first syllable is higher than the third, and both these syllables are higher than the second. Similar tone types are also indicated for disyllabic words and words with four syllables, etc. Doke gives a rather long list of word pairs that are distinguished exclusively by the tone (or tonal variation) of the syllables. The list shows that the corresponding words always belong to two different "tone types." For example, a trisyllabic word that has tones "5," "3," and "9" (tone Type I) can be distinguished from a word "containing the same phonemes" with the tones "2," "7," and "4" (= tone Type V) or "3," "3" to "8," and "9" (= tone Type III), etc. But it cannot be distinguished from such a word with the tones "4," "2," and "9" because such a word would belong to the same "tone Type I." In other words, not the nine tones but only the *tone types* are distinctive in Zulu. The tone types, on the other hand, are only certain combinations of the three tone levels. Thus one also gets for Zulu a system of three tone levels or distinctive registers. Another example: Gweabo, a language of Liberia, already mentioned on several previous occasions, is said to have four distinctive registers, according to information given by E. Sapir.[246] The examples given by Sapir clearly show that these are actually distinctive units and not merely phonetic variants, as in the case of the nine tones of Zulu. However, on page 35 it develops that Gweabo has a special correlation of resonance, in which the "pure" vowels show the so-called normal or second tone, while the remaining three tones are characteristic for the "throaty" or "impure" vowels. Since the purely musical difference between the "second" ("normal") and the "third" ("middle") register cannot be very significant, and since the "normal" register is always related to pure voice, while the "middle" register is always related to impure voice, the contrast between "normal" and "middle" register should probably be considered an irrelevant side phenomenon of the opposition between pure and impure voice. The "high" as well as the "low" tone, on the other hand, are always related to impure voice in Gweabo, so that this is something that is taken matter-of-factly and that is phonologically irrelevant for the extreme tones. Gweabo, therefore, does not have four but three distinctive tone registers: a high, a middle, and a low register. Furthermore, the "correlation of muffling" is present in the vowels of the middle register, in which the pure vowels have a somewhat higher tone than the corresponding impure vowels. Thus we have not come across any sure examples so far of languages that would have more than three distinctive tone registers.[247]

An explanation of this fact must be sought in the nature of tone oppositions. It is clear, of course, that absolute pitch cannot be of importance here. For, as O. Gjerdman[248] observed quite correctly, language is not created only for people with absolute hearing. But the concept of relative pitch must also be strictly delimited. This was recognized by Gjerdman, too. For what may be "low" for a female voice is high for a male voice. Yet oppositions of tone exist for all members of the respective speech community. Each hearer understands immediately which "tone" was meant by the speaker, even though he may never have heard the speaker. Lastly, Gjerdman rightly points out that language was not created only for loud speech but also for whispering. The Swedish phonetician concludes from all this—and rightly so, in my opinion—that for oppositions of tone the relevant factors are changes in vowel and voice quality connected with a change in pitch. If one agrees with this assumption, one may perhaps also get an explanation for the phonological presence of two or three levels fundamental to oppositions of tone. For it is impossible to distinguish among many different tones in whispering, even with the aid of the accompanying qualitative nuances in voice. In loud speech this is only possible for people with a special ear for music. On the other hand, anyone can immediately recognize from the quality of the vowels and the voice of a speaker whether he is speaking in a normal ("middle") pitch or in a pitch that is higher or lower than his normal one. Thus at the most three registers would result therefrom.

But it is not always easy to determine whether a given case involves the correlation of tone register (*Registerkorrelation*) or the correlation of tone movement (*Tonverlaufskorrelation*). Where a low-toned syllable occurs between two high-toned syllables in the same word (as in trisyllabic Type V in Zulu or in the above-mentioned Lonkundo ("_a⁻ta_o⁻ma")), there can be no doubt about the presence of the correlation of tone register since the correlation of tone movement presupposes word accentuation, that is, "the prominence" in each word of some syllable or mora respectively. In those languages, however, where words in principle cannot contain more than two morae, this criterion is inapplicable. But in practice these languages, too, furnish certain indications that make an unambiguous decision possible. Southern Chinese, for example, the Canton dialect, distinguishes six "tones" for bimoric syllable nuclei, a low-level, a high-level, a low-falling, a high-falling, a low-rising, and a high-rising tone.[249] It is clear that this system can only be explained by the assumption of a system with three-tone registers. (The syllable "fan," which has six meanings, depending on "tone," would therefore have to be understood as follows: "faṇ" [share], "fàṅ" [to sleep], "faṅ" [powder], "faṇ" [to get annoyed], "fàn" [to divide], "faṇ" [to burn].) The two "short" (one-mora) tones here should therefore not be interpreted as accented or unaccented, but as "high" and "low." In Northern Chinese, on the other hand, which has only four "tones" (two longer tones, i.e., two bimoric tones, and two shorter ones, i.e., two one-mora tones), it is not necessary to assume registers: in this case an "accent" is present, which in the case of bimoric words puts into relief either the first or the second mora. In the case of one-mora words it is either present or absent.

d. The correlation of accent (*Betonungskorrelation*). In this chapter, which is devoted to the distinctive functions of sound, only the so-called free accent can of course be discussed. In other words, only that type of accent will be discussed for which position in a word is not conditioned externally, and which could, under certain circumstances, differentiate the meaning of words (e.g., Russian "mùkă" [torture]: "mŭkà" [flour]). Accent may be defined as the *culminative prominence* of a prosodeme. Phonetically this prominence can be realized in different ways: by expiratory increase in force, rise in pitch, lengthening, or more precise and more emphatic articulation of the vowels or consonants involved. For languages with a free accent it is phonologically relevant first of all that such prominence occurs only in a single position in every word. The particular prosodeme, or the particular segment of the word, then, stands out from

all other prosodemes and is not second in prominence to any other prosodeme of the same word. Second, it is phonologically relevant that in
words with the same number of prosodemes it is not always the same
prosodeme that is prominent, so that it is possible to have word pairs that
are distinguished from each other exclusively by the position of the peak.

Free accent takes on rather different forms in different languages. The
distinction between syllable-counting languages and mora-counting
languages is very important here. The situation is probably least complicated in those syllable-counting languages where the correlation of accent
occurs as the only prosodic correlation. Portuguese, Spanish, Italian,
Modern Greek, Bulgarian, Romanian, Ukrainian, and Russian belong to
this type in Europe. In some of these languages accented vowels are
lengthened, while unaccented vowels are reduced in quantity and articulation. The situation is more complicated in the syllable-counting languages
that, in addition to free accent, also have a prosodic correlation based on
type of contact, i.e., the correlation of close contact, e.g., German, Dutch,
and English. In these cases two prosodic correlations intersect. Both
show a certain relationship to duration in their phonetic realization: an
accented syllable nucleus is longer than an unaccented one, an unchecked
(*vollablaufender*) syllable nucleus is longer than a checked (*abgeschnittener*)
one. To this is added the presence of grammatically conditioned secondary
accents, which especially complicates the prosodic picture. These never
seem to be present in syllable-counting languages that do not have the
correlation of close contact.

In mora-counting languages with a free accent the word peak can be
formed by either a one-mora syllable or the first mora of a bimoric syllable, or by the last mora of a bimoric syllable. Accordingly "short"
syllables (one-mora syllables) are here divided into accented and unaccented
syllables, "long" (bimoric) syllables, on the other hand, into syllables with
a falling accent, syllables with a rising accent, and unaccented syllables. It
is usually maintained in such cases that short syllables have only "one
accent," while long syllables have two types of accent. The opposition
between the two types of accent on bimoric syllables may be called opposition of tone movement or *correlation of tone movement* (*Tonverlaufskorrelation*). This is a privative opposition. One of the two types of tone
movement is therefore "unmarked." In addition to its distinctly nonlevel
(falling or rising) realization, it may have a "level tone movement" as an
optional variant. Which of the two types of tone movement is unmarked
depends entirely on the language in question.

In addition to the languages with five syllable types, that is, with
accented one-mora syllables, unaccented one-mora syllables, unaccented

bimoric syllables, and two types of accented bimoric syllables, there are languages with only four syllable types. In these either all accented syllables embrace two morae, such as the Slovincian dialect of Kashub,[250] or all unaccented syllables embrace one mora, as, for example, in Slovenian. Accordingly the following systems are the result: in the latter case, a system of low-toned one-mora syllables, high-toned one-mora syllables, bimoric syllables with a positive tone movement (*positiv verlaufend*), and bimoric syllables with a negative tone movement (*negativ verlaufend*); in the former case, a system of always unaccented one-mora syllables, bimoric syllables with prominence of either the first or the second mora, and bimoric syllables in which neither mora is prominent. It is clear that the *absence* of prominence of both morae in a bimoric syllable is essentially equivalent to an *even* prominence of both morae in a bimoric syllable. The Slovincian prosodic inventory thus is in principle identical with that of Estonian described above (see p. 180). It may also be the case, however, that a bimoric syllable with even prominence of both morae is put into distinctive opposition with a bimoric syllable in which neither mora is prominent, and in such a way that both are in a relationship of distinctive opposition with bimoric syllables with a rising accent and bimoric syllables with a falling accent. In this way systems with six prosodically different types of syllables are formed. They are represented in certain Chinese dialects, for example.

The correlation of tone movement need not necessarily be present in all mora-counting languages that have a free accent. There are mora-counting languages that have a free accent, but in which, nevertheless, only one type of accent is present in long (bimoric) nuclei. The clearest examples known to us are Danish on the one hand, and Hopi, which was mentioned above, on the other. It is, perhaps, no coincidence that these languages have a free accent in addition to the prosodic correlation based on type of contact (the correlation of stød [*Stosskorrelation*] in Danish; and the correlation of close contact [*Silbenschnittkorrelation*] in Hopi).

As already mentioned, culminative prominence may extend to both morae of a bimoric syllable, and in some very rare cases may extend over an entire sequence of morae without regard to syllable boundaries. Cases of this type are found in the West Japanese dialects.[251] In the Kyoto dialect such a sequence of high-toned syllables (morae) can only occur word-initially, that is, it may include the stem and possibly the prosodically dependent suffixes immediately following the stem. For example, "úśi" (cow), nominative "úśigà" (but the limitative "ùsimądę"). But in the Tosa dialect such a sequence of high-toned morae may occur in any position in the word. For example, "ąsàgà" (hemp, nom.). The sample text of West Japanese presented by E. D. Polivanov (*op. cit.*, pp. 135 ff.) shows that such sequences of high-toned morae may sometimes be rather long (up to seven morae).[252] However, word peaks of this type which consist of several prosodic units are only attested in a very small number of languages of the world. They are unthinkable, at least for syllable-counting languages.

Since culminative prominence, as was just shown, can sometimes comprise several morae in sequence, one may ask whether conversely it may include only a fraction or a specific portion of a mora. Is it possible to have distinctive differences of tone movement embracing one mora in the presence of free accent? We believe that we can answer this question in the negative. In cases where such oppositions of tone movement over one mora have been observed, they prove to be the realization of the opposition between accented and unaccented mora. The following two examples are especially characteristic: the above-mentioned Kyoto dialect of Western Japan distinguishes an even full-mora accent (transcribed by E. D. Polivanov by a ⌐ to the left of the corresponding mora) and a falling one-mora accent (transcribed by Polivanov by a ∧ over the corresponding vowel symbol). For example: "˪a⌐sa" (hemp): "ˌasâ" (evening); "ˌka⌐me" (vase): "ˌkamê" (turtle); "ˌku⌐ʒu" (old stuff): "ˌkuʒû" (flour). It develops, however, that an even moric prominence in this dialect either occurs word-initially (in which case it embraces either only the first mora of the word or an entire sequence of morae) or it embraces the final mora of a word. In the latter case it may disappear before a word that begins with an accented mora. Optionally it may also occur on the final syllable of a longer word with an accented first syllable (see E. D. Polivanov, *op. cit.*, p. 136, nn. 16 and 20, with respect to "⌐a ˌtamani⌐wa" and "⌐koku˥ˌmocuˌ⌐wo"). Such an even accent becomes obligatory for the final mora of a stem with noninitial accent, if a so-called low-toned suffix is added (e.g., the suffix "-mo" of the additive. See the forms "ˌćot⌐toˌmo ki: ⌐deˌmo," and "nan⌐deˌmo" in the sample text given by Polivanov *loc. cit.*). If, on the other hand, a prosodically neutral suffix is added to a stem with non-initial accent, the even accent is shifted to the final syllable, that is, to the suffix syllable of the entire word. For example, "ˌa⌐sa" (hemp): nominative "ˌasa⌐ŋa." All these facts provide proof that the even accent is only distinctive on the initial mora (or sequence of morae) of a word, and that in all other positions it occurs only with a delimitative function. In contrast, the falling one-mora accent always occurs only on the second syllable of certain stems and retains this position regardless of the suffixes added (see in the above-mentioned text such words as "madôwo," "arâśimaheŋ," "hayêśimaheŋ"). In other words, this accent fulfills exactly the same function on the second syllable as the even accent fulfills on the first syllable of a word. The short falling accent in the Kyoto dialect can therefore only be regarded as a combinatory variant of the distinctive high tone on the noninitial mora of a word. On the other hand, the even one-mora accent on the noninitial mora (insofar as it is not the final member of a polysyllabic word peak) must be regarded as a combinatory variant of absence of tone with the function of a boundary signal: it indicates the boundary between an unaccented morphological unit and the following unit with an initial unaccented mora. In the Kin-chow-fu dialect of China the two so-called shorter tones of Northern Chinese are realized in such a way that the "second" is rising and the "fourth" is falling. This involves only the realization of "one-mora prominence" versus "one-mora nonprominence," however. This is evident from the fact that in the same dialect the "first" tone, which embraces two morae and in which otherwise the onset is prominent while the end is not, is realized as rising-falling. Also, that the "third" tone, which is usually characterized by the prominence of its end and the absence of such prominence on its onset, is realized as falling-rising.[253]

"Freedom" of accent is not always without limitation. Restrictions are found in syllable-counting languages as well as in mora-counting languages with a free accent. In K'üri (Lezghian), Artshi, and certain other syllable-counting languages of the Eastern Caucasus the accent may occur either only on the first or only on the second syllable of a word. The same limitation also holds true for a mora-counting language such as Hopi. In Modern Greek and Italian, which belong to the syllable-counting languages, the accent can occur only on one of the three word-final syllables. In Classical Greek (Ionic-Attic), too, the accent could occur only on one of the last three syllables of a word. But since Classical Greek was a mora-counting language, the formula in reality was somewhat more complicated. According to R. Jakobson, the rule for the accent in Attic can be formulated as follows: the interval between the accented mora and the final mora of a word must not exceed the scope of one syllable.[254] Combinations such as ὐυυ (στέφανος) and ὐ–υ (δέδωχα) therefore were possible, but the combination ὐυ (in which a syllable + one mora would occur between the accented mora and the final mora) was impossible. In Latvian it is always the first syllable that is accented, but long syllable nuclei in this position have a correlation of tone movement. In other words, only one of the first two morae of a word may be accented, and only if it belongs to the first syllable. In Estonian where, as already mentioned, three long accents (degrees of length), that is, a falling, a level, and a rising accent, are distinguished in addition to a short accent, basically the same rule applies as in the case of Latvian. But here the second syllable is accented in some loanwords with short initial syllable, so that from the point of view of the present-day language not only the two morae of the first syllable, but one of the two first morae of the word in general, regardless of whether these belong to the same or different syllables, may be prominent. In the so-called monosyllabic languages, where the word, or more precisely, the morpheme [255] cannot have less than one or more than two morae within a syllable, this fact also acts as a restriction on free accent, should such an accent exist in these languages. Here belong, for example, Northern Chinese,[256] Siamese, and Burmese.

Languages having a correlation of distinctive (free) accent need not accentuate a specific prosodeme in each word. Apart from unaccented proclitic and enclitic particles that exist in almost every language, and that are also "dependent" with respect to their grammatical function, many languages also have grammatically "normal," independent words which do not contain a single accented syllable. Such words can only receive a particular accent optionally in a syntactic context. This accent must be considered a combinatory variant of the absence of accent with a demarcative function. For example, in Classical Greek, the "acute" accent was placed on the final mora of a word in certain word combinations and syntactic positions. In all other cases it was replaced by the "grave" accent, that is, by the absence of accent. The even accent on the final mora of a polysyllabic word in the Kyoto dialect of Western Japan is likewise only a combinatory variant of the absence of accent (see p. 191). In Standard Slovenian, in words that do not have any bimoric syllables, the final (one-mora) syllable bears the accent. If it is an open syllable, the accent may optionally be retracted to the penultimate (also one-mora) syllable. However, statistics of accent distribution in Slovenian poetry teach us that the short accented syllables are treated as unaccented.[257] This is a natural consequence of the fact that the position of the short accented syllables in a word is not free but externally determined, so that it is not capable of differentiation between two words with the same quantitative structure.[258]

The accentual situation of those Štokavian dialects that form the basis of the Serbo-Croatian standard language can also be interpreted in this way. The presence of two kinds of short accent in these dialects is striking in itself. We already know that, wherever the short syllable nuclei show differences in tone movement, one of the two "short accents" must be considered a (combinatory or noncombinatory) realization of the absence of accent.[259] In standard Serbo-Croatian the truly "free" accent is musically rising on short as well as on long syllables. The onset of the following syllable then has the same musical pitch as the end of the accented syllable. This involvement of the following syllable is absolutely essential for the phonetic realization of free accent in Serbo-Croatian. Freedom of accent is therefore limited by the fact that it cannot occur on a word-final syllable. As a rule, the free ("rising") accent can take any position on long as well as on short syllables in polysyllabic words. Many word pairs are differentiated only by the position of this accent. For example: "màlina" (raspberry): "malìna" (small number); "pjèvačica" (cuckoo): "pjevàčica" (songstress); "ràzložiti" (to judge): "razlòžiti" (to take apart); "imānje" (credit): "imánje" (property). The position of this accent within the word is completely independent of syntactic context. The situation is entirely different with respect to the so-called short and long falling accents. In contrast with the "rising" accent, which is characterized almost entirely by its musical quality, and which, insofar as it does not occur in word-initial syllable, is not associated with any significant expiratory increment, the "falling" accent is primarily expiratory. The falling musical movement is only perceptible more or less clearly if the syllable on which it occurs is long. The "short-falling" accent, on the other hand, is very often realized only as an expiratory increment, with the tone movement being musically level on a relatively low register. While syllables that follow a "rising" accent sound rather loud, syllables after a "falling" accent are pronounced in a quite low voice, which is almost a whisper. This clearly underlines the loudness, that is, the expiratory increment of the falling accent. What characterizes the "falling" accent especially in contrast with the "rising" accent, however, is its lack of freedom. The "falling" accent of standard Serbo-Croatian can occur only on the first syllable of a word, or of a close-knit word combination. While the "rising" accent always keeps its position within the word regardless of syntactic context, the "falling" accent disappears from the word-initial syllable as soon as the word enters into a close relationship with a preceding word. For example: "jàrica" (summer wheat): "za jàricu" (for the summer wheat); but "jārica" (young goat): "zā jaricu" (for the young goat); "prèdati" (deliver): "ne prèdati" (not deliver); but "prědati" (to get frightened): "nè predati" (not to get frightened). The "falling" accent of standard Serbo-Croatian, i.e., long as well as short, is therefore only a combinatory variant of the absence of accent which fulfills a demarcative function. It signals that the particular word on which it occurs does not form a close unit with the preceding word. This also explains the fact that earlier Serbo-Croatian grammarians did not label the "short-falling" accent at all and used the same symbol for the "long-falling" accent as for unaccented length.[260]

In the cases discussed above, words not having a distinctive accent are put into opposition with words having a distinctive accent on some syllable or mora. But it was also noted that in some languages, such as the dialects of Western Japan, accentual prominence can comprise a whole sequence of prosodemes, and that this prominent prosodeme sequence may comprise an entire word (e.g., in the Kyoto dialect "ᵓuśiga˥" [the cow], nom. and gen.). One could conceive of a language in which only two types of words exist: on the one hand, words in which all prosodemes are prominent, and on the other, words without such prosodeme prominence. Languages of this type actually appear to exist. The dialect of the Japanese village of Mie (Nagasaki Prefecture), described by E. D. Polivanov, must in our opinion be considered to belong in this category.²⁶¹ Polivanov himself does not speak of prominent and nonprominent words, but of oxytone and barytone words. For the former he considers the musically rising tone movement and for the latter the musically falling tone movement as important. But his description shows that the vowels, in particular *i* and *u*, in polysyllabic "barytone" words are very often realized as voiceless, and sometimes disappear completely in final position (ki̧ta [north], ki̧ku, kiku̧ [listen], haśi̧, haś [bridge]). In "oxytone" words this can never be the case. His description further shows that the musically rising movement does not always comprise the entire final mora of "oxytone" words, and that this mora often ends with a falling movement. In emphatic pronunciation, for example, in the imperative or in exclamation, it is even lower than the penultimate mora. We therefore believe that what is phonologically relevant for the two word types in the dialect of Mie is not the opposition of tone movement but the opposition between total prominence or total absence of prominence of the entire word. This opposition is here found in monosyllabic as well as polysyllabic words.

While, as was shown above, some languages with free accent may sometimes have words without an accented syllable, there are certain other languages in which some words have several accented syllables. Naturally, only one of these syllables can be regarded as the word peak, the rest only being *secondary accents*. What is meant here are, of course, only phonologically relevant secondary accents. In any language with a free accent not all unaccented syllables are equally weak or musically low. But in most languages the dynamic or chromatic gradation of unaccented syllables is quite automatically determined by a specific rhythm, mostly in such a way that the even prosodemes, counted backward or forward from the culminative prosodeme, are somewhat more prominent than the uneven ones, or that the word-final or word-initial syllable receives a secondary ictus, etc. All these phenomena have no distinctive force. However, there are languages in which the position of secondary accents is not determined automatically but "etymologically," and hence has distinctive force. For example, in German, compounded words in addition to a primary accent have secondary accents on every root syllable ("Eísenbàhn" [railroad], "Hóchschùle" [high school]). Certain prefixes and suffixes are also treated as root syllables ("ùnternéhmen" [undertake], "Júdentùm" [Jewry], "Bótschàft" [message], etc.). Insofar as the accent is free in German, that is, insofar as the position of the primary stress can differentiate two words, it is always the opposition "primary stress"/"secondary stress" that is involved (e.g., "ü'bersètzen"/"ü'bersétzen" [to transfer/to translate]). A similar situation is also present with respect to other Germanic languages, insofar as they have a "free" accent. Etymological secondary accents are unknown, on the other hand, in the Romance, Slavic, and Baltic languages which have a free accent. In contrast, this is a common phenomenon in certain American languages, such as Hopi, Tiva, etc. Since among all modern Indo-European languages the Germanic languages are the ones that show the greatest propensity for compounding words, while American languages are famous for their "polysynthetism," one may probably regard this greater utilization of stem composition as a prerequisite for the presence of distinctive secondary accents. The entire phenomenon must be examined in connection with the culminative function.

In conclusion, some remarks on the question of the phonetic realization of accent are in order. In principle, the accent in mora-counting languages is related to a rise in musical pitch, in syllable-counting languages to lengthening. However, a rise in pitch in accented syllables is found also in many syllable-counting languages in addition to lengthening and expiratory increment. Indeed, in many syllable-counting languages a difference in length between accented and unaccented syllables is not present at all. And, conversely, in some mora-counting languages the difference in tone movement in accented syllables is expiratory rather than musical in nature. Many such languages lengthen the accented syllable (or mora). In North Kashubian and Lithuanian unaccented bimoric syllable nuclei are realized as shorter than accented ("semilong") syllable nuclei. In the diphthongal syllable nuclei of Lithuanian the first component is longer than the second in the presence of falling ("acute," *gestossener*) accent, but shorter in the presence of rising ("circumflex," *geschliffener*) accent. In Estonian the realization of differences in tone movement is associated with a gradation in quantity for monophthongal nuclei. All these examples show that the realization of the culminative prominence of prosodemes need not necessarily be in accord with the oppositions valid for nonculminative differentiation of the prosodemes (in which this differentiation is realized by pitch for morae, by intensity for syllables). If a language has a free accent in addition to the nonculminative differentiation of prosodemes, it cannot employ the means utilized for this differentiation for the realization of accent as well. This rule explains the prosodic situation in standard Serbo-Croatian, for the above representation reveals that free accent in that language is realized almost entirely by a musical heightening of the accented syllable.[262] On the other hand, Serbo-Croatian is not a mora-counting language. It does not possess any of the six features by which mora-counting languages are recognized. (The presence of differences in tone movement as in "vrâta" [neck, gen.]: "vráta" [door] proves nothing since the same distinction also exists for short syllable nuclei; cf. "järica" [young goat]: "jàrica" [summer wheat].) Serbo-Croatian may therefore be considered a syllable-counting language. The circumstance that free accent in this language has an entirely musical realization appears to be due to the fact that Serbo-Croatian, in addition to free accent, also has a non-culminative differentiation of prosodemes (syllable nuclei). As in any other syllable-counting language, the latter is realized through the prosodic correlation of intensity. We do not know of any other examples which show the coexistence of free accent with a correlation of nonculminative differentiation.

D   Prosodic Oppositions Based on Type of Contact

a. The correlation of stød (Stosskorrelation). There are two kinds of prosodic oppositions based on type of contact: the correlation of tone interruption (*Tonbruchkorrelation*), or better the correlation of stød (*Stosskorrelation*), and the correlation of close contact (*Silbenschnittkorrelation*). Both have already been mentioned earlier in a different context (pp. 175 ff.) but must be examined here somewhat more closely.

Above all, a warning must be sounded against the confusion of the correlation of stød with some other phenomena that are phonetically quite similar but phonologically very different. Not every combination of a vowel with a complete or incomplete glottal closure can be considered a "vowel with stød" in the sense of the correlation of stød. In languages where the glottal occlusive exists as an independent phoneme, such a combination is simply to be regarded as a phoneme cluster (i.e., as biphonematic). The sequence *a*ᵈ*a* in such a language consists of two syllables. Further, the correlation of stød does not exist in languages such as Achumawi, where a type of glottal catch ("rearticulation") occurs whenever the second mora of a bimoric vowel does not show the same register as the first mora.[263] The glottal closure here is a purely phonetic side phenomenon of register change within a bimoric syllable nucleus. In languages such as Burmese, too, no true correlation of stød is present: here the two "shorter" or one-mora tonemes end in a glottal closure in contrast with the two "longer" tonemes. In the case of the short high tone the glottal closure is formed more vigorously than in the case of the low tone.[264] In this case the glottal closure must be regarded as an ancillary signal of one-mora character.

If one ignores these and similar cases, there still remain a considerable number of languages and dialects with a genuine prosodic correlation of stød. There are languages in which this correlation is found only in bimoric syllable nuclei. In other languages it occurs in bimoric syllable nuclei as well as in one-mora nuclei. However, it seems that there are no languages in which the correlation of stød exists only for short (i.e., one-mora) syllable nuclei, but not for long (bimoric) nuclei. Nor do we know of any languages that have the correlation of stød but no differences of quantity. And since quantity differences in connection with the correlation of stød must be construed as the correlation of prosodic gemination, it follows that the correlation of stød occurs only in languages that have a correlation of prosodic gemination, that is, in mora-counting languages.

For the bimoric syllable nuclei the correlation of stød signifies an opposition in the type of contact between two "morae." In the syllable nuclei with stød the first portion is separated from the second by either a complete or incomplete closure of the glottis. This gives the acoustic impression of two consecutive sounds, or of a sudden transition within the same sound from normal voice to a murmur or whisper. In syllable nuclei without stød, on the other hand, the transition from the initial to the final portion is gradual and direct without any perceptible interruption. For one-mora syllable nuclei the correlation of stød represents an opposition based on the type of contact between the nucleus and the following consonant. The one-mora nucleus (normally a short vowel) may either be separated from the following consonant by a complete closure of the glottis, and hence by a complete pause, or the short vowel may be in direct contact with the following consonant.[265] Accordingly, in the case of bimoric nuclei the stød always occurs within the nucleus itself, while in the case of one-mora nuclei it occurs only at its end. In either case the nuclei with stød are put into opposition with the nuclei with normal articulation, that is, without any such interruption in the middle or at the end of the vowel. Accordingly, what is involved is always the type of contact of a mora with the following element, that is, either with the second mora of a bimoric nucleus (a long vowel, a diphthong, or a combination of vowel plus sonorant) or with the following consonant standing outside of the syllable nucleus. More specifically it bears on the question of whether this contact is direct or whether it is marked by an abrupt glottal closure, that is, a sharp interruption.

b. The correlation of close contact (*Silbenschnittkorrelation*). It is clear that the correlation of close contact (or syllable break) is also a prosodic opposition based on the type of contact. Actually it is nothing more than an opposition between the so-called close and open contact of a vocalic syllable nucleus with the following consonant. If the vowel with "close" contact appears to be shorter than the vowel with "open" contact, this is merely a phonetic side phenomenon. In the case of close contact the consonant begins at a moment when the articulation of the vowel has not yet passed the peak of its normally rising-falling course, while in the case of open contact the articulation of the vowel is fully developed before the onset of the consonant. The close contact, so to speak, "checks" the end of the vowel. The vowel that is "checked" in this fashion must therefore be shorter than the normal unchecked vowel. The correlation of close contact is accordingly based on a privative opposition. Its unmarked member is the "unchecked" vowel with a fully developed articulatory movement which is not in close contact with the following consonant. This also explains the results of neutralization of this correlation: it is neutralized in final position or before vowels. Of course, only the (phonetically long or semilong) unchecked vowel phonemes are found in the position of neutralization (e.g., English, Dutch, German, Norwegian, Swedish, Scottish-Gaelic, Hopi). The fact that vowel length is here phonologically irrelevant can be seen from those cases in which the archiphoneme is realized by a short vowel with open contact, as in unstressed syllables in German ("le-béndig" [live], "Ho-lúnder" [elder tree], "spa-zíeren" [to take a walk], "Ka-pi-tä́n" [captain], etc.).

While the correlation of stød occurs only in mora-counting languages, the relationship of the correlation of close contact to the classification of languages into mora-counting and syllable-counting languages is less clear. German, Dutch, and English, in which the correlation of close contact is found in syllables with primary and secondary stress, are obviously syllable-counting languages. They do not have any of the characteristic features of mora-counting languages. Hopi, on the other hand, where the correlation of close contact is also found in syllables with primary and secondary stress, is a mora-counting language. The correlation of close contact here occurs only in one-mora nuclei (vowels) with primary or secondary stress, while the bimoric nuclei stand outside of this correlation. The correlation of close contact and the correlation of prosodic gemination thus form a three-member bundle in this language: "one-mora nuclei with close contact," "one-mora nuclei without close contact," and "bimoric nuclei (without close contact)." In unaccented syllables the entire bundle is neutralized.

Further, a combination into a bundle of the correlation based on close contact and the correlation of prosodic gemination also seems to be present in Norwegian and Swedish. Carl H. Borgström, to whom we owe an excellent phonological description of standard Norwegian,[266] contends that "standard Norwegian does not divide syllable nuclei into morae" (*op. cit.*, p. 261). However, we believe that this can be questioned. The presence of distinctive oppositions of tone movement in Norwegian speaks in favor of a mora-counting language; for example, "ly'se" (light) with a rising accent, "ly'se" (shine) with a falling-rising accent. True, this correlation of tone movement is found not only with long vowels but also with short vowels. This also seems to be the main reason for the above-mentioned contention of Borgström. However, this obstacle is easily overcome. Borgström recognized quite correctly that accented syllable nuclei in Norwegian are governed by the correlation of close contact; further, that from an objective point of view accented syllables in Norwegian are *always long* "because they either contain a short vowel and a long consonant, or a long vowel and a short consonant" (*op. cit.*, pp. 264 f.). On the other hand, Borgström admits that in accented syllables with a "short" (i.e., checked) vowel the tone movement comprises not only the vowel but also the following consonant. "A short vowel with a following voiceless consonant gives the impression that only a part of the tone movement without voice is intimated. The opposition nevertheless remains clear: where the consonant is voiced, as in 'bønner' (farmer): 'bønner' (beans), part of the tone movement is clearly carried by the consonant" (p. 261). The tone movement is thus carried either by an "unchecked" vowel or diphthong or by a combination of a "checked" vowel and the implosion of the following consonant. The latter—and herein lies the peculiarity of the Swedish-Norwegian type—need not necessarily be a sonorant but may also be an obstruent. All three of these types of accented syllable nuclei may be considered *bimoric*. The presence of two morae is clearly indicated by the correlation of tone movement. In unaccented syllables all of the three types of bimoric nuclei noted occur, as well as *one-mora* nuclei, that is, "short" vowels without close contact with the following consonant (*op. cit.*, pp. 265 ff.). Norwegian thus has the same combination of four possible syllable types as North Kashubian (Slovincian), but in conjunction with the correlation of close contact it has "unaccented one-mora syllables," "unaccented bimoric syllables," "accented bimoric syllables with unmarked tone movement," "accented bimoric syllables with marked tone movement." The correlation of close contact in Norwegian is present only in bimoric syllable nuclei, the final portion of such syllable nuclei coinciding either with the final portion of the unchecked vowel or with the onset of the consonant that is in close contact with the preceding vowel. Thus, the combination of the correlation based on close contact with the correlation of prosodic gemination here also results in a three-member bundle. However, its structure is different from that of Hopi since the correlation of close contact in this language is not found in one-mora syllable nuclei, but just the opposite, in bimoric nuclei. As for Swedish, the same phonological prosodic situation as in Norwegian seems to prevail, but with a somewhat different phonetic realization.[267]

It is not always easy to decide whether the correlation of close contact or the correlation of consonantal gemination is present in a particular language. In languages such as Finnish, Hungarian, or Tamil, where the opposition between long and short vowels is distinctive before simple as well as geminated consonants, there can, of course, be no question of a correlation of close contact. Such a question could, however, be raised with respect to Italian, where accented vowels are always long before a vowel or before a simple intervocalic consonant, but always short before a geminated consonant. But the opposition between geminated and simple consonants exists not only after accented but also after unaccented vowels, and the unaccented vowels before simple consonants are not longer than before geminated consonants. Therefore it is clear that in Italian the correlation of consonantal gemination must be regarded as an independent phenomenon, not as a side phenomenon of the correlation of close contact. Accented vowels in Italian, on the other hand, are short not only before geminated consonants but also before all consonant clusters, except "consonant + r, w, j," and in final position. Differences in vowel quantity are thus conditioned externally, and length in accented vowels before ungeminated consonants, as well as before "consonants + r, w, j," and before heterosyllabic vowels, can be regarded as a combinatory variant. There can be no question of the correlation of close contact in Italian.

On the other hand, the opposition between geminated and simple consonants in languages that have the correlation of close contact is only a phonologically irrelevant side phenomenon. In these languages one should actually not speak of geminated consonants but only of consonants that are in close contact with the preceding vowel, their greater relative length being only a phonetic consequence of this type of contact.

E   Prosodic Oppositions Differentiating Sentences

While the distinctive consonantal and vocalic properties are utilized only to differentiate words, prosodic properties serve to differentiate not only the meaning of words but also of entire combinations of words and sentences. Serving this purpose are the oppositions of tone movement (sentence intonation), change of register, sentence stress, and the pauses.

At the present stage of investigation it is impossible to treat sentence phonology with the same certainty and detail as word phonology. Far too little material is available, and what is available is mostly unreliable. In most available descriptions of "sentence phonetics" the representative function, the appeal function, and the expressive function of sound are generally not even distinguished. Even where such a distinction is made, it is not always in accordance with rigorously applied principles; and in most cases the descriptions are made with definite practical purposes in mind. They are primarily intended for actors, performers, and speakers, for whom a sharp separation of the representative function from the appeal function is of little significance. All these unfavorable circumstances make it difficult to examine the role of prosodic oppositions from the point of view of the representational phonology of the sentence.[268] We will therefore have to content ourselves with only a few remarks on the matter.

Above all, a basic distinction must be made on the basis of whether or not a prosodic opposition that is utilized to differentiate sentences in a particular language also serves to differentiate words. In cases where an opposition that differentiates sentences does not also have the function of differentiating words, its use does not require any particular limitation. But where a syntactically distinctive opposition also serves to differentiate words at the same time, a rather complicated situation arises at times, due to the intersection of these two functions and the subordination of the one to the other.

a. Sentence intonation. Since most European languages do not have oppositions based on tone movement which differentiate words,[269] "intonation" in these languages is a phonological means that is used solely to differentiate sentences. Most often used for this purpose is the contrast between rising and falling intonation. Rising intonation usually fulfills a "nonterminal" function, that is, it indicates that the sentence has not yet been completed, while falling intonation has a "terminal" function. Usually each intonation is realized only with respect to the last word before a pause since only in that position is it important to indicate whether or not the sentence is completed.

In languages with oppositions of tone movement which serve to differentiate words, these oppositions must be modified correspondingly before a pause in order to be subordinated to sentence intonation. For example, in Swedish, where word-differentiating oppositions of tone movement are characterized by the entire tone profile of the accented syllables as well as the posttonic syllables, these tone profiles are realized differently, depending on the character of the sentence intonation. The syllable with the primary accent, provided it is not a final syllable, has a falling tone movement in "grave words" and a level (or slightly rising) tone movement in "acute words." However, posttonic syllables in "grave words" have a rising tone movement in the case of nonterminal sentence intonation and a rising-falling tone movement in the case of terminal sentence intonation, while in "acute words" they show a slightly falling tone movement for nonterminal sentence intonation and an abruptly falling tone movement for terminal sentence intonation.[270] In the Čakavian-Croatian dialect of Castua (Kastav), where two types of tone movement are phonologically distinguished for accented bimoric syllable nuclei, a falling accent on a final syllable always remains falling regardless of sentence intonation. The etymologically long rising accent on a final syllable, on the other hand, is actually rising only in the presence of nonterminal sentence intonation before a pause (or if a word receives special emphasis). It is realized as a musically even long accent in the middle of a sentence (i.e., not before a pause). In the absence of emphasis, and in the case of terminal intonation before a pause, it changes to a falling accent, although from the available description by the poet Ante Dukić one cannot determine whether the two long accents coalesce in this position or whether they are still distinguished. As for the "short" accent on final one-mora syllables, the tone movement of which is not important for the differentiation of words, it is rising in the case of nonterminal sentence intonation and falling for terminal intonation.[271] Unfortunately there are no satisfactory data, let alone systematic descriptions, available on sentence intonation in other European languages that have a correlation of tone movement for the differentiation of words. Sentence intonation in non-European languages, especially in languages that have a correlation of tone for the differentiation of words, have been studied even less. The above (pp. 185 f.) example of Mende shows the types of complications that can arise in languages of this kind in the fitting of the tone profile of words into the tone profile of the sentence. In Mende the tone of all morae in a word in sentence-final position was lowered by one degree, a fact obviously related to a special type of falling terminal sentence intonation.

In addition to the nonterminal and terminal sentence intonation, an *enumerative* intonation is frequently found, which is different from the other two and which has distinctive force. The distinctive opposition between enumerative and nonterminal intonation can be noted particularly in languages such as Russian, in which the so-called nominal clause is quite a common syntactic structure. For example, "l'ud'ï," "zver'ï," "pt'icï" (men, animals, birds) on the one hand, and "l'ud'ï - zver'ï" (man is an animal) on the other.

All other cases where special sentence intonations are posited for European languages involve a confusion of the representational function with the appeal function or the expressive function. The differences produced by these syntactically distinctive intonations do not lie in the conceptual signification but in the emotional content of sentences or combinations of words. It is, of course, not impossible that quite a different situation exists in certain "exotic" languages. But data on sentence intonation from these languages must be used with extreme caution. Observers usually not only fail to distinguish between Bühler's three functions but further, in the sphere of the representative function, also confuse oppositions of tone movement that are distinctive for words with oppositions of tone movement that are distinctive for sentences. It should be stressed that languages with a correlation of tone register distinctive for words use differences of tone register (and consequently also differences of tone movement) for the formation of grammatical forms, just as German uses original vowel gradation or vowel gradation resulting from umlaut for this purpose. In cases such as the German "gib" (give): "gab" (gave), "geben" (to give): "gaben" (gave), "Bruder" (brother): "Brüder" (brothers), the vocalic oppositions cannot be considered distinctive for sentences but only for words. Likewise, in cases such as Fante (Ašanti) ⁻ɔ‿hwɛ (he looks, is looking):⁻ɔ⁻hwɛ-ɛ (looked),[272] one can also only speak of word-differentiating oppositions of tone movement and not of "syntactic tones"—as was unfortunately done even in a valuable handbook for students.

b. Differences of tone distinctive for sentences. Oppositions of tone that are distinctive for sentences must not be confused with sentence intonations. Since oppositions of tone that are distinctive for words are foreign to most languages of the world, there is nothing that would prevent the use of oppositions of tone for the differentiation of sentences. In most languages, nevertheless, this possibility is used either not at all or only sparingly.

Very many languages have a musically rising intonation in yes-no questions (in contrast with information questions). This rising intonation is usually distinguished from nonterminal intonation by a higher pitch only. It generally begins only at the sentence constituent that is put in question.[273] The height of the pitch thus serves here to distinguish an interrogative sentence from a still incomplete declarative sentence. For example, German "er soll kommen?" (he shall come?) and "er soll kommen . . . und sich selbst ueberzeugen" (he shall come and convince himself). Or Russian "on l'ub'ĭt ĭgrat' f-karty?" (he likes to play cards?) and "on l'ub'ĭt ĭgrat' f-kartў . . . no tol'kă n'ĭ-nă-den'gĭ" (he likes to play cards . . . but not for money).

The pitch is usually lowered below the normal level in the case of inter-polated clauses, and also in the case of words (such as direct address, etc.) which are external to the syntactic context. The following clauses will serve as examples: "ich kann nicht kommen, *sagte er*, denn ich bin zu Hause beschäftigt" (I cannot come, *he said*, for I am busy at home), "sehr gerne, *Herr Doktor*" (with pleasure, *Doctor*). (See Karcevskij, *op. cit.*, pp. 217 ff.)[274] By a lowering in pitch a difference is made between the interpolated clause and the normal sentence. But a lowering in pitch is by no means the only indication of an interpolated clause. In such cases it is also associated with a special "level" intonation (i.e., neither falling nor rising) and with an accelerated tempo of speech.

The change of pitch that discriminates between sentences thus never seems to be quite independent in the European languages. It always seems to be related to a particular sentence intonation. An independent change of pitch in European languages occurs only in the sphere of the appeal func-tion or of the expressive function. This circumstance probably also explains its relatively rare use for sentence discrimination.

c. Sentence stress. The expiratory increment of a stressed syllable in many languages is also used to discriminate among sentences. The word that is to be put into relief with respect to its content receives the expiratory increase in force. The matter is relatively simple in those languages where the position of the expiratory accent does not also have the function of differentiating words. In Czech, for example, each of the four words in a sentence such as "tvoje sestra přinesla knihu" (your sister brought a book) can be put into relief by means of stronger expiratory stress on the first syllable. The meaning of the sentence thus receives four different nuances: "*your* sister, not my sister," "your *sister*, not your mother," ". . . already *brought* the book and did not forget it," "brought *the book*, not another object." The remaining words receive less stress on their first syllable, thus in each case creating a hierarchy of stress; one primary stress and as many secondary stresses as the sentence contains words. Only in cases where the principal clause is combined with a subordinate clause (or with several subordinate clauses) may a somewhat more complicated three-level gradation occur. In any event, what is involved in each case is nothing more than a gradation in expiratory force.

In German, too, sentence stress is distinguished only by its degree of force. Word stress is subordinated to sentence stress by means of a grada-tion in force. As far as German is concerned, the situation is complicated only by the fact that individual compounded words may have secondary stresses in addition to the primary word stress. Fundamentally the situation is not as different from Czech as might be supposed. In Czech the position of stress within the word is nondistinctive, but the position of the primary stress within the sentence is distinctive. In German compounded words can be differentiated only by the position of primary stress ("ü′ber-sètzen"/"ü`bersétzen" [to transfer/to translate]). This always involves the opposition "primary stress/secondary stress." The same opposition is also valid for the sentence in German. The force of stress in German thus depends on the meaning of the sentence (i.e., the word complex) and on the meaning of the compounded word (i.e., the stem complex).

A fundamentally different picture is presented by languages such as Russian, where word stress is really completely free (even within the framework of noncompounded words), and where oppositions based on position of stress are very much utilized for lexical purposes, but where secondary accents have no phonemic value. In Russian the force of the stress is dependent on the meaning of the sentence. In other words, the meaning of a sentence can be changed by increasing the stress on a particular word and by weakening the stress on the remaining constituents of the sentence. Sentence constituents not affected by sentence stress generally do not show any expiratory increment on etymologically accented syllables. These syllables nevertheless remain distinct from etymologically unaccented syllables, on the one hand because they are somewhat longer, and on the other because their vowels are not subject to qualitative reduction. It can therefore be said that the qualitative and quantitative difference between vowels of accented and unaccented syllables is phonologically relevant for word stress in Russian, but that differences in expiratory force between the accented syllables of individual syntactic constituents are phonologically relevant for sentence stress.[275] Word stress in Russian is absolute. Russian does not have distinctive secondary accents within a compounded word. But in a sentence primary and secondary stress is distinguished: "ïvàn păjd'ót" (Ivan will go) with secondary stress on the subject, "ïvan păjd'ót" (Ivan *will* go) without secondary stress, "ïván păjd'òt" (*Ivan* will go) with primary stress on the subject and secondary stress on the predicate. Sentence stress in Russian is thus clearly distinguished from word stress. In German, on the other hand, this is not the case. German has distinctive secondary stresses in the sentence and in the word. There is no objective stress feature that would only be relevant for sentence stress or only relevant for word stress.

These few examples may suffice to demonstrate how varied the treatment of sentence stress can be in different languages.[276]

d. Sentence pauses. Pause is probably the only means for differentiating sentences for which there is no exact counterpart among the prosodic properties used to differentiate words, unless one would want to equate the opposition "with pause"/"without pause" with the correlation of stød. Sentence pause, in any event, is a prosodic means like all other means for differentiating sentences and may be counted among the prosodic properties based on type of contact. Sentence pause usually serves to delimit individual sentences or parts of sentences. In other words, it primarily fulfills a boundary (delimitative) function. But the opposition "with pause"/"without pause" frequently also has distinctive value. For example: Russian "ruskaj|arminin|i gruzin" (the Russian, the Armenian, and the Georgian): "ruskaj arminin|i gruzin" (the Russian Armenian and the Georgian).

e. General remarks. In summary it may be said that, although the same phonic properties that furnish prosodic correlations for the differentiation of words are also employed to differentiate sentences, the means used for differentiating sentences are basically different not only from the prosodic phonological properties but also from all other means used to differentiate words. This fundamental difference probably lies in the fact that phonemes and prosodic properties that differentiate words are never *linguistic signs* in themselves but only *parts of linguistic signs*. The phoneme *m* does not have any sign value in itself. It does not designate or signify anything. It is merely a part of different linguistic signs (words, morphemes) such as "Mann" (man), "Mutter" (mother), "Mist" (dung), "dumm" (stupid), "dem" (def. art., masc. sing., dat.), "immer" (always), "Imker" (bee-keeper), etc. Means that differentiate sentences, on the other hand, are independent linguistic signs. Nonterminal intonation *signifies* that the sentence has not yet been completed. Lowering of tone *signifies* that the particular speech segment is not related to what preceded or to what followed, etc. In this respect elements that differentiate sentences, that is, syntactically distinctive elements, are comparable to the delimitative and culminative means.[277]

6   ANOMALOUS DISTINCTIVE ELEMENTS

In addition to the normal phonological system, many languages have still other, special phonological elements which occur with very special functions.

To these belong, in particular, the "foreign sounds," that is, the phonemes that are borrowed from the phonological system of a foreign language. They occur primarily in loanwords, thus underlining the foreign origin of a particular word. In standard German, especially in its southern variety, the nasalized vowels and the voiced (or lenis) equivalent of š are among these, and in Czech there is the phoneme g, and in Serbo-Croatian the phoneme ǧ (dž). It should be noted that usually these foreign phonemes are not realized in exactly the same way in the particular foreign language, but are assimilated to the native system. For example, the ž in German (especially in Vienna) is not a voiced but a voiceless lenis consonant since High German does not have any voiced obstruents. Conversely, the g in Czech is a true voiced occlusive, although in many instances it is intended to render the voiceless lenis g of High German. Furthermore, it may be noted that such "foreign sounds" are not always pronounced in their "proper place" once they have entered the language. They are a sign of foreignism. Accordingly they may occur in a word that is regarded as foreign, regardless of whether or not the sounds are justified in such a word. For example, the loanword "Telephon" is very often pronounced with a nasalized vowel in Vienna (telefõ). Speakers of Czech replace k with g in such loanwords as "plakat" (poster), "balkon" (balcony).[278] It frequently happens that the feeling a word is of foreign origin vanishes and the foreign sounds are incorporated into the native system. It is even possible that new native words are formed with these phonemes. This is the case, for example, with the phonemes f and f′ in Russian. Originally they occurred only in loanwords. Today they are also found in such words as "prăstăf'il'ă" (simpleton), "fŭfajkă" (warm jacket), etc. However, since the loanwords have been "acclimatized" relatively recently, the domain of their use is limited to argot expressions only. These phonemes thus, nevertheless, retain a special function: they signal the alien character and special familiar expressivity that is common to argot vocabulary.

Phonemes that have a special function also occur in interjections, onomatopoetic expressions, and in commands or calls directed toward animals. Words of this type do not have a representative function in the proper sense. Hence they form a special part of the vocabulary, for which the ordinary phonological system is not valid. Even in European languages there are special sounds that are used only in this type of word: for example, the interjection "hmm," the clicks used to set horses moving, the labial r used to stop horses, or the interjection "brrr!" used to express a shudder. In certain "exotic" languages such phonemes, which are external to the phonological system, are very numerous. For example, the Bantu languages have a large number of words that designate the calls or movement of animals. In many of these cases there can hardly be a question of true onomatopoetic expressions. (For example, the roar of a lion is designated by a syllabic palatal ṇ.) In these words there also occur special phonemes that are not found elsewhere in these languages. In the animal fables of the Takelma Indians a voiceless lateral spirant is prefixed to each word in the speech of the grizzly bear, a sound that does not occur elsewhere in Takelma.[279]

[1] L. Hjelmslev, "On principles of phonematics," in *Proceedings of the Second International Congress of Phonetic Sciences* (1935), p. 52.

[2] L. Hjelmslev, "Accent, intonation, quantité," in *Studi Baltici*, VI (1936–1937), 27.

[3] Even in French, where each vowel can form a word by itself (*où, a, ai, est, y, eu, eux, on, an, un*), we find an interjection *rrr!* (command to stop a horse). Thus Hjelmslev's definition proves untenable for this language as well.

[4] P. Menzerath, "Neue Untersuchungen zur Steuerung und Koartikulation," in *Proceedings of the Second International Congress of Phonetic Sciences*, p. 220.

[5] For another definition of the difference between vowels and consonants, cf. p. 222 n. 213.

[6] This has been stressed with particular clarity by Raymond Herbert Stetson, who contributed greatly to the investigation of the phonetic nature of the syllable. See his "Motor Phonetics," in *Archives néerlandaises de phonétique expérimentale* (1928), "Speech Movements in Action," in *Transactions of the American Laryngological Association*, IV (1933), 29 ff. (in particular pp. 39 ff.), and in summary "The relation of the phoneme and the Syllable," in *Proceedings of the Second International Congress of Phonetic Sciences*, pp. 245 ff.

[7] In those languages in which the prosodic units consist entirely of vowels, the prosodic properties appear to be added to the vocalic properties. However, they always form a special group and must not be thrown together with the *properties of vocalic quality proper* in any classification.

[8] In this connection cf. especially the praiseworthy work done by Georg Oskar Russel, "The Vowel," "Speech and Voice" (New York, 1931), and his summary paper "Synchronized X-ray, oscillograph, sound and movie experiments, showing the fallacy of vowel triangle and open-close theories," in *Proceedings of the Second International Congress of Phonetic Sciences*, pp. 198 ff.

[9] Accordingly one should guard against assuming such conditions for reconstructed periods of a language, as unfortunately this is sometimes done.

[10] In connection with what follows, cf. N. S. Trubetzkoy, "Zur allgemeinen Theorie der phonologischen Vokalsysteme," in *TCLP*, I, 39 ff. Incidentally, this article is by now out of date in some respects.

[11] These terms may be retained, subject to the above reservation, as long as no satisfactory acoustic terms have been coined for these concepts.

[12] Cf. M. Rešetar, "Der štokavische Dialekt" (*Schriften der Balkankommission der k. k. Akademie der Wissenschaften in Wien*).

[13] Cf. P. Jaworek in *Materyały i prace komisji językowej*, VII. By *ů* an intermediary sound between *u* and *o* is to be understood, by *y* a vowel of the central series which according to degree of aperture lies between *i* and *e*; *o* and *e* are close before nasals, and open elsewhere. The fact that only the opposition based on lip rounding has distinctive force in this system also affects the realization of the

individual phonemes. For example, *y* is not a front vowel but an unrounded vowel of the central series, *o* and *u* begin with a *u* glide especially after gutturals and labials and in initial position. In many Polish dialects with similarly structured vowel systems the element of rounding is separated, as it were, from the vowels of the class of rounded timbre, so that these vowels are realized as diphthongs: *åu*, *ue*, *uy*.

[14] E. D. Polivanov, "Uzbekskaja dialektologija i uzbekskij literaturnyj jazyk" (Taškent, 1933), p. 14.

[15] This also affects pronunciation in that in the case of *o* lip rounding is detached as a special element: hence the almost diphthongal realization of Russian "o" as *ov*, *uɔ*, *uɛ*, particularly in the speech of Russian women.

[16] N. S. Trubetzkoy, "Die Konsonantensysteme der ostkaukasischen Sprachen," in *Caucasica*, VIII (1931), 44.

[17] Related to this is the feature that the tongue position in the case of *u*, *o*, and *a* is fronted in specific environments (in the vicinity of *ḥ* and *ʕ*). Cf. A. Dirr, "Arčinskij jazyk," in *Sbornik materialov dlja opisanija mestnostej i plemen Kavkaza*, XXXIV (1908), 1.

[18] W. Steinitz, "Chantyjskij (ostjackij) jazyk," in *Jazyki i pis'mennost' narodov Severa*, I (1937), 200–201.

[19] Under these conditions it is probably understandable why Japanese *u* (it seems, in most cases) is realized completely without any lip rounding.

[20] Cf. N. S. Trubetzkoy, "Polabische Studien," in *Sitzb. Wien. Akad., Phil.-hist. Kl.*, CCXI, no. 4, pp. 128 ff.

[21] Certain peculiarities in the realization of the Polabian vowel phonemes seem to be related to this. For example, Polabian α appears to have been pronounced as a back vowel without lip rounding (cf. N. S. Trubetzkoy, "Polabische Studien," pp. 42 ff.). *ü* and *ö*, on the other hand, were pronounced with "uneven rounding," in other words, approximately like *üi* and *öe*, thus lending special emphasis to the element of rounding (see *ibid.*, pp. 50 ff.).

[22] Cf. G. S. Lytkin, "Zyr'anskij kraj pri episkopach permskich i zyrjanskij jazyk" (St. Petersburg, 1889).

[23] Alfred Bouchet, "Cours élémentaire d'annamite" (Hanoi-Haiphong, 1908).

[24] P. K. Uslar, *Etnografija Kavkaza*, Č. I, "Jazykoznanije," vyp. 6 (*Kjurinskij jazyk*) (Tiflis, 1896).

[25] Walter Trittel, "Einführung in das Siamesische," in *Lehrb. d. Semin. f. oriental. Sprachen zu Berlin*, XXXIV (1930).

[26] Cf. A. J. Emel'anov, "Grammatika votjackogo jazyka" (Leningrad, 1927).

[27] Cf. V. L. Ščerba, "Vostočnolužickoje narečije" (1915).

[28] Cf. Ödön Beke, "Texte zur Religion der Osttscheremissen," in *Anthropos*, XXIX (1934).

[29] Neutralization takes place in word-noninitial syllable, the choice of the archiphoneme representative being conditioned externally (by the vowel of the preceding syllable). For example, after a syllable containing *u*, *o*, *a*, and *ə̂*, *a* occurs as the maximally open vowel. After a syllable containing *ü*, *ö*, and *ä*, only *ä* can occur of the maximally open vowels. After a syllable containing *e* and *i*, the maximally open vowel is represented by *à*, etc.

[30] Cf. G. N. Prokof'ev, "Sel'kupskij (ostjacko-samojedskij) jazyk," in *Naučno-issled. Associacija Instituta Narodov Severa, Trudy po lingvistije*, IV, vyp. 1 (Leningrad, 1935).

³¹ J. van Ginneken, *De ontwikkelingsgeschiedenis van de systemen der menschelijke taalklanken* (Amsterdam, 1932), p. 5.

³² Cf. P. K. Uslar, *Etnografija Kavkaza*, Č. I, "Jazykoznanie," Vyp. IV (*Lakskij jazyk*) (Tiflis, 1890), pp. 4–5. However, the description of the pronunciation of the vowels is extremely unclear. Our statements are based on our own observations. It must be stressed, however, that the letters *ä*, *e*, and *ö* are used only in a quite conventional sense.

³³ Incidentally, J. van Ginneken does not seem to deny this: in *op. cit.*, p. 6, he cites Arabic and Modern Persian as examples of triangular systems.

³⁴ Cf. W. H. T. Gairdner, "The Phonetics of Arabic," in *The American University of Cairo Oriental Studies* (Humphrey Milford, Oxford University Press, 1935), Chaps. VI (The Vowels Described) and VII (Influence of Consonants on Vowels).

³⁵ Incidentally, the difference in quality between long and short vowels in Modern Persian is so great that one might be inclined to posit a single quadrangular system consisting of six vowel phonemes (*i*, *o*, *ɔ*, *æ*, *e*, and *i*) and to consider length in *u*(:), *ɔ*(:), and *i*(:) as unimportant. However, this would be in contradiction to the principles of Persian metrics.

³⁶ On both languages, cf. John R. Swanton in *Bulletin of the Bureau of American Ethnology*, XL (= *Handbook of American Indian Languages*, by Franz Boas I).

³⁷ Cf. Harry Hoijer in *Handbook of American Indian Languages* (University of Chicago Press), Vol. III.

³⁸ More precisely, in present-day standard Lezghian and in the dialect studied by Baron P. K. Uslar ("Etnografija Kavkaza," I, in *Jazykoznanije*, Vyp. VI [*K'urinskij jazyk*] [Tiflis, 1896]), where *o* is only an optional combinatory variant of *u*, and where *ä* is on the one hand a combinatory variant of *e*, and on the other the archiphoneme representative of the opposition *a-e* before the pharyngeal occlusive.

³⁹ In K'üri certain consonantal oppositions are neutralized in the vicinity of the close vowels *u*, *ü*, and *i*. Since a "contextually conditioned" neutralization usually takes place in the vicinity of the marked members of an opposition (see Chap. V, 2*d*), the close vowels (*u*, *ü*, and *i*) may be considered as marked in K'üri, and the open vowels (*a* and *e*) as unmarked. On Bulgarian, see pp. 114 f.

⁴⁰ Cf. Carl Hjalmar Borgström, "The Dialect of Barra in the Outer Hebrides," in *Norsk Tidsskrift for Sprogvidenskap*, VII (1935).

⁴¹ A. Martinet, "La phonologie du mot en danois" (Paris, 1937), pp. 17–19 (*BSL*, XXXVIII [1937], 2).

⁴² Cf. Ida C. Ward, *An Introduction to the Ibo Language* (Cambridge, 1936).

⁴³ It is to be noted that the unrounded vowels are here realized much more "open" than the corresponding rounded vowels. From a purely phonetic viewpoint, this system is therefore by no means symmetrical. Dr. Ida C. Ward transcribes the rounded vowel of the second degree of aperture by Θ. We took the liberty of replacing this symbol by ʊ.

⁴⁴ Cf. J. Winteler, *Die Kerenzer Mundart des Canton Glarus* (Leipzig, 1876).

⁴⁵ Cf. D. Westermann and Ida C. Ward, *Practical Phonetics for Students of African Languages* (London, 1933), pp. 172 ff.

⁴⁶ Edward Sapir, "Notes on the Gweabo Language of Liberia," in *Language*, VII (1931), pp. 31 ff.

[47] Cf. A. Thumb, "Handbuch der neugriechischen Volkssprache," p. 6, and B. Havránek in *Proceedings of the International Congress of Phonetic Sciences*, I, 33.

[48] Cf. R. Jakobson in *TCLP*, II, 89.

[49] Cf. A. V. Burdukov, "Rusko-mongol'skij slovar' razgovornogo jazyka, s predislovijem i grammatičeskim očerkom N. N. Poppe" (Leningrad, 1935), as well as N. N. Poppe, "Stroj chalcha-mongol'skogo jazyka" (= *Stroj jazykov*, no. 3) (Leningrad, 1935), pp. 8–10.

[50] Carl Hjalmar Borgström, "Zur Phonologie der norwegischen Schriftsprache," in *Norsk Tidsskrift for Sprogvidenskap*, IX (1937), p. 251.

[51] Charles F. Voegelin, "Tübatulabal Grammar" (*University of California Publications in American Archeology and Ethnology*, XXXIV, no. 2, pp. 55 ff.).

[52] The realization of *U* and *A* is conditioned by the quality of the vowel of the preceding syllable, *U* is realized as *u* after back vowels and after *a*, and as *ü* after *ü*, *ö*, and *e*; *A* is realized as *a* after *u* and *a*, as *o* after *o*, as *e* after *ü* and *e*, and as *ö* after *ö*. Cf. N. N. Poppe, "Stroj chalcha-mongol'skogo jazyka," pp. 10–11.

[53] Cf. V. Brøndal, "La structure des *systèmes vocaliques*," in *TCLP*, VI, 65.

[54] Cf. R. Jakobson in *TCLP*, II, 78, and B. Havránek in *Proceedings of the International Congress of Phonetic Sciences*, I, 28 ff.

[55] Cf. B. Havránek in *Proceedings*, I, 31 ff.; A. Rosetti in *Bulletin linguistique*, II (1934), 21 ff.

[56] A. Isačenko, "Les parlers slovènes du Podjunje en Carinthie, description phonologique," in *Revue des études slaves*, XV (1935), 59.

[57] For Dutch, W. A. de Groot has already suggested a similar classification of the vowel phonemes into diphthongs and monophthongs. See *TCLP*, IV, 118.

[58] Cf. Daniel Jones, *An Outline of English Phonetics*, 3d ed. (Leipzig, 1932), and *English Pronouncing Dictionary* (Leipzig).

[59] "Über die phonologische Interpretation der Diphthonge," in *Práce z vědeckých ústavů*, XXXIII.

[60] "A Phonological Analysis of Present-day Standard English," in *ibid.*, XXXVII.

[61] "Some Observations on the Phonology of the English Vowels," in *Proceedings of the Second International Congress of Phonetic Sciences*, pp. 131 ff.

[62] "Phonemes and Phonemic Correlation in Current English," in *English Studies*, XVIII (The Hague, 1936), 159 ff.

[63] Compare the term "centring diphthongs" proposed by H. E. Palmer and adopted by Daniel Jones.

[64] It follows from what has been said that the class of timbre of the vowel phonemes with an articulatory movement toward the center must be determined on the basis of their point of departure, while that of the vowel phonemes with an articulatory movement away from the center must be determined on the basis of their end point. This should dispose of the doubts raised by A. C. Lawrenson against classifying the phoneme "*au*" with the dark class of timbre (on *oi* see below).

[65] It is true, of course, that only monosyllabic "*aə*" and "*aə*" can be considered monophonematic. In poetry they are treated as monosyllabic combinations (Daniel Jones, *An Outline of English Phonetics*, p. 59). Anglicists may decide to what extent such a monosyllabic pronunciation is normal today. Should it not be normal, the category of vowel phonemes with an articulatory movement toward the center would have only three degrees of sonority.

[66] It would be advisable to adopt a more suitable transcription for the individual phonemes, corresponding to phonological facts. Since o and e function only as a point of departure for vowel phonemes with an articulatory movement away from the center, and $\mathfrak{o}$ and ε only as points of departure of vowel phonemes with an articulatory movement toward the center, it makes no sense to distinguish them graphically: transcribing them by o^u, o^ϑ, e^i, and e^ϑ would be completely unambiguous. For the third degree of sonority, the transcriptions α^u, α^ϑ, a^i, and a^ϑ could be used, and the first degree should accordingly also be transcribed by u^u, u^ϑ, i^i, and i^ϑ. The direction of articulatory movement would then be unambiguously indicated by the exponents ^{u}, ^{i}, and $^\vartheta$, the degree of sonority and the class of timbre by the symbols u, o, α, a, e, and i.

[67] In this connection compare A. Isačenko, "A propos des voyelles nasales," in *BSL*, XXXVIII (1937), pp. 267 ff.

[68] J. R. Firth, "Alphabets and Phonology in India and Burma," in *Bull. of the School of Oriental Studies*, VIII, 534.

[69] Carl Hjalmar Borgström, "The Dialect of Barra in the Outer Hebrides," in *Norsk Tidsskrift for Sprogvidenskap*, VIII.

[70] G. S. Lowmann, "The Phonetics of Albanian," in *Language*, VIII (1932), 281 ff.

[71] Cf. A. Isačenko, "Les dialectes slovènes du Podjunje en Carinthie," in *Revue des études slaves*, XV, 57 ff.

[72] The rule posited by A. Isačenko, according to which such cases are only found in languages with quadrangular systems of nonnasalized vowels (*BSL*, XXXVIII [1937], 269 ff.), must for the present be regarded as a not yet sufficiently tested hypothesis. This hypothesis has something to it, yet the data available to us are still too slight to prove its validity.

[73] Cf. E. N. and A. A. Dragunov, "K latinizacii dialektov central'nogo Kitaja," in *Bull. de l'Acad. des Sciences de l'U.d.R.S.S., Classe des Sciences Sociales* (1932), no. 3, pp. 239 ff. The above diagram is based on the *phonetic* description by Dragunov. Most vowels are realized as diphthongs. u is a very close o with increasing closeness. After sibilants and apicals it is completely unrounded; in other environments it is only rounded in its beginning. o and e are more open in their final portion than in their initial portion ($o\mathfrak{o}$, $e\mathfrak{æ}$). v and $ü$ are the characteristic gingival vowels that occur in many Chinese dialects.

[74] Cf. Anton Pfalz, "Die Mundart des Marchfeldes," in *Sitzb. Wien. Akad., Phil.-hist. Kl.*, CLXX, no. 6 (1912); see also N. S. Trubetzkoy, *TCLP*, IV, 101 ff.

[75] For example, V. G. Bogoraz, who had observed such "muffled" vowels in Chukchi (on Kamchatka), states that these vowels are pronounced with "laryngeal intensification," which "corresponds to a more pronounced intonation" (*Jazyki i pis'mennost' narodov Severa*, III, 12).

[76] A. N. Tucker, "The Function of Voice Quality of the Nilotic Languages," in *Proceedings of the Second International Congress of Phonetic Sciences*, pp. 125 ff.

[77] Ida C. Ward, "Phonetic Phenomena in African Languages," in *Archiv. für vergl. Phonet.*, I (1937), 51.

[78] J. R. Firth, "Phonological Features of Some Indian Languages," in *Proceedings of the Second International Congress of Phonetic Sciences*, p. 181.

[79] A. Dirr, "Grammatičeskij očerk Tabassaranskogo jazyka," in *Materialy dlja opisanija městnostej i plemen Kavkaza*, XXXV (1905), otd. III, 2.

[80] A. Dirr, "Agul'skij jazyk," in *ibid.*, XXXVII (1907), otd. III, 2.

[81] J. P. Grazzolara, "Outlines of a Nuer Grammar," in *Linguistische Bibliothek "Anthropos,"* XIII (1933), 3.

[82] The acoustic effects in the labial series are primarily produced by the impact of the airflow against the soft, wide, but relatively short surface of the lips; in the apical series, by the resonance of the cavity that is bordered from below by the flat, extended tongue, and from above and from the back by the hard and soft palate; in the guttural series, by the resonance of the cavity bordered from below and from the back by the roundish surface of the contracted tongue and the lower teeth, from above by the upper teeth, the hard palate, and possibly the front part of the soft palate.

[83] What is characteristic of this series is the creation of a resonant cavity sideways from the tongue. (The lateral consonants could accordingly be designated as "tongue-cheek sounds" [*Zungenwangenlaute*].) The tongue may either be flatly extended with its tip pointed toward the front of the oral cavity, or it may be contracted, its dorsum raised toward the center or the back of the oral cavity. The latter is irrelevant for the laterals as an independent series of localization. However, in cases where such an independent lateral series of localization is not present, the lateral resonating cavity of individual lateral sounds may in turn seem unimportant, such sounds being then evaluated as realizations of phonemes of the apical or guttural series.

[84] However, what is characteristic is always the contracted shape of the tongue and the frontal position of articulation. Acoustically it is possible to distinguish "more kj-like" or "more tj-like" palatals, or palatals that really lie completely between the "ki-" and the "ti-effect," or assibilated palatals, etc. Cf. E. Šramek, "Le parler de Boboščíca, en Albanie," in *Revue des études slaves*, XIV (1934), 184 f. O. Broch gives a detailed phonetic classification in "Slavische Phonetik" (par. 15, pp. 20–22).

[85] Cf. N. S. Trubetzkoy, "Zur Entwicklung der Gutturale in den slavischen Sprachen," in *Miletič-Festschrift* (1933), pp. 267 ff. On Slovak *h*, see L'. Novák, "Fonologia a študium slovenčiny," in *Spisy jazykového odboru Matice slovenskej*, II (1934), 18.

[86] Cf. William Thalbitzer, "A Phonetical Study of the Eskimo Language," in *Meddelelser om Grönland*, XXXI, 81.

[87] Cf. Clement M. Doke, "A Comparative Study in Shona Phonetics" (Johannesburg, 1931).

[88] For example, in many African languages such as Swahili (Bambara dialect), Herero, etc. (see Carl Meinhof, *Grundriss einer Lautlehre der Bantusprachen* [Berlin, 1910]), as well as in most Indian languages, both Indo-European and Dravidian.

[89] For example, in Nuer and Dinka (Egyptian Sudan). Cf. J. P. Crazzolara, "Outline of a Nuer Grammar," in *Linguistische Bibliothek "Anthropos,"* XIII, and A. N. Tucker, *The Comparative Phonetics of the Suto-Chuana Group of Bantu-Languages* (London, 1929).

[90] For example, in Czech or Hungarian (see below).

[91] Cf. J. Schreiber, *Manuel de la langue Tigraï* (Vienna, 1887).

[92] Cf. E. N. and A. A. Dragunov, "K latinizacii dialektov central'nogo Kitaja," in *Bull. de l'Acad. des Sciences de l'U.d.R.S.S., Classe des Sciences Sociales* (1932), no. 3, pp. 239 ff.

[93] For the same reason it is also not possible to speak of an opposition between occlusives and spirants in French: certain positions of articulation are here related to a firmer closure of the articulatory organs involved (in particular the *p*, *t*, and *k* position), others to a loose stricture (in particular the *s*, *š*, and *f* position). But it is impossible in French to regard the degree of occlusiveness independent of the position of articulation. We therefore believe that we must dispute the classification of the French consonant phonemes given by G. Gougenheim, *Éléments de phonologie française* (Strasbourg, 1935), pp. 41 ff.

[94] This probably also explains why even in cases where the basic series are not split, the spirant of the labial series is realized by *f*, that of the guttural series by *x̌* (as, for example, in Dutch).

[95] Cf. *Bulletin of the Smithsonian Inst. of Ethnology*, XL.

[96] Cf. N. Jakovlev, "Tablicy fonetiki kabardinskogo jazyka," in *Trudy Podrazrjada issledovanija severokavkaszskich jazykov pri Inst. Vostokovedenija*, I (1923).

[97] Cf. A. Schiefner, *Versuch über die Sprache der Uden* (St. Petersburg, 1863); A. Dirr, "Udinskaja Grammatika," in *Sborn. Mat. dlja opis. městn. i plemen Kavkaza*, XXXIII (1904).

[98] See K. E. Mucke, *Historische und vergleichende Laut- und Formenlehre der niedersorbischen Sprache* (Leipzig, 1891), pp. 151 ff.

[99] N. S. Trubetzkoy, "Konsonantensysteme der ostkaukasischen Sprachen," in *Caucasica*, 8.

[100] Cf. Clement M. Doke, *A Comparative Study in Shona Phonetics* (Johannesburg, 1931).

[101] Incidentally, it is not impossible that the *š* series in Shona is not a related series of the two other sibilant series, but an independent *palatal* series.

[102] Cf. R. Jakobson, *K charakteristike evrazijskogo jazykovogo sojuza* (Paris, 1931), in which the Eurasian languages (i.e., the East European and North Asiatic languages) with the correlation of palatalization are enumerated; also Jakobson in *TCLP*, IV, 234 ff., and in *Actes du IVème Congrès International de Linguistes*.

[103] A good phonetic description of the palatalization process is given by A. Thomson, "Die Erweichung und Erhärtung der Labiale im Ukrainischen," in *Zapysky ist. fi. viddilu Ukr. Akad. Nauk.*, XIII–XIV (1927), 253–263.

[104] Cf. N. S. Trubetzkoy, "Die Konsonantensysteme der ostkaukasischen Sprachen," in *Caucasica*, VIII.

[105] Cf. W. H. T. Gairdner, *The Phonetics of Arabic* (Oxford, 1925).

[106] Cf. Franz Boas in *Bulletin of the Bureau for American Ethnology*, XL.

[107] Cf. N. F. Jakovlev, *Kratkaja grammatika adygejskogo (kjachskogo) jazyka dlja školy i samoobrazovanija* (1930).

[108] Cf. Gerhard Deeters, "Der abchasische Sprachbau," in *Nachr. v. d. Ges. d. Wiss. zu Göttingen, Phil. hist. Kl., Fachgr.* III, no. 2 (1931), pp. 290 ff.

[109] Cf. J. R. Firth in *Bull. of the School of Oriental Studies*, VIII, 532–533.

[110] Cf. A. A. Cholodovič, "O latinizacii korejskogo pis'ma," in *Sovetskoje jazykoznanije*, I (1935), 147 ff. The combination "consonant + *w*" is here to be considered monophonematic.

[111] The situation in the Japanese dialect of Nagasaki, on the other hand, is to be interpreted differently. This dialect has four kinds of gutturals: velars, palatals, labiovelars, and labiopalatals. But since in this case the correlation of

labialization is not present in the other series of localization, while the correlation of palatalization comprises all series, one seems to be justified in considering the rounded gutturals (which sound almost like labials) as an autonomous
related series ("labiovelar series") in which the correlation of palatalization
takes place, just as it does in the other series.

[112] Roman Stopa, "Die Schnalze, ihre Natur, Entwicklung und Ursprung,"
in *Prace Komisji Językowej*, no. 23 (Kraków, 1935).

[113] P. de V. Pienaar, "A Few Notes on Phonetic Aspect of Clicks," in *Bantu
Studies* (March 1936), pp. 43 ff.

[114] D. M. Beach, *The Phonetics of the Hottentot Language* (Cambridge,
1938).

[115] Clement M. Doke, "The Phonetics of the Zulu Language," in *Bantu
Studies*, II (1962), Special Number.

[116] See pp. 155 f.

[117] A. N. Tucker, *The Comparative Phonetics of the Suto-Chuana Group of
Bantu-Languages* (London, 1929).

[118] W. H. Bleek and L. C. Lloyd, *Specimens of Bushman Folklore* (London,
1911).

[119] P. Meriggi, "Versuch einer Grammatik des χam-Buschmännischen," in
Zeitschrift f. Eingeborenensprachen, XIX.

[120] A few series also have voiceless spirants, and the labial series has an
"implosive" media.

[121] Clement M. Doke, *A Comparative Study in Shona Phonetics* (Johannesburg, 1931), p. 109, as well as pp. 110–119 and the palatograms, pp. 272 and 273.

[122] Cf. pp. 72 f.

[123] Cf. William Thalbitzer, "A Phonetical Study of the Eskimo Language,"
in *Meddelelser om Grönland*, XXXI, 81.

[124] Cf. Ethel Aginsky, "A Grammar of Mende Language," in *Language
Dissertations* (Ling. Soc. of America), no. 20 (1935).

[125] Cf. Mark H. Watkins, "A Grammar of Chichewa, a Bantu Language in
British Central Africa," in *Language Dissertations* (Ling. Soc. of America), no.
24 (1937).

[126] Above we have mentioned Gilyak and Eskimo. In some Bantu languages
the one liquid is a normal (alveolar) *l*, while the other is a retroflex *ḷ* (which
sometimes is *r*-like). In such languages both liquids are often "localizable,"
as, for example, in Swahili (Mombesa dialect) where a retroflex series is in
opposition with the plain apical series; further in Pedi where the retroflex *ḷ*
clearly belongs to the apical series, while the dental *l* belongs to the lateral
series. On the consonantal systems of these languages, cf. Carl Meinhof, *Grundriss
einer Lautlehre der Bantu-Sprachen* (Berlin, 1910).

[127] Cf. A. Martinet, "La phonologie du mot en danois" (Paris, 1937) (*BSL*,
XXXVIII [1937], 2).

[128] J. R. Firth, *A Short Outline of Tamil Pronunciation* (Appendix to the
second edition of Arden's *Grammar of Common Tamil* [1934]).

[129] This special position of *r* in the Tamil consonant system has as a consequence that the *r* is the only sonorant after which other consonants may occur
(*p, t, k, n*), and which not only occurs after vowels but also after consonants
(especially after *t*). After *l, p*, and *v* are permitted, but it seems only in loanwords,
for example, "reyilvee" (railway).

[130] In any event, English *h* can in no case be considered the spirant of the guttural series. (Here Kemp Malone and A. Martinet are correct in contrast to B. Trnka.) As for French, see above, p. 126.

[131] Based on G. L. Trager in *Maître phonétique*, 3me série, no. 56.

[132] In those North Čakavian dialects where, according to A. Belić and M. Małecki, the *j* originating from Proto-Slavic *j* (as in "jaje" [egg]) is distinguished from the *j* of different origin (as in "zaja" [thirst]); the former is no consonant phoneme from a phonological point of view, but a combinatory variant of the vowel phoneme *i* in direct contact with other vowels.

[133] Cf. A. N. Tucker, *op. cit.*

[134] Cf. R. Bošković, "O prirodi, razvitku i zamenicima glasa *h* u govorima Črne Gore," in *Juž. Fil.*, XI (1931), pp. 179 ff.

[135] A. Martinet (La phonologie du mot en danois) considers Danish *v*, δ, and γ as spirants. However, he is wrong since these phonemes in Danish are treated like *r*, *l*, and *j*. True spirants in Danish are only *f* and *s*. But since these phonemes are not in opposition with any occlusives, and since they are the only representatives of the respective localization series (*f* of the labiodental series, and *s* of the sibilant series), their spirantal character is phonologically irrelevant. On the relationship *v–f*, cf. A. Martinet, *op. cit.*, p. 38.

[136] Various names have been proposed for these consonants. Probably most common is the term "consonants with glottal occlusion." This is somewhat ambiguous, however, since a glottal stop can also be an independent phoneme, and since the closure of the glottis is not a characteristic of these consonants alone. For the same reason one must reject the term "glottocclusive" which I had used in my article "Die Konsonantensysteme der ostkaukasischen Sprachen," in *Caucasica* VIII. The term "consonants of supraglottal expiration," suggested by N. Jakovlev (in his "Tablicy fonetiki kabardinskogo jazyka"), is clumsy and does not express the true nature of these consonants clearly enough. Their character is better described by the term "ejectives" used by English phoneticians (especially by Africanists). Meant hereby is the energetic thrust of the closed glottis which "ejects" the air above it like a piston. The present writer had the same in mind when he chose the term "recursives" for these consonants in 1922 in his article in *BSL*, XXIII. (Incidentally, the term had already been used earlier in Russian Caucasic studies.) The same term is used today in Indological literature; it was probably first used by R. L. Turner in *Bull. of the School of Orient. Stud.*, III, 301 ff. (but, it seems, with reference to "injective" occlusives), now also by the Indic linguist Suniti Kumar Chatterji (cf. his *Recursives in New-Indo-Aryan*, The Linguistic Society of India, Lahore, 1936).

[137] Meant here are those occlusives designated as "injectives" by the English phoneticians. After implosion, the glottis is closed and pushed down. This produces a rarefaction of air in the space between the oral and the glottal closure. The oral closure is then released without the aid of expiration, merely by means of the activity of the respective articulatory organs, and the air from the outside rushes into the oral cavity; but it is expelled immediately by the onset of normal expiration.

[138] Leonard Bloomfield interprets the preaspirated consonants of Fox as combinations (*hp, ht, hk, hč*) ("Notes on the Fox Language," in *International Journal of American Linguistics*, III, 219 ff.). In Hopi no long vowels are permitted before the preaspirated consonants (^hp, ^ht, ^hk, ^hk_o, ^hq, ^hc). According to

the laws of Hopi, this seems to point to the fact that the "preaspirated consonants" must here also be considered consonant combinations.

[139] Cf. Benjamin Lee Whorf, "The Phonetic Value of Certain Characters in Maya Writing," in *Papers of the Peabody Museum of American Archeology and Ethnology, Harvard University*, XIII (1933), no. 2, n. 3.

[140] Cf. G. N. Prokofjev, "Neneckij (juraksko-samojedskij) jazyk," in *Jazyki i pis'mennost' narodov Severa*, I, 13.

[141] Cf. Clement M. Doke, "A Study of Lamba Phonetics," in *Bantu Studies* (July 1928).

[142] Whether Modern Greek belongs to this type as well is difficult to say. It depends on whether the Modern Greek voiced occlusives *b, d*, and *g* are to be considered special phonemes or merely combinatory variants. Medially they occur only before nasals. Neither π, τ, and κ nor the voiced fricatives β, δ, and γ are permitted in that position. Medially *b, d*, and *g* are only found in loanwords. It is difficult to say to what extent these have been assimilated.

[143] Carl H. Borgström, "The Dialect of Barra in the Outer Hebrides," in *Norsk Tidsskr. for Sprogvidenskap*, VIII (1935).

[144] Cf. G. S. Lowman in *Language*, VIII (1932), 271–293.

[145] Cf., e.g., Alf Sommerfelt, "The Dialect of Torr, Co. Donegal," I (Christiania, 1922).

[146] Cf. D. V. Bubrich, *Zvuki i formy erzjanskoj reči* (Moscow, 1930), and N. S. Trubetzkoy, "Das mordwinische phonologische System verglichen mit dem Russischen," in *Charisteria Guilelmo Mathesio* (Prague, 1932), pp. 21 ff.

[147] Cf. P. P. Schumacher in *Anthropos*, XXVI.

[148] In German the situation is more complicated: in the labiodental and sibilant series the weak occlusive is absent (*p̌-f-v, c-s-z*), while in the dorsal series the weak fricative is absent (*k-g-x*).

[149] E. N. and A. A. Dragunov, "K latinizacii dialektov central'nogo Kitaja," in *Bull. de l'Acad. des Sciences de l'U.d.S.S.R., Classe des Sciences Sociales* (1932), pp. 239 ff.

[150] Cf. R. J. Swanton in *Bull. of the Bureau of American Ethnology*, no. 40, pp. 210 ff.

[151] Cf. G. P. Anagnostopulos, "Tsakonische Grammatik," in *Texte und Foschungen zur Byzantinisch-neugriechischen Philologie*, no. 5 (Berlin-Athens, 1926).

[152] Cf. H. A. Jäschke, "Tibetan Grammar," 2d ed., in *Trübners Collection of Simplified Grammars*, VIII (1883).

[153] Cf. Marcel Cohen, "Traité de langue amharique," in *Travaux et Mémoires de l'Institut d'Ethnologie*, XXIV (Paris, 1936), 30 ff.

[154] Mark Hanna Watkins, "A Grammar of Chichewa, a Bantu Language" (*Ling. Soc. of America, Language Dissertations*, no. 24 [1937]). The phoneme ƀ is described by Watkins as a kind of fricative. However, according to its position in the system it is an occlusive (weak affricate?).

[155] Cf. N. Jakovlev, *Tablicy fonetiki kabardinskogo jazyka* (Moscow, 1932). The correlation of rounding is here disregarded with respect to the dorsal consonants.

[156] Cf. J. R. Firth, "Alphabet and Phonology in India and Burma," in *Bull. of the School of Oriental Studies* (1936), p. 533; however, we disregard the correlation of timbre.

157 Cf. Franz Boas in *Bull. of the Bureau of American Ethnology*, XL, 291.

158 In Shona (a Bantu language in Rhodesia) a three-member bundle is present with respect to the occlusives: "voiceless"—"voiced-plosive"—"voiced-injective" (*p-b-bᵘ*, *t-d-dᵘ*). With respect to the fricatives, only the correlation of voice is present; and no correlation based on the manner of overcoming an obstruction is found with respect to the sonorants (cf. Clement M. Doke, *A Comparative Study in Shona Phonetics* [Johannesburg, 1931]). The structure of this system is basically not different from the one discussed above. The same is also true of the consonant system of Fulful.

159 For more details, cf. N. S. Trubetzkoy, "Die Konsonantensysteme der ostkaukasischen Sprachen," in *Caucasica*, VIII.

160 Cf. N. Jakovlev, "Kurze Übersicht über die tscherkessischen (adyghischen) Dialekte und Sprachen," in *Caucasica*, VI (1930), 1 ff., as well as N. S. Trubetzkoy, "Erinnerungen an einen Aufenthalt bei den Tscherkessen des Kreises Tuapse," in *ibid*. II, 5, f.

161 Our assumption that in Tabarasan the sonorants participate in the correlation of intensity (*Caucasica*, VIII, 25 ff.) was based on an error. Involved here was actually the correlation of gemination. Morris Swadesh pointed this out to me.

162 Cf. Boas and Swanton in *Bull. of the Bureau of American Ethnology*, XL, 880. The correlation of aspiration went unnoticed by earlier observers of Dakota. This appears to point to the fact that aspiration in this language is very weak. Such weak aspiration is also characteristic of the unmarked member of the correlation of recursion and the correlation of intensity in the North Caucasian languages. It is therefore possible that what we find in Dakota is not the correlation of aspiration but a correlation of intensity.

163 Cf. R. L. Turner, "The Sindhi Recursives or Voiced Stops Preceded by Glottal Closure," in *Bull. of the School of Oriental Studies*, III, 301 ff.

164 Cf. Suniti Kumar Chatterjee, *Recursives in New-Indo-Aryan* (The Linguistic Society of India, Lahore).

165 Cf. G. L. Trager, "ðə lɛŋwiɟ əv ðə pweblow əv Taos (*nuw meksikow)," in *Le maître phonétique*, 3ᵐᵉ série, no. 56, pp. 59 ff.

166 "Die Sandawe," in *Abhandlungen des Hamburger Kolonialinstituts*, XXXIV (1916).

167 From a phonetic point of view, the production of clicks is completely independent of breathing (and consequently of expiration). However, clicks in Sandawe never occur in isolation: they are always accompanied by a "soft," i.e., voiced offset (which is in free variation with a type of *g*), or by aspiration, or by a "hard" offset. Since all these combinations also occur in initial position where no other consonant clusters are permitted, they must be regarded as monophonematic. In the "dental" and the "lateral" click series the aspirated click is in free variation with the combination "click + *k*." In the "retroflex" click series (which we designate as guttural) the aspirated click is realized exclusively by the combination "click + *k*."

168 The consonantal differences of timbre are not taken into consideration: all obstruents except the labials are found in Sandawe in two varieties, rounded (*dw*, *kw*, *sw*, *λw*, etc.) and unrounded.

169 *The Phonetics of the Hottentot Language* (Cambridge, 1938). We limit ourselves here to the Nama dialect (with which the dialect of the Bergdama is essentially in accord).

[170] After initial nasals, only the homorganic voiced occlusives with unrestricted expiration are permitted of the consonants. In initial position the combinations *mb*, *ŋg*, and *ndz* occur, but not the combination *nd*. This is proof that *n* belongs not to the apical but to the sibilant series.

[171] For languages such as Hottentot, it would perhaps be appropriate to replace the term "apical" by "prelingual," and the term "guttural" by "postlingual," with respect to the opposition existing between the respective click series.

[172] D. M. Beach does not comment here on the relationship of length between types (*b*) and (*d*). He merely notes that these two types of clicks have a greater length than those of type (*a*).

[173] In the correlation of consonant intensity the "weak" opposition members (i.e., the light consonants) are, of course, unmarked. The same can be said of the unaspirated consonants in the correlation of aspiration. This is in accord with the fact that D. M. Beach considers the clicks of type (*a*) "the simplest clicks of Hottentot" (p. 83) and does not mark them with any diacritics in his transcription.

[174] One may perhaps ask why it is that the postlingual affricative clicks have a lateral and not a "frontal" release in the case of retroflex tongue position. We would like to believe that such a realization would not be sufficiently distinct acoustically and could easily be confused with the prelingual affricative or the postlingual plosive click series. The lateral release thus seems to be the only possible solution to the phonetic problem of realizing a postlingual fricative click.

[175] A further peculiarity is represented by the fact that the apical and the guttural series, as the only lingual series, form a bilateral opposition which can even be neutralized: before *i*, *k* and *kx* are not permitted. In this position *t* and *ts* must be regarded as "lingual occlusives in general."

[176] Cf. N. S. Trubetzkoy, "Die phonologischen Grundlagen der sogenannten 'Quantität' in verschiedenen Sprachen," in *Scritti in onore di Alfredo Trombetti* (Milan, 1936), pp. 167 ff.; "Die Quantität als phonologisches Problem," in *Actes du IVème Congrès International de Linguistes* (Copenhagen, 1938), and Morris Swadesh, "The Phonemic Interpretation of Long Consonants," in *Language*, XIII (1937), 1 ff.

[177] Cf. N. S. Trubetzkoy, "Die Konsonantensysteme der ostkaukasischen Sprachen," in *Caucasica*, VIII.

[178] Cf. O. Pletner and E. Polivanov, *Grammatika japonskogo razgovornogo jazyka* (Moscow, 1930), p. 150.

[179] Cf. A. Cholodovič, "O latinizacii korejskogo pisma," in *Sovetskoje azykoznanije*, I, pp. 147 ff.

[180] Cf. R. J. Firth, *op. cit.*, the geminated obstruents are here realized as unaspirated voiceless occlusives (with sustained closure); in other words, they have the same realization (only with a longer sustained closure) as the combinations "*r* + obstruent."

[181] Cf. V. N. Černecov in *Jazyki i pis'mennost' narodov Severa*, I, 171.

[182] Cf. W. Steinitz in *ibid.*, pp. 201 f.

[183] Cf. Morris Swadesh in *Language*, XIII, 5.

[184] This similarity is often even heightened by the fact that the geminated occlusives are unaspirated, while the corresponding ungeminated occlusives are aspirated. Cf., for example, Tamil and Artshi.

185 Cf. N. S. Trubetzkoy in *Caucasica*, VIII.

186 Cf. Paavo Ravila, *Das Quantitätssystem des seelappischen Dialekts von Maattivuono* (Helsinki, 1932); no phonological but an excellent phonetic description.

187 This seems to be the case in the dialect of Inari. Although it is not possible to arrive at the phonological system of this dialect on the basis of the description by Frans Äimäs, which is known for its phonetic exactness ("Phonetic und Lautlehre des Inarilappischen," in *Mémoires de la Société finno-ougrienne*, XLII and XLIII), it is possible to do so on the basis of the texts collected and edited by Paavo Ravila ("Reste lappischen Volksglaubens," in *Mém. de la Soc. finno-ougrienne*, XLVIII).

188 Cf. E. Sapir, "Notes on the Gweabo-Language of Liberia," in *Language*, VII, 36 and 37, and N. S. Trubetzkoy in *Scritti in onore di Alfredo Trombetti* (Milan, 1936), pp. 169 ff.

189 Cf. V. Jochel'son, "Unanganskij (aleutskij) jazyk," in *Jazyki i pis'mennost' narodov Severa*, III, 130 ff.

190 Cf. Pline Earle Goddard in *Handbook of American Indian Languages*, I.

191 Cf. E. Sapir in *ibid.*, II, 9.

192 Cf. John R. Swanton in *Bull. of the Bureau of American Ethnology*, XL.

193 More precisely, the Taz dialect of that language; cf. G. N. Prokofjev, "*Sel'-jkupskaja (ostjakosamojedskaja) grammatika*" (Leningrad, 1935), pp. 5 and 22 ff.

194 Cf. E. Sapir in *Language*, VII, 37.

195 Cf. Mark Hanna Watkins, "A Grammar of Chichewa," in *Language Dissertations*, no. 24.

196 Cf. Franz Boas in *Handbook of American Indian Languages*, I, 289.

197 Cf. Boas, *op. cit.*, p. 565.

198 Cf. Boas, *op. cit.*, p. 429.

199 Cf. Harry Hoijer, "Tonkawa, an Indian Language of Texas" (reprinted from *Handbook of American Indian Languages*, III), p. 3.

200 Cf. N. S. Trubetzkoy in *Caucasica*, VIII.

201 Cf. N. S. Trubetzkoy in *ibid*.

202 Cf. G. L. Trager in *Le maître phonétique*, 3me série, no. 56, pp. 59 ff.

203 Cf. V. Jochel'son, *loc. cit.*

204 The matter is not quite clear. In any event, the opposition *n-ɲ* is much more marked in French and carries a much greater functional load than the opposition between *n* and a nonnasal (cf. Gougenheim, "Éléments de phonologie française" (1935), pp. 44 ff.).

205 Cf. P. K. Uslar, *Etnografija Kavkaza*, Č. I., "Jazykoznanije," vyp. 3 (*Avarskij jazyk*) (Tiflis, 1889), 9.

206 Cf. *ibid.* I, vyp. 4 (Lakskij jazyk) (Tiflis, 1890), 7. Uslar adds that final *n* is pronounced as an *m* before *b*. He notes: "It may be just an auditory deception, for even the natives are not sure of the pronunciation"—a characteristic feature in the neutralization of a distinctive opposition.

207 In the descriptions of living languages with which we are familiar, we have not found any such cases. In Yoruba (Southern Nigeria) nasalized *ỹ* and *w̃* seem to be only (optional?) variants of the palatal and labiovelar nasal (cf. D. Westermann and Ida Ward, *Practical Phonetics for Students of African Languages* [London, 1933], pp. 168 ff.). In certain Slovenian dialects a nasalized *j* (from Proto-Slavic palatal *ɲ*, standard Slovenian *nj*) occurs as an independent phoneme (cf.

A. Isačenko, "Les parlers slovènes du Podjunje en Carinthie," in *Revue des études slaves*, XV ([1935], p. 57). However, apart from this *j̃*, the particular dialects do not have any palatal nasal with a complete oral closure, with which *j* would be in a relationship of bilateral opposition.

[208] Cf. D. Westermann, *Handbuch der Ful-Sprache* (Berlin, 1909), p. 197; Henri Gaden, *Le Poular, dialecte peul du Fouta Sénégalais* (*Collection de la Revue du monde musulman*, I [Paris, 1913]), p. 2. It is interesting to note that at morpheme boundary, the contact between *m* and *b* results neither in a *ḇ* nor in an *mb* but in a geminated *bb* (H. Gaden, *op. cit.*, I, 8, 9, 15). The contact of the phonemes *l*, *d*, *t*, *b* with *ḇ*, *ḍ*, *g̃*, and *j̃*, on the other hand, results in the combinations *mb*, *nd*, *ŋg*, *ɲɟ* (*ibid.*, 9, par. 15, p. 6). After the nasals, the oppositions *ḇ*, *ḍ*, *g̃*, *ɟ*—*b*, *d*, *g*, *ɟ* are neutralized (archiphoneme representative: *b*, *d*, *g*, *ɟ*). On the other hand, the oppositions *m*, *n*, *ŋ*, *ɲ*—*b*, *d*, *g*, *j̃* are neutralized before *b*, *d*, *g*, *j̃* (archiphoneme representative: *m*, *n*, *ŋ*, *ɲ*).

[209] *TCLP*, I, 50 ff.

[210] Cf. N. S. Trubetzkoy, *Anleitung zu phonologischen Beschreibungen* (Brno, 1935), pp. 21 ff.

[211] In *Bulletin de la Maison franco-japonaise*," VIII (1936), no. 1, pp. 126 ff. Cases such as Peking Chinese "*l⁴*" (two) clearly speak against the above view by L. Hjelmslev (toward which B. Trnka, *TCLP*, VI, 62, also seems to tend), according to which a monophonematic word can only consist of one vowel: in contrast with German *s!*, French *rrr!*, and Russian *s! c!* Chinese *l⁴* (two) is no interjection but a quite normal numeral.

[212] This is true only of the standard language in its Stage German pronunciation. In the dialects and in dialectally colored standard German pronunciation, *i* and *j* are different phonemes. This is the case, for example, in those dialects where *ü* changed to *i* and where the combination *ji* is consequently permitted (*jiŋər* = jünger, *jidiš* = jüdisch); or in North German where *j* is only a combinatory variant of the spirant *γ* (before front vowels or after nonback vowels respectively).

[213] In those languages where the syllable nuclei are exclusively monophonematically evaluated vowel phonemes, the difference between vowel phonemes can be defined as follows: vowels are those phonemes capable of functioning as syllable nuclei, while consonants are those phonemes that cannot occur as syllable nuclei. One might be inclined to go even further in this direction: since there is no language in which the vowels would not occur as syllable nuclei, vowels could be defined as those phonemes that function as syllable nuclei either in the form of their basic variants or as unmarked members of a correlation of syllabicity, and consonants as those phonemes that are nonsyllabic in the form of their basic variants or as unmarked members of the correlation of syllabicity. This definition is defended by R. Jakobson. But several objections can be raised against it. First, it is not always possible to establish the basic variant objectively. Second, one can only speak of syllable nuclei in those languages that have distinctive prosodic properties. In languages such as Armenian or Georgian, which do not have any prosodic properties, the "syllable" is not a phonological but a phonetic concept which can only be defined by means of the "vowel" concept but which in no way can serve as basis for the definition of the vowel. The above definition (p. 94) of the difference between "vowel" and "consonant" must therefore be sustained.

[214] Cf. N. S. Trubetzkoy, "Die phonologischen Grundlagen der sogenannten Quantität in den verschiedenen Sprachen," in *Scritti in onore di Alfredo Trombetti* (Milan, 1936), pp. 155 ff.; Trubetzkoy's paper "Die Quantität als phonologisches Problem" (*Actes du IVe Congrès International de Linguistes* [Copenhagen, 1938]); also R. Jakobson, "Über die Beschaffenheit der prosodischen Gegensätze," in *Mélanges offerts à J. van Ginneken* (Paris, 1937), pp. 24 ff.

[215] The "falling" diphthongs are, however, treated differently in Slovak; only their first vowel is considered a syllable nucleus. It is affected by the rhythmic law, only if it is long. Falling diphthongs in which the first vowel is short (e.g., *aj, au*) are considered combinations of a short vowel with a consonant. Accordingly they do not result in a shortening of the long vowels of the following syllable. Cf. R. Jakobson, "Z fonologie spisovné slovenštiny," in *Slovenská miscellanea* (Bratislava, 1931), pp. 156 ff.

[216] Cf. H. W. T. Gairdner, "The Phonetics of Arabic," in *The American University of Cairo Oriental Studies* (1925), p. 71.

[217] Cf. N. S. Trubetzkoy, "Polabische Studien," in *Sitzb. Wien Akad., Phil.-hist. Kl.*, CCXI, no. 4, pp. 126 ff.

[218] Edward Sapir, "Southern Paiute, a Shoshonean Language," in *Proceedings of the American Academy of Arts and Sciences*, 65, nos. 1–3, pp. 37 ff.

[219] Charles F. Voegelin, "Tübatulabal Grammar," in *University of California Publ. in Amer. Archeol. and Ethnol.*, 34, no. 2, pp. 75 ff. In long syllables only the first mora may be accented. If, based on iambic rhythmic law, a secondary accent falls on the second mora of a long vowel, it is shifted to the first mora of that vowel. The secondary accents then continue regularly in distances of one mora.

[220] This can be seen from the data published by Roland B. Dixon in *Handbook of American Indian Languages*, I, 683 ff. (Rare deviations from this scheme can be explained without difficulty.) It seems that the secondary accents in Maidu are distributed in accordance with the same principle as those of Paiute: where R. B. Dixon indicates two accents in a word, the second always falls on one of the "even" morae (e.g., "külü'nanamaä't" [toward evening], "basa'kömoscū'mdi" [at the end of the stick], etc.). In some cases R. B. Dixon heard only this secondary accent (cf. transcriptions such as "ūnī'di," "ākā'nas," "ātsoia," "āā'nkano," "sāmō'estodi," etc.). Incidentally, the Northeast dialect of Maidu geographically borders on Paiute.

[221] In some North Chinese dialects the "short, low tone" is realized as falling, while the "short, high tone" is realized as rising. The "long, rising tone" accordingly has two peaks (i.e., falling-rising), while the "long, falling tone" is rising-falling, so that the longer syllables are still to be equated prosodically with the combination of two short syllables. Cf. E. D. Polivanov and N. Popov-Tativa, *Posobije po kitajskoj transkripcii* (Moscow, 1928), pp. 90 f., and E. Polivanov, *Vvedenije v jazykoznanije dl'a vostokovednych vuzov* (Leningrad, 1928), pp. 118 f.

[222] Cf. R. Jakobson in *TCLP*, IV, 180 f.

[223] *Mélanges . . . van Ginneken*, pp. 32 f.

[224] Cf. Ida C. Ward, *The Phonetic and Tonal Structure of Efik* (Cambridge, 1933), p. 29: "A vowel on a rising or falling tone is generally longer than on a high or low level tone."

[225] It is possible that this is the case in the Gẽ dialect of Ewe. The syllables

"with nonlevel tone" seem here to be somewhat short, even in those cases where they originated from contraction. For example: ".eléy.i" (he is going [from ".el.e," "·ey.i"]). The long syllables, on the other hand, always seem to be level-toned, at least this is the impression one gains from reading the description of this dialect in D. Westermann and Ida C. Ward, *Practical Phonetics for Students of African Languages*, pp. 158-166, and from the examples and the sample text provided there.

226 In these languages the expiratory increment (the "dynamic accent") is bound to word-initial syllable. Accordingly it has no distinctive, only delimitative value.

227 A peculiarity in the realization of the vowels in Hopi should also be mentioned here. It has already been pointed out (in the discussion of the English vocalism, pp. 116 f.) that languages with a correlation of close contact tend to realize unchecked vowel phonemes as diphthongs of movement. A similar case seems to be on hand in Hopi. The maximally dark and maximally close vowel phoneme is here realized as *ou* in syllables of medium length and in long syllables, in short syllables, on the other hand, as *U*.

228 Though long vowels occur in this position, they do so only rarely. B. L. Whorf writes to us: ". . . three lengths do not occur in a word-final vowel. . . . If such a vowel is accentuated, its length is medium, *with very few cases of long*" (italics ours).

229 Neutralization of the opposition between long and medium-length vowels in close syllables in Hopi, is, however, subject to certain restrictions. First, syllables ending in *y* and *w* are treated as open (in other words, before syllable-final *y* and *w* all "three vowel quantities" are distinguished). Second, in monosyllabic words of the type "consonant + vowel + consonant" all three quantities are permitted as well. One may probably assume that syllable-final *y* and *w* in Hopi are considered special syllables (*yi*, *wu*?), and that monosyllabic words (such as the above examples of "păs" [very], "pas" [field], "pās" [quiet]) are interpreted as having two syllables.

230 As for the expiratory accent, primary stress in Hopi falls on the initial syllable in bisyllabic words and on the initial or second syllable in words having more than two syllables. Secondary stress falls either on the first or on the second syllable following primary stress (depending on the grammatical category involved). The remaining accents follow at a distance of one syllable each. In syllables that do not have any accent (neither primary nor secondary), the correlation of close contact and the correlation of gemination are neutralized. The unaccented vowels are here somewhat shorter than the medium-length accented vowels.

231 Cf. Stjepan Ivšić in *Rad Jugoslov. Akad.*, CXCIV, 67–68.

232 Cf. R. Jakobson in *TCLP*, IV, 168.

233 Most recently by G. S. Lowman, "The Phonetics of Albanian," in *Language*, VIII (1932), 286.

234 Cf. Boh. Havránek, "Zur phonologischen Geographie," in *Archives néerlandaises de phonétique expérimentale*, VIII–IX (1933), 29, n. 7.

235 E. D. Polivanov gives a good description of the phonetic situation in Estonian, *Vvedenije v jazykoznanije dlja vostokovednych vuzov* (Leningrad, 1928), pp. 197–202. As for those cases in which genitive, partitive, and illative are differentiated by different degrees of quantity of the stem-final *consonant* (e.g.,

"tükk" [piece], gen. "tüki" with the second degree of quantity, part. "tükki" with the third degree of quantity, and illat. "tükki" with the fourth degree of quantity of long *k*), it is to be noted that not only quantity but the distribution of intensity of the consonant ("falling," "level," and "rising" geminate) and the accentual relationship between the stem syllable and the final syllable play a role as well.

[236] Only the opposition between short (i.e., one-moric) and nonshort (i.e., bimoric) vowels may be considered truly "quantitative" (in an arithmetic sense).

[237] Cf. Ida C. Ward, *An Introduction to the Ibo Language* (Cambridge, 1935), pp. 38–41.

[238] Cf. G. Hulstaert, "Les tons en Lonkundo (Congo Belge)," in *Anthropos*, XXIX.

[239] Cf. Ida C. Ward, *The Phonetic and Tonal Structure of Efik* (Cambridge, 1933).

[240] Cf. Ida C. Ward, *An Introduction to the Ibo Language* (Cambridge, 1935).

[241] Cf. H. J. Uldall, "A Sketch of Achumawi Phonetics," in *Internat. Journ. of American Linguistics*, VIII (1933), 73 ff.

[242] Cf. Clement M. Doke, "A Study of Lamba Phonetics," in *Bantu Studies* (July 1928), pp. 5 ff.

[243] Cf. Ethel G. Aginsky, "A Grammar of the Mende Language," in *Language Dissertations publ. by the Linguistic Society of America*, no. 20, p. 10.

[244] The author herself seems to hint at this. On page 105 in her text analysis she says with respect to the word (77) ye_3e_1 that this stem should actually be ye_4e_2: "lower tonal pattern here due to final position in sentence."

[245] Cf. Clement M. Doke, "The Phonetics of the Zulu Language," in *Bantu Studies*, II (July 1926), Special Number.

[246] *Language, VII* (1931), 33 ff.

[247] This is not contradicted by tone register systems, such as in Nama Hottentot (cf. D. M. Beach, *The Phonetics of the Hottentot Language*, Chap. IX, 124–143), which have three tone registers but distinguish rising and falling "tones" in each of them. A high rising tone seems to presuppose a movement from the high register to an even higher one. The low falling tone (which in Nama is actually falling only in disyllabic words, and "level" elsewhere) likewise presupposes a movement from the low register to an even lower one. In reality each register should not be thought of as a point, but as a range within which either tone movement in Nama takes place. It is also significant that these movements comprise only quite small intervals: the high rising tone and the mid falling tone comprise one tone, the low rising tone and the high falling tone one half tone (cf. the table by D. M. Beach, *op. cit.*, pp. 131 and 141). Only the mid rising tone comprises a third (four half tones) and really shows a movement from the mid to the high register.

[248] Cf. O. Gjerdman, "Critical Remarks on Intonation Research," in *Bull. of the School of Oriental Studies*, III, 495 ff.

[249] Cf. Daniel Jones and Kwing Tong Woo, *A Cantonese Phonetic Reader* (University of London Press), as well as Liu Fu, *Études expérimentales sur les tons du Chinois* (Paris-Peking, 1925); now also Jaime de Angulo in *Le maître phonétique*, 3ᵉ série, no. 60 (1937), p. 69.

[250] Cf. F. Lorentz, *Slovinzische Grammatik* (St. Petersburg, Akad. der Wiss., 1903); N. S. Trubetzkoy in *TCLP*, I, 64.

[251] Cf. E. D. Polivanov, *Vvedenije v jazykoznanije dl'a vostokovednych vuzov* (Leningrad, 1928), pp. 120 ff.

[252] Cf. R. Jakobson in *TCLP*, IV, 172 f.

[253] Cf. E. D. Polivanov, *op. cit.*, pp. 118 ff.; also E. D. Polivanov and N. Popov-Tativa, *Posobije po kitajskoj transkripcii* (Moscow, 1928), pp. 90 f.

[254] Cf. R. Jakobson, "Z zagadnień prozodji starogreckiej," in *Prace ofiarowane Kaz. Wóycickiemu* (Wilno, 1937), pp. 73–88.

[255] Cf. A. Ivanov and E. Polivanov, *Grammatika sovremennogo kitajskogo jazyka* (Moscow, 1930).

[256] But not South Chinese! Compare what has been said about the dialect of Canton (p. 188).

[257] Cf. A. V. Isačenko, "Der slovenische fünffüssige Jambus," in *Slavia* XIV, 45 ff. (particularly p. 53).

[258] R. Jakobson in *TCLP*, IV, 173 f.

[259] Cf. R. Jakobson, *op. cit.*, p. 174.

[260] For more details, cf. the pioneer study by R. Jakobson, "Die Betonung und ihre Rolle in der Wort- und Syntagmaphonologie," in *TCLP*, IV, 164 ff. (particularly pp. 176 ff.).

[261] E. D. Polivanov, *Vvedenije v jazykoznanije dlja vostokovednych vuzov*, pp. 70 ff.

[262] The fact that the accented syllable is here not simply musically high but musically rising (at least in most cases) appears to have its basis in "syntagmatic phonology," i.e., in an effort to distinguish the free accent from the delimitative accent as clearly as possible. For the latter the expiratory force is what is most essential. But insofar as there is also a musical aspect to it, it is falling.

[263] Cf. H. J. Uldall, "A Sketch of Achumawi Phonetics," in *Intern. Journ. of American Linguistics*, VIII (1933), 75 and 77.

[264] Cf. J. R. Firth, "Notes on the Transcription of Burmese," in *Bull. of the School of Orient. Stud.*, VII, 137 ff.

[265] Such short vowels with stød are found, among others, in certain Danish dialects. Prof. Dr. Christen Møller (Aarhus), whose native dialect has this peculiarity, was kind enough to give me some examples. I had the impression that the total length of the short vowel and the pause following the glottal closure corresponded approximately to one normal length. In the case of the bimoric syllable nuclei with stød no pause was audible in the pronunciation of Prof. Christen Møller. However, the syllable nucleus is clearly divided into a loud and a low part. The border between these two parts is very clearly marked. Their total duration corresponds again approximately to one normal length (i.e., to a length without stød). Lauri Kettunen presents a similar picture for Livonian ("Untersuchungen über die livische Sprache," in *Acta et Commentationes Universitatis Dorpatensis*, VII, 3 [Tartu, 1925], pp. 4 ff. and particularly the attached kymograms). R. Ekblom's observations on the acute accent (*Stossakzent*) in Latvian are also instructive (*Die lettischen Akzentarten* (Uppsala, 1933), especially pp. 23 f., 42, and 47 f).

[266] Carl Borgström, "Zur Phonologie der norwegischen Schriftsprache," in *Norsk Tidskrift for Sprogvidenskap*, IX (1937), 250 ff. Of the phonetic descriptions of the Southeast Norwegian prosodic system, I would like to call special attention to the exemplary, clear, and precise presentation by Olaf Broch, "Rhythm in the Spoken Norwegian Language," in *Philological Society Transactions* (1935), pp. 80–112.

[267] Cf. W. Stalling, *Das phonologische System des Schwedischen* (Nijmegen, 1934). A very good, though by no means phonological, but purely instrumental-phonetic study of Swedish intonation is presented under this misleading title.

[268] Cf. S. Karcevskij, "Sur la phonologie de la phrase," in *TCLP*, IV, 188–228.

[269] A correlation of tone movement differentiating words in Europe is found only in Norwegian, Swedish, Lithuanian, Latvian, North Kashubian (Slovincian), Slovenian, Serbo-Croatian, North Albanian (Geg), as well as in some German and Dutch dialects. Cf. R. Jakobson, "Sur la théorie des affinités phonologiques," in *Actes du IVe Congrès International de Linguistes* (Copenhagen, 1938).

[270] Cf. the above work by Stalling, *Das phonologische System des Schwedischen* (Nijmegen, 1934).

[271] Cf. Ante Dukić, *Marija devica čakavska pjesma* (Zagreb, 1935). A short description of the prosodic system of the dialect of the poet is given. Also cf. A. Belić, "O rečeničnom akcentu u kastavskom govoru," in *Juž. Fil.*, XIV (1935), 151 ff., including a rich collection of attestations from the poetic writings of Ante Dukić.

[272] D. Westermann and Ida C. Ward, *Practical Phonetics for Students of African Languages* (London, 1933), p. 178.

[273] On question intonation in various languages, cf. P. Kretschmer, "Der Ursprung des Fragetons und Fragesatzes," in *Scritti in onore di Alfredo Trombetti* (Milan, 1936), pp. 29 ff.

[274] As is known, interpolated vocatives were marked by low tone already in the Rg-Veda.

[275] The accented syllable of an isolated word in Russian not only has its full (unreduced) quantitative and qualitative value, but it is also louder with respect to expiration than the unaccented syllables. This is explained by the fact that an isolated word must be regarded as an independent sentence.

[276] Cf. also A. Belić, "L'accent de la phrase et l'accent du mot," in *TCLP*, IV, 183 ff.

[277] Cf. R. Jakobson in *Mélanges offerts à Jacques van Ginneken* (Paris, 1937), pp. 26 ff., and in *Bulletin du Cercle ling. de Copenhague*, II (1936–1937), 7.

[278] Cf. V. Mathesius, "K výslovnosti cizích slov v češtině," in *Slovo a slovesnost*, I, 36 f., and "Zur synchronischen Analyse fremden Sprachguts," in *English Studies* (1925), pp. 21–35.

[279] E. Sapir, "The Takelma Language of South-western Oregon," in *Handbook of American Indian Languages*, II, 8 (and n. 2).

Translator's note: On p. 107, the terms "low/nonlow," "high/nonhigh" are translations of the German terms "breit" and "eng" (lit., "wide" and "narrow").

Otto v. Essen defines the German terms "weit" (here "breit") and "eng" as synonyms of "offen" and "geschlossen" (open and close). Trubetzkoy does not seem to use the terms "breit" and "eng" in this sense, at least not consistently. See especially pp. 109 and 110, where in addition to "breit" and "eng" (transl. "low" and "high") also the terms "offen" (open) and "geschlossen" (close) are used. But cf. p. 235, where "eng" in the sense of "geschlossen" (close) is in juxtaposition with "offen" (open).—Otto v. Essen, *Allgemeine und Angewandte Phonetik* (Berlin: Akademie-Verlag, 1962), p. 75.

V TYPES OF NEUTRALIZATION OF DISTINCTIVE OPPOSITIONS

1 GENERAL OBSERVATIONS

Individual languages are distinguished from each other not only by their phonemic inventories and their prosodic means but also by the way in which these distinctive elements are utilized. German has the phoneme η ("ng"), but it is only used in final and medial position, never before the "determinate" vowels. In Evenki (Tungus) the same phoneme η is used in all positions, that is, not only medially and finally but also initially and before all vowels. The phoneme r, on the other hand, which in German is used finally, medially, and initially, cannot occur in initial position in Evenki. Similar limitations on the use of certain phonemes are found in all languages. They are just as characteristic of the phonemic system of the individual languages and dialects as are differences in the phonemic inventory.

Very important in this respect are the rules for neutralization of the phonological oppositions. Neutralization takes place in certain positions. The number of phonemes that occur in these positions is hence smaller than in other positions. In addition to the total system of phonemes or of prosodic properties there accordingly also exist *partial systems*. These are valid only for specific positions, and only part of the phonological means of the total system is represented in them. The rules for neutralization differ from language to language, even from dialect to dialect. Still it is possible to uncover certain types that, in the final analysis, form the basis of all kinds of neutralization in the various languages and dialects.[1]

One must particularly distinguish between types of neutralization that are contextually conditioned and types of neutralization that are structurally conditioned. This depends on whether a phonological opposition is neutralized in the environment of specific phonemes or, regardless of phonemes, in specific positions in the word only. Furthermore, one must distinguish between *regressive* and *progressive* types of neutralization, depending on whether the neutralization takes place *after* "something" or *before* "something." But this classification is not exhaustive. In some instances the neutralization is neither regressive nor progressive alone but is both regressive and progressive.

2 CONTEXTUALLY CONDITIONED TYPES OF NEUTRALIZATION

The types of neutralization that are contextually conditioned fall into a *dissimilative* and an *assimilative* class. It all depends on whether the phonemes in question are dissimilated from the "contextual phoneme" with respect to a particular phonic property or are assimilated to it. Since this always involves the loss of a phonological property, it is clear that dissimilative neutralization takes place only in the vicinity of those phonemes that have the property in question, while assimilative neutralization takes place only in the environment of phonemes that do not have this property.

A   Dissimilative Neutralization

With reference to *dissimilative* neutralization, various additional subtypes must be distinguished. The "contextual phonemes," in the vicinity of which a phonological opposition is neutralized, may either have the

229

particular phonological property itself or only a phonologically related property. Further, the contextual phoneme may possess the particular property (or a related property) only positively, or it may possess it positively as well as negatively. In other words, neutralization may take place either in the vicinity of the marked member or in the vicinity of the marked as well as the unmarked member of the same opposition or of a related (privative) opposition. Four possible types of dissimilative neutralization result.

a. The neutralization of a phonological opposition takes place in the vicinity of both members of the same opposition. In very many languages the opposition between voiced and voiceless obstruents is neutralized in the vicinity of voiced as well as voiceless obstruents. (The representative of the archiphoneme in this case is "externally conditioned," that is, it is the same as the contextual phoneme with regard to type of voicing.) For example: Serbo-Croatian "srb" (Serb, masc.): "srpski" (Serbian): "srpkinja" (Serb, fem.); "naručiti" (to order): "narudžba" (the order). In French the opposition between nasalized and nonnasalized vowels is neutralized before all vowels, that is, it is neutralized before nasalized as well as nonnasalized vowels. (The nonnasalized vowels function here as representatives of the archiphoneme because they are the unmarked members of this opposition.)

b. A phonological opposition is neutralized in the vicinity of the marked member of this opposition, but is retained in the vicinity of the unmarked member. In Slovak, for example, the opposition between long and short vowels is neutralized after a syllable with a long syllable nucleus. (The unmarked short vowels function here as the representatives of the archiphoneme.) A rare case of this type is found in Sanskrit. The opposition between dental and "retroflex" *n* is neutralized after a retroflex *ṣ*. (Neutralization takes place not only when it follows directly but also when vowels, labials, or gutturals occur in between.) It is retained, however, not only after nonretroflex *s* but also after all other retroflex consonants (*ḍ, ḍh, ṭ, ṭh*).

c. A phonological opposition is neutralized in the vicinity of both members of a related phonological opposition. "Relatedness" is here based on the classification of phonological oppositions illustrated above. For example, in Lezghian (K'üri) the opposition between rounded and unrounded consonants is neutralized before and after high vowels (*u, ü, i*) because these vowels are members of the opposition of timbre "rounded"/"unrounded." The low vowels *a, e*, on the other hand, do not participate in this opposition.[2]

d. A phonological opposition is neutralized in the vicinity of the marked member of a related opposition, but retains its phonological validity in the vicinity of the corresponding unmarked member. E.g., in Japanese, Lithuanian, and Bulgarian the opposition between palatalized and nonpalatalized consonants is only phonologically valid before back vowels. It is neutralized before front vowels. (The choice of the archiphoneme in this case is conditioned internally in Bulgarian, externally in Lithuanian, and in Japanese internally before *e* and externally before *i*.) In Mordvin the opposition between palatalized and nonpalatalized apicals and liquids (*t-t'*, *d-d'*, *n-ń*, *r-ŕ*, *l-l'*) is neutralized after front vowels. (The choice of the archiphoneme is here conditioned externally.)[3] In the languages of the Eastern Caucasus which have a correlation of consonantal rounding (Ch'ak'ur, Rutulian, Artshi, Aghul, Darghinian, Kubachi), this correlation is neutralized before rounded vowels (the archiphoneme representative being conditioned internally).[4] In French the opposition between nasalized and nonnasalized vowels is neutralized before nasal consonants (i.e., before the marked members of the correlation of consonantal nasalization). This is true at least within a morpheme before *m* (before *n* only one exception is found: *ennui*). In the Maattivuono dialect of the Sea Lapps (as well as in the Inari dialect and in some other dialects) the opposition between long (bimoric) and short (one-mora) vowels is neutralized before long geminated consonants.[5]

Sometimes the neutralization of an opposition in the vicinity of the marked opposition member is proof of the "relatedness" of the two oppositions. For example, in the Štokavian-Evakian dialects of Serbo-Croatian the apical and the sibilant series of localization are "split," that is, they are represented each by two series, so that the entire consonantal system takes on the following shape:

(*p*)	*t*	*ć*	(*k*)	*c*	*č*
(*b*)	*d*	*d*	(*g*)	[*dz*]	[*dž*]
(*m*)	*n*	*ń*			
(*v*)	*l*	*ļ*			
				s	*š*	(*h*)
				z	*ž*	

The relationship of opposition between the *t* and the *ć* series, although it is bilateral, is equipollent. The same is true for the oppositive relationship between the *c* and the *č* series. Both of these equipollent bilateral oppositions are neutralizable. Neutralization in these cases is contextually conditioned: the opposition between the *t* and the *ć* phonemes are neutralized before *t* and *ć* phonemes (type *a*): the oppositions between the *s* and *š* phonemes are neutralized before *č* (type *b*). But further, the opposition between *s* (*z*) and *š* (*ž*) is neutralized before the *ć* phonemes. (The archiphoneme representatives in this case are either *š*, *ž*, or special intermediary sounds *ŝ* and *ẑ*.) This circumstance presents proof that, from the point of view of the phonological system of these dialects, the opposition between the *t* and the *ć* series is "related" to the opposition between the two sibilant series (but not identical with it). In the East Bavarian dialects (as, for example, in Vienna) the opposition between *i*, *e*, *äi* and *ü*, *ö*, *äü* (which originated from *il*, *el*, *eil* and *ül*, *öl*, *äül* respectively) is found in all positions except before liquids: *i*, *e*, and *äi* may occur before *r*, while *ü*, *ö*, and *äü* may occur before *l*. This neutralization of the opposition of vocalic rounding before liquids (which, historically, resulted from the fact that the phoneme combination *lr* did not exist in German) creates a type of relatedness between the opposition *i-ü* (and *e-ö*, etc.) on the one hand, and the opposition *r-l* on the other. From the point of view of the. dialects mentioned, the *r* may be regarded as the clearer, and the *l* as the darker liquid. Thus one cannot always arrive at the "relatedness" of individual oppositions within particular phonological systems from general discussions alone.

B   Assimilative Neutralization

In the case of contextually conditioned *assimilative* neutralization the opposition members lose their opposition mark in the vicinity of those phonemes that do not have the particular opposition mark. In Eastern Cheremis, for example, the opposition between the voiceless occlusives (*p*, *t*, *k*, *c*, *ć*, *č*) and the voiced spirants (*β*, *δ*, *γ*, *z*, *ź*, *ž*) is neutralized after nasals. (Special voiced occlusives, that is, *b*, *d*, *g*, з, з́, з̌, which occur only in this position, function here as archiphoneme representatives.)[6] The nasals are neither voiceless, nor are they spirants, that is, they do not have the marks that are characteristic for the opposition of Cheremis obstruents. But, on the other hand, they are voiced consonants with a complete oral closure. The opposition between *p-β*, *t-δ*, etc., after nasals is neutralized in such a way that the archiphoneme loses the discriminative marks of an obstruent (because, from the point of view of Cheremis, obstruents are either voiceless occlusives or fricatives). But it still remains distinct from a nasal because it does not acquire the characteristic of nasals, namely, nasality.

This example shows that the contextual phoneme must share certain features with the members of the neutralized opposition in the case of assimilative neutralization. It must in some way be closer to them than to the other phonemes of the same system. The mark, however, that distinguishes the members of the neutralized opposition from each other must be completely alien to the contextual phoneme.

We already mentioned that the degree of aperture is a specifically vocalic mark. Assimilative neutralization of the oppositions based on degree of aperture can therefore only take place before those consonants that in some way show more relatedness to vowels than do all other consonants, but nevertheless remain consonants. In standard German the phoneme ŋ (ng) belongs to this category. Before it the oppositions ü-ö and u-o are in fact neutralized. (The "external" members of these gradual oppositions, that is, ü and u, function as the representatives of the archiphoneme.) As a sonorant and as a sound produced with the dorsum of the tongue, ŋ is closer to the vowels than all other consonantal phonemes of German. In many languages and dialects certain differences in degree of aperture are neutralized before nasals or before liquids (or, in particular, before tautosyllabic nasals or liquids). This is explained by the fact that nasals and liquids are closer to vowels than the remaining consonants, yet still are not vowels. In other words, they do not have a distinctive degree of aperture. In order to produce an assimilative neutralization of the differences of degree of aperture, the contextual phoneme must *in some respect* be closer to vowels than the other consonants. Liquids and nasals are closer to vowels because they represent the weakest type of obstacle (i.e., the "lowest degree of obstruction"). In other words, they least possess the properties that are specifically consonantal. But one can also approach vowels from another direction, namely, from the point of view of localization coordinate. For example, in Polabian the opposition between ü and ö was neutralized before gutturals, labials, and palatalized consonants. (The archiphoneme was, of course, always represented by ü.) If one considers that the gutturals were characterized by dorsal articulation, the labials by lip participation, and the palatalized consonants by a shift of the entire bulk of the tongue toward the front, it becomes comprehensible that these series of localization in particular were closest to the front rounded vowels. When we discussed the English vowel system, we saw that, for the unchecked vowel phonemes of standard English, the phonological opposition between direction of articulatory movement away from the center and direction of articulatory movement toward the center was characteristic. This specifically vocalic opposition is neutralizable only before r. (The vowel phonemes with an articulatory movement toward the center, i.e., $u^ə$, $ɔ^ə$, $ɑ^ə$, $a^ə$, $ε^ə$, $i^ə$, represent the archiphonemes.) Of all English consonants, r is the one that is closest to the vowels. But it lacks the specifically vocalic marks of type of contact and direction of articulatory movement.

C   Combined Contextually Conditioned Neutralization

By *combined* contextually conditioned type of neutralization we mean any combination of an assimilative neutralization with a dissimilative neutralization. For example, when in Bulgarian, Lithuanian, and Polabian the opposition between palatalized and nonpalatalized consonants is neutralized before all consonants, this is a case of combined contextually conditioned neutralization: the neutralization is obviously dissimilative in nature before the consonants that are themselves members of the palatalization correlation. It is assimilative, however, before the consonants that do not participate in the correlation of palatalization. Lezghian (K'üri) presents a complicated, yet very instructive, example of a combined contextually conditioned neutralization.[7] The correlation of consonantal intensity is here present only with voiceless (nonrecursive) occlusives, that is, heavy and light tenues are distinguished before accented vowels. But this opposition is neutralized:

(*a*) After a syllable consisting of a "voiceless, nonrecursive occlusive + a high vowel" (archiphoneme representative: the heavy tenuis). For example: "kit·àb" (book).

(*b*) After a syllable consisting of a "voiceless spirant + a high vowel" (the archiphoneme is represented by the heavy tenuis). For example: "fit·è" (veil).

(*c*) After a syllable formed by a "voiceless recursive occlusive + vowel" (the archiphoneme is represented by the light tenuis). For example: "č'utàr" (fleas).

(*d*) After a syllable consisting of a "voiced occlusive + an open vowel" (the archiphoneme is represented by the light tenuis). For example: "gatùn" (to beat, knock).

It is clear that neutralization in position (*a*) is dissimilative, but assimilative in the remaining positions (*b*), (*c*), and (*d*). In cases (*b*), (*c*), and (*d*) the initial consonants of the preceding syllable always have something in common with the nonrecursive voiceless occlusives: voicelessness in the case of (*b*); voicelessness and occlusion in the case of (*c*); and occlusion in the case of (*d*). On the other hand, these consonants do not participate in the correlation of intensity. Neutralization of this correlation in its vicinity can therefore be regarded as assimilative. But in those syllables that begin with sonorants (*r, l, m, n, w, j*) or with voiced fricatives (*v, g, z, ž, γ*), or end in a vowel, the opposition between heavy and light voiceless occlusives is retained. The reason for this is that neither the sonorants nor the voiced fricatives nor the vowels have properties in common with the voiceless occlusives (with the exception of infraglottal expiration, which, however, is too general a property). For example: "rüq·èdin" (ash, gen.): "rug·ùn" (to send); "mekü" (other): "mak·al" (sickle); "jatùr" (calf of the leg): "jat·àr" (waters); "akà" (ovenhole): "ak·ùn" (to see); "γucàr" (God): "γelc·in" (sled, gen.). In the same language the opposition between recursive and nonrecursive occlusives is neutralized before a pretonic close vowel followed by any obstruent. (The archiphoneme is here represented by a nonrecursive occlusive.) Before open pretonic vowels, however, this opposition is retained. For example: "kašàr" (heavy breathings): "k'ašàr" (sledgehammers). There is no doubt that the unaccented close vowels having the specifically vocalic properties in the least degree are the ones that are closest to the consonants.

3 STRUCTURALLY CONDITIONED TYPES OF NEUTRALIZATION

Structurally conditioned types of neutralization in turn are divided into *centrifugal* and *reductive* classes.

A Centrifugal Neutralization

In the *centrifugal* type a phonological opposition is neutralized at the word or morpheme boundaries respectively. In other words, it is neutralized either in initial or final position only, or in both initial and final position. For example, the opposition between voiced and voiceless consonants is neutralized only initially in Erza-Mordvin, only in final position in Russian, Polish, Czech, etc., and initially as well as finally in Kirghiz (previously Karakirghiz).[8] In standard German the opposition between fortes and lenes is neutralized in final position, but the opposition between the two types of *s* (the "soft" lenis *s* and the "sharp" fortis *s*) is also neutralized in initial position. In the Bavarian-Austrian dialects the opposition between lenes and fortes is not neutralized finally, but only initially. In standard German, Dutch, English, Norwegian, and Swedish the opposition between long (unchecked) and short (checked) vowels is neutralized in final position. (The archiphoneme here is represented by the unchecked vowels.) In the Czech spoken language (Middle Bohemian) the opposition between long (heavy) and short (light) vowels is neutralized in initial position. (The archiphonemes here are represented by the short vowels.) In Lithuanian the opposition between vowels with a rising accent and vowels with a falling accent is neutralized in final position. (Vowels with a rising accent function here as archiphoneme representatives.) In most languages where the correlation of consonantal gemination is present, the latter is neutralized in initial as well as in final position.

B   Reductive Neutralization

By *reductive* neutralization we mean the neutralization of a phonological opposition in all syllables of the word except in the syllable that forms the phonological peak. This culminative syllable is generally marked by "accent" (i.e., by an expiratory increase in force or by a musical rise in pitch). Two types can be distinguished.

a. The position of the culminative syllable is free and can have a distinctive function. In such a case it is always "accented," that is, we have a culminative differentiation of the prosodemes. In cases of this type certain phonological oppositions occur only in accented syllables. They are neutralized in all unaccented syllables. For example, in South Great Russian the oppositions *o-a* and *e-i* are neutralized in unaccented syllables, in the dialects of Bulgarian and Modern Greek the oppositions *o-u* and *e-i*, and in Slovenian the opposition between long (bimoric) vowels and short (one-mora) vowels. In the Jauntal dialect of Carinthian-Slovenian the opposition of vocalic nasalization is neutralized in unaccented syllables, and so on. In all these cases neutralization takes place in both directions, that is, before as well as after the accented syllable. But examples are not lacking of neutralizations that are only progressive (pretonic) or only regressive (posttonic). In standard Serbo-Croatian the oppositions of vocalic quantity are neutralized *before* the syllable with primary stress. In Lezghian (K'üri), as we have already mentioned, the opposition between recursive and nonrecursive occlusives is neutralized before high vowels in pretonic syllables, while it is maintained in posttonic syllables. But in the same language the oppositions between rounded and unrounded consonants and between heavy and light tenues are neutralized before *posttonic* vowels.

b. The position of the culminative syllable is not free but bound by a word boundary. In other words, the peak in all words is formed either by the initial syllable or by the final syllable. Certain phonological oppositions then occur only in the particular culminative syllable. They are neutralized in all other syllables of the word. In the Scottish spoken on Barra Island,[9] the opposition between *e* and *æ*, on the one hand, and the correlation of consonantal aspiration, on the other, are neutralized in all syllables except the initial syllable. In Chechen the opposition between recursive and infraglottal consonants (except the pair *q-q'*) and the "correlation of emphatic palatalization" are likewise phonologically relevant only in initial position.[10] In Eastern Bengali the correlation of recursion and the correlation of aspiration are found only initially.[11] In the Maattivuono dialect of the Sea Lapps, which has already been mentioned, the correlation of vocalic gemination is neutralized in all noninitial syllables of a word. Further, the correlation of consonantal gemination and intensity is found only after the vowel (or diphthong) of the word-initial syllable. In the Turkic, Finno-Ugric, Mongolian, and Manchurian languages, which have what is known as "vowel harmony," certain oppositions of vocalic timbre (usually the opposition based on tongue position, but sometimes also the opposition based on lip position) are fully relevant only in word-initial syllables. In the remaining syllables these oppositions are neutralized. The choice of the representative of the archiphoneme is here conditioned externally. In other words, with respect to tongue position, the vowels of the noninitial syllable always belong to the same class as the vowels of the preceding syllable. In all these cases—and the number can easily be multiplied— it is the first syllable that is culminative. In much rarer cases this role falls to the final syllable. In French, for example, the opposition between *é* (phonet. *e*) and *è* (phonet. *ɛ*) is distinctive only in open final position.[12]

If one takes a closer look at the languages in which the position of the peak is not free, one discovers that in most cases the phonologically culminative syllable stands out with respect to expiration as well. This, of course, only involves a delimitative accent without any distinctive meaning. The phonological culminative syllable that is bound to a particular word boundary thus represents only the most appropriate place for such an accent. It is not at all necessary to associate this syllable with the delimitative accent. There are many languages in which the position of the bound delimitative accent does not coincide with the bound phonological word peak. Most Turkic languages in particular are of this type. Vowel harmony indicates that the phonological word peak here occurs on the initial syllable. Still, most Turkic languages do not have the delimitative expiratory accent on the word-initial, but on the word-final, syllable.[13]

It is possible that there are also languages in which the phonological peak is fixed on the penultimate syllable. The system of tone registers that has been described above for Zulu (p. 186) shows that in that language only two tones are distinguished in final syllable—a low tone (Types I, II, III, and VI) and a mid tone (Types IV and V). The antepenultimate syllable also distinguishes only two tones, namely, a high tone (Types II, III, V, and VI) and a mid tone (Types I and IV). But on the penultimate syllable all three tones are distinguished: a high tone by Type I, a mid tone by Type VI, and a low tone by Types II and V, and, further, a falling tone (Types III and IV). Accordingly oppositions of tone are found here on the penultimate syllable which are neutralized on the other syllables. The penultimate thus becomes culminative. It should be noted that the penultimate syllable in Zulu (as in most Bantu languages in general) also receives a (purely delimitative) expiratory increase in force.[14]

It is difficult to evaluate those cases where a prosodic opposition of tone movement is phonologically relevant in a boundary syllable only, as, for example, in Latvian or in Estonian. Since differences of tone movement in final analysis are based on putting the individual morae of a "long syllable nucleus into relief," the accent in such languages (in the sense of a culminative differentiation of morae) is free. On the other hand, this freedom of accent refers only to the two morae of the word-initial syllable. This syllable thereby becomes the phonological peak. But the case of Classical Greek must be distinguished from cases of this type. At first glance it seems as if in Classical Greek the opposition between "rising" and "falling" accent ("acute" and "circumflex") had distinctive force only in word-final syllable. The circumflex accent could not occur on the antepenultimate. On the penultimate the opposition of tone movement was automatically conditioned by the quantity of the final syllable. But in reality the acute accent on final syllables was not an accent in the proper sense, but merely an externally conditioned rise in pitch of the word-final mora. This rise in pitch occurred before a pause, if the word did not have any other high mora, and also before the enclitics, if the penultimate mora of the word was not high (for this reason not only ἀγαθός ἐστι but also δῆμός ἐστι = déemós esti and ἄνθρωπός ἐστι). The difference in tone movement in Classical Greek was thus not only conditioned externally with respect to the penultimate but also with respect to the final syllable.[15]

C   Combined Structurally Conditioned Neutralization

Both forms of structurally conditioned neutralization can combine with one another. In the so-called Turanian languages it often happens that certain consonantal oppositions are neutralized in initial position (the centrifugal type), while certain vocalic or prosodic oppositions are neutralized in noninitial syllables of a word (the reductive type). In Cheremis the consonantal correlation of voice is neutralized in initial position. But in addition this language has strict vowel harmony, which, as already mentioned, requires that the vocalic oppositions of timbre be neutralized in noninitial syllables. In the language of the Sea Lapps of Maattivuono the vocalic and the consonantal correlation of gemination and the correlation of consonantal intensity are neutralized in noninitial syllables, while the correlation of consonantal tension is neutralized initially.[16]

4   MIXED TYPES OF NEUTRALIZATION

Finally, different types of structurally conditioned neutralization can combine with different types of contextually conditioned neutralization.

In the Serbo-Croatian Čakavian dialects of Novi[17] and Castua[18] the opposition between long (bimoric) and short (one-mora) syllable nuclei is neutralized before a syllable with falling primary accent (the archiphonemes being, of course, represented by the short nuclei). Since in these dialects[19] the falling accent is the marked member of the opposition of tone movement, and since the latter is found only on accented long syllable nuclei, this involves the neutralization of an opposition in the vicinity of the marked member of a related opposition. In other words, this is a contextually conditioned dissimilative neutralization of the type (*d*). But at the same time this also involves the neutralization of an opposition in an unaccented syllable, that is, a reductive structurally conditioned neutralization of the type (*a*). In Circassian (Adyghe) the opposition between the maximally open vowel phoneme (*a*) and the vowel phoneme of a mid degree of aperture (*e*) is neutralized in certain positions. The maximally open *a* here always functions as the representative of the archiphoneme. Neutralization occurs in the first place in an accented syllable if the following syllable contains an *e*. It also takes place in initial position regardless of the vowel of the following syllable. The first case involves a dissimilative contextually conditioned type of neutralization of the type (*b*). The second case involves a structurally conditioned centrifugal type of neutralization. In Latin the opposition between *u* and *o* was neutralized before nasals in final syllables. (The archiphoneme was always represented by *u*, as, for example, in the endings *-um*, *-unt*.) This was a combination of the contextually conditioned assimilative type of neutralization with the structurally conditioned centrifugal type.

5   EFFECT OF THE VARIOUS
   TYPES OF NEUTRALIZATION

Combinations of several types of neutralization can have an effect in two opposite directions. They may limit each other to such an extent that a neutralizable opposition is practically neutralized only in very few positions, while it retains its distinctive force in the overwhelming majority of positions. But they may also be cumulative, so that the particular neutralizable opposition functions distinctively only in a very restricted area. In Lithuanian, Polabian, and East Bulgarian the opposition between palatalized and nonpalatalized consonants is found only before back vowels (in other words, it is found only before phonemes that do not share any phonological properties with the palatalized consonants). In all other positions the correlation of palatalization is neutralized in these languages, before consonants by a combined contextually conditioned neutralization;

before front vowels by a dissimilative structurally conditioned neutralization of the type (*d*); and in final position by a structurally conditioned neutralization.

In many languages a preference for certain types of neutralization or for specific positions of neutralization can be observed. In certain positions several phonological oppositions are neutralized, while in certain others all phonological oppositions remain intact. Thus *positions of minimal* and *positions of maximal phoneme distinction* are created in the same language.[20] Incidentally, there need not exist any parallelism in the distinction of vowel phonemes and the distinction of consonantal phonemes. In Bulgarian, for example, all vowel phonemes are differentiated in accented syllables between consonants and in final position. In unaccented syllables, on the other hand, the oppositions *u-o*, *i-e*, and *ă(Ъ)-a* are neutralized (at least in East Bulgarian pronunciation). Accordingly only three archiphonemes (*u*, *i*, *a*) are distinguished here. Before the unaccented vowels *u* and *a*, accented vowels only occur in loanwords, and unaccented *i* is nonsyllabic after vowels. As for the consonants, all thirty-six consonantal phonemes are distinguished before back vowels (*p*, *ṕ*, *b*, *b'*, *m*, *ḿ*, *t*, *t'*, *d*, *d'*, *n*, *ń*, *k*, *ḱ*, *g*, *ǵ*, *x*, *c*, *č*, *s*, *š*, *z*, *ž*, *ć*, *dź*, *ś*, *ź*, *f*, *f'*, *v*, *v́*, *l*, *l'*, *r*, *ŕ*, *j*). The correlation of palatalization is neutralized before sonorants (*l*, *l'*, *r*, *ŕ*, *m*, *ḿ*, *n*, *ń*, *v*, *v́*) and before the front vowels (*i*, *e*), so that in this position only twenty-one consonantal phonemes are distinguished. Before obstruents and in final position, not only the correlation of palatalization but the correlation of voice is neutralized as well. Accordingly only fourteen consonantal phonemes are distinguished in that position (*p*, *m*, *t*, *n*, *k*, *x*, *c* ,*s*, *č*, *š*, *f*, *l*, *r*, *j*). Thus there is no position in Bulgarian in which all phonemes of that language are distinguished. But four typical positions can here be determined: the position of maximal vowel distinction (accented, interconsonantally), the position of maximal consonantal distinction (before back vowels), the position of minimal vowel distinction (before unaccented vowels), and the position of minimal consonantal distinction (before obstruents, and in final position). Similarly four positional types are found in most languages of the world.

Certain languages also show a preference for a particular (progressive or regressive) direction of neutralization. It seems that very often this is a question that is related to the morphonological and grammatical structure of the particular languages.[21]

[1] Cf. N. S. Trubetzkoy, "Character und Methode der systematischen phonologischen Darstellung einer gegebenen Sprache," in *Archives néerlandaises de*

phonétique experimentale, VIII–IX (1933), and "Die Aufhebung der phonologischen Gegensätze," *TCLP*, VI, 29 ff.

[2] Cf. N. S. Trubetzkoy, "Die Konsonantensysteme der ostkaukasischen Sprachen," in *Caucasica*, VIII.

[3] Cf. D. V. Bubrich, *Zvuki i formy erz'anskoj reči* (Moscow, 1930), p. 4.

[4] Cf. N. S. Trubetzkoy, "Die Konsonantensysteme der ostkaukasischen Sprachen," in *Caucasica*, VIII.

[5] Cf. Paavo Ravila, *Das Quantitätssystem des seelappischen Dialektes von Maattivuono* (Helsinki, 1931).

[6] Cf. the Cheremis texts, for example, those published by Ödön Beke, "Texte zur Religion der Osttscheremissen," in *Anthropos*, XXIX (1934).

[7] Cf. N. S. Trubetzkoy, "Die Konsonantensysteme der ostkaukasischen Sprachen," in *Caucasica*, VIII.

[8] Cf. P. M. Melioranskij, *Kratkaja grammatika kazak-kirkizskago jazyka* (St. Petersburg, 1894), I, 24.

[9] Cf. Carl H. Borgström, "The Dialect of Barra," in *Norsk Tidsskrift for Sprogvidenskap*, VIII (1935).

[10] Cf. N. S. Trubetzkoy, "Die Konsonantensysteme der ostkaukasischen Sprachen," in *Caucasica*, VIII.

[11] Cf. S. K. Chatterjee, *Recursives in New-Indo-Aryan* (Lahore, 1936).

[12] Cf. Gougenheim, *Éléments de phonologie française* (Strasbourg, 1935), pp. 20 ff.

[13] Cf. N. S. Trubetzkoy, in *TCLP*, I, 57 ff., and R. Jakobson in *Mélanges . . . van Ginneken*, p. 30.

[14] Cf. Clement M. Doke, "The Phonetics of the Zulu Language," in *Bantu Studies* (1926), Special Number.

[15] Cf. R. Jakobson, "Z zagadnień prozodji starogreckiej," in *Prace ofiarowane Kaz. Wóycickiemu* (Wilno, 1937).

[16] Cf. Paavo Ravila, *Das Quantitätssystem der seelappischen Mundart von Maattivuono*.

[17] Cf. the data by A. Belić, "Zametki po čakavskim govoram," in *Izvestija II. Otd. Akad. Nauk.*, XIV, 2, and N. S. Trubetzkoy in *TCLP*, VI, 44 n. 13.

[18] Cf. Ante Dukić, *Marija Devica, čakavska pjesma s tumačem riječi i naglasa* (Zagreb. 1935).

[19] This can be recognized particularly clearly in the dialect of Castua. The above-mentioned (p. 203) nonuniform realization of the "rising" accent in this dialect (as opposed to the completely uniform realization of the "falling" accent, which is independent of position in the sentence) seems to point to the fact that the phonological content of the "rising" accent is predominantly negative, in other words, that this accent functions as the unmarked member of the correlation of tone movement. But in this case the "falling" accent must be marked in this dialect.

[20] Cf. N. Jakovlev, *Tablicy fonetiki kabardinskogo jazyka* (Moscow, 1923), pp. 70 and 80.

[21] Cf. N. S. Trubetzkoy, "Das mordwinische phonologische System verglichen mit dem russischen," in *Charisteria Guilelmo Mathesio oblata* (Prague, 1932), pp. 21 ff.

VI PHONEME COMBINATIONS

1 FUNCTIONAL CLASSIFICATION OF PHONEMES

The neutralization of phonological oppositions is certainly the most important, but by no means the only important, phenomenon in the sphere of syntagmatic phonology. For only bilateral oppositions can be neutralized, and, as is well known, these are in any system always less numerous than multilateral oppositions. In many, and possibly in most, cases the circumstance that a phoneme is not permitted in a particular phonic position does not even result in the neutralization of any opposition. Such a limitation, nevertheless, represents a very important phenomenon which can be of significance for the typology of the particular system. Any rules that restrict in any way the use of the individual phonemes and their combinations must, therefore, always be carefully stated in the description of a phonological system.

Frequently a classification of phonemes can be undertaken on the basis of such rules. This *functional* classification then complements the other classification that was obtained through a logical analysis of the phonological oppositions.

A good example of this is Classical Greek (specifically the Attic dialect). Classical Greek had only a single phoneme that occurred exclusively in initial position: the *spiritus asper*.[1] The phonemes that could occur initially after the spiritus asper as well as without it were the *vowels*. All other phonemes were *consonants*. Of these ρ occurred initially only after the spiritus asper. All other consonants were never found in that position.

242

Those consonants that could occur initially before ρ formed the class of stops or plosives. All others were continuants. Among the latter there was only a single phoneme, the *spirant* σ, which could occur before plosives in initial position. The remaining continuants were *sonorants*. Among these were two that could occur before σ in medial position. These were the *liquids*. Two others could not occur before σ. These were the *nasals*. Of the liquids only ρ could occur in final position. It could, therefore, be considered the unmarked member of the bilateral opposition ρ-λ. Of the nasals only ν could occur in final position and accordingly be regarded as the unmarked member of the bilateral opposition μ-ν. Besides these only σ occurred in final position, while the plosives were not permitted in that position. Among the stops or plosives there were only three that could occur after other plosives. These were the *apicals* or the *dentals*. Among the plosives not permitted after other plosives there were three that were also not permitted before μ. These were the *labials*. There were three others that were permitted before μ. These were the *gutturals*. Of the plosives only π and κ could occur before τ, only φ and χ before θ, and only β and γ before δ. No syllable that contained θ, φ, or χ could occur before a syllable containing θ, φ, or χ. A syllable with π, τ, or κ could occur, however. Accordingly the bilateral oppositions θ-τ, φ-π, and χ-κ were neutralized; τ, π, and κ, as the unmarked members, represented the archiphonemes. Thus two classes of plosives were characterized by this law: the *tenues* π, τ, and κ and the *aspirates* φ, θ, and χ. As for the remaining plosives, they could not be geminated in native Greek words. This characterized them as a special class of *mediae*. All other consonants, that is, the continuants as well as the stops (plosives), could be geminated after vowels, the long aspirates appearing as τθ, πφ, and κχ. Before σ the bilateral oppositions of

243

"tenues"/"mediae" and "tenues"/"aspirates" were neutralized, so that in that position only a single type of plosive occurred. Its character, however, is no longer evident from the graphs ζ, ψ, and ξ.

The rules governing phoneme combinations thus produce a complete classification of the consonants of Classical Greek as well as a strict division between consonants and vowels. But cases of this type are comparatively rare. There are languages in which the rules of phoneme combination make only a rather rudimentary classification of phonemes possible. For example, in Burmese only two classes of phonemes can be established on the basis of combinatory rules. Vowels are phonemes that are permitted in word-final position. Consonants are phonemes that are not permitted in that position. All words in Burmese are monosyllabic and consist of a vowel (or a monophonematic diphthong) that may be preceded by a consonant. All possible combinations occur within this frame. Accordingly, on the basis of these combinations, phonemes can be classified only as vowels and consonants. However, the phonemic inventory of Burmese is extremely rich: it contains sixty-one consonants and fifty-one vowels (if prosodic differences are included).

In languages such as Burmese the functional division of phonemes is jeopardized by the great uniformity of word types and the limited scope of combinatory possibilities. But there are also languages in which, conversely, word types and combinatory possibilities are so manifold that a clear functional division of phonemes appears almost impossible. All these idiosyncrasies are of great importance for the phonological typology of the world's languages.

2 THE PROBLEM OF GENERAL LAWS GOVERNING PHONEME COMBINATIONS

Combinations of phonemes are subject to special rules in every language. But the question is whether some of these rules at least are valid for all languages. B. Trnka has attempted to solve this problem.[2]

Trnka's attempt could not succeed entirely because he proceeded from an old, already outdated classification of phonological oppositions into correlations and disjunctions. Nevertheless, Trnka contributed toward the solution of the problem and expressed some fruitful thoughts in his article. He believes he is able to formulate a general law according to which two members of a correlational pair cannot occur next to each other within a single morpheme (*op. cit.*, pp. 57 ff.). The law is probably untenable in this form. In languages that consistently have the correlation of constriction, the combination of a fricative with the corresponding occlusive is readily permitted. For example: Polish "ścisłość" (exactness, closeness), "w Polsce" (in Poland), "szczeć" (bristle), "jeździec" (rider), "moždžek" (small brain); Abkhas "ačša" (female of a domestic animal); Tsimshian "txâ'xkᵘdet" (they ate). The vowel combinations *üi* and *uü* occur in various languages. For example, in a large part of the Burgenland (Austria) the diphthong *ui* (as in "fuis" [foot]), which originated from M. H. Ger. *uo*, is distinguished from the *uü* (for example, "guün" [guilda]) that originated from *ul*. In Finnish, though rare, the monomorphemic combination *yi* (= üi) is still quite current. For example: Finnish "lyijy" (pron. *lüijü*, lead). In Annamese *iü* and *üi* are very common. Finally, compare French "huit," "huile," "nuit," "je suis," etc. Combinations of two vowels alike in quality but different in quantity also occur within the frame of one morpheme in some languages, though very rarely. For example, in Haida (cf. "šäada" [woman], "sūus" [say(s)], etc.),[3] and in Prākrit,[4] where combinations of nonnasalized and nasalized vowels within the same morpheme are also permitted.[5] Thus the law formulated by Trnka is not even valid for the oppositions recognized as correlations by Trnka himself. But the most flagrant case is probably represented by the correlation of consonantal nasalization since the combinations *mb*, *nd*, *bm*, *dn*, etc., are found in most languages of the world. Trnka recognized this himself. He believed, however, that he could eliminate these exceptions by not using the term "correlation" but "parallelism" for these cases (*op. cit.*, p. 59). At the same time, however, he found that some languages do not permit the phonemes that do not form correlational pairs (in the sense of the phonological terminology currently in use) to occur next to each other (within the frame of the same morpheme). For example: *s* and *š*, or Czech *n* and *ň*. Trnka then decides to designate such phoneme pairs as correlational pairs as well, thus departing from the terminology in use previously. Above we had defined a correlational pair as a privative proportional opposition. (This is essentially in accord with the definitions of the "Projet de terminologie phonologique standardisée," *TCLP*, IV, 313 ff.). However, on the one hand, Trnka does not wish to recognize the correlation of nasals as such (*b-m*, *d-n*, *g-ŋ*, etc.), and, as was shown above, he cannot recognize the correlation of constriction, the vocalic correlations *ü-i* and *u-ü*, and the "correlation of quantity" either. On the other hand, he designates equipollent bilateral oppositions of the type *s-š* or *n-ň* as correlations. He must therefore give a new definition to the term "correlation." He actually does this on page 59 of the above-mentioned article, when he says: "It is necessary, therefore, to distinguish this kind of phonemic relationship . . . from correlation, which represents such a close affinity that it deprives the members of the same pair of the capacity of being contrasted, as individual phonemes, in one

monomorphemic combination." This, then, is the only possible definition
for Trnka: the term *correlation* is used to designate a relationship between
two phonemes which is so close that it makes it impossible for these
phonemes to be distinguished as individual phonemes in a monomorphemic
combination. But if one replaces the word "correlation" in the "law"
formulated by Trnka with this definition, one notes that the entire law is
no more than a tautology: Phonemes that cannot occur next to each
other within the frame of a morpheme cannot occur next to each other
within the frame of a morpheme! Trnka terms his law the "law of minimal
phonological contrast" (*op. cit.*, p. 58). This term reaches the essence of the
subject matter much better than the mistaken definition that was given.

    The point really is that phonemes (or better the phonological units),
which within the frame of a morpheme are in direct contact with each
other, must represent a certain minimum of distinction. It is to B. Trnka's
credit that he noted this fact. If we regard phoneme combinations from
this point of view, we find that there actually are some phoneme combinations that are not permitted in any language of the world. We can establish
two groups of such *universally inadmissible* phoneme combinations. First,
there are combinations of two consonantal phonemes which are distinguished from each other only by the property of a correlation based on
overcoming an obstruction of the second degree (the correlation of consonantal intensity is excepted).[6] Second, there are combinations of two
consonantal phonemes which are distinguished from each other only by
membership in two "related" series of localization. (In other words, they
are phonemes that stand in a relationship of privative or equipollent bilateral opposition to each other.) All other combinations of phonemes
that are differentiated by a single phonological mark occur in one language
or another.[7]

    The above two groups of "universally inadmissible" phoneme com-
binations were discovered by way of induction. They cannot be combined
under any general formula. Each language has still other inadmissible
phoneme combinations. The "universally inadmissible" phoneme
combinations thus do not constitute a complete system anywhere. They
always form only part of the system of the phoneme combinations that are
inadmissible in a language. Insofar as admissible phoneme combinations
must have a certain minimum of phonological distinctiveness between
their members, this minimum is determined differently for each language.
In Burmese, for example, the opposition between consonant and vowel is
considered such a minimum. Within a morpheme neither combinations of
two consonants nor combinations of two vowels are permitted. (The
phonemes transcribed by "consonant + *y* and consonant + *w*" are in

reality palatalized or rounded consonants. *hl, hm,* etc., represent voiceless
lʻ and *mʻ*, and the diphthongs are to be considered monophonematic.)
The only admissible monomorphemic combination is the combination
"consonantal phoneme + vowel phoneme." Annamese permits within
a morpheme not only combinations of the type "consonant + vowel"
(and "vowel + consonant") but combinations consisting of two or three
vowels as well. But a combination of two consonants is not permitted.
Accordingly all consonantal oppositions (i.e., oppositions based on the
manner of overcoming an obstruction, oppositions of localization, and
oppositions of resonance) in this language are considered so slight that
they do not as yet reach the minimum. The vocalic oppositions, on the
other hand, are evaluated as being above the required minimum of contrast. The Hanakian (Moravian) dialects of Czech offer the opposite
picture. They do not permit any vowel combinations within the frame of a
morpheme but allow many different consonantal combinations. Accordingly the minimum of contrast must be established independently for each
language and given a special definition. The "universally inadmissible"
phoneme combinations are not of much help in this matter.

Only the combination "consonantal phoneme + vowel phoneme"
can probably be considered a *universally admissible* phoneme combination, as B. Trnka correctly recognized (*op. cit.*, p. 59). These combinations
are probably the logical prerequisite for the existence of vowels and consonants. Otherwise the vowels would not be in opposition with the consonants. But a phoneme exists only by virtue of its opposition to another
phoneme. Whatever the case may be, a language without combinations of
the type "consonant + vowel" is unthinkable.

Combinations of occlusives with homorganic nasals, according to
Trnka (*loc. cit.*), exist only in those languages that have the combination
"consonant + vowel." But since combinations of this type are present in
all languages of the world, this rule merely states that the combinations
of nasals with homorganic occlusives are permitted *in some* languages of
the world. The two other laws formulated by Trnka, however, are
acceptable.

Trnka formulates the rule (*loc. cit.*) that combinations of two obstruents
which are distinguished from each other only by membership in different
localization series (e.g., *pt, xs, sf*) occur exclusively in languages which also
permit the combination of other consonants with obstruents (e.g., *sp, tr,
kl, rs*). As far as we can see from the available data, this is really so. Trnka's
next rule states: Languages that permit combinations of consonants
initially or finally also permit consonantal combinations medially. This law
really seems to be valid for languages with polysyllabic words. But in

languages with only monosyllabic words a consonant cluster is only
possible initially (as in Siamese, where obstruents + *r* and *l* are permitted
initially)[8] or finally. It is impossible, however, to find such combinations
in medial position.

In summary, it can be said that the general laws for phoneme combinations which are valid for all languages of the world, insofar as they can be
at all discovered by induction, relate only to a rather insignificant part of
possible phoneme combinations. Accordingly they cannot play a significant
role in syntagmatic phonology.

3   THE METHODS OF SYNTAGMATIC PHONOLOGY

From what has been said it follows that the phoneme combinations in
every language are governed by laws and rules that are valid only for the
particular language and must be established separately for each language.
The variety of combinatory types at first glance seems to preclude any
uniform treatment of syntagmatic phonology. Depending on the type of
language, different methods must be applied. There are languages in which
there are only very few combinatory rules. Burmese, where all words are
monosyllabic and consist either of a vowel phoneme or of the combination "consonantal phoneme + vowel phoneme," has already been
mentioned. But even for a language such as Japanese, where the number of
syllables in a word is unrestricted, syntagmatic rules are no more than
eight in number: (1) no consonantal combinations are permitted in word-
initial position; (2) of the consonantal combinations only the combination
N + consonant is allowed medially; (3) only vowels, or vowels + *N* (*n*),
are permitted finally; (4) palatalized consonants cannot occur before *e*;
(5) nonpalatalized consonants cannot occur before *i*; (6) long (bimoric)
vowels cannot occur before geminated consonants or before syllable-
final *N*; (7) the semivowel *w* occurs only before *a* and *o*; (8) the semivowel
y occurs only before *u*, *o*, and *a* (before initial *e*, *y* is only optional and cannot be considered an independent phoneme in that position). Other
languages, however, have a great abundance of combinatory rules. In
Trnka's study titled *A Phonological Analysis of Present-day Standard
English*,[9] the enumeration of combinatory rules for English comprises no
less than twenty-two pages (23–45). Even if these rules could be formulated
somewhat more briefly, they are still extremely numerous.

Despite this diversity of language types as regards combinatory rules,
it seems not only desirable but absolutely necessary to have as uniform a
method for the study of combinations as possible since a comparison
between the various language types can only be pursued under this con-

dition. At the same time, a typology of sounds cannot be established without such a comparison. The principles underlying a uniform method for the study of combinations can be formulated in the following way.

First, combinatory rules always presuppose a higher phonological unit within the framework of which they are valid. But this higher phonological unit need not always be the word. In many languages not the word but the *morpheme*, which is a complex of phonemes present in several words and always associated with the same (material or formal) meaning, must be regarded as such a unit, This is the case, for example, in German. Word-medially an almost unlimited number of consonantal combinations is allowed. For example: *kstšt* "Axtstiel" (handle of an axe), *ksšv* "Fuchsschwanz" (fox tail), *pstb* "Obsbaum" (fruit tree). Combinatory rules of any kind can be formulated only with great difficulty. The phonemic structure of morphemes that make up German words, on the other hand, is rather clear. It is governed by quite specific combinatory rules. It is therefore only expedient to study combinatory rules within the frame of morphemes and not within the frame of words. The first task in any investigation of combinations is merely to determine the phonological unit within which combinatory rules can be studied most appropriately.

The second task in any investigation of combinations is a suitable division of the "frame units" (words or morphemes) with respect to their phonological structure. In languages such as Burmese this task resolves itself since all frame units here have the same structure. But in a language such as German this task is extremely important. The division of frames must here be undertaken only from the point of view of its appropriateness for the study of phonological combinations. For example, it would be inappropriate from such a point of view to divide morphemes in German according to their grammatical function (i.e., into prefix, root, suffix or final morphemes). From the point of view of a study of German combinations, the only useful division of the morphemes is into those that are *capable of bearing stress* and those that are *incapable of bearing stress*. To the former class belong the morphemes that can have primary or secondary stress in a compounded word (e.g., *aus-*, *-tum*, *tier-*, in words such as "Auswahl" [choice], "Eigentum" [property], "tierisch" [bestial]). To the class of morphemes that are incapable of bearing stress belong the morphemes that never carry primary or secondary stress (e.g., the morphemes *ge-*, *-st*, *-ig* in words such as "Gebäude" [building], "wirfst" [you throw], "ruhig" [calm]). The morphemes that are capable of bearing stress in German are the most numerous. They are very diverse structurally. They can be further divided, according to their number of syllables, into monosyllabic morphemes (e.g., "ab" [off], "Axt" [axe], "-tum" [-dom], "-schaft" [(-i)ty], "schwarz" [black]); bisyllabic morphemes (e.g., "Wagen" [wagon], "Abend" [evening], "Arbeit" [work], "Kamel" [camel]); trisyllabic morphemes (e.g., "Holunder" [elderberry]); quadri- syllabic morphemes (e.g., "Abenteuer" [adventure]). Morphemes that are incapable of bearing stress in German, on the other hand, either form no syllable at all (e.g., -st as in "gib-st" [you give], "fein-st-e" [finest]) or they form only one syllable (e.g., -zig as in "vierzig" [forty]). Accordingly a division on the basis of number of syllables is here impossible. More useful, however, is a division of the German morphemes that are not capable of bearing stress into proclitics and enclitics, that is, into those morphemes that can always occur directly *before* a morpheme capable of bearing stress, as, for example, *be-* in "behalten" (to keep), and those that occur only *after* another morpheme, as, for example, *-er* and *-isch* in "wählerisch" (choosy). This division is also in accord with quite distinct types of phonemic structure. The *proclitic* morphemes incapable of bearing stress always consist of a syllable that contains the vowel *e*. In other words, the syllable consists either of a "media + *e*" (*be-*, *ge-*) or of "(a con- sonant +) *er-*" (*er-*, *ver-*, *zer-*), or of "e + nasal + tenuis" (*ent-*, *emp-*). *Enclitic* morphemes contain either no vowel at all or they contain the vowels *u*, *i*, and *ə*. Of the consonants they contain the following: *t, d, g, x, s, š, l, r, m, n, ŋ*. Of these *š*, *x*, and *g* occur only after *i* (*-ig*, *-lich*, *-rich*, *-isch*), *d* occurs only after *n* (*-end*), *n* occurs only after *u* or *i* ("Jüngling" [young man]), *s* occurs after *i*, *ə*, and *n*, or it occurs without a vowel (*-nis*, *-es*, *-ens*, *-s*, *-st*), *n* occurs after *ə* and *i* or without a vowel (*-en*, *-in*, *-n*); the rest (*-l*, *-m*, *-r*, *-t*) occur either after *ə* or without a vowel. Of the combinations of the type "consonant + vowel" only the combi- nations *n, l, r + i* (*-nis, -lich, -ling, -rich*) and *t + ə* occur within morphemes of this type. Of the consonant combinations only *nd, ns*, and *st* are found.[10] For the morphemes capable of bearing stress the basic types, characterized by the number of syllables, can also be subdivided. For example, the monosyllabic morphemes capable of bearing stress are divided into nine different subtypes. The criterion is whether they begin or end with a vowel phoneme, a consonant, or with a consonantal cluster ("Ei" [egg], "Kuh" [cow], "Stroh" [straw], "Aal" [eel], "Sohn" (son), "klein" [small], "Ast" [branch], "Werk" [work], "krank" [sick]). Still more subtypes are con- ceivable with regard to bi-, tri-, and quadrisyllabic morphemes.

After the division of the frames into structural types has been completed, the phoneme combinations within these structural types are then to be studied. It is clear that in such a study the positions within the particular frames (initial, medial, and final position), on the one hand, and the three basic forms of phoneme combinations (i.e., combinations of vowel phonemes with each other, consonantal phonemes with each other, and vowel phonemes with consonantal phonemes), on the other, must be treated separately.

The method to be used in studying these phoneme combinations is a logically necessary result of the questions to be answered by this study. First, it must be determined *which phonemes* combine with each other in the particular position and which phonemes are mutually exclusive. Second, the *sequence* in which these phonemes occur in the particular position must be determined. And third, the *number* of members of a phoneme combination permissible in a particular position must also be indicated. From a methodological point of view, the study of the phonological structure of English monosyllables by Kemp Malone[11] can be considered exemplary. Malone studied separately the phoneme combinations that are allowed in initial, medial, and final position. He formulated three types of delimitative rules for each of these positions: (*a*) restriction on participation in a combination (restriction in membership), (*b*) restriction in the sequence of combined phonemes (restriction in sequence of members), and (*c*) restriction in the number of members of a combination. These three types of restriction represent an exhaustive answer to three questions so important for the study of phoneme combinations.

As an example, the consonantal combinations permissible in *initial position* in German morphemes capable of bearing stress will be examined here.

a. Restrictions in membership. (1) *s* ("ss"), *z* ("s"), *x* ("ch"), *h* and *ŋ* ("ng") cannot participate in a combination of this type. (2) Mediae and tenues are mutually exclusive (i.e., a media and a tenuis consonant cannot simultaneously participate in one and the same combination). (3) Occlusives are mutually exclusive. (4) Fricatives (*f*, *š*) are mutually exclusive. (5) Sonorants (*r*, *l*, *m*, *n*, *v*) are mutually exclusive. (6) Fricatives cannot be combined with *b*, *d*, *g*, *p̌* ("pf"). (7) *t* and *d* cannot be combined with *l*. (8) *f* cannot be combined with occlusives. (9) *v* ("w") does not combine with labials and labiodentals. (10) *c* ("z") does not combine with *r*, *l*, *s*, *f*. (11) *n* only combines with *š* ("sch"), *k*, and *g*. (12) *m* only combines with *š*.

b. Restrictions in sequence. (1) Fricatives (*f*, *š*) can occur only as first members of a combination. (2) Sonorants (*r*, *l*, *m*, *n*, *v*) can occur only as final members of a combination. (3) No other consonants may occur between *š* and *v*.

c. Restrictions in number of members. (1) Of three-member combinations only *štr*, *špr*, and *špl* are permissible. (2) Combinations of more than three members are not permitted.

From all these restrictions on morphemes capable of bearing stress the following possible combinations of consonants in initial position result: *br, pr, dr, tr, gr, kr, p̆r, fr, šr; bl, pl, kl, p̆l, fl, šl,* gn, kn, šn; šm; dv, (tv), (gv), kv, cv, šv; št, (šk); štr, špr, špl.*

Similar combinatory rules can also be formulated for the final and medial position of morphemes capable of bearing stress. Further, special rules can be established for polysyllabic morphemes. The rules discovered in this way must be compared with each other. It may develop that some of them have a more general sphere of application. For example, rules (2), (4), (6), and (9) of the "restrictions in membership" enumerated above are not only valid for initial position but for all positions within the frame of a German morpheme. Some rules must receive a general formulation. For example, the second "restrictions in sequence" can be replaced by two rules, which are valid for all positions within a German morpheme: (α) Of the liquids (r, l) r can only occur in direct contact with a vowel, while l can occur either in direct contact with a vowel or an r. (β) Of the nasals only m and n can occur in direct contact with either a vowel or a liquid, while η can only occur after a vowel.

Only after phoneme combinations have been studied by the same method in as many languages as possible can a *typology of combinations* be developed by the comparison of various languages, and can the question of the legitimacy of combinatory rules be fruitfully discussed.

4 ANOMALOUS PHONEME COMBINATIONS

The combinatory rules provide each language with a special character. They characterize the language no less than the phonemic inventory. There are languages in which the combinatory rules are rigorously carried out and include all parts of the vocabulary. In such languages even the loanwords are modified in such a way that they obey the normal combinatory rules valid for the native words. In other languages, however, loanwords are changed as little as possible, even if they are in contradiction to native combinatory rules. They continue to exist as foreignisms in the vocabulary. German is among the languages of this type. Take, for example, words such as "Psalm" (psalm), "Sphäre" (sphere), "Szene" (scene), "pneumatisch" (pneumatic) which have "non-German" consonantal combinations initially. It is true of course that words of this type are generally restricted to the area of technical or "erudite" vocabulary. Many of them

---

* *Translator's note: Also gl.*

conform to the normal combinatory rules when they are introduced into everyday vocabulary.[12] Only in the case of very advanced bilingualism do such words with foreign phoneme combinations penetrate the spoken speech in such numbers that they are not felt as foreignisms any more. This means that the combinatory rules of the particular language have undergone a corresponding modification.

The degree to which loanwords do not conform to native combinatory rules seems to depend on several things, especially on the variety of phoneme combinations that are permitted in a given language. In a language such as Japanese, which only allows very few phoneme combinations, the number of admissible phoneme combinations cannot increase greatly. German, on the other hand, which already has numerous and varied phoneme combinations, can add some foreign combinations to those permissible. Yet some fundamental rules must not be violated. For example, a media cannot occur next to a tenuis, r cannot occur without being in direct contact with a vowel, and so on. A word such as Georgian "gvçrtvnis" (he lets us practice) could not be accepted into German without modification.

The presence of particular phoneme combinations at the *morpheme boundary* also plays an important role in the introduction of loanwords. This was emphasized by B. Trnka with good reason.[13] The combinations *sc*, *sf*, *pn* are not allowed in German within the frame of a single morpheme. They do occur, however, in polymorphemic ("compounded") words at the morpheme boundary (e.g.: "Auszug" [exodus], "misfällig" [unpleasant], "abnehmen" [reduce]). This facilitates the unaltered preservation of these combinations in such loanwords as "Szene," "Sphäre," "pneumatisch," where they are transferred to initial position, in the same way as the preservation of the initial combination in "Psalm," "Psychologie," etc., is facilitated by the presence of this combination in medial position in such native words as "Erbse" (pea). In Japanese, on the other hand, the complete absence of consonantal combinations (except for N + consonant) within the frame of a single morpheme but also at morpheme boundary has the effect that loanwords cannot be introduced in unaltered form.

What has been said about foreign phoneme combinations is also valid for dialectal and archaic phoneme combinations. The standard or written language generally admits only dialect words in correspondingly modified form. Dialect words with a phoneme combination that is foreign to the written language present a foreignism in the vocabulary of the written language and are limited to special sections of the vocabulary. Take, for example, such German words as "Kaschperl" (Punch), "Droschke" (carriage), "Wrak" (wreck), "Robben" (seals), "Ebbe" (ebbtide). As for words taken over from the older languages and which have phoneme combinations presently out of use, they also belong to a special section of the vocabulary (the vocabulary of the poetic or of the administrative language). Proper names (i.e., the names of persons as well as places) in many languages form a special class since it is in them particularly that foreign, archaic, and dialectal elements have been retained in unaltered form in the standard language. Examples are such German names as Leipzig, Leoben, Altona, Luick, Treischke, Pschor, which contain either unusual phoneme combinations or belong to very rare morpheme types.[14]

Incidentally, proper names also behave in a very special way with regard to the phonological and morphological system in some other respects.

The most important area of anomalous phoneme combinations is represented by interjections, onomatopoetic expressions, calls or commands directed toward animals, and words with "an expressive" coloration. After what has been said on the subject by V. Mathesius and J. M. Kořínek[15] the problem should be considered as clarified once and for all and does not need any further discussion.

[1] Medially the spiritus asper occurred only in combination with a geminated p. But since it was never absent in that position, it did not have any distinctive force, i.e., it did not have a phonemic function.

[2] B. Trnka, "General Laws of Phonemic Combinations," in *TCLP*, VI, 57 ff.

[3] Cf. John R. Swanton in *Handbook of American Languages*, I (*Bureau of American Ethnology Bulletin*, XL), 211 f.

[4] From the glossary to Hermann Jacobi's *Ausgewählte Erzählungen im Mâhârâshtrî* (Leipzig, 1886), pp. 87 ff., we draw the following evidence: "āara" (respect), "īisa" (such), "ghaṛa-čhāaṇiā" (housewife), "nāara" (townsman), "paāna" (1. give, 2. march, departure), "pāava" (tree)," pāasa" (milk), "vāasa" (crow), "saāsa" (presence), "sāara" (ocean), and the temporal adverbs "kaā" (when), "jaā" (since), "taā" (then), "saā" (always), from which a suffix aā can be abstracted. The opposition between long and short vowels in Māhārāshtrī (as in all Prakrit dialects) is neutralizable: before geminated consonants and before the combination "nasal + consonant" all vowels are short.

[5] Cf. from the same glossary to Jacobi's Māhārāshtrī texts such words as "saā" (even), "saaā" (always), "vaāsa" (companion, friend). Before nasals and before occlusives the correlation of vocalic nasalization is neutralized in Prakrit.

[6] In languages such as Estonian, Lapp, and Gweabo, where light and heavy geminates or geminates with increasing and decreasing intensity are phonologically distinguished, it is the monomorphemic combination of the two members of a correlational pair of the correlation of intensity that is involved.

⁷ In particular it must here be stressed that combinations of two prosodemes that are only distinguished by one prosodic property are permissible without question. Combinations of this type can actually occur only in mora-counting languages. They result in bimoric or trimoric syllable nuclei with falling, rising, etc., tone movement. "Long vowels with stød" are actually also only combinations of two morae, the former of which is the marked, the latter the unmarked, member of the correlation of stød.

⁸ Cf. Walter Trittel, "Einführung in das Siamesische," in *Lehrbücher des Seminars für orientalische Sprachen zu Berlin*, XXXIV (1930).

⁹ *Studies in English by Members of the English Seminar of the Charles University, Prague*, V (*Práce z vědeckých ústavů*, XXXVII [1935]).

¹⁰ R. Jakobson calls our attention to the fact that the phonemic structure of the German enclitic morphemes is related to their grammatical function. *Suffix morphemes* either contain no vowel at all or they contain the vowel ə that occurs only in combination with *n, r,* or *l* in *derivative morphemes*. Of the consonants, the suffix morphemes contain only *s, t, n, m,* and *r,* and the three combinations *ns, nd,* and *st.* Enclitic accentuable morphemes that contain other phonemes or phoneme combinations are derivative morphemes.

¹¹ Kemp Malone, "The Phonemic Structure of English Monosyllables," in *American Speech* (1936), pp. 205 ff.

¹² The word "Sport" is already pronounced with an initial š by many Germans. In this form it no longer bears the mark of a loanword. In Vienna "Sport" as the name of a particular brand of cigarettes is always pronounced with an š.

¹³ Cf. B. Trnka in *TCLP*, VI, 60 ff.

¹⁴ It is to be noted that here also those combinations are found which ordinarily occur only at morpheme boundary. For example: "Leipzig"-"Abzug" (departure), "Leoben"-"beobachten" (observer), "Luick"-"ruhig" (quiet), "Treitschke"-"Deutschkunde" (Germanology), "Pschorr"-"Abschied" (departure).

¹⁵ V. Mathesius, "O výrazové platnosti některých českých skupin bláskových," in *Naše řeč*, XV, 38 ff., as well as J. M. Kořínek, "Studie z oblasti onomatopoje," in *Práce z vědeckých ústavů*, XXXVI (Prague, 1934). Cf. now also V. Skalička, "O mad'arských výrazech onomatopoických," in *Sborník filologický*, XI (1937).

VII PHONOLOGICAL STATISTICS

1 THE TWO WAYS OF COUNTING

The problems of statistics and of the functional load of phonological elements are very closely related to the study of combinations. Phono-statistics has already been studied and used for various practical and scientific purposes. For phonological purposes it must, of course, be modified correspondingly: not letters or sounds, but phonemes and phoneme combinations must be counted. In specifically phonological literature the importance of statistics in phonology was first stressed by V. Mathesius.[1] B. Trnka made a contribution to the statistics of English phonology in his book that we mentioned earlier.[2] W. F. Twaddell attempted a statistical study of the German system of consonants and their combinations.[3] George Kingsley Zipf studies phonological statistics in general.[4] Thus there is now no further lack in phonological statistical investigations. Still, there are by far not enough investigations, and in each one a different method is applied. No uniform method for phonological statistics has so far been developed. We must therefore content ourselves here with a few remarks on the subject.

Statistics is of twofold significance in phonology. First, it must show how often a specific phonological element of a given language (phoneme, phoneme combination, word type, or morpheme type) recurs in speech. Second, it must show the importance of the functional load of such an element or of a specific phonological opposition. For purposes of the

256

former, continuous texts must be examined statistically; for purposes of the latter, dictionaries. In either case it is possible to study the absolute figures for actual occurrences alone or the ratio of these figures to the figures of occurrences theoretically expected on the basis of combinatory rules.

2 STYLISTICALLY CONDITIONED FIGURES AND FIGURES CONDITIONED BY LANGUAGE

Each type of phonological statistical investigation has its own difficulties. In studying the frequency of a particular phonological element in continuous texts, it is the *choice of the text* which is of primary importance.

I open K. Bühler's *Sprachtheorie*[5] randomly at page 23 and take any section of 200 words (starting from "soll es also . . ." to "im Schosse der Sprachwissenschaften längst," in other words, from lines 3 to 28, starting from the top of the page). This section contains 248 accentuable morphemes. Of these 204 are monosyllables, 37 are bisyllabic, and seven trisyllabic. I then select another text, again 200 words in length, namely, the beginning of the first fairy tale in A. Dirr's *Kaukasische Märchen*.[6] I find that this section contains only a total of 220 morphemes capable of bearing stress; 210 are monosyllables, 10 bisyllabic, and not a single one is trisyllabic. The same difference between the two selected texts is also found with regard to word length. In Bühler, words of varying length from 1 to 9 syllables are found. In Dirr only monosyllabic, bisyllabic, and trisyllabic words occur, with an overwhelming preponderance of monosyllables.

257

Words consisting of	K. Bühler		A. Dirr	
	Number of words		Number of words	
	Absolute	Percent	Absolute	Percent
one syllable	95	47.5	134	67
two syllables	57	28.5	56	28
three syllables	27	13.5	10	5
four syllables	7	3.5	—	—
five syllables	6	3	—	—
six syllables	6	3	—	—
seven syllables	1	0.5	—	—
eight syllables	—	0	—	—
nine syllables	1	0.5	—	—
	200	100	200	100

The total number of syllables in the section studied in Bühler is 400, and in Dirr 276. This indicates that the average word length for Bühler is two syllables, and 1.4 syllables for Dirr. Since in German only vowels function as syllable nuclei (syllabic n, r, l* in unstressed syllables phonologically are to be regarded as ən, ər, əl), the number of syllables also indicates the number of vowel phonemes (400 for Bühler, 276 for Dirr). As to consonants, the section examined in Bühler contains 636 consonantal phonemes, and in Dirr 429. In other words, a word in Bühler contains 3.2 consonants on the average, and in Dirr 2.1 consonants. The ratio between consonants and vowels is about the same in both texts. The consonants account for 61 percent, the vowels for 39 percent, of all phonemes. But the total number of phonemes is 1,036 for Bühler, and 705 for Dirr. Accordingly there exists a ratio of about 3:2. It should not be assumed that this difference would disappear in longer sections. It is very closely related to *stylistic differences*. The scholarly language which is geared to a higher intellectual level of hearer is characterized by long words, while short words are preferred in the simple narrative, being geared to a rather primitive level of audience. Another peculiarity of educated speech in German is a superabundance of consonant combinations. While only 55 consonant combinations occur in the section examined in Dirr, with 116 consonants participating, or 27 percent of all consonantal phonemes, 127

* *Translator's note:* Also m (= əm).

consonant combinations occur in the section examined in Bühler's *Sprach-theorie*, with a total of 281 consonants participating, or 44 percent of all consonantal phonemes. As regards the distribution of these consonants within the word or morphemes, in both texts most combinations occur at internal morpheme juncture (in Dirr 40%, in Bühler 42%), and morpheme-finally (in Dirr 33%, in Bühler 32%). Both texts show quite a different relationship in morpheme-initial and morpheme-medial position. In Dirr 22 percent of all consonant combinations occur in morpheme-initial position and 5 percent in morpheme-medial position, while in Bühler 12 percent of all consonant combinations occur in morpheme-initial position and 14 percent in morpheme-medial position. Furthermore, in Bühler combinations such as *cj* ("Situation"), *gm* ("Dogma"), *skr* ("deskriptiv"), are attested in morpheme-medial position. Not only are these absent in the section examined in Dirr, they do not even occur once in his entire collection of Caucasian fairy tales. This is a result of an increased use of borrowings, which is characteristic of any scholarly language.

The two types of style which were chosen as examples, that is, the intellectualized scholarly language and the intentionally simple narrative speech imitative of the primitive, are two poles. Between these, various other types of style are found and each has its specific characteristics. Each text belongs to some kind of style. And if we propose to study the frequency of certain phonological elements in a particular language by means of a text, we must ask ourselves especially which text would be the most appropriate for this purpose. The problem seems to allow for two solutions: one should either choose a text that is "stylistically neutral" or one should choose portions from several texts of different styles. Neither solution is very satisfactory, however. The question remains as to what should be considered "stylistically neutral" and in what proportions should sections of texts of different styles be analyzed?

It seems, therefore, impossible to free phonological statistics completely from the influence of the various types of style. In phonological statistical studies the specific idiosyncrasies of the various types of style must always be taken into consideration. It has to be determined above all which of the phonological phenomena are stylistically conditioned and which exist independently of style. We have already seen that, at least for German, length of semantic units (words or morphemes) and frequency of consonant combinations are stylistically conditioned. The frequency of individual phonemes, on the other hand, appears to be rather independent of the style of the text.

Compare, for example, the frequency of vowel phonemes (in percentages) in the above-mentioned excerpts from Bühler and Dirr:

$$
\begin{array}{c}
\qquad\qquad K.\ B\ddot{u}hler \qquad\qquad\qquad A.\ Dirr \\[4pt]
\begin{array}{l}
a \\ \partial \\[6pt] \\ u \\ o \\ au
\end{array}
\ 57\left\{
\begin{array}{l}
37\left\{\begin{array}{c}15\\22\end{array}\right. \\[10pt]
20\left\{\begin{array}{c}7\\10\\3\end{array}\right.
\end{array}
\right.
\quad
\left.\begin{array}{c}
\left.\begin{array}{c}18\\22\end{array}\right\}40 \\[10pt]
\left.\begin{array}{c}9\\10\\4\end{array}\right\}23
\end{array}\right\}63
\\[30pt]
\begin{array}{l}
i \\ e,\ \ddot{a} \\ ei \\[10pt] \\ \ddot{u} \\ \ddot{o} \\ \ddot{o}\ddot{u}
\end{array}
\ 43\left\{
\begin{array}{l}
39\left\{\begin{array}{c}17\\18\\4\end{array}\right. \\[10pt]
4\left\{\begin{array}{c}3\\0.5\\0.5\end{array}\right.
\end{array}
\right.
\quad
\left.\begin{array}{c}
\left.\begin{array}{c}16.5\\11\\7.5\end{array}\right\}35 \\[10pt]
\left.\begin{array}{c}1\\1\\0\end{array}\right\}2
\end{array}\right\}37
\\[20pt]
\qquad\qquad \underline{100}\qquad\qquad \underline{100}
\end{array}
$$

The small differences in the case of *a*, *e*, and *ei* can hardly be attributed to the influence of style. It is possible that these differences would disappear in a statistical study of a larger section of text.

Phoneme frequency thus does not seem to be stylistically conditioned, at least not in German. To study it statistically any text may be chosen. (An exception are poems and texts of particularly artificial prose, in which an intentional artificial deviation from the natural frequency of phonemes is produced to evoke specific effects.)[7] But as a measure of caution an attempt should be made to neutralize the types of style for these studies as well. Best suited for this purpose appear to be transcriptions of various conversations,[8] or newspapers in which different styles are represented (political headlines, telegrams, semiscientific articles, official communiqués, sports reports, economic reports, serial stories, etc.).[9]

3   PROPOSED INTERPRETATIONS OF PHONEME FREQUENCY

To date far too few languages have been studied statistically with reference to phoneme frequency. Interpretations of statistical data and generalizations on this subject may, therefore, still be premature. But even today studies of this type are not lacking. J. van Ginneken advanced a theory on the cause of frequency differences in individual phonemes within the various languages.[10] According to this theory, each person has a hereditary preference for certain types of articulation. In speaking, he instinctively selects those words in which the respective sounds occur. But since all peoples came into existence through the mixture of different races, a certain combination of hereditary racial characteristics is contained in every representative of a particular people. These characteristics also correspond to articulatory preferences. And since the racial components are the same for different representatives of the same people, the phonemic system, too, is the same for all. Individual fluctuations in phoneme frequency are explained by differences in the numeric ratio of the racial components for individual representatives of the same people. This theory was not attained inductively nor was it deduced from concrete facts. Rather, it was an a priori invention. The phonemic material that was used does not serve as a basis and control for this theory, but is merely explicated by this theory. The explication always remains purely hypothetical: if some phoneme in a particular language indicates an especially high or an especially low frequency count, it is assumed that the racial characteristics of the particular people favor or impede the particular articulatory movements. But this is begging the question, for it must first be shown that a high or low frequency of a phoneme in connective speech depends on the racial characteristics of the speaker. Negro languages do not have the same phoneme frequency as the Indian languages of North America. But this is by far no proof that phoneme frequency is dependent on racial characteristics, since Negro languages are distinguished from Indian languages not only by phoneme frequency but also by their phonemic inventory and their grammatical structure. Objective proof could only be given by an experiment in which the factors in question would be completely isolated from all others. For example, two subjects belonging to a different race, but with the same mother tongue and the same level of education, would have to be examined with respect to phoneme frequency. (Their speech must also belong to the same style.) The results of such an experiment could, however, acquire scientific significance only if the experiment were to be repeated several hundred times with representatives of various races and in different languages. Only then could this question be discussed.

Another theory on the frequency of phonemes was proposed by George Kingsley Zipf.[11] According to this theory, the less complicated the realization of a phoneme, the greater its frequency. In this theory Zipf thus proceeds from a purely scientific point of view. When examining the tenability of this theory one must, therefore, also proceed from a strictly scientific point of view. But the degree of articulatory complexity cannot be measured purely from the standpoint of the natural sciences. The vocal cords are tense in the production of voiced occlusives but, at the same time, the organs of the mouth are relaxed. Conversely, in the case of voiceless occlusives the vocal cords are relaxed while the organs of the mouth are tensed. Which is more complicated? In the case of the aspirated consonants the glottis is wide open, that is, it remains in the same position as in normal breathing, while in the case of unaspirated consonants the glottis must shift position at the moment the consonant is released, lest aspiration follow. But, on the other hand, the greater the flow of air, the more tensed the organs of the mouth. It is therefore also difficult to say, with regard to the opposition of aspiration, whether the aspirated or the unaspirated consonants are "more complicated." The same holds true also for all oppositions based on the manner of overcoming an obstruction. In the case of oppositions based on localization, the degree of complexity can even less be determined. Zipf indicates the opposition *m-n* as an example. He believes it is possible to conclude from the greater frequency in many languages of *n* as compared to *m*, that *m* is the "more complicated." But *m* is articulated with closed lips and a lowered velum. In other words, the speech organs are in a position of complete rest (except that the vocal cords are tensed), while the articulation of *n* entails raising the tip of the tongue to the teeth or alveolar ridge and usually also a corresponding movement of the lower jaw (in addition to tensing the vocal cords, which it has in common with *m*). This theory must therefore also be decidedly rejected, at least in its present formulation.

The two theories discussed above can be considered as subject to attack primarily because they try to explain phonological facts by means of biological, extralinguistic causes. But Zipf's theory can also be "translated into phonological terms," so to speak. Marcel Cohen in his discussion of Zipf's book already hinted at this.[12] In its phonological formulation this theory would be somewhat as follows: "Of the two members of a privative opposition the unmarked member occurs more frequently in continuous speech than the marked member." This formulation should generally hold true, but it should by no means be considered a law without exception. One must make a distinction between neutralizable and nonneutralizable oppositions and also consider the extent of neutralizability. In Russian, where the opposition between palatalized and nonpalatalized consonants exists in twelve phoneme pairs, the rule applies only to eleven of these pairs. Nonpalatalized *p, b, f, v, t, d, s, z, m, n, r* in fact occur much more often than the corresponding palatalized *p', b', f', v', t', d', s', z', m', n', r'* (the ratio being approximately 2:1). But this rule does not apply to the phoneme pair *l:l'*: palatalized *l'* is more frequent in Russian than non-palatalized *l* (*l:l'* = 42:58). It is probably no accident that the opposition *l-l'* can only be neutralized before *e*, while the oppositions *p-p'*, *t-t'*, etc., are neutralized in other positions as well (before apicals, sibilants, and palatalized labials). The correlation of voice is neutralizable in Russian: in word-final position, before a pause, or before words beginning with sonorants only voiceless obstruents are permitted. This marks them as the unmarked members of the correlation of voice. However, the phoneme v (as well as the corresponding palatalized v') occupies a special position: on the one hand, it cannot occur in word-final position; and in medial position, too, it is replaced by f', its voiceless equivalent before voiceless obstruents. On the other hand, voiceless consonants can occur before v (e.g.: "tvoj" [your], "svad'ba" [wedding], "zakvaska" [sour dough]). This is not permitted before the other voiced obstruents. In other words, v does not have the same effect on the other obstruents as do the marked members of the correlation of voice. This is probably related to the fact that v occurs about four times as frequently as f. In contrast, in the remaining phoneme pairs of the correlation of voice, the voiced members are about three times less frequent than the voiceless ones.[13]

The examples given by Zipf can all be reconciled with the above formula. For in languages with a correlation of voice the voiceless obstruents are the unmarked opposition members, just as in languages with a correlation of aspiration the unaspirated obstruents fulfill this function. Languages such as Lezghian (K'üri), in which the aspirated occlusives are the unmarked members of the correlation of consonantal intensity,[14] teach us that it is not aspiration itself but the opposition relationship that is important. Aspirated occlusives are here, as a rule, more frequent than the corresponding unaspirated occlusives (p^h 1.8: P 0.8; t^h 5.2: T 2.2; k^h 8.8: K 0.7; c^h 9.0: C 0.1). The relationship is only reversed with respect to the back velar series of localization (q^h 1.6: Q 3.8). It is to be noted here that in contrast with all other Lezghian oppositions based on the correlation of consonantal intensity, the opposition q^h: Q is not neutralized in posttonic syllables.

There is no doubt that the differences between unmarked and marked opposition members, and the differences between oppositions that can be neutralized and those that cannot, affect phoneme frequency. Yet it is clear that this fact alone is not sufficient to explain the frequency relationships. There always exist oppositions in the various languages for which a privative character cannot be objectively established. For example, in French the correlation of voice is privative and neutralizable. However, it is only subject to a contextually conditioned dissimilative type of neutralization [of the type (a)]. The choice of archiphoneme representative is here conditioned externally so that the unmarked character of the one or the other member of this opposition is not objectively proven.[15] As a

whole, French voiceless obstruents are more frequent than voiced obstruents (approx. 60:40). The ratio is different, however, for each individual
phoneme pair: $\check{z}$ and v are much more frequent than $\check{s}$ and f; d and t have
approximately the same frequency, while in the other pairs (p-b, k-g, s-z)
the voiceless member is much more frequent than the voiced member.

4   ACTUAL AND EXPECTED FREQUENCY

In general it appears hopeless to establish strict rules for phoneme
frequency since phoneme frequency is the result of a whole sequence of
propelling forces. The absolute figures of actual phoneme frequency are
only of secondary importance. Only the relationship of these figures to the
theoretically expected figures of phoneme frequency is of real value. An
actual phoneme count in a text must therefore be preceded by a careful
calculation of the theoretical possibilities (with all rules for neutralization
and combination in mind). Let us imagine, for example, a language in
which a particular opposition of consonantal phonemes is neutralized in
initial and final position, and where only the unmarked opposition member
appears in the position of neutralization. In such a language the unmarked
member of the opposition in question can thus occur in initial position in
each syllable as well as in word-final position, while the marked member
can occur initially in all syllables except the first. If the average number of
syllables in this language equals α, one would expect that the frequency of
the unmarked opposition member behaves to the frequency of the marked
member as $\alpha + 1$ to $\alpha - 1$. In Chechen, where geminated consonants
occur only in medial position (as they do in most languages with a correlation of gemination) and where words contain an average of 1.9 syllables
(at least in folktales), the frequency ratio of geminated consonants to the
corresponding nongeminated consonants should therefore be 9:29 (i.e.,
approximately 1:3). Actually statistics yield the following figures:

$$
\begin{array}{lll}
tt\!:\!t & 12\!:\!90 & (4\!:\!30) \\
qq\!:\!q & 6\!:\!45 & (4\!:\!30) \\
\check{c}\check{c}\!:\!\check{c} & 25\!:\!59 & (13\!:\!30) \\
ll\!:\!l & 16\!:\!32 & (15\!:\!30)^{16}
\end{array}
$$

Geminated $\check{c}\check{c}$ and ll are thus used more frequently than one would have
expected theoretically, while geminated tt and qq are used much more
rarely. The Chechen language also has the correlation of recursion for
occlusives. But it is only found initially. Medially and finally it is neutralized (the archiphonemes being represented by the nonrecursive occlusives). The marked members of this opposition can, therefore, only occur

$\frac{\beta}{\alpha}$ times initially (if one designates the total number of syllables in a text by β and the average number of syllables of a word by α). The corresponding unmarked opposition members, on the other hand, can occur initially in each syllable as well as word-finally, that is, they can occur $\beta + \frac{\beta}{\alpha}$ times. The expected frequencies thus are in a ratio of $\frac{\beta}{\alpha}$ to $\beta + \frac{\beta}{\alpha}$, that is, of 1 to $\alpha + 1$. Since the average number of syllables in a word in Chechen is 1.9, we obtain the ratio of 1:2.9. Actually the following figures are found:

$$
\begin{array}{lll}
\text{t':t} & 33:90 & (11:30) \\
\text{k':k} & 38:47 & (24:30) \\
\text{q':q} & 21:45 & (14:30) \\
\text{c':c} & 17:97 & (5:30) \\
\text{č':č} & 5:59 & (2\frac{1}{2}:30) \\
\text{p':p} & ?:27 & (\ ?\ )^{17}
\end{array}
$$

The ratio of frequency figures for recursives and nonrecursives as a whole corresponds approximately to the expected ratio of (114:365 = 0.9:2.9). However, individual phonemes deviate considerably from this ratio in both directions. The unmarked members, too, always remain more frequent than the marked members. The tabulation of theoretical possibilities is not always as simple as in the examples quoted above. However, one should not be discouraged by the technical difficulties of such a tabulation. For only in a comparison with the *possible* frequency figures obtained on the basis of such a tabulation do the *actual* frequency figures acquire value. They show whether a phoneme is frequently or infrequently utilized in a given language.

When examining a text for phoneme frequency one must not only consider the frequency with which a phoneme occurs in general but also the frequency with which it occurs in a particular position. If, for example, the unmarked member of a neutralizable opposition occurs with special frequency in the position of neutralization (where it represents the archiphoneme), this is evidence that the opposition in question is not much utilized. If, however, such an opposition member occurs particularly often in the position of relevance (in other words, if it occurs more often than one would theoretically expect), this is an indication that the utilization of the opposition in question is favored. The extent to which various oppositions, including nonneutralizable oppositions, are utilized can also be determined statistically. In many languages there are environments in which only very few phonemes are permitted and where accordingly only few distinctive oppositions exist. Depending on whether the theoretically expected frequency for these positions is exceeded or whether that frequency is not reached, it is possible to determine whether the extent to which these oppositions are utilized is great or small.

The gross global statistical tabulation of phonemes must, therefore, be replaced by more detailed specific tabulations. The object of such tabulations no longer centers in phonemes but in oppositions, for in this area of phonology as well as in all others it should always be remembered that it is not the phonemes but the oppositions that represent the true object of phonological study.

5   PHONOLOGICAL STATISTICS AND VOCABULARY

The above discussion clearly shows that a statistical examination of texts alone is not sufficient to gain a picture of the relative utilization of the various phonological elements. Studies of this type must be supplemented by an examination of the vocabulary which is also statistical in nature. Also to be taken into account here is the relationship between the actual figures and the theoretically possible figures. V. Mathesius and B. Trnka have already made important attempts in this direction. The studies by Mathesius give particularly clear evidence for the importance of such investigations for the phonological typology of languages. One easily becomes persuaded thereof if one compares words consisting of two phonemes in various languages. In German 18 consonants (*b*, *p*, *m*, *d*, *t*, *n*, *k*, *g*, *c*, *z*, *š*, *f*, *v*, *p̌*, *h*, *r*, *l*, *j*) can occur word-initially, and 14 consonants (*p*, *m*, *t*, *n*, *k*, *ŋ*, *x*, *c*, *s*, *p̌*, *f*, *š*, *r*, *l*) word-finally, while all stressed vowel phonemes (i.e., 10 phonemes, if one does not distinguish *ä* and *e*) can occur initially as well as finally. Not allowed are the combinations *j* + *i*, *au* + *r*, *au* + *ŋ*, *eü* + *r*, *eü* + *ŋ*, *ai* + *r*, *ai* + *ŋ*, *o* + *ŋ*, and *ö* + *ŋ*. Accordingly 179 ([18 × 10] − 1) words of the type "consonant + vowel" and 132 ([14 × 10] − 8) words of the type "vowel + consonant" are theoretically possible in German. (Differences in type of contact are not taken into consideration.) In reality the type "consonant + vowel" is represented by 57 words in German ("du" [you], "Kuh" [cow], "zu" [to], "Schuh" [shoe], "wo" [where], "loh" [blazing, bright], "roh" [raw], "Bau" [structure], "Tau" [rope, dew], "kau" [chew, imp.], "Gau" [province], "Pfau" [peacock], "Vau" [v], "Sau" [sow], "schau" [look, imp.], "hau" [hew], "lau" [lukewarm], "rauh" [rough], "die" [the], "nie" [never], "Vieh" [cattle], "wie" [as], "zieh" [draw], "sie" [she, they], "hie" [here], "lieh" [lent], "mäh" [mow, imp.], "Tee" [tea], "näh" [sew, imp.], "Weh" [pain], "Zeh" [toe], "See" [sea], "je" [ever], "geh"

[go, imp.], "bei" [near, at], "weih" [bless], "zeih" [accuse, imp.], "sei"
[be, imp.], "reih" [arrange, imp.], "leih" [lend, imp.], "Küh'" [cows],
"Höh'" [height], "neu" [new], "scheu" [shy], "Heu" [hay], "Leu"
[lion, poet.], "Reuh'" [remorse], "da" [there, since], "nah" [near],
"sah" [saw], "ja" [yes], as well as the letters "Be" [b], "Pe" [p], "De"
[d], "Ha" [h], "Ka" [k]). The type "vowel + consonant" is represented
by 37 words ("Uhr" [watch], "Ohr" [ear], "ob" [whether], "Aug'"
[eye], "auch" [also], "aus" [from], "auf" [on], "ihr" [you, pl.; her, dat.],
"im" [in, dat.], "in" [in], "iss" [eat, imp.], "er" [he], "El" [l], "Em" [m],
"En" [n], "eng" [tight], "Eck'" [corner], "ätz" [etch, imp.], "es" [it],
"Esch'" [ash tree], "Eid" [oath], "ein" [a], "eil" [hurry, imp.], "Eich'"
[oak tree], "Eis" [ice], "Eul'" [owl], "euch" [you, pl.], "Aar" [eagle,
poet., or any large bird of prey], "Aal" [eel], "am" [at the, dat.], "an"
[at], "ach" [oh], "ass" [ate], "Aff'" [ape], "ab" [off], "Asch'" [ash]).
In French 15 consonants ($b, p, d, t, g, k, v, f, s, š, ž, m, n, r, l$) are allowed in
initial position, and 18 consonants ($b, p, d, t, g, k, v, f, z, s, š, ž, m, n, ṇ, r,$
l, j) in final position. Of the vowel phonemes 12 are permitted in closed
syllables ($u, o, ɔ, a, ε, i, ø, y, õ, ã, ˜ε, ø̃$), 13 in open syllables (the same phonemes + e). The phonemic sequences "nasal vowel" ($õ, ẽ, ø̃, ã$) + $m, n, ṇ, r,$
l, j are not permitted. Accordingly 195 (15×13) words of the type
"consonant + vowel" and 192 ($[12 \times 18] - [4 \times 6]$) words of the
type "vowel + consonant" are theoretically possible. In reality the type
"consonant + vowel" is here represented by 142 words and the type
"vowel + consonant" by 50 words. In other words, in German only
31.8 percent of the theoretical possibilities of the type "consonant +
vowel" are realized, while in French 73 percent are realized. For the type
"vowel + consonant" the realization of theoretical possibilities amounts
to approximately the same percentage in both languages: 28 percent in
German, 26 percent in French. However, while words of this type in
German make up 40 percent of all monosyllables consisting of two
phonemes, they only account for 26 percent of such monosyllables in
French. One can therefore see that even within such a narrow framework
the individuality of languages is clearly evident. V. Mathesius, in *TCLP*,
I, compares Czech and German with regard to the utilization of phonological means. He finds, among other things, that among the words that
consist of two or three phonemes, words beginning with a vowel amount
to 25.2 percent in German, but only to 8.2 percent in Czech. Further,
consonant combinations in German are utilized more in final position,
while in Czech they are utilized more initially.

All these peculiarities, which lend to each language its particular
character, can be expressed in numbers. By this method of examining the

vocabulary it is also possible to determine for each language in numbers
the extent to which the individual phonological oppositions are utilized
distinctively (their functional load), as well as the average load of the
phonemes in general. It develops that there are "economical" and "wasteful" languages in this respect. In the "economical" languages words that
are only distinguished by one phoneme are very numerous, and the
percentage in which theoretically possible phoneme combinations are
realized is very high. The "wasteful" languages have a tendency to distinguish words by several phonological elements and to realize only a small
percentage of the theoretically possible phoneme combinations.

Against the background of a phonological statistical vocabulary study,
the phonological statistical study of continuous texts takes on a new meaning. Frequency figures acquire a double relativity, so to speak, for the problem is to determine to what extent the theoretical possibilities given by the
combinatory rules, and realized in the vocabulary, are actually exploited
in continuous speech. The greater the number of phonemes in a word type,
the higher the number of theoretically possible words of this type. A
statistical study of the vocabulary shows what percentage of these
theoretical possibilities is realized, in other words, the number of phoneme
combinations of a particular type which have a specific lexical meaning.
But it indicates nothing about the actual frequency of occurrence of words
of this type in normal continuous speech. Only a statistical study of texts
can supply information on this point. It may develop that word types in
which a high percentage of theoretical possibilities is realized are less
frequent than word types with an insignificant percentage of such realization. It is impossible to say, at least for the present, whether there are
generally valid laws or whether languages vary in this regard since far
too little work has been done in phonological statistics. An express warning should be sounded, in any event, against any premature conclusions
and theories in this field.

In conclusion, it should be pointed out that lexical statistics must often
face difficulties similar to those found in statistics of texts. Not all areas of
vocabulary are alike or comparable. There are technical terms known only
to a small circle of experts, though they are not loanwords in the usual
sense of the word. Should such terminology be included in statistical
studies? There are words that in their written shape are probably only
found in dictionaries, and actually exist only in dialectal sound shape, for,
based on what they signify, they belong to the domain of dialects (various
technical terms for farm life, etc.). Which phonic shape should be used for
statistical purposes? Problems of this type appear in studies of lexical
statistics for almost any language. But for certain Oriental written lan-

guages such questions become almost fateful. The matter should, in any event, not be conceived of as being too easy.

---

[1] Cf. his essays, "La structure phonologique du lexique du tchèque moderne," in *TCLP*, I, 67–85, and "Zum Problem der Belastungs- und Kombinationsfähigkeit der Phoneme," in *ibid.*, IV, 148 ff.

[2] B. Trnka, "A Phonological Analysis of Present-day Standard English," in *Práce z vědeckých ústavů*, XXXVII (1935), pp. 45–175.

[3] W. F. Twaddell, "A Phonological Analysis of Intervocalic Consonant Clusters in Modern German," in *Actes du IVe Congrès International de Linguistes à Copenhague* (1938).

[4] G. K. Zipf, *Selected Studies of the Principle of Relative Frequency in Language* (Cambridge, Mass.: Harvard University Press, 1932), and *Psycho-Biology of Language* (Boston-Cambridge, Mass.: Riverside Press, 1935).

[5] Karl Bühler, *Sprachtheorie* (Jena, 1934).

[6] "Kaukasische Märchen selected and translated by A. Dirr," in *Die Märchen der Weltliteratur*, ed. by Friedrich von der Leyen and Paul Zaunert (Jena, 1920).

[7] Cf. J. Mukařovský, "La phonologie et la poétique," in *TCLP*, IV, 280 f.

[8] Peškovskij presents statistics of sound based on such transcriptions of spontaneous discourse for Russian (Peškovskij, *Des'at' tys'ač zvukov russkogo jazyka* [Sbornik statej, Leningrad, 1925], pp. 167–191).

A similar study is available for Swedish, based on stenographic transcriptions of speeches in the Swedish Parliament. Unfortunately both cases involve statistics of phones and not of phonemes.

[9] Cf., for example, B. Eldridge, *A Thousand Common English Words* (Buffalo: The Clement Press, 1911).

[10] Cf. J. van Ginneken, "Ras en Taal" (*Verhandl. d. Kon. Akad. van Wetensch. te Amsterdam, Aft. Letterkunde*, N. R. XXXVI, 1935); *De ontwikkelingsgeschiedenis van de systemen der menschelijke taalklanken* (Amsterdam, 1932), *De oorzaken der taalveranderingen* (Amsterdam, 1930); and "La biologie et la base d'articulation" in *Journ. de psychol.*, XXX, 266–320.

[11] G. K. Zipf, *Psycho-Biology of Language*, pp. 68 ff. Cf. N. S. Trubetzkoy's references in *Slovo a slovesnost*, II (1936), 252 f.

[12] Cf. Marcel Cohen in *BSL* XXXVI (1935), 10.

[13] Furthermore, voiced *ž* occurs more frequently in Russian than voiceless *š*. But this exception does not apply to those Russians who pronounce "*š*" as *šč*.

[14] For the statistics of the Lezghian phonemes, fairy tale no. 5 from the Supplement to P. K. Uslar's "Kjurinskij jazyk" in *Etnografija Kavkaza*, pp. 291–299, was counted.

[15] Cf. A. Martinet in *TCLP*, VI, 51 ff.

[16] Text No. IV in the collection of Karl Bouda, "Tschetschenische Texte," in *Mitteilungen des Seminars für orientalische Sprachen zu Berlin*, Jahrg. XXXVIII, Abt. II *Westasiatische Studien* (Berlin, 1935), 31–35, was counted as follows: the entire text for *tt, t, qqq, čč*, and *č*, only the first 300 words for *ll* and *l*.

[17] Recursive *p* does not occur once in the entire text investigated.

PART II

THE THEORY OF DELIMITATIVE ELEMENTS

The Delimitative Function of Sound

I PRELIMINARY REMARKS[1]

In addition to the phonological means serving to distinguish individual units of meaning (sememes), each language has a number of means that effect the delimitation of such individual units of meaning. These two functions of sound, that is, the distinctive function and the delimitative function, must be carefully distinguished. For language as such the distinctive function is indispensable: it is absolutely necessary that the individual sound complexes which correspond to the units of meaning be different in order not to be confused. For each sound complex to be sufficiently characterized as to its individuality, it must have specific "phonic marks" in specific sequence. Each language has only a limited number of such "phonic marks" which are combined into meaningful sound complexes in accordance with specific rules. This cannot be any other way; it is related to the nature of human speech. The external delimitation of meaningful complexes of sound, on the other hand, is not at all absolutely necessary. In an uninterrupted speech flow these complexes can occur in succession, without their boundaries needing to be indicated. Whether a particular one of these "phonic marks" (= realized phonemes) occurs at the end of a meaningful complex of sound (= word or morpheme), or at the beginning of the immediately following complex of sound, can in most cases be surmised from the entire context. The possibility of a misunderstanding is in most cases very slight, especially as usually when one hears a linguistic utterance one is already attuned to a specific and very limited conceptual sphere, and one needs only to consider the lexical elements that pertain to this sphere. Still, each language possesses specific, phonological means that signal the presence or absence of a sentence, word, or morpheme boundary at a specific point in the sound continuum. But these means are only ancillary devices. They can probably be compared to traffic signals in the street. Until recently no such signals existed even in big cities. Even today they have not been introduced in all cities. It is possible to get along without them: one need only be more careful and attentive. Therefore they are not found on every street corner but only on some. Similarly, linguistic delimitative elements generally do not occur in all positions concerned but are found only now and then. The difference lies only in the fact that traffic signals are always present at "particularly dangerous" crossings, whereas the distribution of linguistic delimitative elements in most languages seems to be quite accidental. This is probably due to the fact that traffic is artificially and rationally regulated, while language shapes and develops organically. Yet, according to their psychological nature, linguistic delimitative elements do resemble traffic signals: every now and then the ones as well as the others permit a relaxation of attentiveness.

We designate the linguistic delimitative means as *boundary signals*. They can be classified on the basis of various principles: first, on the basis of their relationship to the distinctive function; second, on the basis of their homogeneous or complex character; third, according to whether they indicate the presence or the absence of a boundary; and fourth, according to what type of boundary they signal (that is, whether a word, morpheme, or sentence boundary is involved). In order to characterize a language, it is very important to determine what types of boundary signals dominate in that language, as well as the frequency of their use. The delimitative function of sound thus requires special statistics.

[1] Cf. N. S. Trubetzkoy, *Anleitung zu phonologischen Beschreibungen* (Brno, 1935), pp. 30 ff., and "Die phonologischen Grenzsignale," in *Proceedings of the Second International Congress of Phonetic Sciences* (Cambridge, 1936), pp. 45 ff.

II PHONEMIC AND NONPHONEMIC BOUNDARY SIGNALS

In the discussion of structurally conditioned types of neutralization above (p. 235) we noted that some languages have certain distinctive oppositions found only in initial or final position in the units of meaning (words or morphemes). In all other positions they are neutralized. In such cases the marked members of the particular oppositions also have the value of boundary signals in addition to their phonemic (that is, distinctive) value because they occur only at the (initial or final) boundary of a unit of meaning. This is true, for example, for the aspirated occlusives of the Scottish-Gaelic dialect of Barra Island, the aspirated and recursive consonants of East Bengali, the recursive occlusives and emphatic palatalized consonants of Chechen, and others. The nasalized vowels, the long vowels, and the vowels of the central series (y, $ø$, $ə$) in the Scottish dialect of Barra Island, and all rounded vowels ($ū$, u, $ō$, o) in (the Kazum dialect of) North Ostyak[1] are likewise phonemes and boundary signals at the same time since they occur only in initial syllables. However, in this position they form distinctive oppositions (oppositions differentiating meaning) with the corresponding unmarked vowels. All cases mentioned involve a reductive neutralization of entire correlations in "nonboundary position." In "boundary position" entire categories of marked phonemes thus become boundary signals. But it may also be the case that only individual privative oppositions of phonemes, not correlations, are subject to reductive neutralization. However, the result in this case too must be the merger of the distinctive function of a particular marked opposition member

275

with the delimitative function. The unmarked opposition member, on the other hand, fulfills in this as in the case discussed above only a distinctive function. Classical Greek, for example, had the contrast between aspirated and unaspirated vowel onset in initial position only. Accordingly the aspirated vowel onset (spiritus asper) was simultaneously a phoneme with distinctive force (e.g.: "ὣς" [as], "ὣς" [ear], "ἕξ" [six], "ἔξ" [out]) and a signal marking the beginning of a word. Western Nuer has the opposition of voice in the occlusives of all localization series. While this opposition cannot be neutralized in the labial and the two apical series, it is subject to reductive neutralization in the guttural and palatal series. Accordingly the phonemes g and j occur only word-initially, where they are simultaneously phonemes and boundary signals.[2]

In addition to these *phonemic* boundary signals, many languages have special *nonphonemic* boundary signals. By this term we understand a combinatory variant (permissible in a boundary position only) of a phoneme that is permitted in other positions as well. For example, in Tamil obstruents are realized as aspirated voiceless occlusives (p^h, t^h, k^h) word-initially. However, in medial position they are realized in part as voiced and in part as spirantized (and in the case of gemination as unaspirated occlusives).[3] p^h, t^h, and k^h are therefore here only boundary signals: the opposition k^h-x or k^h-g (or p^h-v or p^h-b and t^h-δ or t^h-d) has no distinctive force. In short, it cannot be used to differentiate words, but serves exclusively to delimit words: k^h (or p^h, t^h) here always signals the beginning of a word. In the same language short u in final position is realized as a high back unrounded vowel ("u"). Since it is not realized in this way in any other position, u signals only the end of a word, and the opposition u-u has no distinctive but only delimitative force. In Japanese a relationship of combinatory variance exists between g and $ŋ$. g only occurs word-initially, and $ŋ$ only intervocalically. Accordingly the contrast between g:$ŋ$ cannot here distinguish word pairs, but it does serve to delimit words, g always signaling the beginning of a word. In several languages certain fricatives are realized as "affricates" in initial position: in Upper Sorbian the voiceless guttural fricative x is always pronounced as a guttural affricate kx (written "kh") in morpheme-initial position. The same phenomenon can also be observed in some dialects of the Buryat language (Buryat Mongolian), as, for example, in the Alar dialect.[4] In the Sosva dialect of Vogul word-initial s is realized as a type of affricated "c."[5] And in the earlier-mentioned Western dialect of Nuer the phoneme that is elsewhere realized as an f is pronounced as a labiodental affricate $p̆$ ("pf") word-initially. In all these languages the affricates in question are only combinatory variants of the respective fricatives. They serve only to signal the beginning of a word (or of a morpheme). A nonphonemic boundary signal is likewise "the vowel onset preceded by a glottal stop" which is found in languages such as German, the Southern dialects of Polish, the Bohemian dialects of Czech, Armenian, etc. It is not a phoneme but merely a "natural way of pronouncing" vowels in morpheme-initial position.[6] In Finnish, on the other hand, the glottal stop is a phonemic boundary signal. It occurs only after vowels in word-final position, where it is in distinctive opposition, however, with "final vowels without a glottal stop" (e.g., "vie'" [lead]: "vie" [he leads]).

Finally, the so-called "nonfree" or "fixed" accent is also a non-phonemic boundary signal. Since all words with the same number of syllables (or morae) always carry this accent on the same syllable (or mora), the position of the accent cannot differentiate the meaning of words. However, it always indicates the relationship of the accented prosodeme to the word boundary.[7] In by far the majority of languages in question the "fixed" (dynamic) accent falls on the word-initial syllable. Take, for example, Gaelic, Icelandic, Lapp, Finnish, Livonian, Upper and in part also Lower Sorbian, Czech, Slovak, Hungarian, Chechen, Darghinian, Lak, Yurak-Samoyed ("Nenets"), Tavgi Samoyed ("Nganasan"), Yenisei-Samoyed ("Enets"), Vogul, Yakut, Mongolian, and Kalmuk. In other languages the fixed accent always occurs on the final syllable, as, for example, in Armenian, the Tawda dialect of Vogul, the overwhelming majority of Turkic languages, and in Tübatulabal (Shoshonean group of Uto-Aztecan). In all these languages the dynamic accent thus indicates directly with which syllable the word begins or ends. In some other languages the fixed accent is separated from the word boundary by a prosodeme. In other words, it falls on the second or on the penultimate prosodeme of the word. This type of fixed accent is not rare, but it seems to occur only in a geographically limited area. In Europe the fixed accent on the penultimate *syllable* is represented in Polish (with the exception of the Kashub dialects), in the neighboring dialects of Czech and Slovak, and the Eastern dialects of Lower Sorbian.[8] This same "accentuation of the penultimate" is further found in certain Bulgarian dialects of Macedonia and Albania.[9] The accent in the now extinct Polabian fell on the penultimate *mora* of the word.

However, the most important range of distribution in which the fixed expiratory accent falls on the penultimate syllable of a word is not in Europe but in Africa. It seems to comprise all the Bantu languages. As for the fixed accentuation of the second prosodeme, it appears to be especially widespread in American languages: above (in the discussion of the features of the mora-counting languages), reference has already been made to Southern Paiute and Maidu, where the expiratory primary accent falls on the second mora of the word (p.174). In all these cases where a prosodeme separates the accent from the "word boundary," the accent does not signal the word boundary directly but merely the vicinity of the word boundary. The distance between accent and word boundary, however, is always the same. There are even more complicated cases, as, for example, the fixed accent on the antepenultimate syllable in certain Bulgarian dialects of Macedonia,[10] or the accent on the penultimate mora before the final syllable in Classical Latin. All these types of accentuation which are automatically determined by the number of prosodemes are incapable of differentiating meaning between word pairs. They serve only to signal the proximity of a word boundary, that is, they are nonphonemic boundary signals.

Inasmuch as the "fixed accent" signals a word boundary, it is actually only meaningful within a sentence. In a language where the final syllable of every word is accented, thus signaling the word boundary, this final accent should actually be omitted with respect to the last word of the sentence since the final boundary of the word is already sufficiently signaled by the final pause of the sentence. And this is in fact the case in many languages. According to E. D. Polivanov,[11] Korean accentuates the final syllable of every word. Only in the last word of the sentence is the initial syllable accented. In Uzbek the accent in all words falls on the final syllable. Only the verb forms of the preterite have the primary accent on the first syllable. This, according to Polivanov's very plausible opinion, is related to the well-known syntactic idiosyncrasy of Turkic languages, namely, that the finite verb occurs in sentence-final position. This idiosyncrasy might also explain the "retraction" of the accent in certain verbal forms of Ottoman Turkish, for example, in the present tense in -jor- and in the interrogative forms. In Czech, where the fixed accent falls on the word-initial syllable, monosyllabic conjunctions such as "a" (and), "že" (that), etc., are not accented. The reason for this is that they generally occur sentence-initially, and the initial boundary of a sentence need not be signaled. It is true, of course, that in most languages with a fixed accent the rules of accentuation have already become so automatic that sentence boundaries are no longer taken into consideration.[12]

[1] Cf. W. Steinitz, "Chantyjskij (ostjackij) jazyk," in *Jazyki i pis'mennost' narodov Severa*, I (1937), 200 ff.
[2] Cf. J. P. Crazzolara, "Outlines of a Nuer Grammar," in *Linguistische Bibliothek "Anthropos,"* XIII (1933).
[3] Cf. J. R. Firth, *A Short Outline of Tamil Pronunciation* (offprint of the new and revised edition of Arden's *Grammar of Common Tamil* [1934]).

[4] Cf. N. N. Poppe, "Alarskij govor" in *Materialy komissii po issledovaniju Mongol'skoj i Tuvinskoj Narodnych Respublik*, II (Leningrad, Akad. Nauk SSSR, 1930).

[5] Cf. V. N. Černecov, "Manzijskij (vogul'skij) jazyk," in *Jazyki i pis'mennost' narodov Severa*, I (1937), 171.

[6] In German the same pronunciation is also found medially in "hiatus position" (e.g., in "Theater"). However, words containing a sequence of two vowels which cannot be divided up morphologically are loanwords in German. Accordingly this is a case where a boundary signal is used to mark loanwords (see below).

[7] Cf. R. Jakobson, *O češskom stiche* (Berlin, 1923), pp. 26 ff., and in *Mélanges ... van Ginneken*, pp. 26 f.

[8] Cf. L. Ščerba, *Vostočnolužickoje narěčije* (Petrograd, 1915), pp. 35 ff.; and Zd. Stieber, *Stosunki prokrewieństwa języków łużyckich* (Kraków, 1934), pp. 70 ff.

[9] Among others, for example, the dialect of Boboštica, cf. A. Mazon, *Documents, contes et chansons slaves de l'Albanie du Sud* (Paris, 1936).

[10] Cf. B. Conev, *Istorija na bălgarskij ezik*, I (Sofia, 1919), 465 ff.

[11] E. D. Polivanov, "Zur Frage der Betonungsfunktionen," in *TCLP*, VI, 80 f.

[12] French represents a very special case. Accentuation has nothing to do here with word boundaries. Its sole function is to organize speech into sentences, sentence sections, and sentence rhythm. The circumstance that a word in isolation is always accented on its final syllable is solely due to the fact that such a word is treated as a unit of sentence rhythm. French accent does not signal the end of a word as such but the end of a unit of sentence rhythm, a sentence section, or a sentence. Retraction of accent in French serves solely "phonostylistic" purposes.

III INDIVIDUAL SIGNALS AND GROUP SIGNALS

The boundary signals discussed in the preceding chapter may be designated as *individual signals*. They either involve a single phoneme that occurs only at a word or morpheme boundary, or they involve a combinatory variant of an individual phoneme, which can only occur in a specific boundary position.[1] But there is still another type of boundary signal, namely, special combinations of (phonemic or nonphonemic) units which occur only at the boundary between two words or morphemes and therefore signal such a boundary. These may be designated as *group signals*.

Phonemic group signals are combinations of phonemes which occur only at a boundary between two units of meaning. The first part of such a combination belongs to the end of the preceding unit of meaning, the second to the beginning of the following unit. Boundary signals of this type are extremely numerous and varied. For example, with reference to German, the following combinations may be cited, to mention only two-member group signals: "consonant + h" ("ein Haus" [a house], "an-halten" [stop], "Wesen-heit" [essence], "der Hals" [the neck], "ver-hindern" [prevent], "Wahr-heit" [truth]); "nasal + liquid" ("an-liegen" [to border on], "ein-reden" [to convince oneself], "irrtüm-lich" [erroneous], "um-ringen" [to surround]); further, *nm, pm, km, tzm, fm, mw, mg, mch, mtz, nb, np, ng* (i.e., *ŋg* in contrast with *ŋ*), *nf, nw, pw, pfw, fw, chw, spf, schpf, schf, schz, ssch, fp, k, fch, chf, chp, chk*, etc.* With respect to

---

* *Translator's note:* In phoneme terms these are *nm, pm, km, cm, fm, mv, mg, mx, mc, nb, np, ŋg, nf, nv, pv, p̆v, fv, xv, sp̆, šp̆, šf, šc, sš, fp, k, fx, xf, xp, xk.*

French, the phoneme sequence "nasalized vowel + *m*" may be mentioned (e.g., *un marin, on mange, grand'mère, emmener, nous vinmes*); for English, the combinations *θs, δz, sθ, zδ, čt, čs, šs, sš, dz*, and very many others.

Similar phonemic group signals can probably be cited for most European languages,[2] but they are not rare in other geographical areas either. In Northern Greenlandic there are two types of consonant combination: "*r* + consonant" and "occlusive + consonant." The former occurs only in medial position, while the latter always occurs at the word boundary, the occlusive (*p, t, k,* or *q*) ending the preceding word, the following consonant beginning the next word. In Tonkawa (an isolated Indian language in Texas) the combination "two consonants + *d̓* " occurs only at the word boundary, the first consonant belonging to the preceding word. The combination "*d̓* + *š* + consonant" is here likewise a phonemic word boundary signal. In this case the boundary occurs between *š* and the following consonant.[3] In the Santee dialect of Dakota the combinations *tx̌, mt, mk, ms, mč, mx̌, sk', x̌k', gs, gč, gb,* and *np* occur only at the morpheme boundary.[4] It follows from the rules for the use of consonants and consonant combinations in initial and final position given by Ida C. Ward that in Efik the combinations "*k, d, p* + consonant," "*t* + consonant except *r*," "*m* + nonlabial consonant," and "*n* + nonapical consonant" can only arise upon contact between two words in syntactic context.[5] Accordingly they are phonemic group signals. With respect to the Turkic languages, a great deal of instructive material can be found in chapter 12 of W. Radloff's *Phonetics*. In the Altai and Abakan dialects and in Kazakh-Kirghiz (now Kazakh) the combination "(voiceless) obstruent + sonorant (*j, m, n, r, l*)" occurs only at the place of contact between two words. In the Altai dialects the combinations *tp, ts, tč* (= *čč*)*, pp, st, sč, sp, št, šč, šp,*

281

šs, *čq*, *čk*, *čt*, *čs*, and *čp* signal either the morpheme (*op. cit.*, pp. 226 f.) or the word boundary. In Kazakh-Kirghiz (p. 231), the Northern Abakan dialects (p. 229), and the Altai dialects, with the exception of Teleut, original *pq* and *pk* became *qp* and *kp* in medial position (so far as it could not be divided morphologically). The combinations *pq* and *pk* in these dialects today accordingly always signal a morpheme (or word) boundary. The same is true for the combinations *qs* and *ks* in the Abakan dialects (p. 229). In Yakut the phoneme sequences $t + k$, $t + s$, and $s + t$ always signal a word boundary (pp. 236 and 238). In Lak consonant combinations that include a liquid or a nasal are permitted within a morpheme. The combinations of two obstruents are always boundary signals. The combinations "obstruent + *s*" occur at the morpheme as well as the word boundary. The remaining combinations of obstruents occur only at the place of contact between two words in syntactic context. Avar, which otherwise permits a great variety of consonant combinations within a morpheme, does not allow the phoneme sequence "labial + liquid" within a word. In cases where it should occur metathesis takes place. For example: "qomòr" (wolf): ergative *qormìc·a* (< **qomrìc·a*); "xibìl" (side): ergative *xolbòc·a* (< **xilblòc·a*); also such loanwords as "ilbis" (satan) = Arabic "iblis," "q'ilba" (south) = Arabic "quibla." The phoneme sequence "labial + liquid" therefore occurs here only at the place of contact between two words within a sentence (e.g., "k'udìjab ròso" [big village], "qàḥab lèmag" [white sheep]). It must be regarded as a phonemic group boundary signal.

There are languages in which units of meaning are delimited in advance by their phonemic structure. This is the case in the so-called "monosyllabic" or "isolating" languages. In Burmese, where all words (i.e., morphemes) are monosyllabic and consist either of a vowel phoneme or of the phoneme sequence "consonant phoneme + vowel phoneme," the phoneme sequences "vowel phoneme + vowel phoneme" or "vowel phoneme + consonant phoneme" can only occur at the place of contact between two words in a sentence. They are therefore phonemic group boundary signals. In Northern Chinese, where a morpheme can either end in a vowel or in a diphthong, or in an indeterminate nasal (or in an indeterminate liquid, but not in all dialects), and where it can begin either with a vowel or with a consonant, the boundary between two morphemes is usually also signaled quite unambiguously by phoneme sequences (e.g., by the sequences "nasal + consonant," "liquid + consonant," "vowel + consonant"). The sequences "vowel + vowel" are usually unambiguously phonemic group signals since not all vowels form diphthongs with each other. And only in exceptional cases is the phonemic structure of such a sequence not sufficient to delimit the morphemes from each other (e.g., in a sequence such as *u̯ai̯o* = *u̯ai̯* + *o*, or *u̯a* + *i̯o*). In cases of this type nonphonemic factors will decide.

Just as common as phonemic group boundary signals are nonphonemic group boundary signals. The opposition between velar and palatal *x* as well as *g* in German may be cited as an example. The syllables *xə* and *gə* ("che," "ge") are pronounced with a velar *x* and *g* after back vowels (*u, o, a, au*: "suche" [seek], "Woche" [week], "Wache" [watch], "rauche" [smoke], "Fuge" [fugue], "Woge" [wave], "sage" [say], "Auge" [eye]), but with a palatal *x* and *g* in all other positions. One may therefore be led to believe that the opposition between palatal and velar *x* and *g* is quite irrelevant before a *ə*. In reality the velarizing effect of the preceding *u, o, a*, and *au* does not extend beyond the scope of one morpheme. In "im Zuge stehen" (to stand in a draught/in a train) the *g* is velar because it belongs to the same morpheme as the preceding *u*. In "zugestehen" (to confess), however, the *g* is palatal because a morpheme boundary exists between it and the *u* (*cu-gə-šte-n*). Likewise, in "machen" (to make) the *x* is velar because it belongs to the same morpheme as the *a* (*max-n*); but in "Mama-chen" (mother, dimin.) the *x* is palatal because a morpheme boundary exists between it and the *a* (*mama-xən*). The palatal realization of *g* and *x* after a back vowel in German is thus a nonphonemic group boundary signal. As for English, reference may be made to the distribution of the two types of *l*. The rule says that *l* is pronounced "clear" before vowels but "dark" before consonants and in final position. But instead of "before vowels" one should rather say "before a vowel of the same word." For this rule is not effective across word boundaries. Accordingly the *l* in "we learn" (phonet. *wilə:n*) is "clear" but "dark" in "will earn" (phonet. *wiḷə:n*). Clear and dark *l* in English are therefore only two combinatory variants of a single phoneme. But in the phoneme sequence "vowel + *l* + vowel" the opposition between the clear and the dark variant of the phoneme *l* has a delimitative function. "Dark realization" of the phoneme *l* in such a phoneme sequence indicates that there is a word boundary between the *l* and the following vowel. In Russian (as in German or English) the contrast between palatal and velar *k* is nonphonemic: before *e* and *i*, *k* is pronounced as a palatal; in all other positions it is pronounced as a velar. But this rule does not apply across the boundaries of a word. If a word ends in a *k* and the next word begins with an *e* or an *i*, the *k* remains velar, and the vowels *i* and *e* are shifted toward the back correspondingly (*e > ɛ, i > ʉ*). For example: "k etomu" (to this) pronounced *kɛtəmʉ* (but "keta" [a Siberian type of fish] pron. *k'etă*); "mog eto" (could this) pronounced *mɔkɛtə*; "k izbam" (to the huts) pronounced *kʉzbəm* (but

"kis by" [would become sour] pronounced *k'izby*); "drug i prijatel'"
[bosom friend] pronounced *drùkŭ pr'ĭjǽt'ĭl'* (but "ruki prijatel'a" [the
hands of a friend] pronounced *ruk'ĭ pr'ĭjǽt'ĭl'ə*). The sequences *kE* and
ku in Russian thus are group boundary signals that indicate the presence
of a word boundary between the phoneme *k* and the following vowel
phonemes *e* or *i*. Before *e* only palatalized consonants are permitted within
a morpheme in Russian. The correlation of palatalization is thus neutralized in this position. However, if a morpheme boundary occurs before
the *e*, the preceding consonant can also remain unpalatalized. For example:
"s-etim" (with this), "iz-etogo" (from this), "v-etom" (in this), "pod-
etim" (under this), "ot-etogo" (from/of this). These are pronounced
set'ĭm, iztəvə, vɛtəm, pădetĭm, ătɛtəvə respectively. The absence of a palatalization before the phoneme *e* is a nonphonemic group signal for a morpheme boundary. The Russian phoneme *ă* (unaccented *a*) is realized as an *a*
in initial position, after vowels, and in directly pretonic syllable, but as a *ə*
elsewhere. In a sequence such as in the following phrase "zvùkabrŭʋà-
(j)icəràzəm" a morpheme boundary has to occur before the first *a* (*a* would
have to be realized as a *ə* after a *k* in an unaccented, directly pretonic
syllable). But a word boundary must also occur between *ə* and *r* because in
a directly pretonic syllable in the same word *a* could not be realized as a *ə*
but has to be realized as an *a*. Accordingly there is only one way in which
to divide the above phoneme sequence: "zvuk ăbrŭʋàjĭcə ràzəm" (phonol.
"zvuk ăbrĭvajĭcă razăm" [the sound stops abruptly]). The phones *a* and *ə*
in Russian are thus combinatory variants of the phoneme *a*. In their
relationship to the accented syllable they form a part of group signals for
word boundaries.

A special type of nonphonemic group signal is represented by what is
called "vowel harmony." Certain border cases exist here between nonphonemic and phonemic boundary signals. We have already discussed
the vowel system of Ibo, where a word can either contain only open or
only close vowels (p. 109). If in this language a syllable with an open vowel
occurs next to a syllable with a close vowel within the context of a sentence, a word boundary has to be present between these syllables. It is
obvious that a group signal is involved here, but it is not quite clear
whether this signal is phonemic or nonphonemic. On the one hand, open
and close vowels are different phonemes that have distinctive force in
certain positions (namely, in the first syllable of the root). On the other
hand, the opposition between open and close vowels is neutralized in
noninitial root syllable (in accordance with the law of vowel harmony).
A similar case appears to exist in Finnish. As already mentioned (p. 102),
the oppositions *u-y*, *o-ö*, and *a-ä* are there neutralized in noninitial syllable

after a syllable containing *u, y, o, ö, a,* or *ä*. Only *u, o,* and *a* can occur after *u, o,* and *a,* and only *y, ö,* and *ä* after *y, ö,* and *ä*. Should these vowels occur in a different sequence in syntactic context (e.g., "hyvä poika" [good boy], "iso pyssy" [big can]), this signals the presence of a boundary between the two words. But there are also clearer cases of nonphonemic boundary signals associated with vowel harmony. In Lamba unaccented *e* and *o* in word-initial syllable are realized as close *e* and *o* after a syllable containing *ē, ō, ī, i, ū,* and *u*. In all other cases they are realized as open *ε* and *ə*.[8] Open realization of these phonemes after a syllable containing *i* and *u* is thus a sign that a word boundary falls between these phonemes. Likewise in Zulu, where *e* and *o* are close before a syllable containing *i, u, m,* and *n* of the same word, and open elsewhere (*ε* and *ə*),[9] open realization of the phonemes *e* and *o* before a syllable with *i, u, m,* and *n* signals the presence of a word boundary immediately after *e* and *o*. In Tamil *e, ē, o,* and *ō* are realized as close vowels before *i* and *ī* and as open vowels before *a* and *ā*.[10] Where this law is disturbed, a word boundary is found after the phonemes *e, ē, o,* and *ō*. From "vowel harmony" in the proper sense, the so-called *synharmonism* must be distinguished. It is found most clearly in certain Turkic languages, for example, in Volga Tatar, or Kazan Tatar, Bashkir, Kazakh-Kirghiz or Kazakh, and in the Kipchak dialects of Uzbek. From a purely phonetic point of view, synharmonism consists in that each word in the particular language can either contain only front vowels and palatalized consonants or only back vowels and velarized consonants.[11] Since such synharmonism is only effective within the frame of a word, the sequences "palatalized consonant or front vowel + velarized consonant or back vowel" and "velarized consonant or back vowel + palatalized consonant or front vowel" are a sign of the presence of a word boundary between the two constituents of that sequence. In the same languages a different series of nonphonemic group signals for word boundaries also results from the laws of so-called labial attraction. According to these, vowel phonemes in word-noninitial syllable which phonologically are not characterized by any class of timbre are realized as rounded vowels after certain rounded vowels.[12] A word boundary is found at the point of the sound continuum where this law is violated. Phenomena related to synharmonism and labial attraction outside the Turkic languages are also found in some Finno-Ugric languages and in the Mongolian and Tungus languages. They always function as signals of word boundaries.

Synharmonism can be compared to tonality in music. In a "synharmonic" language each word is like a string of sounds moving within a particular key. But there are only two such keys in the language, and synharmonism utilizes the change in key in the context of a sentence to signal the word boundary. But just as the word in "synharmonic" languages is, as it were, a unit of timbre, there are other languages in which the word is regarded as a specific *rhythmic unit*. These are languages with unfree, fixed accentuation which, in addition to a primary accent, also have secondary accents (which are also automatically determined). Sometimes all quantity relationships, and even the qualitative marks of the vowels and consonants, are affected by the distribution of the expiratory accent. For example, in Southern Paiute (Shoshonean group of the Uto-Aztecan language family), in which the primary accent falls on the second mora, and the secondary accent on the even morae of a word (i.e., on the fourth, sixth, eighth, etc.), the "weak" morae (i.e., morae that have neither primary nor secondary accent) are voiceless before geminated consonants. Before such voiceless vowels the occlusives are pronounced as voiceless aspirates, and the continuants (fricatives, nasals, and *r*) as voiceless consonants. Before voiced vowels, on the other hand, the occlusives are (voiceless but) unaspirated, and the continuants are voiced except for the sibilants. A short vowel in word-final position is always voiceless, regardless of accent distribution.[13] The rhythmic structure of the word is accordingly reinforced here by the realization of all phonemes. Any disturbance of this rhythmic inertia, which always signals the end of a word and the beginning of another, thereby acquires a special potency. In most Finno-Ugric and Samoyed languages with a fixed initial accent, the secondary accents fall on uneven syllables or morae (i.e., on the third, fifth, seventh, etc.).[14] This produces a certain rhythmic inertia that, when disturbed, is a signal of the word boundary. In some of these languages this rhythmic inertia of the word is reinforced by various other means that are partially phonemic and partially nonphonemic. For example, in the Sea Lapp dialect of Maattivuono neither *c*, *ʒ*, *č'*, *ʒ'*, *d'*, *γ*, *δ*, *ŋ*, *n'*, *l'*, nor geminated consonants can occur directly after the vowel of an even syllable (i.e., the second, fourth, sixth, etc.). The number of consonant combinations that occur in this position is also very limited (*sk, st, sn, št, šD, jD, lD, rD, lG, rG, lm*). In addition to these phonemic means that serve to underline the opposition between even and uneven word syllables, there also exist non-phonemic means: the vowels of even syllables are "excessively short" and whispered when they occur between voiceless consonants; the fortes *p, t, k* are always aspirated after vowels of even word syllables. The trochaic rhythm of the word is thereby anchored not only in the accentual relationships but also in the entire phonic makeup of the individual syllables. Further, the "tempo" in which the word syllables are realized depends on the total word. The length of the same etymologically long or short vowel in the same consonant environment is determined by whether it occurs in word-initial syllable or noninitial syllable, and further by the number of syllables of the word in question.[15] The word in this Lapp dialect thus is a rhythmic unit. A violation of the rhythmic inertia of individual points in the context of a sentence is a signal of the word boundaries. It may be noted that in languages such as Lapp the tendency for a nonphonemic (phonetic) joining of words into rhythmic units appears especially clearly. But this tendency is also found in many other languages in a less clear form (not all of these are languages with a fixed accent).

That the word can also be a *melodic* unit is readily evident. This is, of course, especially the case in those languages where the accent is primarily "musical," in other words, in mora-counting languages. In Lithuanian pretonic syllables are musically rising within the frame of a word, while posttonic syllables are musically falling.[16] Where this relationship is disturbed in the speech continuum, that is, in places where a musically falling syllable occurs before a musically rising syllable, a word boundary must occur between the two syllables. Accordingly a nonphonemic group signal for the word boundary results here too from the total melodic structure of the word.

In conclusion it should be mentioned that in certain cases it is difficult to decide whether a nonphonemic or a phonemic boundary signal is involved. In certain Middle Indic ("Prākrit") dialects, for example, in Mahârâshtrî, the occlusives *p, ph, b, t, th, d, dh, k, kh, g, gh, c, ch, j, jh* were always geminated after a short vowel medially or in a noncompounded word. In ungeminated form these occlusives occurred after a short vowel only when they were found initially in the second member of a compound. For example: "digghakaṇṇo" (long ear) = "diggha" (long) + "kaṇṇo" (ear). The geminated and the nongeminated occlusives of the labial, apical, guttural, and palatal series thus could be regarded as two combinatory variants, and the combination "vowel + nongeminated occlusive" as a nonphonemic group signal of the word boundary (or of the boundary between the constituents of a compound). But this relationship was disturbed in that in Mahârâshtrî certain consonants participated in a distinctive correlation of gemination (namely, the voiced retroflex occlusives *ḍ* and *ḍh*, the nasals *ṇ* and *m*, the liquid *l*, and the spirant *s*).[17] This would create a feeling of evoking a sense for the phonemic value of the oppositions of consonant gemination, so that the *k* (in "digghakaṇṇo" [long ear]) and *kk* (in "vakkala" [cow]) were perhaps not regarded as combinatory variants, but as two different phonemes. (In such event the combination "vowel + nongeminated labial, apical, guttural, or palatal" had to be considered a phonemic group signal.)

Following this chapter some remarks will be made on combinatory variants. Recently a voice has been raised among phonologists to remove the study of combinatory variants from the domain of phonology.[18] According to this view, combinatory variants belong to the domain of parole. They owe their existence to the physiology of speech sounds. Consequently they have nothing to do with phonology. If phonologists still make mention of combinatory variants and take them into consideration, this is a vestige of the old phonetic orientation, or it is done in consideration of the diachronic (historical) study of sounds. A misinterpretation of the role of combinatory variants is obviously involved here. Combinatory variants are not merely causally but also teleologically conditioned phenomena that have a specific purpose and perform a definite function.[19] This function always consists of signaling the direct proximity of another linguistic element, which may be either a specific phoneme or a (word or morpheme) boundary, or both. Now, it is clear that where a combinatory variant signals a word or morpheme boundary directly, its function belongs to the domain of the system of language (langue). For the de-limitation of morphemes within a word is no less "glottal" than the differ-entiation of words. On the other hand, a combinatory variant that merely signals the proximity of a phoneme clearly belongs to the domain of the act of speech. For only insofar as the speech act is concerned is it meaning-ful to assure the perception of a phoneme, not only by its own realization but also by specific peculiarities in the realization of the neighboring phonemes. Such an "assurance of perception" presupposes an orientation toward speech, which is characteristic for the domain of parole but alien to the system of language (langue). Those combinatory variants that signal at the same time the proximity of a phoneme and the relationship to the (word or morpheme) boundary represent a case of transition. Combinatory variants of this type (i.e., nonphonemic group signals), hover between the system of language and the speech act, thus requiring the attention of the phonologist as well as that of the phonetician. Specific word sequences, of course, in which nonphonemic group signals mark the word boundaries, occur only in the speech act. However, the rules for pronunciation, which yield these group signals, belong to the domain of the system of language, just as do the syntactic rules for word ordering and concordance.

[1] Likewise the "fixed accent" is nothing more than a special combinatory variant of an individual syllable nucleus (marked by loudness of voice).

[2] For Czech, compare, for example, the list given by B. Trnka in his study "Pokus o vědeckou teorii a praktickou reformu těsnopisu," in *Facultas Philo-sophica Universitatis Carolinae, Sbírka pojednáni a rozprav*, XX (1937), 40 ff.

INDIVIDUAL SIGNALS AND GROUP SIGNALS 289

[3] Cf. Harry Hoijer, "Tonkawa, an Indian Language of Texas," in *Handbook of American Indian Languages*, III (The University of Chicago Press).

[4] Cf. Franz Boas and R. J. Swanton in *Handbook of American Indian Languages*, I (*Bureau of American Ethnology*, Bulletin XL), 882.

[5] Cf. Ida C. Ward, *The Phonetic and Tonal Structure of Efik* (Cambridge, 1933).

[6] W. Radloff, *Vergleichende Grammatik der nördlichen Türksprachen*, I: *Phonetik der nördlichen Türksprachen* (Leipzig, 1882).

[7] Cf. N. Jakovlev, *Tablicy fonetiki kabardinskogo jazyka* (Moscow, 1923), pp. 70 f.

[8] Cf. Clement M. Doke, "A Study of Lamba Phonetics," in *Bantu Studies* (1928).

[9] Cf. Clement M. Doke, "The Phonetics of the Zulu Language," in *Bantu Studies*, II (1926), Special Number.

[10] Cf. J. R. Firth, *A Short Outline of Tamil Pronunciation* (1934).

[11] Cf. Halimdžan Šaraf, *Palatogrammy zvukov tatarskogo jazyka* (Kazan, 1927), especially pp. 35 ff. Phonologically the matter appears differently. The consonant *j* does not have any palatalized or velarized variants, and many words consist only of vowels and *j* ("aj" [moon], "aju" [bear], etc.). Accordingly it is possible for vowel phonemes to have a specific property of timbre independent of consonantal environment, while the consonants are palatalized or velarized only in connection with vowels. (The vowelless interjections such as *pšt*, *k'l't'*, etc., which are cited by H. Šaraf, are no ordinary words.) Oppositions of timbre are therefore phonemic for vowels. The palatalized and velarized variants of the consonants represent only combinatory variants without distinctive (but with delimitative) force.

[12] On this point, cf. W. Radloff, *op. cit.* (Chaps. I–III), and a clear survey by V. A. Bogorodickij, *Étjudy po tatarskomu i tjurkskomu jazykoznaniju* (Kazan, 1933), pp. 58–73.

[13] Cf. Edward Sapir, "The Southern Paiute Language," in *Proceedings of the Amer. Acad. of Arts and Sciences*, LXV, nos. 1–3, pars. 8–10, 12.

[14] The uneven morae of a word receive secondary accents in Tavgy-Samjoyed ("Ngasan"). For example: "kúa" (birch): loc. "kúatànu"; but "lū" (dress): loc. "lū'tànu," etc. Otherwise most of these languages have the secondary accent on the uneven *syllables* (G. Prokofjev in *Jazyki i pis'mennost' narodov Severa*, I, 56).

[15] Paavo Ravila, *Das Quantitätssystem des seelappischen Dialektes von Maattivuono*, pp. 56 f., 59 ff., and 78 f.

[16] A similar situation may probably also be assumed for Proto-Slavic.

[17] Cf. R. Pischel, "Grammatik der Prakrit-Sprachen" (*Grundr. d. indoarischen Philol.*, Strassburg, 1900), and H. Jacobi, "Ausgewählte Erzählungen im Mâhârâshtri."

[18] L'udovít Novák, "K základným otázkám štrukturálnéj jazykovedy" (*Sborník Matice Slovenskej*, XV (1937), no. 1).

[19] Cf. N. Jakovlev, *Tablicy fonetiki kabardinskogo jazyka* (Moscow, 1923), pp. 73 ff.

IV POSITIVE AND NEGATIVE BOUNDARY SIGNALS

The boundary signals discussed so far were positive. In other words, they indicated expressly that a word or morpheme boundary was present at the particular position. But there may also be *negative* boundary signals whose express function is to indicate the absence of a boundary in a particular position. Their role could be compared to the green lights that indicate to the traveler that all is well at the particular crossing and that he may proceed safely. However, in addition to such *generally negative* boundary signals, language also possesses *bilaterally negative* boundary signals. These merely indicate that no new word can begin or no word can end in a particular position. All negative boundary signals can either be phonemic or nonphonemic. They may be group signals or individual signals. Several examples of each of these types of negative boundary signals will follow.

1 PHONEMIC NEGATIVE BOUNDARY SIGNALS

A Individual Signals

By phonemic negative individual signals those phonemes are to be understood that are permitted only word- or morpheme-medially in a language. In Finnish the phonemes *d* and *ŋ* (always geminated, *ŋŋ* written *ng*) belong to this category. In Tamil *ŋ*, retroflex *ṭ*, and *ḷ*, and the guttural liquid λ belong here. In Kazakh (formerly Kazakh-Kirghiz) and in Kirghiz (formerly Karakirghiz), as well as in the Turkic dialects of the Irtysh Basin, the voiced gutturals γ and *g* occur neither initially nor finally, only medially. In Tübatulabal all voiced obstruents (b, d, g, з, ž) occur exclusively medially. In Efik h and r are found medially only.

As bilateral negative signals the ŋ in German, English, Dutch, Danish, Norwegian, and Swedish, and French ɲ (gn), can be mentioned. They are permitted in medial and final position, but not initially. The same is also true as follows: for r in Chechen and Tungus; for the "only liquid" in Korean (which is realized as an r intervocalically and as an l finally); for p, t, k, ḍ, з, ž, θ, δ, γ, ṇ, and l in the Sea Lapp dialect of Maattivuono; for b, d, k, g, c, and ć of Yurak Samoyed; and for p of Efik. On the other hand, the h in German, English, Yurak Samoyed, Artshi, etc., is only permitted in initial and medial but not in final position. The same holds true for g, k, and k' in Haida, and for f, s, ṇ, and kp in Efik. There are languages that finally only permit vowels, or in addition to vowels, only a very small number of consonants: ν, ρ, σ in Classical Greek, n, r, and l in Italian, and n, t, and s in Finnish, etc. In languages of this type all consonants, except those mentioned, may be regarded as signals that "negate final position."

B Group Signals

Finnish does not permit any consonant combinations initially and finally. Furthermore, only vowels and the consonants n, t, and s occur in final position. Any consonant combination in which n, t, or s does not occur as a first member is, accordingly, a negative phonemic group signal. In words such as "kahdeksan" (eight), "hupsu" (stupid), "selkä" (back), etc., the combinations hd, ks, ps, and lk point to medial position. The same function is here also fulfilled by all geminated consonants (with the exception of nn, ss, and tt; these may occur not only medially but also at the word boundary. For example: "mies seisoo" [the man is standing], "pojat tansivat" [the boys dance], "nainen neuloo" [the woman sews], etc.). In languages such as Russian, where obstruents are always voiceless in final position, the combination "voiced obstruent + vowel or sonorant" is always a sign that no word boundary is present between the components of this combination. In Northern Greenlandic, where *r* cannot occur in final position, the combination "*r* + consonant" is always a sign of medial position. The same is also true for the combination of "*l* + consonant" (except *s*) in Classical Greek. In German the combination *dl*, which occurs only word-medially, seems to be the only negative phonemic group signal. Negative phonemic group signals in general are a relatively rare phenomenon.

2   NONPHONEMIC NEGATIVE BOUNDARY SIGNALS

A   Individual Signals

In cases where a phoneme is realized in a particular way initially or finally, any other realization of this phoneme is consequently a negative boundary signal. As already discussed above, aspiration of p^h, t^h, and k^h in Tamil must be regarded as a positive nonphonemic boundary signal. It is only realized in this way word-initially. The realization of the same phonemes as fricatives (*v*, δ, *x*, or *h* respectively) must be regarded accordingly as a negative nonphonemic boundary signal since it occurs only medially (intervocalically). In Japanese, where "*g*" initially is realized as the voiced obstruent *g*, and medially as a nasal *ŋ*, *g* is a positive and *ŋ* a negative nonphonemic boundary signal. In Korean, where the "only liquid" is realized as an *l* finally, and as an *r* medially, the *l* is a positive, the *r* a negative nonphonemic boundary signal. In many Turkic languages of Siberia (e.g., in the dialects of Altai of the Baraba Steppe, in Teleut, in Shor, and in the Küärik dialect) all obstruents are realized as voiceless in initial and final position (i.e., as *q* or *x* respectively, and as *k*, *p*, *t*, *s*, *š*, and *c* or *č* or *ṭ* respectively). They are realized as voiced medially between vowels, however (γ, *g*, *b*, *d*, *z*, *ž*, and *ǯ*),[1] thus creating negative nonphonemic boundary signals. In Ostyak, too, the obstruents are voiceless in initial and final position. But medially they are more or less voiced.[2] In German and Hungarian *h* is voiceless initially (in Hungarian also finally), but voiced medially between vowels (Uhu! Oho).[3]

B   Group Signals

What has been said with regard to individual signals also holds true for negative nonphonemic group signals. As a rule, a positive nonphonemic group signal has a negative counterpart. For example, in German the sequence "back vowel + palatal *g*" is a sign of the existence of a morpheme boundary between these two phones. The sequence "back vowel + velar *g* (before ə)," on the other hand, indicates the absence of a boundary between the vowel and *g*. In English the sequence "dark *l* + vowel" is a positive nonphonemic boundary signal. The sequence "clear *l* + vowel," on the other hand, indicates that no word boundary is present between these two components. Most of the examples for positive nonphonemic group signals, cited above, have negative group signals as their counterparts. However, this is not always the case. In a language with consistent synharmonism the disturbance of such synharmonism represents a positive boundary signal (e.g., the contact of a front vowel with a velarized consonant). However, synharmonism of this type has neither positive nor negative signaling value since it is very possible that two words "with back vowels" or two words "with front vowels" occur next to each other without affecting the synharmonism.

To the negative nonphonemic group signals belongs also lengthening of medial accented vowels in Italian. As is known, final accented vowels are never lengthened. Only accented vowels of the penultimate and antepenultimate syllable are lengthened, and, more precisely, they are only lengthened before a vowel, before an intervocalic consonant, or before the combination "consonant + liquid (*r*, *u̯*, and *i̯*)." If one considers that the word-final syllable in Italian can be accented only if it ends in a vowel, and, on the other hand, that in Italian a word can either begin only in a vowel or in a single consonant, or in a cluster "consonant + *r*, *u̯*, *i̯*," or in the combination "*s* + consonant," the purpose for lengthening the accented vowel in Italian becomes perfectly clear. Such lengthening precludes the presence of a word boundary after an accented vowel. Accordingly it occurs only in those positions where such a word boundary could be surmised, that is, before those phones and combinations of phones that can also occur initially. Before "*m*, *n*, *l*, *r* + consonant" a lengthening of accented vowels would serve no purpose. For after an accented vowel these combinations are already (phonemic) negative group signals. Only before the sequence "*s* + consonant" can the absence of a lengthened accented vowel lead to misunderstandings. For example, one could analyse the sequence "velocità straordinaria" as "velocitastra ordinaria." However, words beginning with "*s* (or *z*) + consonant" account for only somewhat less than 8 percent of the entire vocabulary in Italian. Cases in which the possibility for such misinterpretations exists are therefore not very numerous. Lengthening of accented vowels accordingly remains one of the most important negative nonphonemic group signals of Italian.

---

[1] Cf. W. Radloff, *op. cit.*, pp. 128 ff., 173 ff., and 199 f.

[2] However, only optionally with strong individual fluctuations. Cf. W. Steinitz in *Jazyki i pis'mennost' narodov Severa*, I, 202.

[3] Likewise also in Yurak-Samoyed, cf. G. N. Prokofjev in *Jazyki i pis'mennost' narodov Severa*, I, 13.

V THE USE OF BOUNDARY SIGNALS

Individual languages vary considerably in their use of boundary signals. In some languages it is the morpheme boundaries that are signaled primarily or even exclusively, in others it is the word boundaries. To the first type belongs German, for example. All boundary signals valid for word boundaries in German are also valid for morpheme boundaries. In addition, there are several signals that are valid only for morpheme boundaries, but not for word boundaries. The consonant cluster *dl* (as in "redlich" [honest], "Siedlung" [settlement]) seems to be the only signal in German which does not relate to the morpheme but to the word. It is a negative phonemic group signal. Conversely, there are many languages where morpheme boundaries are not signaled at all but where word boundaries are indicated by specific boundary signals. Among these is Finnish, where word boundaries are characterized positively by a fixed initial accent, and negatively by *d* and *ŋ*, geminates (except for *tt, nn,* and *ss*), and consonantal clusters (except for *n, t,* and *s* + consonant). Morpheme boundaries, on the other hand, have no specific marks, and sometimes even fall within a "long" (geminated) phoneme (e.g., "talo" [house]: illative "taloon"; "vesi" [water]: partitive "vettä"). Mixed types can be found in many languages, to be sure. For most languages, however, a certain preference for either morpheme boundaries or word boundaries can be noted. These two basic types are important for the entire structure of the vocabulary. The positive phonemic boundary signals are also used without a delimitative function in loanwords as a substitution for foreign phonemes and phoneme combinations. This is done without any difficulty in the case of positive individual signals. But it is not so easy to transfer a negative phonemic individual signal to an unusual phonic position. For a German it is not easy to pronounce "exotic" proper names beginning with an *ŋ* ("ng"). Equally difficult for a Finn are loanwords beginning in a *d* or ending in a *v*. As far as phonemic group signals are concerned, their use without a delimitative function to reproduce foreign phoneme combinations is only possible in those languages where these boundary signals already characterize morpheme boundaries. In German, words such as "pneumatisch" (pneumatic), "Sphäre" (sphere), "Szene" (scene), "Kosmos" (cosmos), etc., are easily pronounceable because the phoneme clusters *pn, sf, sc, sm* occur also in native German words as phonemic group signals for morpheme boundaries (e.g., "abnehmen" [reduce], "Ausfuhr" [export], "Auszug" [departure], "ausmachen" [amount to]). But in Avar, where the combination "labial + liquid" is a group signal not of the morpheme boundary but of the word boundary, this combination is not even permitted in loanwords. The way in which individual languages signal morpheme or word boundaries thus exerts a certain influence on the receptivity of these languages to loanwords.

Phoneme combinations that function as boundary signals in native words, but occur without this function in loanwords, are, of course, quite bothersome. Too frequent a use of loanwords in which such combinations are present weakens their delimitative capacity. Styles marked by the frequent use of loanwords are therefore also characterized by a weakening of the delimitative function because the phonemic boundary signals themselves are weakened. In a language otherwise rich in phonemic boundary signals, and specifically oriented toward morpheme delimitation, a large discrepancy arises between the "ordinary" style and the style

295

characterized by the use of loanwords. The latter style appears as a particularly cumbersome, strenuous style. This is one of the reasons for the purism found in certain languages, that is, the endeavor to create a scholarly language without loanwords. Such organic purism, which has its roots in the phonological structure of the language, must in principle be distinguished from an external type of purism conditioned by culture history. The German type of purism is more of the organic type. The German language did not have to fight for its existence or emancipation. For the role of German as an international language, the absorption of as many loanwords as possible would be rather advantageous (as is the case, for example, with English). The fact that in German from time to time strong puristic tendencies make themselves successfully felt nevertheless is due for the most part to the specific phonological structure of German, to the relatively small number of morpheme types, to their pregnant phonological structure, and to the large number of phonemic boundary signals by which the morphemes are clearly delimited from each other.

The distinction between languages that are predominantly delimitative with respect to words and those predominantly delimitative with respect to morphemes is not the only distinction of significance for the typology of the delimitative function. It is also very important to determine what types of boundary signals are preferred and how these signal types are distributed. For example, it is important to determine whether non-phonemic boundary signals are utilized to mark word boundaries, and phonemic signals to mark phoneme boundaries. Of importance is, further, the direction of bilaterally negative boundary signals and the position of positive individual signals; most languages show a preference for signaling the beginning of a new word. However, there are also those languages that primarily signal the end of a word.

Certainly most important for the characterization of a language with reference to its delimitative capacity is the statistical tabulation of boundary signals in continuous texts. Boundary signals in general are distributed with great irregularity. In a sentence containing six syllables, such as "die Hausfrau wäscht mein Hemd" (the housewife is washing my shirt), all six morpheme boundaries are signaled: *di-haus-frau-vɛšt-mæin-hemt*.[1] Yet in another sentence, consisting of ten syllables, not a single morpheme or word boundary is phonologically marked. For example: "Am Boden sassen drei kleine Buben" (three little boys were sitting on the floor). In larger continuous texts such irregularity of distribution is balanced out, so that one obtains a mean value for every language. Such a mean value is different for each language. There are languages that do not only have very few boundary signals but also use them only very sparingly. Accordingly only a very insignificant percentage of all word or morpheme boundaries is "signaled" in a continuous text. French, for example, belongs to languages of this type. It attaches very little importance to the delimitation of words or morphemes in a sentence. Other languages, on the other hand, show an exaggerated preference for boundary signals. In addition to a fixed accent that marks all word boundaries, they employ a profusion of other boundary signals, so that the number of boundary signals in a continuous text is at times greater than the number of delimited units. For example, in Tamil approximately 80 percent of all word boundaries are marked by special boundary signals (at least in the sample texts included by J. R. Firth in his *A Short Outline of Tamil Pronunciation*). This despite the fact that Tamil already has a fixed accent on word-initial syllables (as well as a secondary accent on the final syllable of longer words), by which the delimitation of words is sufficiently assured. German, too, is among the languages "with a predilection for delimitation." About 50 percent of all boundaries of accentuable morphemes and proclitic unaccentuable morphemes are marked by special boundary signals. This is only true, however, of those styles that do not use loanwords excessively.

Statistics are therefore also indispensable for the study of the delimitative sound function. And in this case the statistical tabulation of texts is almost entirely possible. Of course, the same difficulties as in a statistical study of phonemes emerge here also, and must be overcome in the same way. But too little has been done so far with respect to detailed statistical investigations of various languages. Accordingly almost nothing can be said on this subject.

---

[1] Cf. the analysis of this example by N. S. Trubetzkoy in *Proceedings of the Second International Congress of Phonetic Sciences*, pp. 49 f.

APPENDIX I   PHONOLOGY AND LINGUISTIC GEOGRAPHY

1

The phonic differences between two dialects may be of three types: they may involve the *phonological system*, or the *phonetic realization* of individual phonemes, or the *etymological distribution* of phonemes within words. Accordingly we speak of phonological, phonetic, and etymological dialect differences.

The *phonological* dialect differences, in turn, are divided into differences based on inventory and differences in function. A phonological difference based on inventory exists when a dialect possesses a phoneme that is not known in another dialect. A difference in phonological function is present when a phoneme in one dialect occurs in a phonological position in which it is not found in another dialect. A difference in phonological inventory exists, for example, between North Great Russian and South Great Russian. North Great Russian has four unaccented (reduced) vowel phonemes (*ŭ, ŏ, ă,* and *ĭ*), while South Great Russian has only three unaccented vowel phonemes, namely, *ŭ, ă,* and *ĭ*. It does not have an unaccented *ŏ*. A difference in phonological function exists, for example, between various South and Central Great Russian dialects. Some of these allow the phoneme *ă* only after hard (nonpalatalized) consonants, while others permit it after hard as well as soft (palatalized) consonants. In this second group of dialects a difference in phonological function in turn exists between those dialects in which the unaccented *ă* after soft consonants can occur only

298

before a hard consonant (e.g., *v̆ădu*: *v̆ĭd'oš*) and those that do not have this restriction (e.g., *v̆ădu*: *v̆ăd'oš*).

The phonetic differences may be *absolute* when they affect the realization of a phoneme in all positions, or *limited* (combinatory) when they occur only in certain positions. An absolute phonetic difference exists, for example, between the Polish dialects that realize the *l* as *ḷ* (a somewhat retracted *l*) and those that realize the *l* as *u̯*. A combinatory phonetic difference, for example, is found between the South Polish dialects in which *l* is palatalized before *i* ("l'is"/"las") and the North Polish dialects in which it is not modified in that position ("lis"/"las").

Among the etymological phonic differences there are likewise two types that can be distinguished. There are etymological phonic differences that are related to differences in phonological function. Should the function of a particular phoneme be restricted in one dialect as compared with another dialect, such restriction would generally occur in favor of the greater use of a different specific phoneme (in those positions in which the first phoneme cannot occur). The functional restriction of the first phoneme is thus, as it were, compensated for. In cases of this type one can speak of *compensatory* etymological sound differences. However, in other cases, where the etymological phonic differences are not related to any functional difference, these differences may be designated as *free* etymological phonic differences. The relationship between West and East White Russian may be cited as an example of a compensatory etymological sound difference. Although in West White Russian the unaccented *ă* occurs in all positions, it cannot occur before a syllable containing an accented *á* in East White Russian. Words that in West White Russian have an *ă* in that position generally appear with an *ĭ* in East White Russian. As an example of a free etymological sound difference, the dialects of Little Poland may be cited. In some of these the "close *é*" of Proto-Polish is changed to *i*, in others, in the principality of Łowicz, for example, it is changed to *e*. If one compares these dialects with one another, and in so doing disregards any historical explanation, the only fact that can be established is that some words that in the dialects of the first group have the phoneme *i*, occur with the phoneme *e* in the second group. This phenomenon is here not bound by any particular phonological environment.

2

Up to now dialectology has always operated in diachronic terms. Any difference in sound was consequently interpreted as the result of a divergence in phonic development. In a conscious reaction against the doctrine that sound laws are without exception, modern dialectology or linguistic geography claims that each individual word that shows a sound change has its own distributional boundaries, that accordingly the geographical boundaries of a sound change can never be precisely and sharply drawn.

This claim has its foundation in the fact that the three types of phonic differences discussed above (i.e., the phonological, the phonetic, and the etymological) are generally not distinguished.

The thesis of the imprecision and vagueness of dialect boundaries is entirely correct if by dialectal differences one understands the etymological differences in sound alone. As far as such differences are concerned, there can be no question of any complete distributional regularity. An area in which a particular sound change has been rigorously carried out, that is, in which an old phoneme (or an old phoneme combination) has been replaced by a specific new phoneme in all words concerned, is generally bordered by areas where a portion of these words shows a phoneme different from the one expected, without any discernible reason for such "exceptions." Not far from these areas, however, there are generally still others in which these "exceptions" actually form the "rule." Accordingly one can say that between the areas of maximal etymological phonic differences (that is, between the areas where a given phonic difference occurs in the majority of words) there are always transition areas. In these the individual words sometimes show the one and sometimes the other of the particular "treatments" of the old phoneme. The distributional boundaries for the different sound forms of the individual words are here completely independent of one another.

As regards *phonetic* sound differences, the situation is quite different. If a phoneme is realized differently phonetically in two dialects, it must be realized in that way in all words in which the given phoneme occurs in the same position. If this were not so, the different ways of phonetic realization would take on a distinctive function in the linguistic consciousness. Consequently they would acquire phonological validity. In other words, the phonetic distinction would become a phonological distinction. As far as phonetic dialect differences are concerned, it is at times difficult to draw any exact boundary between two areas. The reason for this is that between regions of maximally opposed phonetic realizations there are often either areas of "intermediate" or "intermediary" phonetic realization, so that the transition from one type of phonetic realization to the other is a gradual one. Or it may be that there are areas in between where both types of phonetic realization occur as optional variants of the same phoneme. However, in either case, such a phonetic phenomenon must occur in all words that contain the particular phoneme. Here the term "transition area" thus takes on quite a different meaning from that in the context of etymological sound differences.

Turning to *phonological* differences in sound, we are forced to note that the term "transition area" cannot here be used in any sense. A phoneme or a phoneme combination either can occur in a dialect or it cannot. There is no third possibility. It is frequently the case that a phonetic opposition in one dialect, so to speak, paves the way for a phonological opposition in an adjacent dialect.[1] We mentioned above the contrast of West White Russian *văda*: *vădi̧* with East White Russian *vi̧da*: *vădi̧*. East White Russian proper is bordered by those White Russian dialects in which *ă*, when it precedes a syllable with an accented *á*, is realized as an indeterminate vowel *ə̆*. Objectively, this vowel is neither identical with *i̧* nor with *ă*. However, it is not felt as an independent phoneme by linguistic consciousness, but as a combinatory variant of the phoneme *ă*. The area that has the pronunciation *və̆da*: *vădi̧* may, so to speak, be considered as the transition area between East White Russian (*vi̧da*: *vădi̧*) and West White Russian (*văda*: *vădi̧*). However, this is only correct from a purely phonetic standpoint. Phonologically, this area belongs to West White Russian. In more precise terms, the difference between the region that is "totally West White Russian" and the *və̆da-vădi̧* area is purely phonetic. The difference between the latter region and East White Russian is phonological in nature. And while the delimitation against the "totally West White Russian" area may present certain difficulties (especially because of the gradual transitional shadings between *ă* and *ə̆*), the delimitation against East White Russian is quite simple. Where the vowel of the initial syllable of *vi̧da* is felt as identical with the vowel of the initial syllable of *bi̧la*, East White Russian phonology is involved. Where this is not the case, White Russian phonology is present. The situation is the same in all similar cases. In contrast with the gradual character of phonetic transitions of sound, which make the delimitation of phonetically different dialect areas difficult, phonological differences always have clear and sharp boundaries.

The above considerations result in a guide for the mapping of dialectal sound differences. *Etymological* differences cannot be mapped simply in the form of uniform isoglosses. The methods of word geography alone are suitable for differences of this type. The isoglosses for each individual word showing the particular sound change must be entered on separate maps, which must then be placed on top of one another. The synthetic map produced in this fashion reveals the common (i.e., coinciding) isoglosses in thick and dark lines. Those isoglosses that do not coincide appear as thin and pale lines. The transitional areas are marked by an accumulation of such pale lines, while the areas in which "the sound change is carried out rigorously" is completely, or almost completely, free of these lines. The *phonetic* differences can best be mapped by using different colors or a different type of marking. The areas of transitional sounds, or the areas of optional cooccurrence of both sounds, can be indicated by mixing the colors of both sounds, or by merging the respective markings. This would then express the gradual transitions of phonetic realization symbolically. As far as *phonological* differences are concerned, their geographical boundaries can either be represented by simple lines drawn sharply and clearly on the map, or the "phonological areas" may be represented by different colors, or both media may be used simultaneously. In any case, the mapping of phonological differences is very simple since there are no transitional areas to be considered.

3

In order to determine etymological differences in sound and their distributional boundaries, one has to take down the dialectal pronunciation of the same words in various parts of the linguistic area. The questionnaire that is prepared for these purposes will contain the question: "How is this word pronounced in dialect ——?" The study of *etymological differences in sound*, accordingly, always presupposes the presence of a more or less *uniform vocabulary*. A study of this type is therefore only possible within a uniform language, or, at the most, within a group of closely related languages.

In order to determine phonetic differences in sound and the boundaries thereof, it is necessary to study the pronunciation (i.e., the phonetic realization) of the same phoneme in various localities. It does not matter, of course, whether the same words are selected as examples everywhere. What is important is to choose words in which the given dialect shows the particular phoneme. The study of *phonetic differences in sound* is thus independent of the nature of the vocabulary. What it presupposes is the presence of the *same phonological system* in all dialects under study, or at least the existence of similar systems.

In examining phonological differences in sound, the phonological inventory and the functions of the individual phonemes must be determined for each dialect. The questions here to be answered by the dialectologist are as follows: "Does this phoneme occur at all in dialect ——?" and "In which phonological position is this phoneme used in dialect ——?" It is, of course, quite irrelevant whether all dialects under study have the same vocabulary or the same grammatical structure. In contrast with the study of etymological differences in sound, the *study of phonological sound differences can also be pursued outside the boundaries of a language*, even outside the boundaries of *a language family*. Everything that has been said before on the mapping of phonological sound differences also applies if several languages are examined.

There is no question that such an extension of phonological dialectology across the boundaries of individual languages (without regard to linguistic relatedness) can be useful. Certain phonological phenomena are distributed geographically in such a way that they occur in several unrelated, but geographically adjacent, languages, or, vice versa, that they are absent from the larger geographical areas in which several languages are spoken. Roman Jakobson has demonstrated this for the consonantal oppositions of timbre and the vocalic pitch oppositions. The same could also be shown for other phonological phenomena. For example, the correlation based on type of expiration "with glottal stop"/"without glottal stop" is common in all languages of the Caucasus without regard to their origin (that is, not only in the North and South Caucasian languages, but also in the Indo-European and Turkic languages of this area). On the other hand, this correlation does not occur elsewhere in Europe or in the adjacent areas of Asia and Eurasia. Such geographical distributional areas can also be determined for individual phonemes. It should be noted here that the distributional boundaries for phonological phenomena coincide by no means always with language boundaries. Very often they cut across the area of one language. Distributional boundaries in such cases can only be established by phonological dialect investigation.

The existence of common phonological peculiarities in several adjacent, yet unrelated, languages or dialects has already been confirmed on several

304 PHONOLOGY AND LINGUISTIC GEOGRAPHY

occasions. But one was too quick to explain these facts on the basis of substratum theory or by assuming the influence of a "dominant" language for this purpose. Such interpretations are of no value as long as they only explain individual cases. In general it would be better for the present to refrain from any interpretation, until such time as all data have been gathered. Of importance today is the exhaustive collection of data and the establishment of facts; a comparative description of the languages of the world from the standpoint of phonological geography is now on the agenda. But such a study presupposes a phonological study of the dialects in the individual languages.

[1] Or conversely a phonological difference degenerates into a phonetic difference in an adjacent area. Both conceptions are equally justifiable from a static point of view.

APPENDIX II   THOUGHTS ON MORPHONOLOGY

By morphonology or morphophonology we understand, as is well known, the study of the utilization in morphology of the phonological means of language. Morphonology in Europe has so far been the most neglected branch of grammar. If one compares the studies of ancient Greece and Rome with the studies of the Hebrew, Arab, and particularly Sanskrit grammarians, one is struck by the lack of understanding with which classical antiquity and the Middle Ages in Europe treated morphonological problems. This situation has hardly changed in essence, even in modern times. In modern Semitic studies the morphonological doctrines of the Arab and Hebrew grammarians were merely taken over without being adapted to a modern scientific viewpoint. Indo-Europeanists took over the morphonological doctrines of India as the basis for a morphonology of the Indo-European protolanguage. They developed this morphonology thoroughly, and thus the so-called Indo-European *Ablaut* system and the entire Indo-European root and suffix theory came into existence. But when we consider these results of modern Indo-European studies we see that they completely lack the true essence of a morphonological treatment. The roots ("bases") and suffixes take on the character of metaphysical entities, and apophony becomes a type of magical operation. In any event, these studies are characterized by the lack of any relation to a living language. Root theories, systems of vowel gradation, etc., only appear to have been possible and necessary in a hypothetical protolanguage.

Historically attested languages show only vestiges thereof, and even these have been so overlaid by subsequent development that there can be no question of a system. For Schleicher, who had made the basic distinction between a primitive period of language evolution and a historical period of language decay, such a point of view had been entirely justified. Today it is still subconsciously followed by most Indo-Europeanists, though the theoretical bases of Schleicher are rejected by all. Ablaut relationships and the various types of sound change in the individual Indo-European languages are always represented from a historical point of view. All existing types of sound change, apart from their present value, are then traced to their historical origin. Since productive and unproductive morphonological facts are treated without distinction, and since their function is not taken into account at all, any regularity in these facts must, of course, go unrecognized. Indo-Europeanists never liked to admit that morphonology formed a separate and independent branch of grammar, not only as far as the protolanguage was concerned but also in every individual language. Morphonology was regarded as the result of a compromise or an interaction of the history of sound and the history of forms. A part of the morphonological phenomena was therefore discussed in phonology, another part in morphology.

This state of affairs cannot be permitted to continue. As a link between phonology and morphology, morphonology must take the place it deserves, not only in the grammars of the Semitic and Indo-European languages but in any grammar. Only those languages that have no morphology in the proper sense can also do without morphonology. But in languages of this type certain chapters that would generally be part of morphonology (as, for example, the phonological structure of morphemes) are shifted to phonology.

A complete morphonological study comprises the following three parts: (1) the study of the phonological structure of the morphemes; (2) the study of combinatory sound changes that take place in the morphemes in morpheme combinations; (3) the study of sound alternation series that fulfill a morphological function.

Only the first of these three sections applies to all languages. In all languages that distinguish various morpheme types, the individual morpheme types have special phonic characteristics. These characteristics are different for each language. Root morphemes, in particular, show a variety of structural types. As is known, the nominal and the verbal root morphemes of the Semitic languages usually consist of three consonants. These limitations do not hold, however, for pronominal roots. But rules of this type can also be formulated for other non-Semitic languages. For

example, in certain languages of the Eastern Caucasus verbal and pronominal root morphemes always consist of one consonant. However,
these limitations are not valid for nominal root morphemes. Indo-European
languages also have similar rules. In the Slavic languages root morphemes
consisting of only a single consonant occur as pronominal roots. Root
morphemes that consist of only a vowel without a consonant are not
found at all in present-day Slavic languages, apart from such relics as *u* in
Polish "obuć." In Russian nominal and pronominal root morphemes must
have a consonant in final position, etc. Other types of morphemes (such as
final morphemes, prefix morphemes, suffix morphemes, etc.) also show a
limited number of possible types of phonological structure in every language. It is the task of morphonology to determine the types of phonic
structure of the various morpheme types.[1]

The study of combinatory sound changes of morphemes conditioned by
the morpheme combinations corresponds to what is called "internal
sandhi" in Sanskrit grammar. This part of morphonology is not of like
importance for all languages. In certain "agglutinative" languages it
constitutes all of morphonology (together with the study of the phonic
structure of morphemes discussed above). In certain other languages, on
the other hand, it plays no role at all.

Mutatis mutandis, the same can also be said for the third section of
morphonology, that is, for the study of whole series of sound alternations
that fulfill a morphological function.

It is very important, especially for this section of morphonology, to
draw a clear line between productive and nonproductive phenomena, and
to be cognizant of the functional specialization of the various alternation
series. An examination of the morphonology of the Russian language
reveals, for example, that the sound alternation series in the nominal forms
in this language are not the same as those in the verbal forms. It further
reveals that there is a big difference between the series of sound alternations
that are used to make up paradigmatic forms and those used to make up
derivational forms. A similar situation can probably be found in many
other languages.

The change of the phonic shape of morphemes does not play a role only
in the so-called inflectional languages, such as Indo-European, Semitic,
and East Caucasian. We need only to call attention to the morphologically
utilized quantitative and qualitative vowel gradation of Ugric and the
consonant alternation of the Finnish languages. There is no doubt, however, that in many languages morphemes remain unchanged phonically.
For languages of the latter type, this third section of morphonology is, of
course, omitted.

Morphonology is thus a part of grammar which plays an important role in almost all languages, but there is hardly any language in which it has so far been studied. The study of morphonology will considerably deepen our knowledge of languages. To be stressed in particular is the importance of this branch of grammar for the typology of languages. The old typological classification of languages into isolating, incorporating (polysynthetic), agglutinative, and inflectional languages is unsatisfactory in many respects. Morphonology, as mentioned, represents a link between phonology and morphology. Already by reason of its central position in the grammatical system it is best qualified to furnish a comprehensive characterization of the peculiarities of each language. It is possible that those language types that would result from a morphonological treatment would make it easier to work out a rational typological classification of the languages of the world.

[1] As for languages that do not have different morpheme classes (e.g., Chinese), one has to establish the possible phonic types of words. However, this is not to be accomplished in morphonology but in a special chapter on phonology.

APPENDIX III AUTOBIOGRAPHICAL NOTES ON N. S. TRUBETZKOY

AS RELATED BY ROMAN JAKOBSON

"I was born in Moscow on April 16, 1890. My father, Prince Sergius Trubetzkoy (1862–1904), was professor of philosophy at the University of Moscow. He also took part in the liberal political movement as a writer for the liberal party and held the post of rector of the University of Moscow at the time of his death in 1904.

"By the age of thirteen I had already become interested in the sciences. Originally I studied primarily ethnography and ethnology. In addition to Russian folk poetry, my interests lay particularly with the Finno-Ugric peoples of Russia. After 1904 I regularly attended all meetings of the Moscow Ethnographic Society and established personal contacts with its president, Professor Vsevolod Fedorovič Miller, the noted authority on Russian folk epic and Ossetic. At the same time I maintained a close relationship with Stefan Kirovič Kuznecov, a distinguished archaeologist who specialized in the study of the Volga Finns. He guided and encouraged me in my studies in Finno-Ugric ethnography with his suggestions and his references to literature. Under the influence of S. K. Kuznecov I began to occupy myself with the Finno-Ugric languages and soon became interested in general linguistics. As early as 1905 I published two articles on Finno-Ugric folklore in *Ethnografičeskoje Obozrenije*, the journal of the Moscow Ethnographic Society. One of these articles discussed traces of an ancient common Finno-Ugric pagan funeral rite found in a West Finnish folk song. The other attempted to prove that there existed traces of the cult of the Northwest Siberian pagan goddess 'Zolotaja Baba,' which had been mentioned on several occasions by ancient travelers, in the folk beliefs of the present-day Voguls, Ostyaks, and Votyaks. In 1907 my attention was drawn simultaneously to the problems of two isolated language families, the so-called Paleo-Asiatic languages on the one hand, and the Caucasian on the other. S. K. Kuznecov introduced me to the Paleo-Asiatic languages of Eastern Siberia. At his instigation I collected all the data contained in ancient travel reports on the Kamchadal language (on the peninsula of Kamchatka), which today is almost extinct. On the basis of this material I compiled a vocabulary and a short grammatical sketch of that language. Through this work I established correspondence with three scholars of East Siberian ethnography: Jochelson (for Yukhagir), Bogoraz (for Chukchi and Koryak), and Šternberg (for Gilyak). I discovered a series of striking correspondences in the vocabulary of Kamchadal and Chukchi-Koryak on the one hand, and Samoyed on the other. Unfortunately I had to interrupt this work because I was preparing for my baccalaureate examinations. Subsequently I never had an opportunity to come back to this interesting problem. A lecture given by V. F. Miller before the Moscow Ethnographic Society on the importance of Caucasian linguistics for the historical ethnology of Asia Minor stimulated my interest in Caucasian languages. Originally I had considered Caucasian languages and folklore only from the standpoint of the historical ethnology of Asia Minor. (In this sense I treated, for example, the North Caucasian stone birth legends in an essay in *Etnografičeskoje Obozrenije*, 1908.) However, I soon began to study the Caucasian languages for their own sake. In addition to all these individual problems, I was also interested in culture history in general, sociology, the philosophy of culture, and the philosophy of history.

"After graduation from the fifth gymnasium in Moscow I entered Moscow University, in 1908. At that time the university curriculum was based on the principle of a strictly separated program. Each department was divided into several special sections. Each of these sections had a fixed program of lectures, seminars, and examinations. The student could choose the section himself. After he had enrolled in a section, however, he had to complete the entire program and could not make any changes. A combination of subjects from different sections was not permitted. Ethnography and ethnology were part of the geography-anthropology section of the Department of Natural Sciences. The head of that section, Professor D. N. Anučin, conducted his classes strictly in accordance with the principles of natural history. Since ethnography and ethnology attracted me primarily in their philological and humanistic aspect, the

status of these sciences in the official program was unacceptable to me. I
first enrolled in the philosophy-psychology section of the History-Philology
Department (Humanities), since I intended to study primarily ethno-
psychology, the philosophy of history, and methodological problems. But
I soon recognized that the philosophy-psychology section had little relation
to my special sphere of interest. In my third semester I transferred to the
linguistic section. This section, headed by Professor W. Porzeziński,
offered classes in general linguistics, Sanskrit, and Indo-European languages. Indo-European studies were pursued with special emphasis on
Slavic and Baltic languages. Latin, Greek, Gothic, and Old High German
were considered only secondarily, and the remaining Indo-European
languages were not taught at all. For Armenian there was only a lecture-
ship that remained vacant after the death of the lecturer, Chalatianz. The
scope and direction of instruction in the linguistic section left me dis-
satisfied. My main interest lay outside Indo-European languages. I nevertheless decided in favor of this section for the following reasons. First, I
had already become convinced that linguistic science was the only branch
of "anthropology" which had a truly scientific method, and that all other
branches of anthropology (ethnology, history of religion, culture history,
etc.) could pass from the "alchemic" stages of development to a higher
stage only if, with regard to method, they would follow the example of
linguistics. Second, I knew that Indo-European linguistics was the only
thoroughly studied area of linguistics, that through it one could study the
correct linguistic method. Accordingly I concentrated diligently on the
studies prescribed by the program of the linguistic section. At the same time,
however, I continued my own studies in the field of Caucasian linguistics
and folklore. In 1911 Professor Miller invited me to spend part of my
summer vacation at his estate on the Caucasian coast of the Black Sea
and study the Circassian language and folk poetry in the adjacent Cherkess
villages. I accepted his invitation and in the summer of 1912 I continued my
studies in Circassian. I was able to collect rather extensive data. I had to
postpone its analysis and publication until after my graduation from the
university, however. My personal contact with Professor Miller was
highly profitable for my work, although his opinions on linguistics were
somewhat antiquated. As a folklorist and specialist in Ossetic ethnography, however, he gave me valuable advice and references.

"I spent the academic year 1912–13 preparing for my final examinations
and working on my thesis for the degree of *Kandidat** titled 'On the Desig-

---

* *Translator's note:* This roughly corresponds to the American Ph.D. degree.

nations of the Future Tense in the Most Important Indo-European Languages.' The head of the linguistics section, Professor Porzeziński, approved my dissertation, presented it to the faculty, and requested my affiliation with the university for purposes of preparation for university teaching. This recommendation was unanimously accepted by the faculty. After I completed my final examinations in linguistics in the spring of 1913 I went to Tiflis, where I participated in the meeting of an All-Russian Congress of naturalists, geographers, and ethnologists. I gave three lectures ('Vestiges of Paganism in the Cherkess People on the Coast of the Black Sea,' 'North Caucasian Fire Abduction Legends,' and 'The Morpheme Structure of the East Caucasian Verb'). I spent the summer in the country and worked primarily on the analysis of my Cherkess data and on a comparative grammar of North Caucasian languages.

"In the fall of 1913 the faculty approved a trip abroad to complete my scientific education. I went to Germany as a Fellow of the Russian Ministry of Education and enrolled in the University of Leipzig. I attended the lectures of Professors Brugmann, Leskien, Windisch, and Lindner, and participated in the seminars and exercises supervised by them. My main interests at that time centered on Sanskrit and Avestan. In Leipzig I also bought a quantity of books, so that my personal library doubled after my stay there. I intended to go to Göttingen for the summer semester, but a personal matter prevented me from doing so, and I was forced to return to Russia. Soon after that the [First] World War broke out.

"During the years 1914 and 1915 I was preparing myself for the *Habilitation*.* The procedure for attaining competency in comparative linguistics and Sanskrit was extremely strict at that time. It included five examinations that had to be taken within the course of one semester: (*a*) comparative grammar of the Indo-European languages, (*b*) Sanskrit, (*c*) Greek, (*d*) Latin, and (*e*) another Indo-European language chosen by the candidate and approved by the professor who taught it. A specific number of questions was given for the examinations in the theoretical subjects (for example, twenty-five questions in the comparative grammar of the Indo-European languages). The content of these questions was determined by agreement between the candidate and the examiner. At the examinations, in which all faculty members could participate, three questions were put to the candidate. Each of these questions had to be answered by a half-hour detailed discussion including the cogent literature. Each of the faculty members present had the right to ask other questions on the same subject

---

* *Translator's note:* Tests designed to qualify a scholar to hold a professorial position.

which had not been provided for in the program. In my case, for example, the examinations in comparative grammar lasted three hours (in addition to Professor Porzeziński and A. A. Hruška who was then dean, the classical philologist M. M. Pokrovskij and the Slavicists R. F. Brandt and V. N. Sčepkin participated). For the examinations in the individual languages, texts with detailed linguistic and philological commentary, critical commentary, and culture history commentary had to be prepared, as well as a certain number of questions from historical grammar. For the examination in Greek I had prepared as a text the second book of the *Iliad*, for the examination in Latin, Petronius' *Cena Trimalchionis*. For the examination in Sanskrit, samples of all main categories of Sanskrit literature had to be selected. For this examination I prepared a translation with a detailed commentary of twenty-five Vedic hymns, three longer episodes from the epic (*Nala* and *Sāvitrī* from the *Mahābhārata*, and the *Battle of the Apes* from the *Rāmāyana*), two dramas (Kālidāsa's *Vikramorvaśiya* and *Mālavikāgnimitra*), with particular attention to the Prakrit sections, and a text from prosaic literature (I selected the *Vētālapañcaviṅśati*). My competency examinations lasted the entire winter semester 1915–16. They were concluded by two public trial lectures ('The Various Aspects of Veda Studies' and 'The Problem of Reality of the Protolanguage and the Modern Methods of Reconstruction'). I was then granted the *venia legendi* and joined the faculty of Moscow University as a *Privatdozent*.

"Professor W. Porzeziński, who had so far conducted all lectures in general linguistics provided for by the program of that section, assigned the lectures and exercises in Sanskrit to me for the academic year 1915–16. I had the intention of teaching Avestan and Old Persian the following year, since Iranian languages had not been taught at all at Moscow University. In 1915 a book by A. A. Šakhmatov titled *Očerk drevnejšego perioda istorii russkogo jazyka* appeared, and it was of great importance for my linguistic biography. This book was devoted to the reconstruction of Proto-Slavic and Proto-Russian, and Šakhmatov as a faithful disciple and follower of F. F. Fortunatov proceeded in the spirit of his mentor. All the shortcomings of the method of reconstruction followed by the Fortunatov (Moscow) school stood out with particular clarity in his book. This imperfection made a very strong impression on me, I had always been very much interested in questions of methodology. I wrote a detailed critical review of the book, which I read at the meeting of the Moscow Dialectological Commission. My paper had the effect of a bomb. Up to that time Fortunatov's school had ruled the Moscow arena and all Moscow linguists had accepted the dogmas and methodological principles of that school without reservation. A lively debate developed, in which representatives of the older generation of linguists polemicized against my views and tried to defend the methods of Šakhmatov, while the younger generation was on my side. I believe that my paper was of decisive importance for the further development of linguistic science in Moscow. It was the first expression of a turning away from Fortunatov's method of reconstruction. Many concluded from this that linguistic reconstruction in general was a hopeless undertaking and turned away from the entire area of historical linguistics. They were soon reinforced by the influences of the school of Ferdinand de Saussure which had been little known in Russia prior to the war. Even today most young linguists in Moscow work in the direction of 'static' or 'synchronic' linguistics and show little interest in historical linguistics. For myself, however, the discussion that ensued from my paper had quite a different meaning. After deciding that the method applied by F. F. Fortunatov, A. A. Šakhmatov, and other disciples was untenable, I merely concluded that one must look for a more suitable method for historical linguistics and linguistic reconstruction. I made it my task to search for such a method. Since Šakhmatov's book, which had convinced me of the untenability of the old method, was devoted to Slavic languages, my attention was directed to these languages. Previously I had been more occupied with Iranian languages (since of all Indo-European languages these had most influenced the Caucasian languages which were my main interest). The Slavic languages now came more into the foreground. I decided to write a book titled *Prehistory of the Slavic Languages*, and in it I planned to illustrate the process of development of the individual Slavic languages from Proto-Slavic, and of Proto-Slavic from Indo-European, by means of an improved method of reconstruction. . . ."

Here end the autobiographical notes. During the summer of 1917 Trubetzkoy visited the Caucasus which soon became enveloped in the turmoil of civil war. After many dramatic journeys and adventures he was able to resume his work toward the end of 1918. About two hundred letters, which were miraculously saved, tell us of Trubetzkoy's scientific life from that time until his death on June 25, 1938. The first of these letters is dated December 12, 1920, the last May 9, 1938. An edition of all these letters is now in preparation. They contain many valuable thoughts, observations, and discoveries by Trubetzkoy which are still unknown. Here only a selection of remarks is given which illuminate the development of his views on basic questions of linguistics, and especially of phonology.[1*]

"After a really very intensive life in Moscow during these past years, I

---

* *Translator's note:* According to a personal communication from Roman Jakobson, the publication of these letters is imminent.

was first in Kislovodsk in the deepest provinces, and later in Rostov. Despite the existence of a university (which conferred upon me the chair of comparative linguistics), there was not a trace of intellectual life and not a soul with whom one could have discussed anything. . . . For better or for worse, one is forced to become self-sufficient, to work all by oneself without discussing one's work with anyone. . . . During my stay in Kislovodsk I had begun writing a treatise titled 'Attempt at a Prehistory of the Slavic Languages.' I attempted to reconstruct the history of the development and division of Common Slavic, I applied the method I had opposed to that of Šakhmatov in my [Moscow] paper. The results were not uninteresting. . . . I had to break rather radically with the dogmas of the 'Moscow School.' . . . I had to break with many other dogmas as well. If my work should ever be published, it will probably be strongly attacked, and not only on the part of the 'Muscovites.' But it also contained some thoughts that, I hope, will ultimately find general acceptance. It was very difficult for me to write because I had taken along only a few books, and the university library in Rostov was absolutely useless in my area. Nevertheless, I completed the history of phonology in outline form and prepared a sketch of the morphology. But just then we had to leave Rostov, and during our evacuation all my manuscripts and books remained there [and vanished without a trace]" (12–12–1920).

From 1920 on Trubetzkoy is in Bulgaria. He is appointed lecturer in Slavic philology by the University of Sofia, with the privilege of giving lectures in comparative linguistics. There he wrote and published a book on culture theory, which he had already planned in 1909 and 1910 as the first part of a trilogy titled "Justification of Nationalism." The first part was to be titled "On Egocentricity." It was changed to the more meaningful title "Europe and Humanity." The original dedication to Copernicus was omitted as being too pretentious. The aim of this book is purely negative and destructive. The first task is to revolutionize consciousness. "The essence of such revolution consists in completely overcoming egocentricity and eccentricity and to pass from absolutism to relativism" (3–7–1921). At the same time Trubetzkoy was trying to reconstitute his manuscript of the *Prehistory*.

"I am proceeding from the viewpoint that Common Slavic is not only a short moment but an epoch, or rather, a sequence of epochs. The first dialectal particularities which appear in the 'Proto-Slavic dialects' (in other words, in those dialects of Indo-European from which Common Slavic subsequently developed) toward the end of the Proto-Indo-European era, may be viewed as a point of departure. Those last phonic phenomena which spread through all Slavic languages may be considered the end of

Common Slavic; for example, the loss of the vowels *ŭ* and *ĭ* which generally had the same character in all Slavic languages. This means that the era of Common Slavic comprised several millennia, at least two and one-half millennia. . . . I consider the twelfth century as the end of the era of Common Slavic" (12–12–1920). "In view of these conditions it would be just as meaningless to determine the phenomena of Common Slavic without precisely establishing the period in which each of these phenomena occurred, as it would be for a historian to indicate on the same map the boundaries of the conquests of Napoleon and of Alexander the Great. I am therefore attempting to establish a reciprocal relative chronology of the various phenomena of Common Slavic. In this way I obtained a chronological table that includes not only almost all phonic phenomena of Common Slavic, but also the majority of phenomena of Common Russian, Common Polish, etc. For many of the particularities of the various dialects of Common Slavic had already appeared, while phenomena that appeared in all dialects continued to occur. Some morphological innovations, among which relative chronology also holds, may be included in this table of phonic phenomena as well. One thus obtains a table that indicates the successive development of phonological and morphological features as they occur in the dialects from which the autonomous Slavic languages developed" (2–1–1922).

"In the summer of 1922 I accepted an appointment to the chair of Slavic at the University of Vienna. . . . I have to give five lectures weekly. These lectures may not be repeated for three years. They are to comprise six Slavic languages and the most important works in literature. . . . For the coming year I will be so deluged by work that I cannot even think of writing a book. I will only be able to publish some articles from time to time. This, of course, is very regrettable. But perhaps it is useful that the 'Prehistory' has time to mature in my mind. I am continually having new ideas that force me to make improvements on the entire work. . . . At present I am completely absorbed by the preparation of my lectures on the historical grammar of Russian and Old Church Slavic" (1923).

"With regard to the history of the Russian language, as with Slavic studies in general, I am above all trying to recognize the forest before the trees. In my opinion this is feasible today. Yet there are few people who make an attempt to do so. Taking a brief look at the history of the development and the divisions of Common Russian, I am amazed at the logical harmony of this survey. . . . Up to the fourteenth century the development of the history of Russian sounds is determined by a single principle: it follows logically from the relationship of the geographical position of the Russian area to the other Slavic languages" (7–12–1923).

"At the present I am extensively applying the methodological procedures I had already used in the sound history of Russian to the sound history of the other Slavic languages, and to a comparative study of the sounds of Slavic. This leads to very peculiar results. The disintegration of Common Slavic offers an entirely new picture. The relationships between the various languages frequently appear in a completely different light. Most important, one always discovers a certain inner logic in the development. Very often the discovery of this logic is a surprise to the scholar himself " (Letter to Durnovo, 2–24–1925).

At the same time Trubetzkoy continued the study of other language families, especially those of the Northern Caucasus. He attentively follows the development of general linguistics. Above all he studies and discusses the first concrete attempts of a phonological analysis of language. He warns about certain erroneous views in linguistics, and vehemently condemns the doctrine of Marr, which at that time was undermining linguistic science in Russia.

"The essay by Marr[2] surpasses anything he has so far written. . . . I am firmly convinced that a critical review of this article should not be undertaken by a linguist but by a psychiatrist. It is unfortunate for linguistics that Marr is not sufficiently insane to be put into an institution; but it is clear to me that he is crazy. This is pure Martynov.[3] Even the format of the article is characteristic of a lunatic. It is terrible that most people have not yet noticed this" (11–6–1924).

While "again seriously" thinking about his *Prehistory of the Slavic Languages*, Trubetzkoy reaches the conclusion that it can only be beneficial if the publication of that book be delayed. "This type of thing must mature slowly" (1–15–1925).

In search of new methods, he tries a new field of investigation—"stylistics and poetry."

"I do not occupy myself any more with linguistics. . . . I can see that I am giving the lectures on Old Russian literature with much more enthusiasm than the lectures on comparative grammar. . . . They in no way resemble the usual lectures on Old Russian literature. . . . You would probably also enjoy it since the formal methods come very much into their own here. But I still cannot consider myself a true formalist, for the formal method for me is only a means to bringing out the spirit of the work. . . . After grasping the 'literary devices' of the Old Russian writers and the purposes of these literary devices, we begin to understand the work itself. We gradually penetrate into the mentality of the ancient Russian reader and make his viewpoint our own. One can make a series of unexpected discoveries in this area. Seen from this vantage point, the literary development shows itself in a completely new perspective. . . . You can see that my attention is channeled in a completely new direction. But at the bottom of my heart I certainly am above all a linguist" (2–18–1926).

The discussion of the possibility of applying the phonological method to the area of diachronic linguistics again leads to Trubetzkoy's plunging himself, and this time definitively, into the problems of linguistics. A long and ardent letter, which I had sent from Prague to Vienna, had brought up the questions that I subsequently developed in the introductory chapters of my "Remarques sur l'évolution phonologique" (*TCLP*, II). The letter had stressed above all the necessity of bridging the chasm that existed between the synchronic analysis of the phonological system and the history of sounds. Any change in a system of meaning-forming components can only be understood in its relation to such a system. I did not have long to wait for Trubetzkoy's reply.

"I fully agree with your general views. Many things in the history of language appear fortuitous, but the historian cannot be satisfied thereby. Upon a bit of attentive and logical reflection we notice that the general lines of language history are not at all accidental, and that accordingly small details are by no means accidental either. One must only grasp their meaning. The logical character of language development is a result of the fact that 'language is a system.' In my lectures I always try to demonstrate the logic of the development. This is possible not only in the domain of phonetics but also in morphology (perhaps also in the domain of the lexicon). There are examples that lend themselves particularly well to illustration, such as the development of the numerals in the Slavic languages, the development of the conjugation in Russian, etc. (The development of the former depends entirely on whether or not the dual was preserved as a productive category.)

"Ferdinand de Saussure, though he teaches that 'language is a system,' has not dared to draw the consequences from his own theory. This can be explained principally by the fact that such a conclusion would not only have been a contradiction of the traditional conception of language history, but also of the customary ideas about history in general. One does not concede that history has any meaning other than the notorious one of 'progress.' This is a mistaken conclusion, in which meaning is deduced from absurdity. From the viewpoint of the historian, only 'laws' such as the following can be ascertained in the development of language: 'The progress of culture destroys the dual' (Meillet). But, strictly speaking, these laws are neither definitive nor purely linguistic. Yet we are taught by a careful reflection on languages, which is oriented toward an inner logic in their development, that such logic exists, and that a whole series of purely linguistic laws can be established which are independent of extra-linguistic factors such as 'culture,' etc. Naturally, these laws will not tell us anything about 'progress' or 'regression.'. . .

"The various aspects of culture and the existence of peoples also develop in accordance with an immanent logic, and their own laws have nothing in common with 'progress' either. It is specifically for this reason that ethnology and anthropology do not wish to examine these laws. In the history of literature the formalists have finally begun to study the immanent laws, thus unveiling the meaning and inner logic of literary development. All sciences that deal with development are so neglected methodologically that the 'problem of the day' now is to improve the method of each of these sciences separately. The time is not yet ripe for a synthesis. But there is no doubt about a certain parallelism in the development of the various aspects of culture. Accordingly there must be laws that deny such parallelism. . . . A special science must be created which focuses on a synthetic study of a parallelism in the development of the various aspects of life.

"All this would also be applicable to the problems of language. . . . Accordingly one may not only ask oneself in the final analysis why a particular language, after choosing a particular direction, has developed in one way rather than in another, but also why a given language, spoken by a particular people, has developed just in this direction and not in another. For example, why has Czech preserved vocalic quantity and Polish the palatalization of consonants" (12–29–1926).

Trubetzkoy immediately recognized the comprehensive revision that would result for all our previous postulates from the application of the phonological method to the history of sounds. "You disconcerted me," he told me in jest when we met, and in the above-mentioned letter he confesses with reference to his *Prehistory of the Slavic Languages*, "I am afraid it is already too late for that."

He realized that a teleological explanation of the origin of sound change could and must reveal many essentially new and important things. But in the beginning he found it difficult to detach himself from the traditional view that useless sound change only created disorder in the system and was due only to "mechanical causes" (1–12–1927).

However, his doubts were soon dispersed. Trubetzkoy replied to my proposal of topics for historical phonology, which were to be read at the First International Congress of Linguists in The Hague in 1928, as follows:

"I am in agreement with your proposal. I would only like to add that in view of the novelty of the problem . . . it would be desirable to keep the arguments in their simplest and clearest form, and not to be afraid of going into details. Put yourself in the place of a person who has never heard anything about these questions. Please do not forget that, on the average, linguists are narrow-minded routineers who, furthermore, are hardly used to abstractions. . . . But this is only a matter of form. With regard to content, I am in complete agreement with you. Please add my signature" (10–22–1927).

The success of phonology at the Congress in The Hague encouraged Trubetzkoy. He took part effectively in the activities of the Cercle Linguistique de Prague which then appeared for the first time in the international arena, by preparing for the first International Congress of Slavicists (Prague, September 1929) the first two volumes of the *Travaux* (*TCLP*). They contained a series of collective papers devoted to the problems of structural linguistics in general and phonology in particular. Progress in historical phonology requires a great deal of preliminary work in the area of synchronic phonology. A historian by training and predilection, Trubetzkoy begins a brilliant attempt to reconstruct the phonological system of Polabian, an extinct language. However, he is becoming increasingly aware of the necessity to concentrate his efforts on the description of modern languages and on the analysis of their general structural laws. These investigations, which later were to become the center of Trubetzkoy's work, seemed at first to be only an interlude. He announces the most important of his discoveries—the phonological analysis of vowels (subsequently published in *TCLP*, I)—as follows:

"This summer I worked little. For the most part I went for walks. The weather was beautiful. I made good progress with my 'Polabian Studies,' but have not yet completed them. In the meantime I have started working on something else which fascinates me. I have compiled all vocalic systems I knew by heart (thirty-four in all), and tried to compare them with each other. I continued this work here in Vienna and now I already have forty-six systems. By and by I will continue my work on them, until I have collected about one hundred languages. The results are extremely strange. All systems can be reduced to a small number of types and can always be represented by symmetrical diagrams (triangles, parallel series, etc.). There are some laws about the 'formation of systems' which can be seen without difficulty . . . I believe that the empirical laws discovered in this way will be of great importance, in particular for language history and reconstruction. . . . They must be applicable to all languages, for the theoretically reconstructed protolanguages as well as for the various developmental stages of the historically attested languages" (9–19–1928).

From here on the problem of general laws is formulated more and more precisely in the investigations of Trubetzkoy.

"I believe that there are some laws of phonological structure which are actually valid universally, while others are limited to a particular type of morphological and perhaps even lexical structure. Since language is a system, a close link must exist between the grammatical and phonological structure of language. Only a limited number of phonological systems are compatible with one and the same grammatical structure. This is a fact that limits the developmental possibilities and restricts the application of comparative phonology" (2-25-1930).

Another fundamental discovery by Trubetzkoy in the field of phonological structure was soon to follow. This was the observation that one of two terms of a binary opposition "is to be considered as positive, characterized by a specific mark, while the other is simply to be regarded as lacking that mark" (7-31-1930). This discovery was closely linked with the feverish preparations for the First International Phonological Conference which took place in December 1930 in Prague. The conference had a very full program and fruitful discussions. It represented an accounting of the first stage of phonological studies. Trubetzkoy's informative contributions to the discussions fascinated the audience. At the same time the work done at the conference, the enthusiastic letters of linguists such as Meillet and Sapir, and the close cooperation with the Prague Circle made a deep impression on Trubetzkoy. In a letter to V. Mathesius on the occasion of the tenth anniversary of the Prague Circle he referred to the past as follows, when he wrote:

"The various stages of development of the Prague Circle which I have experienced come alive in my memory: first the heroic period, the preparation for the First Congress of Slavicists, the unforgettable days at the phonological conference, and many other wonderful days I have spent with my Prague friends. All these memories are for me linked with a wonderful feeling of excitement. With each contact with the Prague Circle, I felt a new wave of creative joy which died away again and again during my lonely work away from Prague. This stimulation and inspiration are reflective of the spirit of our circle. They emanate from the collaborative efforts of the scholars who, in agreement among themselves, direct their efforts toward the same methodological goals and are inspired by the same leading idea" (November 1936).

While Trubetzkoy continues to develop the theoretical and practical investigations in the field of phonological analysis, he studies the works of his precursors in phonology, especially those of de Saussure and Baudouin de Courtenay. As early as July 18, 1929, he writes:

"In reading Baudouin, I grasp with particular clarity what it is by which he distinguishes himself from us. The ground we have covered since then is indeed much more significant than one would have believed." And on October 27, 1931, he notes in a draft of a rebuttal to his critics:

"I am moving further and further away from Baudouin's system. This is, of course, inevitable, but it seems to me that, if one disregards the later definitions by Baudouin and Ščerba, which in my opinion are often insufficient and inexact, and if one only considers the essence of their systems, in other words, how they applied these systems in practice, one would recognize that our present-day conceptions (those of Jakobson and myself) are a further development of those systems rather than a contradiction of them."

Subsequently, when Trubetzkoy came back to this topic, he ascribed the errors in the phonological attempts of Baudouin's school "to the influence of historical methods and the phonetic conception of the phoneme" (12-3-1937). Of the prephonological studies he appreciates above all the work by the Swiss, J. Winteler: *Die Kerenzer Mundart des Kanton Glarus in ihren Grundzügen dargestellt* (Leipzig, 1876):

"The book is remarkable for its time. The phonetic nature of sound and the role of sound in a system are here distinguished with surprising precision. He strictly distinguishes between those sounds that are physiologically possible and those sounds that are actually used in a given language with a significative value. In general, the author constantly reaches the borders of phonology. . . . It is evident that many of his thoughts were ahead of his time and were not understood" (1-28-1931).

The spiritual isolation of the Swiss innovator which caught the attention of Trubetzkoy is in marked contrast to the recognition accorded phonology sixty years later in 1936 at the International Congress of Linguists in Copenhagen:

"Generally speaking, I am very much satisfied with the Congress. To be exact, not so much with the Congress itself as with its atmosphere. The sense of isolation which is so oppressive to me in Vienna and handicaps me in my work, it seems to me, is disappearing. It has turned out that we are many. . . . This is a step forward, compared to Rome [Congress of Linguists, 1933]. And disregarding all other considerations, a change in generation has taken place. Generations always advance by steps. In Copenhagen it was discovered for the first time that we are not alone in being active as an outpost. We are followed by the younger generation which has learned from our work and which can work independently. In any event, the Congress gave me wings. Upon my return I diligently set upon writing my introduction to phonology which had not seemed to make any headway prior to my trip [to Copenhagen]. Ideas are again beginning to take form" (10-5-1936).

This introduction, the first draft of *Principles of Phonology*, had long been conceived by Trubetzkoy. Early in 1935 he noted: "Meillet suggested that I write a manual of phonology in French which would be published by the Société de Linguistique." Trubetzkoy notes that modern linguistics has left behind its *Sturm und Drang* period, and that his own activity as well as that of his comrades-in-arms has entered a new phase. "In place of a violent storm, an even flood, though still mighty and unrelenting. It appears vexing at first. What is it? Should it be true that youth has passed and that this is the beginning of old age? But in addition to youth and old age there is, after all, also a period of maturity" (1–25–1935).

Trubetzkoy is concentrating his efforts on his main work. He rejects with determination any tendencies to philosophize blindly about the facts apart from actual study. In short, he rejects any tendencies to neglect details in favor of the whole. On the other hand, he severely reprimands the neglect of the whole in favor of details, or of theory in favor of practice. "A mathematician can do without an engineer, but an engineer cannot do without a mathematician" (2–21–1935).

He prepared a card index of phonological descriptions of numerous languages of the world. He attempted to formulate the methods for their analysis with precision and to discover the universal laws of human language behind the particularities of individual languages. He was aware with equal lucidity of the deadly sickness that was draining him of his energy, and of the catastrophe that was befalling Europe. During the last years of his life Trubetzkoy suffered from angina pectoris. He poked fun at the naiveté of his doctors who promised him a long life provided he lived quietly. "How can one fulfill this condition in Europe today?" he added with a smile. Hitler's occupation of Austria was disastrous for Trubetzkoy. He had never attempted to conceal his antinational-socialist views. In an article on the racial question he had subjected the racist theory to devastating criticism. He neither could nor wanted to remain at the University of Vienna. Trubetzkoy's last hope was to emigrate to America to continue his scientific work there. The Gestapo looked for him and subjected him to an impudent house search and interrogation. His files were confiscated. As a direct consequence of this visit, Trubetzkoy suffered a severe heart attack. In the hospital he still hurried to complete his book. He dictated it up to his final days. Except for a final review, the volume was almost completed. Only about twenty pages remained to be written when, on June 25, 1938, Trubetzkoy suddenly died.

[1] If I mention a letter that is addressed to somebody else but me, I indicate this.

[2] N. Marr, *Ob jafetičeskoj teorii* (Novyj Vostok, 1924–1925), pp. 303–339.

[3] A Russian mental patient at the end of the nineteenth century, who had published a pamphlet: "Entdeckung des Geheimnisses der menschlichen Sprache oder die Offenbarung des Bankrotts der gelehrten Sprachwissenschaft." He tried to prove that all words of human languages can be traced back to the root meaning "to eat."—R. Jakobson.

APPENDIX IV   BIBLIOGRAPHY OF
N. S. TRUBETZKOY'S WORKS*

COMPILED BY BOHUSLAV HAVRÁNEK
TRANSLATED AND ENLARGED BY C. BALTAXE

List of Abbreviations
  BSL Bulletin de la Société de Linguistique (Paris)
  JevrazChr Jevrazijskaja Chronika (Berlin-Paris)
  MSL Mémoires de la Société de Linguistique (Paris)
  RESl Revue des études slaves (Paris)
  Slavia Slavia. Časopis pro slovanskou filologii (Prague)
  SlSl Slovo a slovesnost (Prague)
  TCLP Travaux du Cercle linguistique de Prague (Prague)
  ZslPh Zeitschrift für slavische Philologie (Berlin)

1905. Finnskaja pěsn' "Kulto neito" kak preživanije jazyčeskago obyčaja (*Etnografičeskoje obozrěnije* XVII, 2–3, 1905, pp. 231–233).

1906. K voprosu o "Zolotoj Babě" (*Etnografičeskoje obozrěnije* XVIII, 1–2, 1906, pp. 52–62).

1907. V. J. Mansikka: Das Lied von Ogoi und Hovatitsa. Finnisch-Ugrische Forschungen VI, 1906 (*Etnografičeskoje obozrěnije* XIX, 3, 1907, pp. 124-125), review.

---

* Originally published in *Études phonologiques dédiées à la mémoire de M. le prince N. S. Trubetzkoy* (Prague: Jednota cěských matematiků a fysiků, 1939—*TCLP* 8).

1908. Kavkazskija paralleli k frigijskomu mifu o roždenii iz kamnja (= zemlji) (*Etnografičeskoje obozrěnije* XX, 3, 1908, pp. 88–92).

Sbornik materialov dlja opisanija městnostej i plemen Kavkaza. Vyp. XXXVII, otd. III, Tiflis 1907 (*ibid.*, pp. 146–151), review.

1911. Rededja na Kavkaze (*Etnografičeskoje obozrěnije* XXIII, 1–2, 1911, pp. 229–238).

1913. Stefan Kirovič' Kuznecov. Ličnyja vpečatlenija (*Etnografičeskoje obozrěnije* XXV, 1–2, 1913, pp. 325–331).

1914. O stiche vostočno-finskich pesen (summary of a presentation to Etnografičeskij otdel Obščestva ljubitelej jestestvoznanija, antropologii i etnografii) (*Izveštija Obščestva ljubitelej jestestvoznanija . . .* 1914).

1920. Jevropa i čelověčestvo. Sofija, Rossijsko-Bolgarskoje knigoizdatel'stvo, 1920, 82 pp. (translated into German and Japanese).

Predislovije (*G. D. Wells: Rossija vo mglě*. Sofija, Rossijsko-Bolgarskoje knigoizdatel'stvo, pp. iii–xvi).

1921. La valeur primitive des intonations du slave commun (*RESl* I, 1921, pp. 171–187).

Ob istinnom i ložnom nacionalizmě (*Ischod k Vostoku*, Sofija, 1921, pp. 71–85).

Verchi i nizy russkoj kul'tury. Etničeskaja osnova russkoj kul'tury (*ibid.*, pp. 86–103).

1922. O někotorych ostatkach isčeznuvšich grammatičeskich kategorij v obščeslavjanskom prajazykě (*Slavia* I, 1922, pp. 12–21).

La forme slave du nominatif-accusatif singulier des thèmes neutres en *-n-* (*MSL* XXII, 1922, pp. 253–258).

Essai sur la chronologie de certains faits phonétiques du slave commun (*RESl* II, 1922, pp. 217–234).

Remarques sur quelques mots iraniens empruntés par les langues du Caucase Septentrional (*MSL* XXII, 1922, pp. 247–252).

Les consonnes latérales des langues caucasiques septrionales (*BSL* XXXIII, 1922, pp. 184–204).

Religii Indii i christianstvo (*Na putjach*, Berlin, 1922, pp. 177–229).

Russkaja problema (*Na putjach*, Berlin, 1922, pp. 294–316).

1923. Les adjectifs slaves en ŭkŭ (*BSL* XXIV, 1923, pp. 130–137).

Soblazny jedinenija (*Rossija i Latinstvo*, Berlin, 1923, pp. 121–140).

U dverej. Reakcija? Revolucija? (*Jevrazijskij Vremennik* III, 1923, pp. 18–29).

Vavilonskaja bašnja i smešenije jazykov (*ibid.*, pp. 107–124).

1924. Les langues caucasiques septentrionales (*Les langues du monde*, Paris, 1924, pp. 327–342).

Zum urslavischen Intonationssystem (*Streitberg-Festgabe*, Leipzig, 1924, pp. 359–366).

R. Jakobson, O českom stiche, preimuščestvenno v sopostavlenii s russkim (*Slavia* II, 1923/24, pp. 452–260), review.

1925. Einiges über die russische Lautgeschichte und die Auflösung der gemeinrussischen Spracheinheit (*ZslPh* I, 1925, pp. 287–319).

Polab. *Staup* (Hennig B₁) "Altar" (*ibid.*, pp. 153–156).

Les voyelles nasales des langues léchites (*RESl* V, 1925, pp. 24–37).

Staroslavjanskoje скврьна (*Sbornik v čest' na Vasil N. Zlatarski*, Sofia, 1925, pp. 481–483).

Die Behandlung der Lautverbindungen *tl*, *dl*, in den slavischen Sprachen (*ZslPh* II, 1925, pp. 117–122).

Nasledije Čingischana. Vzgljad na russkoju istoriju ne s Zapada, a s Vostoka. Berlin, 1925, 60 pp.

Nas otvet. Paris, 1925, 11 pp.

My i drugije (*Jevrazijskij Vremennik* IV, 1925, pp. 66–81).

O turanskom elemente v russkoj kul'ture (*ibid.*, pp. 351–377).

Trudy Podrazrjada issledovanija severno-kavkazskich jazykov pri Institute Vostokovedenija v Moskve, vyp. 1–3 (*BSL* XXVI, 3, 1925), review.

K. H. Meyer, Historische Grammatik der russischen Sprache (*Archiv für slav. Philologie* XXXIX, 1925, pp. 107–114), review.

1926. Otraženija obščeslavjanskago *o v polabskom jazykě (*Slavia* IV, 1925–26, pp. 228–237).

Zur Quellenkunde des Polabischen (*ZslPh* III, 1926, pp. 326–364).

Studien auf dem Gebiete der vergleichenden Lautlehre der nord-kaukasischen Sprachen (*Caucasica*, fasc. 3, 1926, pp. 7–36).

Gedanken über den lateinschen *a*-Konjunktiv (*Festschrift für P. Kretschmer*, Vienna, 1926, pp. 267–274).

"Choženije za tri morja" Afanasija Nikitina, kak literaturnyj pamjatnik (*Versty* I, Paris, 1926, pp. 164–186).

1927. Urslav. *dǔždžǔ* "Regen" (*ZslPh* IV, 1927, pp. 62–64).

Russ. семь "sieben" als gemeinostslavisches Merkmal (*ibid.*).

O metrike častuški (*Versty* II, Paris, 1927, pp. 205–223).

K probleme russkogo samopoznanija. Paris, Jevrazijskoje Knigoizdatel'stvo, 1927, 94 pp.

Vatroslav Jagić, ein Nachruf (*Almanach der Akademie der Wissenschaften in Wien, für das Jahr 1927*, 1927, pp. 239–246).

K ukrainskoj probleme (*Jevrazijskij Vremennik* V, 1927, pp. 165–184).

Redakcionnoje primečanije [Introduction to the study by V. Nikitin "Ivan, Turan i Rossija"] (*ibid.*, pp. 75–78), coauthored by P. Savickij.

O gosudarstvennom stroje i forme pravlenija (*JevrazChr* VIII, 1927, pp. 3–9).

Obščejevrazijskij nacionalism (*JevrazChr* IX, 1927, pp. 24–31).

1928. Ob otraženijach obščeslavjanskogo ę v češskom jazyke (*Slavia* VI, 1927–28, pp. 661–684).

(*Reply to the question:*) Etablissement et délimination des termes techniques. Quelle est la traduction exacte des terms techniques dans les différentes langues? (*Premier Congrès international des Linguistes*, La Haye, 1928, *Propositions*, and *Actes du premier Congrès international de Linguistes à la Haye*, April 10–15, 1928, Leiden [1930], pp. 17–18). Quelles sont les méthodes les mieux appropriées à un exposé complet et pratique de la grammaire d'une langue quelconque? Proposition cosigned by R. Jakobson, S. Karcevskij, and N. S. Trubetzkoy, *ibid.*, pp. 33–36, and reprinted in Roman Jakobson, *Selected Writings I*, Mouton & Co., pp. 3–6.

Ideokratija i armija (*JevrazChr* X, 1928, pp. 3–8).

N. V. Gogol (*Radio Wien*, 1928, no. 16).

Otvet D. I. Dorošenku (*JevrazChr* X, 1928, pp. 51–59).

1929. K voprosu o chronologii stjaženija glasnych v zapadnoslavjanskich jazykach (*Slavia* VII, 1928–29, pp. 205–807).

Zur allgemeinen Theorie der phonologischen Vokalsysteme (*TCLP* I = *Mélanges linguistiques dédiés au premier Congrès des philologues slaves*, 1929, pp. 39–67). (Reprinted in J. Vachek, *A Prague School Reader in Linguistics*, Indiana University Press, 1964, pp. 108–142.)

Sur la "morphonologie" (*ibid.*, pp. 85–88). (Repr. Vachek, 183–86.)

Problèmes slaves relatifs à un atlas linguistique, surtout lexical.— Problèmes de méthode de la lexicographie slave (*ibid.*, pp. 25–27), *theses* 7 and 8. = Problémy všeslovanského atlasu linguistického, zvláště lexikálního.—Methodické problémy slovanské lexikografie (*I. sjezd slovanských filologů v Praze*, 1929, sekce II, these k diskusi, 7. a 8.).

Notes sur les désinences du verbe des langues tchétchéno-lesghiennes (*BSL* XXIX, 1929, pp. 153–171).

Caucasian languages (*Encyclopaedia Britannica*, vol. V, p. 54).

Lettre sur les dipthongues du protoslave (*TCLP* II, 1929, 104).

1930. Polabische Studien (*Sitzungberichte der Akademie der Wissenschaften in Wien*, Philos.-hist. Kl., Bd. 211, Abh. 4) 1930, 167 pp.

Das Münchner slavische Abecedarium (*Byzantinoslavica* II, 1930, pp. 29–31).

Nordkaukasische Wortgleichungen (*Wiener Zeitschrift zur Kunde des Morgenlandes* XXXVII, 1930, pp. 76–92).

Über die Entstehung der gemeinwestslavischen Eigentümlichkeiten auf dem Gebiete des Konsonantismus (*ZslPh* VII, 1930, pp. 383–406).

† Viktor K. Poržezinskij (*Slavia* IX, 1930–31, pp. 199–203).

T. Lehr-Spławiński, Gramatyka połabska (*Slavia* IX, 1930–31, pp. 154–164), review.

1931. Die phonologischen Systeme (*TCLP* IV = International Phonological Conference held in Prague, December 18–21, 1930, 1931, pp. 96–116).

Gedanken über Morphonologie (*ibid.*, pp. 160–163). Transl. herein.

Phonologie und Sprachgeographie (*ibid.*, pp. 228–234). Tr. herein.

Principes de transcription phonologique (*ibid.*, pp. 323–326).

Zum phonologischen Vokalsystem des Altkirchenslavischen (*Mélanges de philologie offerts à M. J. J. Mikkola = Annales Academiae Scientiarum Fennicae*, XXVII, 1931, pp. 317–325).

Die Konsonantensysteme der ostkaukasischen Sprachen (*Caucasica*, fasc. 8, 1931, pp. 1–52).

Lettre sur la géographie de la déclinaison (*R. Jakobson, K charakteristike evraz. jezyk. sojuza*, 1931, pp. 51–52).

1932. Das mordwinische phonologische System verglichen mit dem russischen (*Charisteria Gvil. Mathesio quinquagenario . . . oblata*, Prague, 1932, pp. 21–24).

1933. La phonologie actuelle (*Journal de Psychologie* XXX, 1933, pp. 227–246).

Les systèmes phonologiques envisagés en eux-mêmes et dans leurs rapports avec la structure générale de la langue (*Actes du deuxième Congrès international de Linguistes, Genève 25–29 août 1931.* Paris, 1933, pp. 109–113, 120–125).

Charakter und Methode der systematischen phonologischen Darstellung einer gegebenen Sprache. (*Proceedings of the International Congress of Phonetic Sciences, Amsterdam, July 3–8, 1932* [Archives néerlandaises de phonétique expérimentale VIII-IX, 1933], pp. 18-22 = *Conférences des membres du Cercle linguistique de Prague au Congrès des sciences phonétiques tenue* . . . , 1933, pp. 1-5).

Die Entwicklung der Gutturale in den slavischen Sprachen (*Sbornik v čest' na prof. L. Miletič*, Sofia, 1933, pp. 267-279).

Zur Struktur der mordwinischen Melodien (*Sitzungsberichte der Akademie der Wissenschaften in Wien*, Philos.-histor. Kl., Bd. 205., Abh. 2., 1933, pp. 106-117).

Il problema delle parentele tra i grandi gruppi linguistici (*Terzo Congresso internazionale dei Linguisti, Roma, 19-26 settembre, 1933*, and *Atti del III Congresso internazionale dei Linguisti*, 1935, pp. 326-327).

Mysli ob avtarkii (*Novaja epocha*, Narva, 1933, pp. 25-26).

1934. Das morphonologische System der russischen Sprache (*TCLP* V₂ = *Phonological description of modern Russian*. Second part), Prague, 1934, 94 pp.

Ein altkirchenslavisches Gedicht (*ZslPh* XI, 1934, pp. 52-54).

Erinnerungen en einen Aufenthalt bei den Tscherkessen des Kreises Tuapse (*Caucasica*, fasc. 11, 1934, pp. 1-39).

Die sogenannte Entpalatalisierung der ursl. *e* und *ě* vor harten Dentalen im Polnischen vom Standpunkte der Phonologie (*Księga referatów, II międzynarod. zjazd slawistów*, Warsaw, 1934, pp. 135-139).

Peuples du Caucase. Excerpt from a letter of Prince N. S. Trubetzkoy (June 18, 1932) (*The Universal Adoption of the Latin Alphabet*. Paris, Institut International de Coopération Intellectuelle, 1934, pp. 45-48).

Altkirchenslavische Sprache, Schrift-, Laut- und Formenlehre (based on lectures given at the University of Vienna in the winter semester 1932-33 and the summer semester 1933). Vienna, 1934, 142 pp. and 11 pp. of corrections.

G. Dumézil, Études comparatives sur les langues caucasiennes du Nord-Ouest, Paris, 1932.—Recherches comparatives sur le verbe caucasien (*Orientalistische Literaturzeitung*, 1934, pp. 629-635), review.

Quelques remarques sur le livre de M. Dumézil "Études comparatives sur les langues caucasiennes du nord-ouest," n.d., 34 pp.

1935. Anleitung zu phonologischen Beschreibungen. Association internationale pour les études phonologiques (published by the Prague Linguistic Circle), Brno, 1935, 32 pp.

Ob idee-pravitel'nice ideokratičeskogo gosudarstva (*JevrazChr* XI, 1935, pp. 29–37).

Psaní (*SlSl* I, 1935, p. 133) [review of "Die Schrift"]

Ke skladbě starého církevněslovanského jazyka (*SlSl* I, 1935, pp. 188–189, and *ibid.* III, 1937, p. 128) [review of J. Stanislav "Dativ absolutný v starej cirkevnej slovančine"].

O poměru hlaholské a řěcké abecedy [summary of a meeting held on 10–6–1934 by the Prague Linguistic Circle] (*SlSl* I, 1935, pp. 135–136).

1936. Die phonologischen Grenzsignale (*Proceedings of the Second International Congress of Phonetic Sciences, London, July 22–26, 1935.* Cambridge, 1936, pp. 45–49).

Die Aufhebung der phonologischen Gegensätze (*TCLP* VI, 1936, pp. 29–45). Repr. in Vachek, *Prague School Reader,* pp. 187–205.

Essai d'une théorie des oppositions phonologiques (*Journal* de *Psychologie* XXXIII, 1936, pp. 5–18).

Die phonologischen Grundlagen der sogenannten "Quantität" in den verschiedenen Sprachen (*Scritti in onore di Alfredo Trombetti,* Milan, 1936, pp. 155–176).

Die altkirchenslavische Vertretung der urslav. *tj, *dj (*ZslPh* XIII, 1936, pp. 88–97).

Die Aussprache des griechischen χ im 9. Jahrhundert n. Chr. (*Glotta. Zeitschrift f. griech. u. latein. Sprache* XXV, 1936, pp. 248–256).

Die Quantität als phonologisches Problem (*IVe Congrès international de Linguistes, Copenhague, 1936. Résumés des communications,* pp. 104–105).

Americká kniha podnětných nápadů o jazyce [review of G. K. Zipf, The Psycho-Biology of Language, 1935] (*SlSl* II, 1936, pp. 252–253).

Ida C. Ward, An Introduction to the Ibo Language. Cambridge, 1936 (*Anthropos* XXXI, 1936, pp. 978–980), review.

1937. Über eine neue Kritik des Phonembegriffes (*Archiv für die vergleichende Phonetik* I, 1937, pp. 129–153).

Gedanken über die slovakische Deklination (*Sborník Matice slovenskej* XV, 1937, pp. 39–47).

O pritjažateľnych prilagateľnych (possessiva) starocerkovnoslavjanskogo jazyka (*Zbornik u čast A. Belića = Mélanges linguistiques et philologiques offerts à M. Aleksandar Belić*, Belgrade, 1937, pp. 15–20).

W sprawie wiersza byliny rosyjskiej (*Prace ofiarowane Kazimierzowi Wóycickiemu*. Z zagadnień poetyki, no. 6, Wilno, 1937, pp. 100–110).

Zum Flussnamen *Upa* (*ZslPh* XIV, 1937, pp. 353–354).

Zur Vorgeschichte der ostkaukasischen Sprachen (*Mélanges de linguistique et de philologie offerts à Jacq. van Ginneken*, Paris, 1937, pp. 171–178).

K voprosu o stichě "Pěsen zapadnych slavjan" Puškina (*Bělgradskij Puškinskij Sbornik*, Belgrade, 1937, pp. 31–44).

Projet d'un questionnaire phonologique pour les pays d'Europe, Prague, 1937, 7 pp.

Erich Berneker. Ein Nachruf (*Almanach der Akademie der Wissenschaften in Wien, für das Jahr 1937*, 1937, pp. 346–350).

Upadok tvorčestva (*JevrazChr* XII, 1937, pp. 10–16).

Nová kniha o indoevropské pravlasti (*SlSl* III, 1937, pp. 105–108).

Myšlenky o problému Indoevropanů [summary of a meeting held 12–14–1936 by the Prague Linguistic Circle] (*SlSl* III, 1937, pp. 191–192).

1938. Die Quantität als phonologisches Problem (*Actes du quatrième Congrès international de Linguistes tenu à Copenhague du 27 août au 1er septembre 1936*. Copenhagen, 1938, pp. 117–122).

1939. Grundzüge der Phonologie (*TCLP* VII), Prague, 1939, 272 pp.

Wie soll das Lautsystem einer künstlichen internationalen Hilfssprache beschaffen sein? (*TCLP* VIII, 1939, pp. 5–21).

Aus meiner phonologischen Kartothek (*ibid.*, pp. 22–26 and 343–345).

Zur phonologischen Geographie der Welt (*Proceedings of the Third International Congress of Phonetic Sciences, Geneva 1938, 1939*, p. 499).

Les rapports entre le déterminé, le déterminant et le défini (*Mélanges offerts à M. Ch. Bally*, 1939).

Gedanken über das Indogermanenproblem (*Acta linguistica* I, 1939).

Mysli o indojevropejskoj probleme (*JevrazChr* XIII, 1939).

Fol'klornoje obščenije meždu vostočnymi slavjanami i narodami sěvěrnago Kavkaza (*Zapiski Russkago Naučnago Instituta*, Belgrade).

Očerki russkoj literatury XVIII-go věka i russkoj poezii XIX-go. Pariž, Russkaja naučnaja biblioteka.

Dostojevskij kak chudožnik. Pariž, Russkaja naučnaja biblioteka.

Beach, D.M. The Phonetics of the Hottentot Language (*Anthropos*), review.

Addenda
Posthumous publications and translations of Trubetzkoy's works

1949. *Principes de Phonologie*, trans. J. Cantinean. Paris: C. Klincksieck, 1949.

1952. *The Common Slavic Element in Russian Culture*, ed. Leon Stilman. New York, 1949, 2d rev. ed. 1952. Translated by a group of graduate students of the Department of Slavic Languages, Columbia University, from a study included in a volume of the author's collected writings which appeared in 1927 in Paris under the general title *K probleme russkogo samopoznanija*.

1954. *Altkirchenslavische Grammatik, Schrift-, Laut- und Formensystem, von Nikolaus S. Trubetzkoy*. Im Auftrage der Akademie hrsg. von Rudolf Jagoditsch. Vienna: In Kommission bei R. M. Rohrer, 1954.

1956. *Die russischen Dichter des 18. und 19. Jahrhunderts*. Abriss einer Entwicklunsgeschichte. Nach einem nachgelassenen russischen Manuskript hrsg. Rudolf Jagoditsch, Graz, H. Böhlaus Nachf. 1956.

1960. Translation of *Grundzüge* into Russian: *Osnovy fonologii*, tr. A. A. Xolodoviča, ed. S. D. Kacnel'sona. Postscript by A. A. Reformatskogo. Foreign Languages Publishing House, Moscow, 1960.

1964. *Dostoevskij als Künstler*. The Hague: Mouton & Co., 1964.

1968. *Introduction to the Principles of Phonological Descriptions*. The Hague: Martinus Nijhoff, 1968. Translation of *Anleitung zu phonologischen Beschreibungen*, 1935, by L. A. Murray, ed. H. Blume, 46 pp.

INDEX OF TOPICS

INDEX OF LANGUAGES

Language groups, language families, and linguistic "unions" are listed only insofar as their general characteristics are concerned.